The Jeffersonian Republicans in Power

Party Operations,
1801-1809

The Institute of Early American History and Culture is sponsored jointly by the College of William and Mary and Colonial Williamsburg, Incorporated.

THE JEFFERSONIAN REPUBLICANS IN POWER

Party Operations, 1801-1809

by

Noble E. Cunningham, Jr.

PUBLISHED FOR THE
Institute of Early American History and Culture
AT WILLIAMSBURG, VIRGINIA
BY
The University of North Carolina Press · Chapel Hill

Copyright © *1963 by*
THE UNIVERSITY OF NORTH CAROLINA PRESS

Library of Congress Catalog Card Number 63-21074

To

My Wife

Preface

In this book I have attempted to carry forward the study of the practical operation of the Jeffersonian political party begun in *The Jeffersonian Republicans: The Formation of Party Organization, 1789-1801* (Chapel Hill, 1957), which traced the rise of the early Republican party through the Jeffersonian triumph in the election of 1800. The years from 1801 to 1809 covered by the present volume were still formative years in the development of the nation's political system, and the structure and role of political parties had not yet become fully established. These are thus important times to study in seeking a better understanding of the development and operation of the political system which forms a basic part of the American way of life. It is also hoped that the work's focus on the period of Jefferson's administration will contribute to a fuller portrait of Jefferson the President.

Attention has been concentrated on the practical aspects of Jeffersonian democracy: party machinery, campaign methods, party leadership, and such problems as party unity, the patronage, and the party press. I have tried also to display the relationship of President Jefferson, as the head of the party, to the practical operation of Republican organization: Jefferson's relationship to the press, his leadership of the party in Congress, his policies in regard to the patronage, and his position in regard to state party organizations and internal party schisms. I have attempted to keep the narrative focused on the central theme of party operations and have made no effort to present a full political history of the period.

This is a study of the Jeffersonian Republican party as a national organization, but I have aimed at presenting the national party structure with its components in the various states. Since American political parties then as now operated both on the state and national level, a full view of the party nationally is impossible without including state organizations. A state by state survey of party machinery has thus been presented as an essential part of this book. Since there has been very little written relating to the operation of parties in many states in the Jeffersonian era, this section is aimed at making available a summary of party machinery throughout the nation. I have not explored the internal political history of any state, however, beyond that point necessary for explaining the operation of the party as a national institution. Since the extent of party machinery differed markedly from state to state and the availability of evidence also varies considerably, it has not been possible to devote equal attention to each state, but a balanced presentation has been attempted. The role of the press, although inseparable from state and local politics, has been examined from the broad perspective of national politics. The subject of the party patronage has been restricted to that involving federal offices.

The findings of this study are based primarily on a fresh reading of the primary sources for the period and a search for new evidence, particularly that relating to the minor figures in the party as well as to the well-known leaders. Many direct quotations from contemporary sources have been included, both to offer as much as possible of the insight which original evidence affords and to provide a substantial body of concrete evidence for interpreting the history of parties and of the Jeffersonian era. It is hoped that this material will lessen the difficulties and the dangers which have faced historians in dealing with the operation of politics in this early period.

Although the name *Democratic Republican* was used occasionally during this period, principally in New Jersey and Delaware, and the term *Democrat* was used at times in Pennsylvania, I have continued to use the designation *Republican,* which clearly remained the most commonly accepted name for the Jeffersonian party throughout the country.

Since the material upon which this study has been based was widely scattered, I am indebted to numerous libraries and their staffs for aiding my research. I gladly acknowledge the use of the collections and facilities of the following institutions and express my appreciation for the help of their staffs: American Antiquarian Society, Columbia University, Duke University, Filson Club, Georgia Department of Archives and History, Harvard University, Historical Society of Pennsylvania, Kentucky State Historical Society, Library of Congress, Maryland Historical Society, Massachusetts Historical Society, National Archives, New Jersey Historical Society, New-York Historical Society, New York Public Library, North Carolina Department of Archives and History, Rutgers

University, University of Georgia, University of North Carolina, University of Richmond, University of South Carolina, University of Virginia, Virginia Historical Society, Virginia State Library, Yale University.

For reading portions of the manuscript of this study I am indebted to Dr. Richard P. McCormick, Rutgers University, Dr. John A. Munroe, University of Delaware, Dr. Sanford W. Higginbotham, Rice University, and Dr. Spencer D. Albright, Jr., University of Richmond. For his thoughtful and competent editorial guidance, I am grateful to Dr. James Morton Smith, Editor of Publications of the Institute of Early American History and Culture. Finally, I am indebted to my wife, Dana Gulley Cunningham, for continuing assistance in many laborious tasks of research and publication.

The research and the writing of this book were made possible by a John Simon Guggenheim Memorial Fellowship and grants from the Research Council of the University Center in Virginia, the University of Richmond, and the Southern Fellowships Fund.

NOBLE E. CUNNINGHAM, JR.

Richmond, Virginia

Contents

CHAPTER		PAGE
	Preface	vii
I	THE REPUBLICAN PARTY TAKES POWER	3
II	THE PARTY AND THE PATRONAGE: THE INITIATION OF POLICY	12
III	THE PARTY AND THE PATRONAGE: PROBLEMS AND PRACTICES	30
IV	THE PARTY IN CONGRESS	71
V	NATIONAL PARTY MACHINERY	101
VI	PARTY MACHINERY IN NEW ENGLAND	125
VII	PARTY MACHINERY IN THE MIDDLE STATES	148
VIII	PARTY MACHINERY IN THE SOUTH AND THE WEST	176
IX	PROBLEMS OF PARTY UNITY	203
X	THE PARTY AND THE PRESS	236
XI	THE PARTY AND THE VOTER	275
XII	A BROAD VIEW	299
	Bibliographical Note	306
	Index	311

Illustrations

	PAGE
Invitation to the Republican Nominating Caucus of 1808	113
Circular by the Republican General Committee of Virginia, 1804	181
Circular by the Chairman of the Republican General Committee of Virginia, 1804	182
Republican Campaign Handbill, New York, 1807	295

The Jeffersonian Republicans in Power

Party Operations,
1801-1809

CHAPTER ONE

The Republican Party Takes Power

Nearly a thousand persons packed the old semicircular Senate chamber in the unfinished Capitol on March 4, 1801. Senators, representatives, and others fortunate enough to crowd into the room strained to hear the President's inaugural address delivered in a barely audible tone, and they watched intently as Chief Justice John Marshall administered the oath of office to Thomas Jefferson as the third President of the United States. "I have this morning witnessed one of the most interesting scenes, a free people can ever witness," declared a thoughtful observer. "The changes of administration, which in every government and in every age have most generally been epochs of confusion, villainy and bloodshed, in this our happy country take place without any species of distraction, or disorder."[1] The scene which Mrs. Samuel Harrison Smith, wife of the editor of the Washington *National Intelligencer,* thus appreciatively witnessed has been so periodically repeated in American history as to make the inheritors of this enduring political system unmindful of the great importance of the events of March 4, 1801. What occurred on that day was far more than the first inaugural ceremony in the new capital at Washington. It was the first time in the nation's history that political power in the national government was transferred from one political party to another.

That such a change should take place without incident seems less eventful today to Americans, conditioned by the history of an uninterrupted pattern of such political behavior, than to contemporaries, who two weeks before the inauguration had feared the disastrous consequences of the House of Representatives failing to decide the electoral tie between Jefferson and Aaron Burr. Although the election of 1800 had clearly demonstrated the nation's wish that Jefferson should be president, the

---

1. Mrs. Samuel H. Smith to Susan B. Smith, Mar. 4, 1801, Gaillard Hunt, ed., *The First Forty Years of Washington Society, portrayed by the Family Letters of Mrs. Samuel Harrison Smith* . . . (New York, 1906), 25-26.

verdict of the electorate was threatened when the tie vote threw the election into the House. There, until the new Congress convened, the Federalists had a majority. Nearly a week of voting and thirty-five ballots produced no decision; it was conceivable that such a deadlock could continue through March 4, when President John Adams's term came to an end. What then would have been the consequences? Fortunately for the future of the American political system this question did not have to be faced; on February 17, on the thirty-sixth ballot, Jefferson, receiving the votes of ten of the sixteen states, was elected.

Thus on March 4 the executive branch passed without disruption from Federalist to Republican control. Since President John Adams had retained all of President Washington's Cabinet when he took office in 1797, Jefferson's appointment of a new Cabinet was to mark the first time that a complete change in the executive department had occurred. The most important Cabinet posts went to men prominent in Republican leadership and in service to the party. The President's close political confidant James Madison, who had played a major role in the formation of the Republican party, became Secretary of State. Pennsylvania's Albert Gallatin, who had recently headed the Republican leadership in Congress, received the Treasury post. The appointment of two leading Massachusetts Republicans—Henry Dearborn as Secretary of War and Levi Lincoln as Attorney General—emphasized the national basis of the party. Another New England Republican, Gideon Granger of Connecticut, was named Postmaster General, an office of influence though not of Cabinet rank. After considerable difficulty in obtaining a Secretary of the Navy, Jefferson settled on Robert Smith of Maryland, brother of Congressman Samuel Smith, to complete his official family. In the new Seventh Congress, a Republican majority in both the House and the Senate was to replace what had previously been a Federalist majority in both houses. In both executive and legislative branches, the transfer of political power, so significant for the future of the American party system, was thus complete.

The political parties which participated in this party changeover were of even more recent origin than the national government installed only twelve years before. Although George Washington had begun his presidency in 1789 under non-party conditions, two parties were fairly distinctly formed by the time he left office in 1797. In the presidential election of 1796, Federalist John Adams and Republican Thomas Jefferson faced each other in the nation's first party contest for the presidency, and the campaign left little doubt that the political groupings which had emerged under the new government had assumed the definite character of political parties. The clear-cut party conditions created by the results of this election—the inauguration of a Federalist president and the convening of a Federalist-controlled Congress—speeded the party system toward maturity. As the opposition party the Republicans, in resorting to extensive organizational and electioneering efforts to turn the Federalists out of office, contributed markedly to the development and to the permanency of the party system. The Republicans and the Federalists who faced each other in the vigorous political campaign of 1800 displayed a degree of organization, party discipline, and effective campaign methods largely unknown a decade before. Although a system of political parties had not come to be accepted in theory and neither party recognized the validity nor usefulness of its opponent, in practice the operation of parties had become an essential feature of the nation's political life.[2]

The discharge of artillery which greeted the President-elect as he entered the Capitol for the inauguration[3] was echoed throughout the country as Republicans celebrated the election victory. One of the most vivid childhood memories of a Connecticut writer was the inauguration day in Ridgefield when "the old fieldpiece, a four-pounder, which had been stuck muzzle down as a horse-post at Keeler's tavern, since the fight of 1777, was dug up, swabbed, and fired off sixteen times, that being the number of States then in the Union."[4] In Richmond, Virginia, an artillery company fired sixteen-gun salutes at sunrise, at noon, and at sunset on inauguration day, the expense of which was defrayed from the proceeds of a subscription ball held as part of the Republican festivities. This was followed by a dinner celebration on March 11.[5] Republican festivals and dinners, which had begun before March 4, continued for some weeks after the inauguration. The President, the Vice-President, and the heads of the departments attended a Republican celebration in

2. Details of the rise of the Republican party and the means by which it came to power in 1800 are presented in Noble E. Cunningham, Jr., *The Jeffersonian Republicans: The Formation of Party Organization, 1789-1801* (Chapel Hill, 1957).

3. For a description of the inauguration day in Washington see Washington *National Intelligencer*, Mar. 6, 1801.

4. Samuel G. Goodrich, *Recollections of a Lifetime* . . . , 2 vols. (N. Y., 1857), I, 115.

5. Richmond *Examiner*, Feb. 27, Mar. 13, 1801; Noble E. Cunningham, Jr., "Virginia Jeffersonians' Victory Celebrations in 1801," *Virginia Cavalcade*, 8 (1958), 4-9.

Alexandria on March 14 and joined in the sixteen toasts filled with phrases from the President's inaugural address.[6] At a "General Thanksgiving, for the Election of Thomas Jefferson to the Presidency," Connecticut Republicans listened to a stirring oration by Abraham Bishop, who had led the Republican assault on Federalism in that state in 1800.[7] In New York, a Federalist lamented: "Our people in this county are running perfectly mad with enthusiasm about the man of the people, the savior of his country (as they term him). Drunken frolicks is the order of the day, and more bullocks and rams are sacrificed to this newfangled deity than were formerly by the Israelitish priests."[8]

The victory which Republicans so enthusiastically hailed in 1801 was basically a party triumph. The election of Jefferson and of a Republican Congress had been accomplished through four years of party organizing, vigorous political campaigning, and realistic fashioning of party machinery, made effective by the ability of the Republican party to sense and to conform to the temper of the electorate. In the post-mortems held by Federalists following their fall from power, Federalist leaders privately credited Republican success to superior party organization and methods, and, though professing to abhor Republican methods, they sought to imitate their rivals. "I hope it is not too late to wrench the name *republican* from those who have unworthily usurped it . . . ," wrote Fisher Ames, early in 1801. "Names and appearances are in party warfare arms and ammunition. It is particularly necessary to contest this name with them now." The new administration "must not begin with an impression on the popular mind that we are a disgraced if we are a disappointed party. We must court popular favor, we must study public opinion, and accommodate measures to what it is and still more to what it ought to be."[9] Delaware's James A. Bayard, discussing Federalist policy with Alexander Hamilton, similarly suggested: "We shall probably pay more attention to public opinion than we have heretofore done, and take more pains, not merely to do right things, but to do them in an

---

6. *Alexandria Advertiser*, Mar. 16, 1801.

7. Abraham Bishop, *Oration delivered in Wallingford, on the 11th of March 1801, before the Republicans of the State of Connecticut, at their General Thanksgiving, for the Election of Thomas Jefferson to the Presidency* . . . (New Haven, 1801), pamphlet, Library of Congress.

8. Francis Crawford to Ebenezer Foote, Mar. 7, 1801, Ebenezer Foote Papers, Lib. Cong.

9. Ames to John Rutledge, Jan. 26, 1801, John Rutledge Papers, University of North Carolina.

acceptable manner."[10] Hamilton, replying with a proposal for an extensive organization of the Federalist party, agreed that Federalists had "erred in relying so much on the rectitude and utility of their measures as to have neglected the cultivation of popular favor, by fair and justifiable expedients.... Unluckily, however, for us, in the competition for the passions of the people, our opponents have great advantages over us.... unless we can contrive to take hold of, and carry along with us some strong feelings of the mind, we shall in vain calculate upon any substantial or durable results."[11] Although Federalists overstated the case in contrasting their own reliance on principles to the Republican appeals to passion, the Republican party had taken the initiative in organizing party machinery, providing for popular participation in party affairs, and effectively presenting the party's program and its candidates to the electorate.

The Federalist party never recovered from its defeat in the election of 1800 and was never to return to power in the national government, but it did continue to maintain sizable support in some areas; and there was always an active Federalist opposition in Congress throughout Jefferson's two terms. New England Federalists remained most loyal to their party; one state, Connecticut, remained Federalist throughout Jefferson's presidency. There were important Federalist minorities in New York, Pennsylvania, New Jersey, and Maryland; Delaware, although partially recruited into the Republican camp in 1801 and 1802, returned to Federalism in 1804. The Federalists were also supported by a powerful press. Overwhelming Republican strength in some areas and a strong majority in Congress made Republicans at times careless of party unity, but Republican leaders never discounted the possibility of a Federalist resurgence. The likelihood of the Federalists profiting from Republican divisions was, in fact, realistically feared.

John Quincy Adams, in 1802, found the Republicans unduly alarmed, "constantly trembling . . . lest the old administration should recover in the eyes of the people." He saw Republicans in Congress as driven by unnecessary fears in the attempts of a House investigating committee to discredit the previous administration which "never can and never will

---

10. Bayard to Hamilton, Apr. 12, 1802, John C. Hamilton, ed., *The Works of Alexander Hamilton* . . . , 7 vols. (N. Y., 1850-51), VI, 539.

11. Hamilton to Bayard, Apr. 1802, *ibid.*, VI, 541. See also Broadus Mitchell, *Alexander Hamilton: The National Adventure, 1788-1804* (N.Y., 1962), 512-14.

be revived." Although Adams believed that "the alarm of the pilots at the helm" was "without cause," Republican leaders took no chances.¹²

It is important to remember that the future failure of the Federalist party to return to power, though hopefully predicted, could not be foreseen by the Republicans who came to power in 1801. "You ask what I think the condition of the adversary?" Senate Republican leader Stevens T. Mason wrote to James Monroe in July 1801. "They are at present certainly down, but yet they do not despair of rising again. I have no doubt that they will soon be re-organized, and should an opening be given by too much supineness on our part or by any unfortunate schism among ourselves, that they will come forward under some more puissant leader than John of Braintree and that taught by the fatal consequences of their late divisions they will form a phalanx not to be despised but perhaps seriously to be dreaded."¹³

Jefferson in his inaugural address voiced a hope for the reconciliation of parties, and at the beginning of his administration he made some steps in that direction. "The people have come over in a body to the republican side, and have left such of their leaders as were incurable to stand by themselves," he wrote shortly after his inauguration, "so that there is every reason to hope that that line of party division which we saw drawn here, will be totally obliterated."¹⁴ That Jefferson, like most of his contemporaries, did not fully appreciate the party system which he was helping to establish was reflected in other letters, written soon after taking office, in which he hopefully anticipated the end of political parties. "The symptoms of a coalition of parties give me infinite pleasure," he wrote, March 22, 1801. "Setting aside only a few only, I have been ever persuaded that the great bulk of both parties had the same principles fundamentally, and that it was only as to our foreign relations there was any division. These I hope can be so managed as to cease to be a subject of division for us. Nothing shall be spared on my part to obliterate the traces of party and consolidate the nation, if it can be done without abandonment of principle."¹⁵ But the consolidation of

12. Adams to Rufus King, Oct. 8, 1802, Worthington C. Ford, ed., *Writings of John Quincy Adams*, 7 vols. (N.Y., 1913-17), III, 8-9.
13. Mason to Monroe, July 5, 1801, James Monroe Papers, Lib. Cong.
14. Jefferson to Thaddeus Kosciuszko, Mar. 14, 1801, Thomas Jefferson Papers, Lib. Cong.
15. Jefferson to Joseph Fay, Mar. 22, 1801, *ibid*. See also Jefferson to Henry Knox, Mar. 27, 1801, Paul Leicester Ford, ed., *The Writings of Thomas Jefferson*, 10 vols. (N.Y., 1892-99), VIII, 35-36. Hereafter cited as Ford, ed., *Jefferson Writings*.

parties did not take place, and Jefferson early abandoned his hopes of reconciling the Federalists. "The attempt at reconciliation was honourably pursued by us for a year or two and spurned by them," he later explained.[16] In fact, as early as December 1802 he confessed that "instead of conciliation their bitterness is got to that excess which forbids further attention to them."[17] Jefferson was to leave the presidency with no more amity toward, nor from, the Federalists than when he had taken office.

The Federalists in the presidential election of 1804 made no national contest, and Jefferson's sweeping victory of 162 electoral votes to 14 for Charles Cotesworth Pinckney appeared to foretell the doom of the Federalist party. Jefferson in 1807 affirmed his belief that the Federalists were "compleately vanquished, and never more to take the field under their own banners. They will now reserve themselves to profit by the schisms among republicans."[18] But that the Federalist party had not disappeared was soon demonstrated in the presidential election of 1808. Federalist candidate Charles Cotesworth Pinckney carried all of New England, except Vermont, and also won Delaware, two of Maryland's eleven votes, and three of North Carolina's fourteen electoral votes. James Madison's 122 electoral votes represented a substantial victory over Pinckney's 47 electoral votes, but the Federalist party could by no means be dismissed from the political scene. Although the party conflict during Jefferson's administration was an unequal contest, the majority party was never without significant active or potential opposition from the Federalist minority.

As he took the oath of office on March 4, 1801, Jefferson could have little anticipated the problems which would most occupy the attention of his administration. His inaugural address, devoted almost exclusively to the domestic scene, referred but briefly to foreign policy, where he was to accomplish his greatest success, the purchase of Louisiana, and experience his greatest disappointment, the failure of the Embargo. His immediate goal was to put into operation the program which he and his party had promised in the election of 1800: a policy of retrenchment or, in Jeffersonian terms, "simplicity and frugality." In the opening years of his administration, a Republican majority in both houses of Congress

16. Jefferson to William Short, Jan. 23, 1804, *American Historical Review*, 33 (1928), 834.
17. Jefferson to John Steele, Dec. 10, 1802, Henry M. Wagstaff, ed., *The Papers of John Steele*, 2 vols. (Raleigh, 1924), I, 338; see also pp. 52-53 below.
18. Jefferson to James Sullivan, June 19, 1807, Ford, ed., *Jefferson Writings*, IX, 77.

enacted the President's program, demonstrating the maturity of the party system by this revision of public policy through the party process. In his first message to Congress in December 1801, Jefferson recommended the abolition of all internal taxes, reductions in the army, navy, and civil government, and announced the steps which had already been taken to reduce officers under executive authority. Philip Norborne Nicholas, chairman of the Virginia Republican General Committee, rejoiced: "The presidents communication to congress has met the warmest approbation of the Republicans here both on account of the manner and the matter. The idea of such a diminution of the taxes will secure to the administration the hearts of the people more than any thing which could happen. This is an argument which will have weight in every part of the Union and with all parties."[19] Delaware's Caesar A. Rodney agreed: "The message of the President must have a wonderful effect on the Country. Nothing can be better calculated to answer the public expectation at this important period. . . . When the people find Mr. Jefferson in his first communication to congress recommending the abolition of all internal taxation—of the *'odious stamp act,'* of the excise *'the horror of all free states,'* of the carriage tax . . . they will look up to him as the 'Father of the Commonwealth.' "[20]

Federalists generally opposed the Jeffersonian program and constantly complained of too many changes for the sake of change, as Connecticut Congressman Roger Griswold cynically protested in December 1801:

Under this administration nothing is to remain as it was. Every minutia is to be changed. When Mr. Adams was President, the door of the president's House opened to the East. Mr. Jefferson has closed that door and opened a new door to the West. General Washington and Mr. Adams opened every Session of Congress with a speech. Mr. Jefferson delivers no speech, but makes his communication by a written message. I fear that you Aristocrats of New England will think these important changes unnecessary and be apt to say that they are made with a view only to change, but you ought to recollect that you are neither Philosophers or skilled in the mysteries of Democratic policy.[21]

19. Philip N. Nicholas to Wilson C. Nicholas, Richmond, Dec. 14, 1801, Wilson Cary Nicholas Papers, University of Virginia.
20. Rodney to Joseph H. Nicholson, Dec. 14, 1801, Joseph H. Nicholson Papers, Lib. Cong.
21. Griswold to David Daggett, Dec. 8, 1801, William Griswold Lane Collection, Yale University.

The incoming Republican administration, however, was faced with a new set of political circumstances that called for more fundamental changes in policy and in strategy than those deplored by Griswold. The Republican party now found itself under vastly changed conditions; no longer the opposition party but the party in power, its future success rested on its ability to function and prosper under the pressures of national responsibility. Would the cement supplied by common opposition to the Federalist regime now dissolve? How would the party act in regard to such practical political problems as the patronage? How could party supremacy be maintained? The Jeffersonian Republican party, which through the successful operation of practical political machinery and well-developed party methods had turned the Federalists out of office, was now faced with the equally challenging problem of staying in power.

As the development of the Republican party entered a new and significant phase, Jefferson and his party lieutenants did not overlook the importance of completing party organization in states where it was still incomplete, nor did they underestimate the need to utilize political patronage for party purposes, yet at the same time neither did the party leaders lose sight of the necessity to keep the Republican party attuned to the hopes and the needs of the American people.

CHAPTER TWO

The Party and the Patronage: The Initiation of Policy

Among the many important questions raised by the transfer of national political power from one party to another, the most immediate and pressing problem to face the new administration was that of the federal patronage. What policy was to be followed in regard to Federalist officeholders? Were they to be swept out of office and replaced by Republicans? Were the Republican party faithful to be rewarded by the new administration? Jefferson's inaugural address suggested a policy of moderation. He warned against political intolerance, affirmed that "every difference of opinion is not a difference of principle," and concluded: "We have called by different names brethren of the same principle. We are all republicans—we are all federalists." Jefferson, who shared the common reluctance of his contemporaries to think in terms of a permanent two-party system, began his presidency with the hope of reconciling political parties. Although soon abandoned, this sentiment, so repeatedly expressed by Jefferson in many letters written in the first weeks after taking office, strongly influenced his initial expressions of opinion concerning removal and appointment policies.

Three days after his inauguration, Jefferson elaborated on his address in a letter to Monroe. He emphasized that he distinguished between the Federalist leaders and the mass of their supporters. Conciliation, he wrote, "is impracticable with the leaders of the late faction, whom I abandon as incurables, and will never turn an inch out of my way to reconcile them. But with the main body of the federalists, I believe it very practicable." These were ready to support the administration, he believed, "if it avoids in the outset acts which might revolt and throw them off." In regard to appointments and removals he explained:

I have firmly refused to follow the counsels of those who have advised the giving offices to some of their leaders, in order to reconcile.

I have given, and will give only to republicans, under existing circumstances. But I believe with others, that deprivations of office, if made on the ground of political principles alone, would revolt our new converts, and give a body to leaders who now stand alone. Some, I know, must be made. They must be as few as possible, done gradually, and bottomed on some malversation or inherent disqualification. Where we shall draw the line between retaining all and none, is not yet settled, and will not be till we get our administration together; and perhaps even then, we shall proceed *à talons*, balancing our measures according to the impression we perceive them to make.[1]

These explanations made privately by the President were not apparent in his public declarations, which suggested a general policy of conciliation. Many Republicans thus were alarmed by what they believed to be the President's policy. "I like the sentiment in the President's speech, as coming from him—(we are all Republicans, we are all Federalists)," observed one South Carolina Republican. "I would to God it were so."[2] Others admitted that "the Speech of the President was well received by the people of every political description," but they suggested that his hopes of reconciling the Federalists were unrealistic. "Every Democrat appointed to office will sting them to the heart, and every officer removed will give them new cause of offence," wrote Congressman John A. Hanna of Pennsylvania. "To expect they will be satisfied with the conduct of a Republican Executive is to reckon against all experience. If Mr. Jefferson were an Angel sent of God, they will never heartily be reconciled to his administration. . . . I would as soon expect to see the heavens and the Earth pass away as to find the body of them supporting him. The burden of their song will be about offices."[3] William B. Giles praised the President's inaugural address, commended it for containing "the only American language I ever heard from the Presidential chair," but explained:

Many of your best and firmest friends already suggest apprehensions, that the principle of moderation adopted by the administration, although correct in itself, may by too much indulgence degenerate into feebleness and inefficiency. . . . A pretty general purgation of office, has been one of the benefits expected by the friends of the new order of things, and although an indiscriminate privation of office, merely from a difference

1. Jefferson to Monroe, [Mar.] 7, 1801, Ford, ed., *Jefferson Writings*, VIII, 9-10.
2. John Hunter to Madison, Apr. 16, 1801, James Madison Papers, Lib. Cong.
3. Hanna to Gallatin, Mar. 22, 1801, Albert Gallatin Papers, New-York Historical Society.

in political sentiments, might not be expected; yet it is expected, and confidently expected, that obnoxious men will be ousted. It can never be unpopular, to turn out a vicious man and put a virtuous one in his room; and I am persuaded from the prevalence of the vicious principles of the late administration, and the universal loyalty of its adherents in office, it would be hardly possible to err in exclusions.[4]

Giles's apprehensive letter prompted confidential explanations from Jefferson, who outlined more specifically than in his letter to Monroe the policies contemplated by the administration. The President proposed to be guided by the following considerations:

1. All appointments to *civil* offices *during pleasure,* made after the event of the election was certainly known to Mr. A[dams], are considered as nullities.... 2. Officers who have been guilty of *official* malconduct are proper subjects of removal. 3. Good men, to whom there is no objection but a difference of political principle, practised on only as far as the right of a private citizen will justify, are not proper subjects of removal, except in the case of attorneys and marshals. The courts being so decidedly federal and irremovable, it is believed that republican attorneys and marshals, being the doors of entrance into the courts, are indispensably necessary as a shield to the republican part of our fellow citizens, which, I believe, is the main body of the people.[5]

These projected policies were explained by Jefferson to numerous other correspondents during March and April 1801. It was "perfectly just," he told Benjamin Rush, "that the republicans should come in for the vacancies which may fall in, until something like an equilibrium in office be restored."[6]

Jefferson was determined to "expunge the effects of Mr. A[dams]'s indecent conduct, in crowding nominations after he knew they were not for himself, till 9 o'clock of the night, at 12 o'clock of which he was to go out of office."[7] Removals, however, were not to be confined to these immediate midnight appointments, but to all appointments (except those not removable) made after December 12, 1800, when the result of the South Carolina election, assuring Adams's defeat, was known in Washington.[8] That Adams had far exceeded normal or necessary appointments in his last months in office was clear, and the only reasonable ex-

4. Giles to Jefferson, Mar. 16, 1801, Jefferson Papers, Lib. Cong.
5. Jefferson to Giles, Mar. 23, 1801, Ford, ed., *Jefferson Writings,* VIII, 25.
6. Jefferson to Rush, Mar. 24, 1801, *ibid.,* 31.
7. *Ibid.,* 32.
8. Jefferson to Henry Knox, Mar. 27, 1801, *ibid.,* 36-37; [List of appointments, May 1802], Jefferson Papers, CXIX, 20542, Lib. Cong.

planation appeared to be a design to embarrass the incoming administration. Congressman Joseph Eggleston must have expressed the sentiments of many Republicans when he wrote in February 1801: "More nominations, both military and civil, have been made by the President and confirmed by the Senate, within the last month, than for a year past. This is merely intended, either with a view to clog the new President with men in whom he has no confidence, and who may take every opportunity to thwart his plans; or with a view to compel him to remove a great number from their places, with a hope of exciting a clamor which may promote the reinstatement of their party in power."[9] Numerous places created by the Judiciary Act of February 1801 had been speedily filled with Federalists, and the judges, appointed for life, were not subject to removal. "The conduct of the *Feds* in the last days of Mr. Adams was abominable," protested Samuel Smith to Federalist Congressman John Rutledge. *"The organization of your new Judiciary, the hurried appointments—what were they for?* There was no misunderstanding the intention. As you fixed the Judiciary you cannot think it wrong for the President to have a few attornies and marshals that think him an honest man. If any of that class should be removed charge yourselves with it— you only are to blame."[10]

Jefferson's early appointments indicated that the political faithful were to be rewarded. Party leaders who had played important roles during the election of 1800 were prominent among the first officers appointed. Charles Pinckney who had worked to carry Republican electors in the crucial contest in South Carolina was chosen as minister to Spain. Several important appointments were made in New York, where the Republican victory in May of 1800 had carried a critical state for Jefferson and had given spirit to Republican efforts in other states: Robert R. Livingston was chosen as minister to France, and Edward Livingston was appointed district attorney for New York. Offices were also conferred on several of Aaron Burr's party lieutenants who had been active during the election of 1800: John Swartwout became United States marshal and David Gelston was named collector of the port of New York.[11] In Connecticut, Samuel Bishop, the father of Abraham Bishop who had boldly championed the party's cause in that state in 1800, was

9. Eggleston to Joseph Jones, Feb. 26, 1801, Joseph Jones Papers, Duke University.
10. Smith to Rutledge, May 12, 1801, Rutledge Papers, Univ. of N.C.
11. The subject of Jefferson's appointments in New York is treated in more detail, pp. 38-44 below.

appointed collector of New Haven, a post to which the younger Bishop was to succeed upon his father's death in 1803. In Rhode Island, Jonathan Russell, Republican leader in the state in 1800, was named collector of Bristol, Rhode Island. Peter Muhlenberg, whose influence with the Pennsylvania Germans was unequaled, was early appointed supervisor of revenue of Pennsylvania. Former Congressman James Linn, who had helped to swing the New Jersey delegation to Jefferson during the House contest between Jefferson and Burr, was appointed supervisor of New Jersey; William C. C. Claiborne, who as Tennessee's only Representative had cast his state's vote for Jefferson, became Governor of the Mississippi Territory. All of these appointments were made during the first months of Jefferson's administration and reflected, as did nearly all of Jefferson's early choices, strong political considerations.

Under the policy of nullifying Adams's last appointments, removing officials for misconduct, and appointing Republican attorneys and marshals, the first removals took place. These measures dispelled a belief that the President's inaugural had meant that no Federalists would be removed and encouraged many Republicans to expect more extensive removals. A Pennsylvania office seeker, writing his congressman to renew an earlier application, explained: "At that time, it was uncertain what steps the President would take. But circumstances have since occurred, which warrant an opinion that he intends to make an extensive removal among the present officers."[12] Delaware Republicans were convinced "that some of our federal officers ought to be changed, and from the recent changes made in the state of Pennsylvania and elsewhere of those officers, we are led to suppose the Executive of the U.S. are of the same opinion."[13] Noticing the changes in Pennsylvania, Thomas Boylston Adams, son of the former President, concluded: "This I expected, it could not be otherwise and the federalists who expect, that the President will be able, if disposed, to persevere in a system of moderation and forbearance with respect to appointment, will be disappointed. It begins to be well understood by both or *all* parties and us, that success in obtaining a Candidate of their own, at the head of government, is sufficient to authorize a system of proscription with regard to the opponents. This is Republicanism."[14]

12. John Porter to John Smilie, Mar. 20, 1801, Gallatin Papers, N.-Y. Hist. Soc.
13. Nehemiah Tilton to Isaac Griffin, Apr. 1, 1801, *ibid.*
14. Adams to Joseph Pitcairn, Mar. 27, 1801, "Letters of Thomas Boylston Adams," Historical and Philosophical Society of Ohio, *Quarterly Publications*, 12 (1917), 44.

Jefferson was soon feeling the pressure for more removals and finding that "it is the business of removal and appointment which presents the serious difficulties. All others compared with these, are as nothing."[15] From New Jersey came word that "the republicans in Jersey are anxious to have some persons who hold appointments under the general government in that state displaced, and particularly the supervisor. The influence of this office in politicks is considerable, and it has been asserted in the federal interest to the utmost extent."[16] Jefferson confessed that the demands from New Jersey and Delaware were "moderately importunate" and that in Pennsylvania "there is a strong pressure on me, and some discontent."[17] The Philadelphia *Aurora* declared: "Elective government would then be contemptible indeed, if a change of a few superior individuals, without regard to the virtues or integrity of subordinate agents were to be the only consequences. A change of characters has become a matter of necessity. The administration can have no choice, but the will of the people."[18] From Virginia, William B. Giles reported to the President: "I find the soundest republicans in this place and throughout the country are rising considerably in the tone which they think ought to be assumed by the administration."[19]

New York Republicans differed on what patronage policies the President should follow. The *American Citizen* declared that "nothing will satisfy that description of people in this quarter, to whom Mr. Jefferson is indebted for his elevation, but the removal from office of the foes of our constitution, and the appointment of its friends." Privately the editors wrote to Jefferson that a "thorough change in the different offices" was "absolutely necessary to preserve that republican majority in this State which has contributed so essentially towards placing you in that elevated situation which you now hold." Removals would also "be extremely useful in the eastern States," they noted. "Republican exertions will certainly be relaxed in this quarter if unhappily the people ever be convinced that all their efforts to change the Chief Magistrate, have produced no consequent effects in renovating the subordinate stations of

---

15. Jefferson to John Dickinson, June 21, 1801, Jefferson Papers, Lib. Cong.
16. James Linn to Gallatin, May 14, 1801, Gallatin Papers, N.-Y. Hist. Soc. See also George Logan to Jefferson, May 10, 1801, Jefferson Papers, Lib. Cong.
17. Jefferson to Wilson Cary Nicholas, June 11, 1801, Ford, ed., *Jefferson Writings*, VIII, 64.
18. *Aurora*, June 18, 1801.
19. Giles to Jefferson, June 1, 1801, Jefferson Papers, Lib. Cong.

our government."[20] More boldly the *American Citizen* proclaimed on June 5 that the removals had been so "solitary and unfrequent" that the Republicans had more cause for complaint than the Federalists. The editors explained:

> It was ardently desired and confidently expected by the Republicans of New-York ... that by this time *one half at least* of the Tories *now in office* in the United States, would have been removed; and its not being done has occasioned, we solemnly and reluctantly confess, very serious apprehensions and doubts in the public mind, which are every day increasing. ... It is rational to suppose that those who removed John Adams from office, because of his manifold transgressions of the constitution, and his pointed hostility to liberty ... would naturally expect the removal of lesser culprits in office. If this should not be the case, for what, in the name of God, have we been contending? Merely for the removal of John Adams, that Mr. Jefferson might occupy the place which he shamefully left?[21]

But Aaron Burr, disturbed by this piece, wrote to Gallatin asking him to assure the President that "notwithstanding any ebullitions of this kind, he may be confidently assured that the great mass of republicans in this State are determined that he shall do things at his own time and in his own manner."[22] Jefferson, hoping to reconcile the differences among the New York Republicans, decided: "We shall yield a little to their pressure, but no more than appears absolutely necessary to keep them together. And if that would be as much as to disgust other parts of the union, we must prefer the greater to the lesser part."[23]

Under the pressure of Republican demands and the fading prospects of Federalist reconciliation, Jefferson began to modify his patronage policies. To New York Governor George Clinton, he wrote on May 17: "Disposed myself to make as few changes in office as possible, to endeavor to restore harmony by avoiding everything harsh, and to remove only for malconduct, I have nevertheless been persuaded that circumstances in your state, and still more in the neighboring states on both sides, require something more."[24] A further modification of earlier sentiments was indicated in June, when Jefferson decided in regard to

20. New York *American Citizen,* June 4, 1801; David Denniston and James Cheetham to Jefferson, June 1, 1801, Jefferson Papers, Lib. Cong. See also Jefferson to Denniston and Cheetham, June 6, 1801, Denniston and Cheetham to Jefferson, June 12, 1801, *ibid.*
21. New York *American Citizen,* June 5, 1801.
22. Burr to Gallatin, June 8, 1801, Gallatin Papers, N.-Y. Hist. Soc.
23. Jefferson to Wilson Cary Nicholas, June 11, 1801, Ford, ed., *Jefferson Writings,* VIII, 64.
24. Jefferson to Clinton, May 17, 1801, *ibid.,* 52-53.

Connecticut that "a general sweep seems to be called for on principles of justice and policy. Their legislature now sitting are removing every republican even from the commissions of the peace and the lowest offices. There then we will retaliate. Whilst the Feds. are taking possession of all the state offices, exclusively, they ought not to expect we will leave them the exclusive possession of those at our disposal. The republicans have some rights: and must be protected."[25] Jefferson's hopes of Federalist conciliation were being rudely shattered. His changing attitude was reflected in his reply to the New Haven remonstrance which constituted the first public statement of removal policies to be made by the President since the general expressions of his inaugural address. As the most important public policy statement in regard to patronage made by Jefferson during his two terms, it is important to examine the background of this declaration before noticing its content and effect.

In March, Jefferson had written Connecticut Republican leaders requesting their opinions on the removal of Elizur Goodrich as collector of New Haven. Goodrich, who had been appointed by President Adams among his last hurried appointments, fell under Jefferson's policy of removing such officials, but Jefferson wanted those "who best know all the circumstances which ought to weigh, to consult and advise us on this subject; taking a broad view of it, general as well as local."[26] After consulting with other party leaders in the state, Pierpont Edwards, a prominent Connecticut Republican, replied, May 12, 1801:

> There is but one opinion among the intelligent republicans in Connecticut, respecting the case of Mr. Goodrich; all agree, that a removal will be right in itself, and that the measure is necessary, as it regards the general cause in Connecticut. . . . we are convinced, that his being continued in office, instead of reconciling his friends, or any part of the federalists to republicanism, and to your administration, will strengthen them in their Opposition. They boldly assert that you dare not dismiss any federal officer in Connecticut. And they assign two reasons: "That you know, that if your administration is supported at all in Connecticut, it must be supported by the federalists," and "that you have no confidence in any of the republicans, because you consider them men unfriendly to all regular Government."[27]

25. Jefferson to Wilson Cary Nicholas, June 11, 1801, *ibid.*, 64-65.
26. Jefferson to Pierpont Edwards, Mar. 29, 1801, Jefferson to Gideon Granger, Mar. 29, 1801, *ibid.*, 44-45.
27. Edwards to Jefferson, May 12, 1801, Appointment Papers, National Archives. Also printed in Gaillard Hunt, "Office-seeking during Jefferson's Administration," *Amer. Hist. Rev.*, 3 (1898), 274-77.

Edwards reported that all Republicans agreed on Samuel Bishop as Goodrich's successor. Less than two weeks later, on May 23, 1801, Bishop was appointed to replace Goodrich as collector of New Haven.

On June 18, a committee of New Haven merchants headed by Elias Shipman addressed a remonstrance to the President. Signed by seventy-eight merchants, who were certified by the president of the New Haven Chamber of Commerce to be "owners of more than seven-eights of the navigation of the port of New Haven," the address protested against the removal of Goodrich and the appointment of Bishop. The character of Goodrich as an officer was pronounced unexceptionable, while Bishop was declared too old and infirm. It was further asserted that his son Abraham Bishop would do the actual work of the office and that he was "entirely destitute of public confidence."[28] The remonstrance, Madison thought, was couched "in the strongest terms that decorum would tolerate."[29]

Jefferson decided to make his reply to the New Haven remonstrance the vehicle for a public statement of his policies in regard to appointments and removals. Meanwhile, he had received detailed reports from Connecticut Republican leaders on the party situation in that state, and these played an important part in determining the stand which he should take. One of the reports was a lengthy letter signed by twenty-four Connecticut Republicans, who, according to Gideon Granger, included all but two or three of the most influential Republican leaders in the state. These Connecticut Republicans were convinced that "even if it should be judged good policy in all other States, to retain the federalists in office, yet in this State, we could contemplate, in such policy only the certain ruin of republicanism and even by delays we apprehend a relapse, from which it will be difficult, perhaps impossible to recover." They pointed to the lack of any spirit of conciliation on the part of the Federalists—demonstrated by the actions of the state legislature in removing Republicans from state offices—and recommended that Jefferson abandon his policy of conciliation in regard to Connecticut. They explained:

Considering the facts in our own State as a basis, and perhaps somewhat under the influence of irritation, we have judged that a very

28. Elias Shipman and others, committee of the merchants of New Haven, to Jefferson, [June 18, 1801], Jefferson Papers, Lib. Cong.

29. Madison to Wilson C. Nicholas, June 10, 1801, Gaillard Hunt, ed., *The Writings of James Madison* . . . , 9 vols. (N.Y., 1900-1910), VI, 426n.

extended system of removals would aid our cause—that republicanism was established at the Southward, and had so far advanced in New England that nothing was wanting but presidential patronage to compleat it —that it was more important to retain the confidence of the majority than to conciliate apparently men who can never be republicans. . . . we have been, and continue to be opposed to any conciliatory system from a persuasion that it cannot succeed and that a continuance of attempts to compose this object will throw us into imminent hazard. . . .

The operating republicans here are few: they need every aid in advancing the cause. The Federal leaders are numerous, they have the influence of the Clergy, of several papers, State offices and federal officers. Without the aid of these last, the republicans cannot encounter the others. . . . The republicans expect that the President will remove the federalists from office. . . . They are all mortified to see their enemies triumphing in a day when they expected triumph and to be daily insulted and abused as not having merited the confidence of the administration, whose advocates they have been. They are naturally ambitious that the confidence of the President should be openly extended to their friends and that he should repel from himself the unmerited reproach of indecision and timidity. . . .

The proposed removals would bring the federalists into action, we will not conceal it. They would denounce the measure as the result of a vindictive spirit, as the act of the President of a party, but this they have already said in respect to the removals made in other States. We conceive it better to meet them with all their force now, than three years hence, and we know, that they who seek occasion, will always find occasion for blame against any administration, and that their leaders will be opposed to Mr. Jefferson's re-election at any rate. . . . We cannot conceive, Sir, that our cause is to yield any sacrifices to any false construction of Mr. Jefferson's Speech nor can we place a moments confidence in our cause, if it depends in the least on the conversion or acquiescence of a single federal leader.[30]

After conferring with other New England Republicans, Attorney General Levi Lincoln, in forwarding the above letter to the President, agreed that the proposed removals should be made in Connecticut. However, he advised that they not be made all at once, but gradually, perhaps over a period of a year. Large-scale immediate removals, he felt, "would appear more like the effect of resentment and a persecution for a past political difference of opinion than a provision for the benefit of Government."[31] Gideon Granger supported Lincoln's position that re-

---

30. Pierpont Edwards and others to Levi Lincoln, June 4, 1801, enclosed in Lincoln to Jefferson, June 15, 1801, Jefferson Papers, Lib. Cong.
31. Lincoln to Jefferson, June 15, 1801, *ibid*.

movals should take place gradually, but advised that "they ought to be made in the forepart of the Administration, that all consequent agitations may be quieted before the next Electoral Election." Granger, having recently visited in most of the New England states, was convinced that a sudden general removal in Connecticut would be felt throughout the entire region. "Can it be wise to strike a general blow and throw a whole State with a powerful majority into agitation?" he asked. "By such a measure the whole phalanx will be united; by removing one by one, those who are spared, with all their friends, will at least be silent, hoping to hold each one his office." Granger stressed the regionalism of New England and suggested that "the different habits and tempers of the people in the various parts of the Union appear to require different treatment." The people of New England could not be frightened into supporting the administration, he said; they must be persuaded. From the point of view of practical politics, he advised delay. "We all duly appreciate the importance of carrying the Elections in Vermont next fall," he wrote; "whoever coolly considers that one half of the people of Vermont emigrated from this State, where they have many kindred whom they usually visit in Autumn just before their Election I think will be ready to admit that any great agitation in Connecticut will sensibly affect and endanger the Elections in that State. I cannot therefore avoid hoping that but little will be done with us before the issue of that Election."[32]

In the midst of this Republican concern in Connecticut regarding the patronage, the President received the remonstrance from the New Haven merchants. At the same time he received a confidential letter from Pierpont Edwards explaining its origin and supplying the President with the factual information to refute the Federalist charges voiced in the remonstrance. Edwards explained:

It is my duty to inform you of the state of facts as they respect Mr. Samuel Bishop; he is about seventy-seven years of age, possesses his faculties of mind perfectly, and a more pure, upright, unblemished character New England cannot afford. As a proof that his mental faculties are good, I need only tell you, that he is Mayor of our City, which office, though bestowed by the City, he holds during the pleasure of our Legislature. Our Judges of every description are appointed annually in May; Mr. Samuel Bishop was in May last, appointed chief Judge of our County Court, and Judge of our Court of Probates. . . . The Assembly

32. Granger to Jefferson, July 6, 1801, *ibid*.

also appointed him a Justice of the Peace. I trust no further proof as to his (Samuel Bishop) capacity can be demanded by the friends of order —for these proofs are from them.[33]

The real object of Federalist bitterness, Edwards pointed out, was Abraham Bishop, "whom they hate above all men."

In his reply to the New Haven merchants, July 12, 1801, Jefferson used many of the facts furnished by Edwards to defend the qualifications of Samuel Bishop for office and to challenge the contention of the remonstrance that he was unfit to be the collector of New Haven. He also vindicated the removal of Goodrich on the basis of his having been appointed in the last moments of Adams's administration. From a defense of the particular case involved in the protest, Jefferson turned to explain more fully than he had ever before done publicly the principles to be followed by the administration in regard to appointments and removals. It is this general statement of policy that makes his reply to the New Haven remonstrance his most important public statement on the question of the patronage.

Although not specifically mentioning his inaugural address, Jefferson began by suggesting the sentiment expressed there had been misinterpreted:

Declarations by myself in favor of *political tolerance*, exhortations to *harmony* and affection in social intercourse, and to respect for the *equal rights* of the minority, have, on certain occasions, been quoted and misconstrued into assurances that the tenure of offices was to be undisturbed. But could candor apply such a construction? . . . When it is considered, that during the late administration, those who were not of a particular sect of politics were excluded from all office; when, by a steady pursuit of this measure, nearly the whole offices of the U.S. were monopolized by that sect; when the public sentiment at length declared itself, and burst open the doors of honor and confidence to those whose opinion they more approved, was it to be imagined that this monopoly of office was still to be continued in the hands of the minority? Does it violate their *equal rights,* to assert some rights in the majority also? Is it *political intolerance* to claim a proportionate share in the direction of the public affairs? Can they not *harmonize* in society unless they have everything in their own hands? If the will of the nation, manifested by their various elections, calls for an administration of government according with the opinions of those elected; if, for the fulfilment of that will, displacements are necessary, with whom can they so justly begin as with persons ap-

33. Edwards to Jefferson, June 10-18, 1801, *ibid.*

pointed in the last moments of an administration, not for its own aid, but to begin a career at the same time with their successors, by whom they had never been approved, and who could scarcely expect from them a cordial co-operation? ... If a due participation of office is a matter of right, how are vacancies to be obtained? Those by death are few; by resignation, none. Can any other mode than that of removal be proposed? This is a painful office; but it is made my duty, and I meet it as such. I proceed in the operation with deliberation and inquiry, that it may injure the best men least, and effect the purposes of justice and public utility with the least private distress; that it may be thrown, as much as possible, on delinquency, on oppression, on intolerance, on incompetence, on ante-revolutionary adherence to our enemies.

... It would have been to me a circumstance of great relief, had I found a moderate participation of office in the hands of the majority. I would gladly have left to time and accident to raise them to their just share. But their total exclusion calls for prompter correctives. I shall correct the procedure; but that done, disdain to follow it, shall return with joy to that state of things, when the only questions concerning a candidate shall be, is he honest? Is he capable? Is he faithful to the Constitution?[34]

Jefferson wrote privately that he had welcomed the opportunity afforded by the New Haven remonstrance "of correcting the *misconstructions*" of what he had said on March 4.[35] But whatever interpretations may have been placed upon his inaugural declarations, Jefferson's own papers suggest that his own interpretation of what he had meant had changed. The private explanations which he made in March and April did not indicate the removal policy outlined in this July statement. In March he had affirmed that "for mere difference of principle, I am not disposed to disturb any man."[36] "Malconduct is a just ground of removal: mere difference of political opinion is not." "Those who have acted well have nothing to fear, however they may have differed from me in opinion."[37] In July, on the other hand, he indicated that Federalists would be dismissed on political grounds if necessary to afford Republicans a proportionate share of the federal offices. There was to be no waiting for deaths or resignations, and, although the least capable

---

34. Jefferson to Elias Shipman and others, committee of the merchants of New Haven, July 12, 1801, Ford, ed., *Jefferson Writings*, VIII, 67-70.
35. Jefferson to Thomas McKean, July 24, 1801, Jefferson to Pierpont Edwards, July 21, 1801, *ibid.*, 74, 79.
36. Jefferson to John W. Eppes, Mar. 27, 1801, Jefferson Papers, Univ. of Va.
37. Jefferson to William Findley, Mar. 24, 1801, Jefferson to Elbridge Gerry, Mar. 29, 1801, Ford, ed., *Jefferson Writings*, VIII, 27, 42.

were to be dismissed first and removals were to be founded as far as possible upon malconduct, offices were to be vacated. He urged his department heads to be "inflexible against appointing Federalists till there be a due portion of Republicans introduced into office." Efforts to reconcile the Federalists should not be pushed to such an extent as to revolt "our tried friends," he said. "It would be a poor manoeuvre to exchange them for new converts."[38] Under the pressure of Republican demands and the influence of continuing Federalist opposition, the President's earlier sentiments of moderation and conciliation had undergone noticeable modification.

The full meaning of this change in Jefferson's policy did not immediately appear clear even to Albert Gallatin, one of his closest advisers on patronage decisions. On July 25, the Secretary of the Treasury sent to the President for approval the draft of a circular to be sent to collectors. Part of the circular concerned the policies to be followed by collectors in appointing subordinate officers. In this, Gallatin instructed that "the door of office be no longer shut against any man merely on account of his political opinions, but that whether he shall differ or not from those avowed either by you or by myself, integrity and capacity suitable to the station be the only qualifications that shall direct our choice." Another paragraph stated that the exercise of official influence to restrain or control the freedom of suffrage at public elections would not be tolerated. Gallatin explained that these instructions were "intended to let them know that it is expected that they will, although Federal, divide the offices in their nomination" and "that an electioneering collector is commonly a bad officer as it relates to his official duties."[39]

Jefferson, who opened Gallatin's circular in Madison's presence, replied: "I approve so entirely of the two paragraphs on the participation of office and electioneering activity, that on the latter subject I proposed very early to issue a proclamation, but was restrained by some particular considerations; with respect to the former, we both thought it better to be kept back till the New Haven remonstrance and answer have got into possession of the public; and then that it should go further and require an equilibrium to be first produced by exchanging one-half of their subordinates, after which talents and worth alone to be inquired into in the

38. Jefferson to Gallatin, Aug. 14, 1801, Henry Adams, ed., *The Writings of Albert Gallatin*, 3 vols. (Philadelphia, 1879), I, 37.
39. Gallatin to Jefferson, July 25, 1801, *ibid.*, 28-29; Henry Adams, *The Life of Albert Gallatin* (Phila., 1880), 278-79.

case of new vacancies."⁴⁰ Although Jefferson's reply to the New Haven remonstrance had not specified what he regarded as a due participation of Republicans in office, his letter to Gallatin suggested that he considered that one-half of the offices should be placed in Republican hands. This interpretation was also advanced by the press.⁴¹ On the other hand, Jefferson's vagueness led some Republicans to think in terms of more extensive removals. Jefferson himself admitted that his New Haven statement had "given more expectation to the *sweeping* Republicans than I think its terms justify."⁴² Later, Jefferson clearly indicated that he did not consider an equal number of Republican and Federalist officeholders as constituting a due proportion. In June 1803, he noted that Federalists "can now bear to talk themselves of an *equal number,* instead of a monopoly of offices. This is well, as a first symptom; and we hope, in the progress of convalescence, they will become able to bear the idea of a *due proportion.* On this ground we are ready to compromise with them: and I ask what is their due proportion? I suppose the relative numbers of the two parties will be thought to fix it; and that, judging from the elections, we over-rate the Federalists at one third or fourth of the whole mass of our citizens."⁴³

Jefferson's reply to the New Haven remonstrance was major news. Both the remonstrance and the answer were published in full in newspapers throughout the country.⁴⁴ The Federalist Boston *Columbian Centinel* accused the President of "hypocrisy" and "equivocation,"⁴⁵ while the Republican Newark *Centinel of Freedom* declared: "It is hoped that the different federal Editors and federal scribblers, will no longer be deceiving their readers with the cries of *political intolerance,* on account of the removal of some of their partizans from office—that they will not by distorted construction of detached sentences in Mr. Jefferson's inaugural speech, attempt to palm a belief on the public mind that he is a deceiver, whose practices are at variance with his professions—the falsehood of these assertions we conceive to be amply proved by his conduct, as well

40. Jefferson to Gallatin, July 26, 1801, Adams, ed., *Gallatin Writings,* I, 29-30.
41. Hartford *American Mercury,* Aug. 13, 1801; Philadelphia *Aurora,* Aug. 10, 1801.
42. Jefferson to Gallatin, Aug. 14, 1801, Adams, ed., *Gallatin Writings,* I, 37.
43. Article written by Jefferson, published in Boston *Independent Chronicle,* June 27, 1803, printed in Ford, ed., *Jefferson Writings,* VIII, 236n. See pp. 255-56 below.
44. Boston *Independent Chronicle,* July 27, 1801, extra; Philadelphia *Aurora,* July 28, 1801; Newark *Centinel of Freedom,* July 28, 1801, extra; Washington *National Intelligencer,* July 29, 1801; Raleigh *Register,* Aug. 11, 1801; Nashville *Tennessee Gazette,* Sept. 2, 9, 1801.
45. *Columbian Centinel,* July 29, 1801.

as his reply to the remonstrance of the merchants of New-Haven."[46] The Philadelphia *Aurora* expressed satisfaction that the "insolent, indecent, and intolerant" remonstrance had served the useful purpose of drawing forth an elucidation of the principles of the administration,[47] and the *Albany Register* affirmed: "An equal distribution of the offices at his disposal, between the contending parties which divide the country, is the object of the President. Can reasonable OPPOSITIONISTS expect or hope for more? Can liberal and enlightened republicans be disposed to give less? . . . the PEOPLE will be highly pleased with this wise, liberal, and magnanimous policy of the President."[48]

The President's answer was rebutted at great length in a pamphlet, *An Examination of the President's Reply to the New-Haven Remonstrance,* signed Lucius Junius Brutus. Criticizing the President for becoming "a party to an altercation respecting his official acts," Brutus vigorously assailed Jefferson's reply, protesting that "it is here we are to look for the real sentiments of the President, and not to the delusive Address by which, on the threshold of office, he sought to lull the fears, and win the confidence of the people." He exclaimed: "Instead of pursuing that mild and conciliatory system of conduct, tending *to restore harmony to social intercourse,* for which he pledged himself, and thus gradually to wear off the asperities of party, he has suddenly, and unexpectedly, departed from this just and honorable policy; divided the people into two distinct classes; branded one as an odious Sect; and in the true spirit of a bigot, he now wages a war of extermination against all who are not within the pale of his established Church."[49]

Several replies to Brutus soon appeared, the most able of which declared:

The people have done *their* duty; it is the business of their agents to perform *their's.* In every instance in which the aggregate mass of the citizens had the right, by election, to remove the federal officers, they have uniformly done so. . . . If the people had possessed the right of removing, by election, those who have been removed by the President, a prompter and a more efficient "corrective" would have been applied by them than has been applied by the executive. The minor tyrants, such as collectors, naval officers, surveyors, supervisors, marshals, district attornies, and even

46. *Centinel of Freedom,* Aug. 4, 1801.
47. *Aurora,* July 29, 1801.
48. *Ibid.,* Aug. 10, 1801, reprinted from *Albany Register.*
49. Lucius Junius Brutus [pseud.], *An Examination of the President's Reply to the New-Haven Remonstrance* (N.Y., 1801), pamphlet, Historical Society of Pennsylvania.

justices of the peace . . . with myriads of others of a still lower grade, would all have been removed by the people with a force little less prompt than an electrical shock. . . . Can you then suppose, that if Mr. Jefferson be faithful to his trust, faithful to the constitution, faithful to the people, he has any choice beween removal and non-removal?[50]

Reaction to the President's reply was divided strictly along party lines. "The answer to the Newhaven remonstrance is a recantation of the Speech," said Federalist Harrison G. Otis, "and probably an expiatory sacrifice to the *resentment* of many who made no secret of their disapprobation of the tolerant and specious language of that instrument. Jefferson is not the first chieftain of a party who has realized that the hour of success was also the hour of the decline of his personal influence among his own adherents. By proclaiming himself the head and champion of a party, he secures the continuance of their zeal and exertions."[51] Another Federalist, Henry W. DeSaussure, agreed: "It would have been greatly desirable that he would have forgotten that he was the head of a party, and have become what the Constitution intended, the head of the nation. It would have made his administration a healing one. But as he does not chuse so to act, he could not have chosen a mode of expression and action better calculated to ruin himself and his party, with reasonable men, than that which he has adopted."[52]

Republican response on the other hand was overwhelmingly in support of the President. "Your answer to the New Haven remonstrance is much admired here, by the republicans, and will be productive of very salutary effects," wrote Levi Lincoln from Massachusetts. "The principles it contains alarm the gentlemen in office, and will put them on their behavior, and prove to some of them a converting ordinance and of course an useful one."[53] Governor Thomas McKean reported enthusiastic support in Pennsylvania for the President's reply; and Caesar A. Rodney wrote that in Delaware "our Republicans to a man have been delighted with the sentiments which it breathes. It will have no doubt a very happy effect on the approaching elections throughout the United

---

50. Leonidas [pseud.], *A Reply to Lucius Brutus's Examination of the President's Answer to the New-Haven Remonstrance* (N.Y., 1801), pamphlet, Hist. Soc. of Pa. See also Tullius Americus [pseud.], *Strictures on a Pamphlet Entitled, "An Examination of the President's Reply to the New-Haven Remonstrance"* (Albany, 1801), pamphlet, N.-Y. Hist. Soc.

51. Otis to John Rutledge, Oct. 18, 1801, Rutledge Papers, Univ. of N.C.

52. DeSaussure to John Rutledge, Sept. [11?], 1801, *ibid.*

53. Lincoln to Jefferson, July 28, 1801, Jefferson Papers, Lib. Cong.; see also Lincoln to Gallatin, July 29, 1801, Gallatin Papers, N.-Y. Hist. Soc.

States."⁵⁴ Secretary of War Henry Dearborn also concluded that "the Presidents Answer to the New Haven remonstrance has had a good effect. Some of the leading characters among the federalists say the New Haven people were D——d fools for giving the President such an opportunity of expressing his sentiments."⁵⁵ Albert Gallatin was not in unison with most other Republicans when he voiced his concern that "the answer to New Haven seems to have had a greater effect than had been calculated upon. The Republicans hope for a greater number of removals; the Federals also expect it." But Jefferson promptly denied the suggestion of his Secretary of the Treasury and defended his declaration as "indispensably necessary."⁵⁶

By July 1801, the President's patronage policy had thus been formulated. His earlier uncertainty as to where to draw the line between all or none in removals had now been resolved. Federalists would be removed from office and replaced with Republicans until a proportionate share of the federal offices was filled by Republicans. As later defined this meant Republicans were entitled to from two-thirds to three-fourths of all offices. In making removals, Adams's midnight appointees, delinquent officials, and Federalist attorneys and marshals would be removed first. In other removals, the conduct and performance of Federalists in office would be carefully considered in order to effect the removal of the least capable officials first. Only Republicans would be appointed to offices until Republicans held their proportionate share of the appointments; after this, political affiliation was not to be considered in qualifications for office. After formulating his rationale for patronage policy, Jefferson moved to implement it.

54. McKean to Jefferson, Aug. 10, 1801, Rodney to Jefferson, Aug. 11, 1801, Jefferson Papers, Lib. Cong.
55. Dearborn to Gallatin, Aug. 8, 1801, Gallatin Papers, N.-Y. Hist. Soc.
56. Gallatin to Jefferson, Aug. 10, 1801, Jefferson to Gallatin, Aug. 14, 1801, Adams, ed., *Gallatin Writings*, I, 32-33, 37.

CHAPTER THREE

The Party and the Patronage: Problems and Practices

The advent of the Jeffersonian administration brought a flood of applications for office, and the contest for places, although abating after the initial fury, continued throughout both terms. Some office seekers wrote directly to the President, or to a member of his Cabinet, recommending themselves for office. The more successful in obtaining appointments wrote to their representative or senator, or had influential friends send letters of recommendation to the President or a department head. Applications received by members of Congress were frequently turned over to the President or to the department involved; often they were enclosed in letters adding the congressman's endorsement. In the National Archives there are twenty ream-size boxes of applications and recommendations for office for the period of Jefferson's administration. The private papers of Jefferson, Gallatin, and Madison contain hundreds of additional letters relating to offices.

An example of a successful applicant was John Smith, who was appointed marshal of the eastern district of Pennsylvania. His application for office was supported by: (1) a glowing letter of recommendation from John Beckley, who praised Smith's efforts in behalf of the Republican party in the presidential election of 1796, noting that he had spent twenty-five days at his own expense and had traveled seven or eight hundred miles during the campaign; (2) a letter of recommendation from the citizens of Northumberland County, signed by fifteen persons headed by Daniel Montgomery, a leading Republican of the county; (3) a very similar letter from the citizens of Berks County, the fifteen signers headed by Joseph Hiester, Republican member of Congress; (4) a letter from eighteen citizens of Philadelphia, headed by Hugh Ferguson, active Republican in state politics; (5) a letter signed by twenty-nine commissioned officers of the Militia Legion of Philadelphia; and (6) a note in Jefferson's handwriting that Smith was recommended by Dr. Michael Leib, prominent Republican congressman.[1] On March 28, 1801, Jefferson removed John Hall, the Federalist marshal of eastern Pennsylvania, on the ground of packing juries and commissioned Smith to replace him.

Not all candidates, of course, were able to muster such support for their applications, but they were wise to follow similar methods. Jefferson, like other Presidents, relied heavily on the opinions of members of his party in Congress from the state where the appointment was to be made. The same was true of department heads. "Your success probably will depend on the recommendation of the delegation of the State of Tennessee, as that is the Channel from whence information is sought by the Executive in this case," explained South Carolina Senator Thomas Sumter to a Tennessee friend seeking an army appointment.[2] Sometimes, a group of congressmen would make a recommendation. Six Republican members from Pennsylvania, for example, successfully recommended Peter Muhlenberg for the office of supervisor of revenue for that state in 1801, citing him as a "uniform and able supporter of the Republican cause."[3]

An example of a consistently unsuccessful applicant was David Austin, whose entreaties to the President must have become exceedingly tiresome. During Jefferson's first ten months in office Austin wrote to the President no less than seventeen times in regard to some sort of appointment. In March 1801, he wrote repeatedly seeking a commission to go to Europe to treat with both France and England to establish world peace. He was distracted from this ambition when he saw an item in the newspaper stating that no appointment of a private secretary to the President had been announced. This prompted him to apply for this post, although he stated that he would be agreeable, should that appointment have been made, to accept the headship of a department. Getting no response from these suggestions, he proposed in June that he be appointed to succeed Rufus King as ambassador to England. By the end

---

1. John Beckley to ———, Mar. 10, 1801; Citizens of County of Northumberland to Jefferson, [1801]; Citizens of County of Berks to Jefferson, Mar. 14, 1801; John Smith to Jefferson, Mar. 11, 1801; Hugh Ferguson and others to Jefferson, Mar. 5, 1801; Peter Christian, adjutant, and others to Jefferson, Mar. 5, 1801, Appointment Papers, Nat. Archives.

2. Sumter to Andrew Butler, July 17, 1808, Butler to George W. Campbell, Sept. 15, 1808, George W. Campbell Papers, Lib. Cong.

3. Michael Leib, Robert Brown, Joseph Hiester, John Smilie, John A. Hanna, and Andrew Gregg to Jefferson, Feb. 20, 1801, Appointment Papers, Nat. Archives.

of June and early July, Austin was seeking a clerkship in either the Treasury or Navy Department. Jefferson's delay in appointing a Secretary of the Navy encouraged him to ask for that post in mid-July. By August he was suggesting a position as assistant secretary in one of the departments. In 1802, he renewed his application to be ambassador to England; in 1803, he applied to be collector of New Haven. By 1804, the unsuccessful applicant was writing for any sort of appointment that Jefferson might have at his disposal. The President, personally going over all the letters of application which he received, was not spared this sort of nuisance.[4]

Most applications or letters of recommendation made some reference to the candidate's contribution to the party cause or to his steady attachment to Republicanism. "Being one of those Citizens whose Politicks has ever been congenial with your own, and having long been a faithful labourer in the vineyard of Republicanism," wrote one applicant; "beg leave on the authority of the enclosed recommendatory vouchers, to offer myself as an applicant for the Collectorship of the District of Delaware."[5] Less modestly another wrote from Pennsylvania:

My pretensions to the appointment of Supervisor are founded, First on my zealous, laborious, *daring* and efficient exertions to promote the great objects of the late Election. No one in this State exposed himself more to aristocratic vengeance than I did. No one spent more time and money in writing and circulating pamphlets and pieces. I am assured that owing to the circulation of several hundred copies of my "Sketch of Address" in Frederick County, Maryland, the republican members for their State Legislature were carried . . . and I am assured . . . that it was also owing to the circulation of several hundred copies of the same Address in the English and German Languages that the republican Ticket prevailed in York and Adams.[6]

Letters of recommendation contained such assurances as that a candidate for office "was a zealous labourer in 1800 to bring about the present pleasing order of things,"[7] or that "his sound republican Principles are such as Government may rely on."[8] Or it might be stressed that "very

4. Austin to Jefferson, Mar. 9, 15, 16, 21, May 26, 31, June 11, 30, July 6, 17, Aug. 31, Sept. 4, 1801, Mar. 20, 1802, Aug. 20, 1803, Oct. 6, 1804, *ibid.*
5. Leonard Vandegrifte to Jefferson, Mar. 16, 1801, Jefferson Papers, Lib. Cong.
6. Samuel Bryan to Albert Gallatin, Apr. 3, 1801, Gallatin Papers, N.-Y. Hist. Soc.
7. Arthur Campbell to Madison, Jan. 25, 1802, Madison Papers, Lib. Cong.
8. Letter, recommending Abraham Bissent for collector, to Albert Gallatin, signed by 56 residents of the Town of St. Mary's, Camden County, S.C., Oct. 5, 1806, Appointment Papers, Nat. Archives.

few, if any of our Republican friends, in this quarter, stand higher in point of character. . . . the appointment of no man, would give more general satisfaction, and be productive of more advantage to the party."[9]

Other letters pointed out that the applicant "has been open and active in displaying his active disapprobation of the preceding administration," or "has always manifested a warm attachment to Republicanism."[10] Six Republican members of the legislature of New Jersey in petitioning for the appointment of Oliver Barnet as United States marshal for the district of New Jersey wrote: "We beg leave to add, that he has ever distinguished himself for his attachment to the Principles of the Revolution and most particularly in the late Elections, in support of the present Administration, and we think the appointment will most essentially serve the cause of Republicanism in New Jersey."[11] John Taylor in recommending a friend stressed: "He is a republican, and an admirer of the present administration; not from accident or influence, but from conviction, the effect of examination and reflection."[12] Supporting the Rev. John Hargrove for "an upper clerk's" position in one of the departments, Arthur Campbell explained: "What lays us under obligation, he wrote last Summer and Fall some pieces that was printed in defence of the present President that had a good effect in removing prejudices relating to religious opinions, and moral principles. A liberal clergyman now-o-days is a valuable Man."[13]

Assurances of party support were in fact absolutely necessary if an applicant expected to receive an office. Jefferson made it clear that only Republicans would be appointed, and he requested information as to party attachments before making his decisions. When letters of recommendation said nothing of the politics of a candidate, it was his belief that this "generally authorises a presumption that they are not with the government."[14]

The letters of application and recommendation reveal the hopes and ambitions, the strengths and the weaknesses, of human character; they

9. Nathaniel Hazard to Christopher Ellery, Feb. 9, 1804, enclosed in Ellery to Jefferson, Feb. 27, 1804, *ibid*.
10. Larkin Smith to Madison, Aug. 14, 1801, Madison Papers, Lib. Cong.; Thomas Proctor and others to Peter Muhlenberg, May 1, 1801, Gallatin Papers, N.-Y. Hist. Soc.
11. John Lambert and others to Jefferson, May 24, 1802, Appointment Papers, Nat. Archives.
12. John Taylor of Caroline to Gallatin, Dec. 26, 1803, Gallatin Papers, N.-Y. Hist. Soc.
13. Campbell to Madison, Mar. 23, 1801, Madison Papers, Lib. Cong.
14. Jefferson to Wilson Cary Nicholas, Aug. 8, 1804 [photostat of original in private collection], Jefferson Papers, Univ. of Va.

display the personal and the party motives. Their mass and their content help to explain why Jefferson found the task of making appointments the most burdensome of his duties. Nor were the members of his Cabinet spared the importunities of the office seekers. When Madison was appointed Secretary of State, several former classmates at Princeton decided to renew acquaintances. "You have not had a letter from me in twenty years," wrote one who explained: "I saw you engrossed by national business.... the splendor of your talents threw me at a distance.... I was content with the humbler ambition of telling my friends, when you became the subject of discourse, that I had the honor of being known to you at College."[15] He sought a clerkship for his son. Another classmate seeking an office for himself wrote: "You and I were at College but a little time together, so that you may have but a faint recollection of me; though you may recollect the Commencement, in which I pronounced the Valedictory Oration. If therefore you should render service to an old College-friend, it will be gratefully remembered."[16]

Although Jefferson and his department heads made it a practice not to reply to letters seeking appointments, their numbers, especially in the first years of the administration, created a heavy burden. Perhaps a letter such as the following provided a moment of relief. From near Middletown, Kentucky, Richard Taylor wrote to Madison:

I should be very glad to get Some publick office of moderate emolument, and the duty of which not very intricate, So as I Could discharge the duty of, with Credit and ease. You will I presume Say that one Foible I possest, aught to be done away, before it would be prudent to trust any publick post or office to me. I am perfectly Sensible from experience that the long habit in drinking to excess rendered me less Capable of doing my duty, as I aught to have done, which on reflection, hurt my feelings as it hurt my Consequence. You may be assured Sir I have quitted that dissipation. I have not drunk one Quart of ardent Spirits for near twelve months put it all together, of that little it was in way of Safety against the Colick. Nor have I the least desire to drink, although I Seldom See a day but I am in Company where Spirits is drank. I drink wine and water, Beer, and Syder Sometimes. I am satisfied within my own breast, that I dont want for resolution and fortitude to refrain from any thing I undertake.[17]

15. Nathaniel Irwin to Madison, Mar. 31, 1801, Madison Papers, Lib. Cong.
16. Isaac Story to Madison, Jan. 11, 1802, *ibid.*
17. Taylor to [Madison], Sept. 12, 1803, Madison-Todd Family Papers, Univ. of Va.

The President and the department heads, while patiently enduring unsolicited applications and recommendations, did not depend upon this source of information in making appointments. They especially sought the advice of party leaders in the various localities and regularly requested members of Congress to submit names of suitable candidates and to make recommendations. Despite the flood of applications for office, it was not always easy to find qualified persons willing to accept appointments.

Jefferson devoted a great deal of time to the mechanics of assigning offices. He kept lists of the names of persons proposed for offices, with notes on their qualifications, politics, and by whom they were recommended. His papers are filled with correspondence relating to offices and with numerous worksheets used in reaching decisions on appointments. The following memorandum which Jefferson sent to Gallatin in 1802 illustrates the procedure followed by the President in making appointments.

Candidates for the office of Surveyor of Smithfield

Doctor Purdie.	His father I know. He is a good man. But they are tories.
Wilson Davies.	He was collector of the direct tax, which is sufficient evidence he is a tory. He is recommended too by John Parker appointed by our predecessors, ergo a tory.
Dr. Southall.	His father was an excellent man and whig. His brother is said to be a very bad man. Of himself I know nothing. Col. Davies's favor makes his politics suspicious.
Cuningham.	Recommended by T. Newton junr. but not on his own knolege. A republican of 75. He does not live at the place and would be to remove.
John Easson.	Strongly recommended by Col. Newton the father, from an intimate knolege of him, as a very honest man, republican, and living on the spot. He was not long since a member of the Senate of Virginia, chosen by a district of several counties, which is good testimony of respectability, and a shield for us in his appointment.

It appears to me that Easson is the preferable candidate. If you think so let the commission issue. Such a paper as this you would not of course let go into the office bundles, but burn or otherwise dispose of as a private communication, and confidential.[18]

18. Jefferson to Gallatin, Oct. 28, 1802, Gallatin Papers, N.-Y. Hist. Soc. Easson was appointed, Nov. 2, 1802. Jefferson, [list of appointments, 1801-1809], Jefferson Papers, CLXXXVI, 33095-101, Lib. Cong.

Frequently the administration received conflicting testimony in regard to candidates for office. Noticing that "the task of removing and appointing officers continues to embarrass the Executive," Madison explained in July 1801: "The degree, the mode, and the times of performing it are often rendered the more perplexing by the discord of information and counsel received from different persons whose principles and views are the same."[19] This difficulty increased when Republican divisions disrupted party harmony in several important states.

The perplexities of making appointments were well illustrated by the appointment of Joel Lewis as marshal of Delaware. Since Delaware's representation in Congress was Federalist, Jefferson had to depend upon information from state Republican leaders. In June 1801, Dr. John Vaughan arrived in Washington with a letter of introduction from John Dickinson, Republican elder statesman, who recommended Vaughan as a sound Republican and a well-informed leading man in the state. Vaughan called on Gallatin, and the Secretary of the Treasury insisted that he confer with the President, who requested his recommendation in regard to a suitable choice as marshal of Delaware. Vaughan promised to comply after consulting Republicans back home, and Jefferson hurried a note off to Dickinson thanking him for acquainting him with Vaughan, explaining: "It is extremely important . . . for me to be on terms of confidence with some persons of dispassionate judgment and integrity in every state."[20] Soon after his return to Delaware, Vaughan wrote the President that, "having consulted several . . . Republican friends," he wished to recommend Joel Lewis as marshal of Delaware.[21] Construing John Dickinson's letter of introduction as a certification of Vaughan as a spokesman for Delaware Republicans, Jefferson issued the marshal's commission to Lewis.

Meanwhile, on the way to Washington was Caesar A. Rodney, recommended as the spokesman of Delaware Republicans by James Tilton, one of the most active Republican leaders in the state. At the insistence of "a number of ingenuous republicans, Mr. Rodney is prevailed upon to make a visit to Washington for the express purpose of representing the

19. Madison to Wilson Cary Nicholas, July 10, 1801, Hunt, ed., *Madison Writings*, VI, 426n.
20. Dickinson to Jefferson, May 25, 1801, Jefferson to Dickinson, June 21, 1801, Gallatin to Jefferson, June 20, 1801, Jefferson Papers, Lib. Cong.
21. Vaughan to Jefferson, June 24, 1801, *ibid*.

true interest of republicanism in Delaware," Tilton explained. "We have chosen him for this important duty, because we think him known and known to be irreproachable." Of consistent republican principles, he is "justly placed, at the head of the republican party. I am bold in making this declaration, from a wish that you may enquire into the truth of the allegation, and employ the result of your investigation, for the interest of Delaware." Tilton further suggested that "we have reason to think and are persuaded that insidious attempts have been made to precipitate certain appointments, which, though wished and expected, may be timed to great advantage."[22]

But before Jefferson was to read this letter, Lewis had been appointed marshal of Delaware. What Vaughan had neglected to tell the President was that Lewis was his father-in-law; and when the appointment of the new marshal was announced, a wave of Republican protest followed. Caesar A. Rodney, quickly taken into the President's confidence and henceforth relied upon for information in regard to Delaware politics, was requested to explain what had happened. Rodney reported that "not one Republican character we know of, was consulted by Dr. Vaughan on the subject of the appointment. Even Mr. Dickinson himself who had given the letter of introduction, knew not a syllable of it, until at or about the time the commission came on."[23] Dickinson also sent the President a letter protesting Lewis's appointment,[24] and he and other Delaware Republican leaders held a conference where it was decided to ask Lewis to resign. To this request Lewis agreed only *to offer* his resignation. Fearing adverse effects on the party in the fall elections in Delaware, Rodney earnestly hoped that the resignation would be accepted. "It is important also to consider that this is the first appointment under the Republican administration," he suggested. "It is most earnestly to be desired that in the conduct to be adopted relative thereto, the people should behold a pledge of attention to their wishes from which they will calculate with great confidence as to the future."[25]

Lewis's letter to the President, however, was a rather reluctant proposal to resign. "I valued the reception of the commission, as a tenor of your good opinion, and I do not wish to retain it under the denounce of

22. Tilton to Jefferson, June 30, 1801, *ibid*.
23. Rodney to Madison, July 17, 1801, James Madison Papers, New York Public Library.
24. Dickinson to Jefferson, July 18, 1801, Jefferson Papers, Lib. Cong.
25. Rodney to Madison, July 17, 1801, Madison Papers, N.Y. Pub. Lib.

your disapprobation," he wrote. "If, when the present clamor subsides, you have reason to believe it is in your power to make a better choice, I shall resign my commission with pleasure into your hands."[26] Meanwhile, Gallatin offered to write to Dr. Vaughan, if the President thought it proper that Lewis should resign, advising Lewis's resignation "on the grounds of public utility."[27]

In August, with elections approaching, Rodney wrote the President that every day furnished new proofs that Lewis should resign, "for I really do scarcely know a dissenting voice among the Republicans here."[28] But Jefferson, who pointed out that he had asked Vaughan for a recommendation, was unwilling to accuse him of improper efforts and refused to reverse the appointment. After conferring with Madison he explained to Gallatin that "we both think that as the appointment of Mr. Lewis is made, we ought not to meddle in it. If he offers to resign, certainly we may accept it, but not propose it to him. He is admitted to be a good republican, and not a word alledged against his moral character, nor any reason given why he should be removed but that he is disagreeable without saying for what."[29] Lewis was still in office in 1808.[30]

New York presented one of the administration's most difficult patronage problems. Initially when Jefferson took office he accepted Vice-President Aaron Burr as the spokesman of New York Republicans in regard to the patronage in that state. Burr submitted a list of removals which the Republicans of the New York delegation in Congress had unanimously agreed should be made, recommending David Gelston for collector, John Swartwout for marshal, Theodorus Bailey for supervisor, Matthew L. Davis for naval officer, and Edward Livingston for district attorney. Burr noted that one member preferred that Bailey and Davis should change places, otherwise all agreed on this arrangement.[31] Burr himself was strongly opposed to Bailey as naval officer, considering him unqualified for the post and an unpopular choice for that office; and

26. Lewis to Jefferson, July 16, 1801, Appointment Papers, Nat. Archives.
27. Gallatin to Jefferson, July 29, 1801, Jefferson Papers, Lib. Cong.
28. Rodney to Jefferson, Aug. 11, 1801, *ibid.*
29. Jefferson to Gallatin, Aug. 7, 1801, *ibid.*
30. Wilmington *Museum of Delaware*, July 23, 1808. I am indebted to Herbert T. Pratt for supplying this information.
31. Unsigned paper in handwriting of Aaron Burr, [1801], endorsed by Jefferson "from Col. Burr," printed in Hunt, "Office-seeking during Jefferson's Administration," *Amer. Hist. Rev.*, 3 (1898), 290. See also Jefferson, note on New York appointments, filed under David Gelston, [1801], Appointment Papers, Nat. Archives.

should Bailey be appointed as naval officer instead of Davis he advised against appointing Davis as supervisor.[32]

Under the President's policy of removing Federalist marshals and attorneys, prompt removals were made in these posts in New York, and before the end of March 1801, John Swartwout was appointed marshal and Edward Livingston, district attorney. Burr anticipated that these changes would have a happy effect on the state elections at the end of April.[33] The other recommendations were not immediately acted upon. Meanwhile, the administration received suggestions from New York that other voices besides that of Burr should be heeded. Samuel Osgood, a prominent New York Republican and Clinton connection, wrote confidentially to Madison suggesting that Burr had tried to win the presidency for himself and that "we have strong Evidence that the three Gentlemen appointed in this City are entirely devoted to the Vice President; and had it been in their Power, we have Reason to believe, that Mr. Jefferson would not have been President." Osgood recommended that Governor George Clinton be consulted on appointments in New York.[34] United States Senator John Armstrong also wrote to Gallatin inquiring "whether it would not be at once safe and civil to consult Gov. Clinton" on appointments.[35]

As allegations of Burr's intrigues relating to the electoral tie of 1800 reached the President, an immediate change in his handling of New York patronage was noticeable. He now began to consult Clinton, to whom he wrote at length on May 17: "It is represented that the Collector, Naval officer, and Supervisor ought all to be removed for the violence of their characters and conduct. The following arrangement was agreed on by Col. Burr and some of your Senators and representatives. David Gelston, collector, Theodorus Bailey, Naval officer, and M. L. Davis, Supervisor." Jefferson had thus listed Bailey and Davis contrary to the recommendations of Burr, but he went on to point out that he had received letters stating that Bailey was not fitted for naval officer and that Davis was not a proper choice for supervisor. "Unacquainted myself

32. Burr to Gallatin, Apr. 21, 1801, Gallatin Papers, N.-Y. Hist. Soc.
33. *Ibid.*
34. Osgood to Madison, Apr. 24, 1801, Madison Papers, Lib. Cong. On Burr's conduct in relation to the electoral tie with Jefferson in 1800, see Irving Brant, *James Madison, Secretary of State, 1800-1809* (Indianapolis, 1953), 23-24; Morton Borden, "The Election of 1800: Charge and Countercharge," *Delaware History*, 5 (1952), 42-62. On Jefferson's attitude toward Burr's actions, see Dumas Malone, *Jefferson and the Ordeal of Liberty* (Boston, 1962), 593-98.
35. Armstrong to Gallatin, May 7, 1801, Gallatin Papers, N.-Y. Hist. Soc.

with these and the other characters in the state which might be proper for these offices, and forced to decide on the opinions of others, there is no one whose opinion would command with me greater respect than yours, if you would be so good as to advise me, which of these characters and what others would be fittest for these offices."[36] Clinton's reply has not been located. David Gelston was named collector as Burr had recommended; Bailey and Davis were not appointed. To the office of supervisor, Samuel Osgood, who had warned Madison of Burr, was appointed. Osgood had been recommended by DeWitt Clinton, and also by Burr's friend David Gelston, who wrote that "should he be appointed, it *will meet* the entire approbation, as well as the *wish* of our friend Gov. Clinton for this I will be responsible."[37]

The question of the proposed appointment of Matthew L. Davis as naval officer developed into one of the most serious patronage disputes of Jefferson's administration, and it ultimately displayed the light in which the President regarded the Vice-President. Davis was one of Burr's closest political lieutenants; he had been one of the most active party workers in the critical New York City election of 1800 in which, under Burr's management, the Republicans had carried the city and thereby the state. Burr had been opposed to appointing Davis as supervisor because he believed that an older man would be more acceptable; he had been supported in this view by other New York Republicans such as Marinus Willett who explained that "Mr. Davis is a young man of promising parts and a very good republican, but his standing in the community such as to render the appointment improper."[38] But though Davis's lack of pretensions for this important office was admitted, Burr felt strongly that "we must provide for Davis in some other way," and repeatedly urged that he be appointed as naval officer. He was supported in this recommendation by Marinus Willett; John Swartwout, the newly appointed marshal; David Gelston, the recently named collector; and a number of other prominent Republican friends of Burr.[39]

36. Jefferson to George Clinton, May 17, 1801, Ford, ed., *Jefferson Writings*, VIII, 53.
37. DeWitt Clinton to Gallatin, July 21, 1801, David Gelston to Gallatin, July 28, 1801, Samuel Osgood to Gallatin, Aug. 4, 1801, Gallatin Papers, N.-Y. Hist. Soc.
38. Burr to Gallatin, Apr. 21, 1801, *ibid.;* Burr to Jefferson, Sept. 4, 1801, Marinus Willett to Jefferson, May 4, 1801, Appointment Papers, Nat. Archives.
39. Burr to Gallatin, Apr. 21, 1801, Gallatin Papers, N.-Y. Hist. Soc.; John Swartwout to Gallatin, Sept. 1, 1801, David Gelston to Gallatin, Sept. 4, 1801, Marinus Willett to Jefferson, Sept. 7, 1801, Henry Rutgers to Gallatin, Sept. 7, 1801, Daniel Ludlow, John Broome, Brockholst Livingston, and John B. Prevost to Jefferson, Aug. 26, 1801, Appointment Papers, Nat. Archives.

Near the end of June 1801, Burr wrote to Gallatin from New York that reports were in circulation there "respecting secret Machinations against Davis." Burr was more confirmed than ever in his opinion that Davis's talents for the naval office were superior to any other who might be proposed and that opposition to him "must proceed from improper motives, as no man dare avow an opinion hostile to the measure." Davis's character was in some measure at stake; he had refused lucrative employment in expectation of the appointment. "This thing has in my opinion gone too far to be now defeated," warned Burr, ". . . Davis is too important to be trifled with."[40] He asked Gallatin to show this letter to the President. But no decision was made in regard to removing the Federalist naval officer at New York, Richard Rogers, and Davis grew impatient, though there is no evidence that Jefferson was proceeding any slower in regard to this office than in many other similar cases. In September, Davis, armed with a stack of letters of recommendation, arrived in Washington on his way to Monticello to carry his case in person to the President. "Mr. D[avis] has been goaded into this Journey by the instances of an hundred friends of whom I am not one," confessed Burr. "Yet I have not opposed it and am rather gratified that he undertakes it." The business had been "too often talked of and too long left in suspense," Burr wrote to Gallatin. "The Matter is now arrived at a crisis which calls for your opinion. This I presume you will give in unqualified terms. . . . and I do entreat that there may now be a determination of some kind; for it has become a matter of too much speculation here why R[ogers] is kept in and why D[avis] is not appointed."[41]

Gallatin attempted to dissuade Davis from going to Monticello, but he found that "he had left New York with that intention, and is not easily diverted from his purpose." Gallatin added his letter of recommendation to those which Davis carried to the President, but he expressed doubts as to whether the removal of Rogers should take place. "I feel a great reluctance in yielding to that general spirit of persecution which, in that State particularly, disgraces our cause and sinks us on a level with our predecessors," he wrote, referring to the removals which Republicans were making in state offices. But, "if Rogers shall be removed, I have no hesitation in saying that I do not know a man whom I would

---

40. Burr to Gallatin, June 28, 1801, Gallatin Papers, N.-Y. Hist. Soc.
41. Burr to Gallatin, Sept. 8, 1801, *ibid.*

prefer to Mr. Davis for that office."[42] By mail which would reach Monticello the day after Davis's arrival, Gallatin wrote at length his thoughts on the difficulties presented by Davis's application. It was intimately related to Burr's future in the Republican party, he suggested, concluding that "it is not to be doubted that after all that has been said on the subject his refusal will, by Burr, be considered as a declaration of war. . . . I do know that there is hardly a man who meddles with politics in New York who does not believe that Davis's rejection is owing to Burr's recommendation. On that as well as on many other accounts I was anxious to prevent Davis's journey."[43]

When Davis arrived at Monticello, after stopping to visit Madison en route, Jefferson gave him no encouragement. He would only say that the matter would be decided after the Cabinet reassembled in Washington. Gallatin, who was well acquainted with New York politics, had made it clear that failure to appoint Davis would be a declaration of war on Burr. Jefferson's procrastination indicates that he had withdrawn his confidence from Burr and was prepared for a public break with his Vice-President. He had put off the decision until it became clearly a matter of supporting Burr or not supporting him, and Jefferson pointedly chose the latter.

How much this decision was influenced by reports from Burr's rivals in New York, especially the Clintonians, it is impossible to say. What was in a "very confidential letter from DeWitt Clinton" which Madison forwarded to Jefferson by Davis has not been discovered. Madison regarded it as "very apropos" to Davis's visit.[44] There is insufficient evidence, however, to warrant the conclusion that Jefferson in 1801 was in league with DeWitt Clinton to destroy Burr. There are, in fact, no known extant letters of DeWitt Clinton to Jefferson in 1801 relating to Davis's appointment.[45] It is also important in this connection to note that Burr's followers were not being totally excluded from state offices

---

42. Gallatin to Jefferson, Sept. 12, 1801, Adams, ed., *Gallatin Writings*, I, 47-48.
43. Gallatin to Jefferson, Sept. 14, 1801, *ibid.*, 51-53.
44. Madison to Jefferson, Sept. 17, 1801, Jefferson Papers, Lib. Cong.
45. Only one letter, DeWitt Clinton to Jefferson, Sept. 14, 1801, Gallatin Papers, N.-Y. Hist. Soc., has been discovered for 1801. This letter is a recommendation of James Nicholson, Gallatin's father-in-law, for loan officer of New York. No other correspondence between Jefferson and DeWitt Clinton is listed in the master file (microfilm) to the Jefferson Papers edited by Julian P. Boyd. There are two known letters from George Clinton to Jefferson listed by Boyd: July 29, 1801, a letter of introduction (Pierpont Morgan Library), and Oct. 14, 1801, relating entirely to plans for fortifying the port of New York (Jefferson Papers, Lib. Cong.).

by DeWitt Clinton's supporters in the state government, as has frequently been asserted.[46]

That Jefferson's attitude toward Burr had changed, however, was subtly revealed in his answer to Burr's letter of September 4, 1801, in which the Vice-President had urged Davis's appointment. Jefferson did not reply until November, when he wrote coolly: "Your favor of the 10th has been received, as have been those of Sept. 4, and 23 in due time. These letters all relating to office, fall within the general rule . . . of not answering letters on office specifically, but leaving the answer to be found in what is done or not done on them."[47] This was the type of reply which Jefferson might send, out of respect, to a prominent solicitor for office, but it was not the way he wrote to political confidants and friends. To these he frequently gave explanations relating to appointments. That Burr was no longer in the President's confidence was unmistakable in this reply. Nevertheless, Burr continued to work for Davis's appointment, but with increasing despair. To Gallatin he wrote in March 1802: "As to Davis it is a small very small favor to ask a *determination*. That 'nothing is determined' is so common place that I should prefer any other answer to this only *request* which I have ever made."[48]

By 1802 Burr's alienation from the administration was becoming clear.[49] John P. Van Ness, a close political friend of Burr and a Representative from New York, wrote confidentially in April that Burr's "influence and weight with the Administration is in my opinion not such as I could wish" and suggested that the influence of DeWitt Clinton, who was then in the Senate, was of great importance.[50] That DeWitt Clinton came to be increasingly consulted on appointments in New York is clear, and it is not surprising that when Rogers was finally removed from the naval office in May 1803, Davis was not appointed.

---

46. Evidence that, although Livingstonians and Clintonians were favored in the distribution of the state patronage in 1801, Burrites were not rigidly excluded is presented in Howard L. McBain, *DeWitt Clinton and the Origin of the Spoils System in New York* (N.Y., 1907), 126-37. McBain also shows that the New York Council of Appointments in 1801, dominated by DeWitt Clinton, did not make a clean sweep of Federalists from office, as is frequently claimed. *Ibid.*, 97-125.

47. Jefferson to Burr, Nov. 18, 1801, Ford, ed., *Jefferson Writings*, VIII, 102; Burr to Jefferson, Sept. 4, 1801, Appointment Papers, Nat. Archives.

48. Burr to Gallatin, Mar. 25, 1802, Gallatin Papers, N.-Y. Hist. Soc.

49. See pp. 204-5 below.

50. John P. Van Ness to William P. Van Ness, Apr. 2, 1802, William P. Van Ness Papers, N.Y. Pub. Lib.

Samuel Osgood, who had earlier sounded the warning against Burr, was transferred from the supervisor's post to the naval office.[51] "It seems to be a prevailing opinion," concluded Gouverneur Morris in November 1803, "that the Clinton party have exclusively the ear of our President as to what regards this State and it is presumed, that his arrangements are taken with them for the next election."[52]

Although Jefferson on numerous occasions yielded to local political pressures in regard to particular removals, in some instances he stood firm against what appeared to be overwhelming sentiment in favor of removal. One such case was that of Allen McLane, collector of customs of the port of Wilmington, Delaware. Appointed marshal of Delaware by President Washington in 1789, McLane had been transferred to the more lucrative post of collector in 1797. Soon after taking office, Jefferson heard charges against the official and electioneering conduct of McLane, and his removal was considered; but the President decided against it.[53]

In the spring of 1802, demands for McLane's removal were again vigorously pressed upon the administration. Governor David Hall, recent Republican victor for Delaware's chief magistracy, transmitted an address to the President from "a number of respectable citizens of the County of Kent" soliciting the removal of McLane; and the Governor displayed his own sentiments by adding: "I know of no Character more obnoxious to the republicans of this State than Mr. McLane, no one who has taken more undue means to crush the republican Interest, . . . a removal of this man from office (if consistent with the plan you have laid down to walk by) would I am convinced be very gratifying to every Republican in the State of Delaware."[54] About the same time, Jefferson received another address from "a Democratic Republican Meeting held at Dover," also soliciting the removal of McLane. The address explained

---

51. On the administration consulting DeWitt Clinton, see Gallatin to Jefferson, July 27, Aug. 11, 1803, Adams, ed., *Gallatin Writings,* I, 134, 135.

52. Morris to Robert R. Livingston, Nov. 28, 1803, Jared Sparks, *The Life of Gouverneur Morris, with Selections from his Correspondence and Miscellaneous Papers* . . . , 3 vols. (Boston, 1832), III, 188.

53. Gallatin to Jefferson, June 20, 1801, Gallatin to Jefferson, enclosing summary of charges against McLane, [June 1801], Jefferson Papers, CXIV, 19574, 19578-79, Lib. Cong.; Jefferson, note written on a letter from Gallatin, Dec. 21, 1801, Gallatin Papers, N.-Y. Hist. Soc.; Jefferson to David Hall, July 6, 1802, Ford, ed., *Jefferson Writings,* VIII, 156n.

54. Hall to Jefferson, May 31, 1802, Jefferson Papers, Lib. Cong.

that "the conduct of this officer has assumed a shape the most violent and intolerant towards those of his fellow Citizens who have opposed him on points of a political nature," and the petitioners concluded: "If Hostility to the measures of the present rulers of our public affairs should be encouraged by suffering the authors of such conduct to enjoy posts of influence and wealth, the ardor of Republicanism will be damped, and the exertions of our friends will be parylized by disappointment."[55]

In view of these addresses, Jefferson wrote confidentially to Caesar A. Rodney, seeking more specific information. "If he has been active in electioneering in favor of those who wish to subvert the present order of things, it would be a serious circumstance. I do not mean as to giving his personal vote, in which he ought not to be controuled; but as to using his influence (which necessarily included his official influence) to sway the votes of others."[56] Rodney replied at great length. Personally a friend of McLane, he had no desire to see him lose his office. "The current [for removals] was however so very strong in this State," he wrote, "that in my candid opinion it cannot without manifest hazard be resisted. You can scarcely meet any of the principal Republicans who do not express the strongest anxiety that a removal should take place. The rest are more warm." In regard to the charges against McLane, Rodney confessed that McLane now acted less openly in politics than in the past, but insisted that Republican demands for dismissal were based on his conduct in office. "I am sensible it must be a painful task which the Republicans of this state have imposed on you," he continued. "Could any conduct of mine have prevented it, . . . I would cheerfully have done it, but from the temper which seems universally to pervade our friends, I should have fallen a victim in the unequal conflict of resistance to the general wishes and will of the Republicans. The county of Kent, and particularly the leading men will be paralized, unless their remonstrances succeed, it appears to me. I hope by your wise and prudent conduct we shall [be] able in a little time by yielding certain lengths to the strong impulse of the people to restrain it at a future period within due bounds."[57]

Rodney's advice was unmistakable; and Jefferson had great confidence in Rodney.[58] Yet Jefferson resisted the strong demands for removal,

55. [Dover Address], Daniel Blaney, Chairman, June 5, 1802, *ibid.*
56. Jefferson to Rodney, June 14, 1802, Ford, ed., *Jefferson Writings,* VIII, 154-55.
57. Rodney to Jefferson, June 19, 1802, Jefferson Papers, Lib. Cong.
58. See pp. 75-76 below.

rejected Rodney's recommendations, and, after a personal conference with Governor Hall and Rodney in July 1802, convinced them (at least in his own opinion) that if McLane did not take an active part in elections, he need not be removed.[59] Jefferson reasoned that, because he had inquired into McLane's conduct shortly after taking office and acquitted him of misconduct, some evidence of misconduct or electioneering activity since his acquittal was necessary to justify his removal. To replace McLane solely on the grounds of his unpopularity would injure the Republican cause in other states.[60] But though Jefferson had believed that Rodney and Hall were satisfied with his decision, Rodney wrote frankly to the President after the October elections that the Republican loss in Kent County could be attributed to the failure to remove McLane. "I feel little hesitation in saying that had the advice from this State been attended to," he declared, "we should have succeeded there and that the loss is to be attributed to this circumstance principally. I could enclose you letters from our most active, influential and intelligent men there, to me, declaring that they would not exert themselves unless their memorial was attended to."[61]

McLane made it plain that he had no intention of surrendering his office unless dismissed. He denounced his accusers as office hunters and emphasized his service in the Revolutionary War. In a letter to Gallatin, in June 1802, he declared that "it is a great point with me to retain my office, after wading through a bloody war of eight long years, to the detriment of constitution and fortune under almost unsurmountable difficulties. . . . How I have acquitted myself as Collector the Treasury department have full information. If I am hunted out of office at this moment I shall be injured beyond any person's conception. . . . Sir, I have been tried in those times that tried men's souls and never betrayed the trust reposed in me by those it become my duty to act with."[62]

McLane's insistence that his removal would be political persecution and his reminders of his Revolutionary service undoubtedly contributed to the President's hesitation to remove him, but Jefferson was quick to grasp at a suggestion that McLane might resign. After the fall elections in 1802, the clamor for McLane's office was revived, and McLane wrote

59. Jefferson to Gallatin, July 13, 1802, Jefferson Papers, Lib. Cong.
60. Jefferson to Rodney, June 24, 1802, Jefferson to Hall, July 6, 1802, Ford, ed., *Jefferson Writings*, VIII, 155n-57n.
61. Rodney to Jefferson, [received Nov. 4, 1802], Jefferson Papers, Lib. Cong.
62. McLane to Gallatin, June 12, 1802, *ibid.*

again to the Secretary of the Treasury assuring him that the accusations against him were unfounded and expressing his confidence that the President would not gratify his accusers. He also added that he especially desired to keep the post until the end of 1803 by which time his income would have afforded him enough money to stock a small farm.[63] How Jefferson interpreted these remarks was indicated when he wrote to Gallatin: "With respect to Col. McLane, his letter was fairly construed as a request to remain in office to a certain day only, and consequently a resignation, and has been the foundation of ulterior arrangements, no longer revocable. And in fact it must be so evident to himself that his continuance in office excites perpetual irritation, that I considered his letter as an evidence of his candor and attention to our peace as well as his own."[64] But McLane apparently had no intention of resigning at the end of 1803 or at any time; subsequent attempts to dislodge him led him to assure the President: "I shall continue to treat their slander with silent contempt, execute the office with fidelity, and integrity, as long as it is the pleasure of the President to continue me."[65]

There is no indication that the demands for McLane's removal subsided. In July 1803, Rodney had again impressed upon the President the strong feelings of Delaware Republicans. "The public sentiment is so fixed on this subject that it [is] difficult to reconcile our leading active politicians," he wrote. "You may rely on it in this state it is not the *interested few* but the *disinterested many* who are extremely anxious about it and manifest the strongest sensation. . . . patriotism and the sincerest attachment to the Republican cause, to yourself and to your administration will induce them to acquiesce in what those whose 'positions command a view of the whole ground' may consider upon mature reflection and after full information to be most productive of the Public good." The next election would be of little importance; if it were, it would be cause for apprehension. The 1804 election would be exceedingly important, however. "It will decide the fate of this state and I anticipate every aid and assistance consistent with principle from a virtuous administration."[66] But McLane was not dismissed before the 1804 election. This contest reversed the Delaware Republican victories in the gubernatorial election of 1801 and in the congressional election of

---

63. McLane to Gallatin, Nov. 3, 1802, Gallatin Papers, N.-Y. Hist. Soc.
64. Jefferson to Gallatin, Dec. 21, 1802, *ibid.*
65. McLane to Jefferson, Oct. 13, 1804, Appointment Papers, Nat. Archives.
66. Rodney to Jefferson, July 7, 1803, Jefferson Papers, Lib. Cong.

1802 and brought the Federalists a striking victory at the time of the sweeping national Republican triumph in the re-election of Jefferson.[67] In spite of the overwhelming sentiment of Delaware Republicans in favor of McLane's removal and the strong recommendations of the party's leaders in the state, McLane was not dismissed. When Jefferson went out of office, McLane was still at his post as collector of the port of Wilmington, and there he remained until his death in 1829.

McLane had been assured by Federalist Congressman James A. Bayard, at the time of Jefferson's election by the House of Representatives, that he would not be removed on political grounds. As Delaware's only member of the House of Representatives, thus casting that state's vote, Bayard had been a key figure in the contest to decide the tie between Jefferson and Burr. On the very day that the election was decided, February 17, 1801, Bayard wrote to McLane that he had "direct information" that Jefferson would not pursue a plan of sweeping all Federalists from office, and he added: "I have taken good care of you, and think if prudent, you are safe."[68] Five years later Bayard explained that he had received assurances from Samuel Smith on the authority of Jefferson that subordinate public officers would not be removed solely on grounds of their political character. Bayard also testified that he had specifically mentioned the offices held by George Latimer, collector of the port of Philadelphia, and Allen McLane, collector of Wilmington. Smith verified that he had conferred with Jefferson and had in the light of his conversation conveyed to Bayard assurances that Jefferson did not intend the removal of such officers on political grounds alone and that McLane would not be removed on these grounds. Smith, however, testified that he did not act on Jefferson's authority and that there had been no bargains; this was also strongly affirmed by Jefferson.[69] Years later Smith admitted that he had conferred with Jefferson "*without his*

---

67. On Delaware elections see John A. Munroe, *Federalist Delaware, 1775-1815* (New Brunswick, N.J., 1954), 232-33.

68. Bayard to McLane, Feb. 17, 1801, Elizabeth Donnan, ed., *Papers of James A. Bayard, 1796-1815* (American Historical Association, *Annual Report, 1913* [Washington, 1915], II), 128-29.

69. Deposition of James A. Bayard, Apr. 3, 1806, deposition of Samuel Smith, Apr. 15, 1806, printed in Matthew L. Davis, *Memoirs of Aaron Burr, with Miscellaneous Selections from his Correspondence,* 2 vols. (N.Y., 1838), II, 129-33, 133-37; Jefferson, "Anas," Apr. 15, 1806, Jefferson to Monroe, Feb. 15, 1801, Ford, ed., *Jefferson Writings,* I, 312, VII, 491. The depositions of Bayard and Smith were made in 1806 for the case of *James Gillespie v. Abraham Smith* but they were not used and were not made public until 1830. Davis, *Memoirs of Burr,* II, 100-101.

having the remotest idea of my object."⁷⁰ There is thus no evidence to indicate that Jefferson was committed to Bayard to retain McLane in office, although it may be assumed that the President was influenced in his decisions by his early statements of patronage policy such as those made to Smith. It should be noted, at the same time, that George Latimer, the Philadelphia collector whom Bayard had also mentioned in 1801, was removed from office in August 1802.

Much of the President's reluctance to take precipitant action in regard to McLane is undoubtedly explained by the fact that McLane had powerful friends and connections in Delaware and was determined to make an issue of it, should he be removed. The tactics that could be expected from McLane in the event of his removal were clearly hinted at in his references to his Revolutionary record. The longer Jefferson delayed, the better McLane fortified his position and the more difficult it became to remove him. It was also to McLane's advantage that many people wanted his job and that his enemies were unable to agree on a candidate to succeed him.

Although Jefferson never publicly announced any change in the policy which he indicated in his reply to the New Haven remonstrance, in practice and in his own thinking he did modify that policy. In his answer to New Haven, removals on purely political grounds had been justified, but Jefferson did not persist in defending removals on such grounds. He preferred, if possible (as it frequently was), to find other reasons for removals. As early as March 1802, Congressman John P. Van Ness reported:

The President has become of late very cautious as to removals without some complaint of *official misconduct.* He has asked me two or three times in conversation upon the subject of Doctor Malcom whether there was any such complaint. This embarrassed me considerably as I had no evidence of any kind of the fact in my possession or knowledge. . . . I suppose the great noise which the Federalists have made throughout the Continent about removals on account of political difference of sentiment only has made the President so reluctant as he has lately been in several

---

70. Samuel Smith to Richard H. Bayard and James A. Bayard, Apr. 3, 1830, Davis, *Memoirs of Burr*, II, 107-9; for details of the controversy relating to Bayard and Smith in the election of 1800, see Borden, "The Election of 1800: Charge and Countercharge," *Delaware History*, 5 (1952), 42-62; Morton Borden, *The Federalism of James A. Bayard* (N.Y., 1955), 80-95.

Instances to proceed any further than he has done upon that ground only: indeed he has expressed himself to me in that way.[71]

In November 1802, in reply to an address from a general meeting of Connecticut Republicans suggesting further removals in that state, Jefferson wrote:

> Exercising that discretion which the constitution has confided to me in the choice of public agents, I have been sensible, on the one hand, of the justice due to those who have been systematically excluded from the service of their country, and attentive, on the other, to restore justice in such a way as might least affect the sympathies and the tranquility of the public mind. Deaths, resignations, delinquencies, malignant and active opposition to the order of things established by the will of the nation, will, it is believed, within a moderate space of time, make room for a just participation in the management of the public affairs; and that being once affected, future changes at the helm will be viewed with tranquility by those in subordinate stations.[72]

This was a much milder declaration than had been made in answer to the New Haven remonstrance a year before.

Jefferson also began to place a more moderate interpretation upon what he had said in his reply to the New Haven remonstrance. In July 1803, in reference to that declaration, he wrote: "The purpose there explained was to remove some of the least deserving officers, but generally to prefer the milder measure of waiting till accidental vacancies should furnish opportunity of giving republicans their *due proportion* of office. To this we have steadily adhered. Many vacancies have been made by death and resignation, many by removal for malversation in office and for open, active and virulent abuse of official influence in opposition to the order of things established by the will of the nation. Such removals continue to be made on sufficient proof."[73]

What Jefferson had actually said in 1801, however, placed far more emphasis on direct political removals. "If a due participation of office is a matter of right, how are vacancies to be obtained?" he had asked. "Those by death are few; by resignation, none. Can any other mode

---

71. John P. Van Ness to William P. Van Ness, Mar. 8, 1802, Van Ness Papers, N.Y. Pub. Lib.
72. Jefferson to William Judd, chairman [of Republicans of Connecticut], Nov. 15, 1802; [address from Republicans of Connecticut], Oct. 27, 1802, Jefferson Papers, Lib. Cong.
73. Jefferson to William Duane, July 24, 1803 (not sent), Ford, ed., *Jefferson Writings,* VIII, 257-58.

than that of removal be proposed?" As far as possible these removals would be based "on delinquency, on oppression, on intolerance, on incompetence, on ante-revolutionary adherence to our enemies." Had he found "a moderate participation of office" in Republican hands, he "would gladly have left to time and accident to raise them to their just share. But their total exclusion calls for prompter correctives."[74] Jefferson's 1803 interpretation of this strongly worded statement indicates a shift toward a more moderate removal policy.

That Jefferson in 1803 was emphasizing moderation is also suggested by an editorial in the Washington *National Intelligencer,* a paper whose editor, Samuel Harrison Smith, was very close to the administration.[75] Written in answer to Republican demands for more removals, the editorial asked the question: "Is it the duty of the executive to remove all federalists from office?" After detailed consideration, it was concluded that "the removal of all federalists is indefensible on the ground of justice" and that "no motive of policy . . . can justify it." The editorial concluded:

Without extending these remarks by quotations from the President's Inaugural Address, or Reply to the Memorial of the Merchants of New Haven it may be said that he has put this subject upon its true footing. . . . The monopoly of office created by the preceding administration was unjust. . . . The true principle which ought to regulate appointments is the representative principle. . . . Notwithstanding the removals which have taken place and the new appointments, it is not believed that the republicans have the full participation of office, to which, on abstract principles their numbers entitle them. This has undoubtedly arisen from the indisposition of the chief magistrate to remove a good officer, who had faithfully discharged the duties of his office, whatever might be his politics. And notwithstanding the vehement denunciations of his enemies, and their constant cry of intolerance and persecution, we have always considered this moderation and forbearance on his part as one of the brightest ornaments of a character, that in the exercise of great power, far from cherishing a disposition to extend or abuse it, has sought every fit occasion to limit and control it.[76]

Although moderation appeared to be the theme in 1803, Jefferson continued to insist that only Republicans be appointed to office. In May 1803, he instructed: "Considering that the republican description of

74. Jefferson to Elias Shipman and others, committee of the merchants of New Haven, July 12, 1801, *ibid.,* 70. See pp. 23-24 above.
75. On *National Intelligencer,* see pp. 258-63 below.
76. Washington *National Intelligencer,* Apr. 15, 20, 1803.

our citizens has not yet nearly received that share in the public offices to which they are entitled, and from which they were so long excluded, such an one of equal qualifications for the public service ought to be preferred to a federal competitor."[77] Jefferson also wanted it to be clearly understood that the administration would not tolerate active opposition by officeholders. In 1804, he requested Gallatin to insert in a letter of dismissal a statement that "the President considering that the patronage of public office should no longer be confided to one who uses it for active opposition to the national will, had, some time since, determined to place your office in other hands." Jefferson thought that "the declaration of this principle will meet the entire approbation of all moderate republicans, and will extort indulgence from the warmer ones. Seeing that we do not mean to leave arms in the hands of active enemies, they will care the less at our tolerance of the inactive."[78] These comments also suggest the President's efforts to keep Republicans, with varying sentiments on removals, reconciled in an election year.

Jefferson never reached the point where he was ready to adopt a policy of appointing Federalists to office. In November 1804, he explained: "If the federalists would have been contented with my giving a very moderate participation in office to those who had been totally excluded, I had hoped to have been able to effect a reconciliation, and would sincerely have attempted it. But they spurned every overture of conciliation. I have therefore long since given up the idea, and proceed in all things without caring what they will think, say or do. To me will have fallen the drudgeory of putting them out of condition to do mischief. My successor I hope will have smoother seas."[79] In 1805, he again instructed: "With respect to Federalists, whether they are in opposition because hostile to the principles of our constitution or to the measures of it's administration, legislative and executive, we must not strengthen the effect of their opposition by the weight of office."[80]

The acquisition of Louisiana required many new appointments, but there was no division of the offices between the parties. Jefferson always

---

77. Jefferson to Christopher Ellery, May 10, 1803, Jefferson Papers, Lib. Cong. See also Jefferson to Francis Peyton, Mar. 31, 1802, Emmett Collection, N.Y. Pub. Lib.; Jefferson to Monroe, May 9, 1802, James Monroe Papers, N.Y. Pub. Lib.; Jefferson to Thomas Newton, Oct. 13, 1802, Jefferson Papers, Lib. Cong.
78. Jefferson to Gallatin, May 30, 1804, Ford, ed., *Jefferson Writings*, VIII, 304.
79. Jefferson to William Short, Nov. 10, 1804, Jefferson Papers, Lib. Cong. See also Jefferson to William Short, Jan. 23, 1804, *Amer. Hist. Rev.*, 33 (1928), 834.
80. Jefferson to Robert Williams, July 6, 1805, Jefferson Papers, Lib. Cong.

found some justification for excluding Federalists. In 1807, he explained: "The Federalists have so decidedly made common cause with Burr, that to send a Federalist or a Burrite to the Orleans territory I consider as the same thing. Sound republicans alone can be trusted there."[81]

Federalists in general saw little moderation in the President's removal policies. "The freedom of our Elections, has been virtually destroyed, by the conduct of the President in making new appointments—he has incited a spirit of rivalship, passion and resentment, which is utterly uncontrollable," declared Oliver Wolcott. "Every four years, while the present government lasts we shall be called to elect a President and with him a compleat sett of executive officers, down to the most subordinate grades. The passions which will be incited by rival Candidates, will soon render peacable Elections impracticable."[82] Federalist Congressman Simeon Baldwin wrote in 1804:

I do consider the wanton abuse of the necessary power of removal, as one of the darkest traits in the character of our present chief magistrate. That those who are the constitutional advisers of the executive should be of the same political sentiments with him I readily admit, for a change in such officers, I never blamed him—but I cannot forgive him for removing a host of inferior officers who were *honest, faithful and capable,* and whose political sentiments had no connexion with the discharge of their official Duties. It was an extension of the arm of power, that I believe no prime minister, or even monarch in Europe ever dared to use.[83]

On the other hand, throughout both terms, Jefferson's administering of the federal patronage was never quite partisan enough to satisfy all of his supporters. Many continued to regard any policy which did not sweep all Federalists from office as too moderate; others felt the President was too timid in employing the power of the patronage for political advantage; almost all judged the administration policy on the basis of what changes had taken place in their state or locality.

From one quarter or another there was always a demand for more removals. Although some of Jefferson's earliest removals had taken place in Pennsylvania, Congressman Michael Leib began in December

---

81. Jefferson to Gallatin, Mar. 13, 1807, Gallatin Papers, N.-Y. Hist. Soc.
82. Oliver Wolcott to John Steele, Mar. 12, 1802, Wagstaff, ed., *Papers of John Steele,* I, 260-61.
83. Simeon Baldwin to Jared Mansfield, Jan. 16, 1804, Baldwin Family Papers, Yale Univ.

1802 to organize public pressure on the executive for more dismissals. Writing from Washington to publisher Mathew Carey in Philadelphia, he suggested:

> The opinion that the enemies of the representative system should not be continued in office has gained ground among the Members of the Legislature. The example of Pennsylvania and the intolerance and abuse of the federalists have concurred in the progress and soundness of this policy. I have good reason to believe, that the President is desirous of superseding the obnoxious men among us, and that he only wants a pretext for so doing—this can certainly be found in the will of the people, and I am of the opinion, that if this will be expressed to him in the form of memorial or remonstrance, that our wishes will be gratified. Can you not make a movement which will effect this object?
>
> It is truly astonishing that there should be found men among us, and professors of democratic principles too, who exert themselves to counteract the wish of the people of our State. The President is much importuned by such men to continue the present incumbents in office. . . . He ought to know the public sentiment on this point.[84]

Despite divided sentiment among Pennsylvania Republicans on the issue of federal patronage,[85] the movement to address the President on removals succeeded; and in July 1803, Jefferson received an address from "The Ward Committees of Philadelphia in General Committee assembled" strongly supporting a policy of general removals. "On the subject of removal from office the opinion of Pennsylvania has long been well known"; that sentiment had been displayed by the "unanimous applause and confidence" which followed the extensive removals made by Governor McKean in state offices. The address continued:

> The same intolerant spirit governs the federal officers in this section of the union, which has ever been characteristick of their party; their official influence is exerted to excite prejudices against the administration, their official expenditures to purchase proselytes to their cause. It is a fact deeply affecting that in Philadelphia, publick employment under the federal administration in all its grades, with scarcely an exception,

---

84. Michael Leib to Mathew Carey, Dec. 12, 1802, Lea and Febiger Collection, Hist. Soc. of Pa.

85. Six Republican congressmen from Pennsylvania in February 1803 signed a letter to the President assuring him of their confidence in his removal policies, but it was not sent after Michael Leib refused to sign and leaked its contents to Philadelphia. Andrew Gregg, Robert Brown, Isaac Van Horne, John A. Hanna, John Smilie, and William Jones to Jefferson, Feb. 12, 1803 (not sent); Andrew Gregg to William Jones, Mar. 1, 1803; William Jones to John Randolph, Mar. 19, 1803, William Jones Papers, Uselma Clarke Smith Collection, Hist. Soc. of Pa.

is confined not to federalists merely but to apostates, persecutors, and enemies of Representative Government.

We believe we express the sentiments of the people of Pennsylvania, we know we speak of those of our immediate constituents....

Three years have nearly passed away in unexampled efforts of conciliation, and we have witnessed as the consequence, increased audacity and the circulation of the most unfounded slanders and misrepresentations of the government and those who administer it, while not a few who disseminate discontent are fostered by a too indulgent administration.

We look, Sir, to an election fast approaching when our whole strength must of necessity be exerted. Our opponents have already commenced their operations.... We look up to you, Sir, for that aid which a good cause requires, to enable us to resist the combination of Mercantile and Banking influence, which cooperating with that of men in office, menaces us with an opposition which though formidable, is not such as to dismay if we continue united and receive that support from the General Government which it is in their power to afford, and which the people confidently hope for and expect.

... a continuance of the power to do good must depend much on the removal from office of men, who abuse the power entrusted to them and pursue their incurable propensity to do mischief.[86]

Jefferson drew up a detailed answer to the Philadelphia address in which he reviewed the general principles of his removal policy and undertook a particular examination of his appointments in Pennsylvania. He pointed out that of eight offices subject to his appointment and removal in Pennsylvania five were in Republican hands and three in Federalist, or a ratio of 5 to 3; and, citing figures showing the more extensive patronage of the offices held by Republicans, he demonstrated that "taking emolument and patronage as the measure, our actual share is much greater." He could "not therefore suppose that our friends had sufficiently examined the fact" when they alleged that federal employment in Philadelphia was confined to the opponents of Republicanism.[87] Jefferson had planned to send this reply to William Duane, one of the signers of the address, but Gallatin persuaded him not to do so: "Unforeseen circumstances may produce alterations in your present view of the subject, and if you shall hereafter think proper to act on a plan somewhat different from that you now consider as the best, a com-

---

86. The Ward Committees of Philadelphia to Jefferson, [received July 17, 1803], signed by 39 representatives of 14 wards, Jefferson Papers, Lib. Cong.

87. Jefferson to William Duane, July 24, 1803 (not sent), Ford, ed., *Jefferson Writings*, VIII, 255-59.

mitment would prove unpleasant." Jefferson had thought that an explanation of his policies might help to remove the cause of division of Republicans in Pennsylvania and "perhaps to cure the incipient schism." But Gallatin thought it improbable "that abstract reasoning, or even a statement of facts already known to them, will make converts of men under the influence of passions or governed by self-interest," and Jefferson yielded to the arguments of his Secretary of the Treasury.[88]

Republicans everywhere expected to see Federalists removed from offices in *their* state, preferring that if the administration was determined to leave some Federalists in office they be left in some other state; and they brought pressure on the President to heed their requests. In February 1804, Senator Wilson Cary Nicholas of Virginia wrote the President that he had been informed by both of the senators from Rhode Island that their state "was very much discontented with all the most valuable offices remaining in the hands of Federalists; and from recent letters they did fear, that spirit would manifest itself, by a rejection of the amendment to the Constitution" to change the electoral procedure in presidential elections. Nicholas suggested that there was "no part of the country where the conflict of parties has been greater than in that State. This perhaps may make it necessary to make some sacrifice to appease the republicans."[89]

What was done to satisfy Rhode Island Republicans cannot be definitely established, but Senator William Plumer maintained that after information of the danger of Rhode Island rejecting the amendment was communicated to the administration, "assurances were conveyed post haste to the file leaders in that degraded State that the obnoxious federalists should be removed from office. I believe there is no doubt of the fact."[90] Though Plumer's charge cannot be confirmed, Rhode Island did ratify the amendment. Rhode Island Republicans, however, remained dissatisfied with their share of the patronage. Congressman Joseph Stanton wrote frankly to the President early in 1806: "Permit me to observe that an opinion is prevailing in Rhode Island among the Republicans that they have served the Republican cause and the Adminis-

88. Jefferson to Gallatin, July 25, 1803, Gallatin to Jefferson, Aug. 11, 1803, Jefferson to Gallatin, Aug. 18, 1803, Adams, ed., *Gallatin Writings*, I, 129, 134-35, 138. See also Gallatin, [memorandum to Jefferson on the Philadelphia address, 1803], Jefferson Papers, CXIX, 20389, Lib. Cong.
89. Nicholas to Jefferson, Feb. 21, 1804, Jefferson Papers, Lib. Cong.
90. Plumer to Jeremiah Smith, Mar. 15, 1804, William Plumer Papers, Lib. Cong.

tration faithfully; But in the distribution of Favours they have been forgotten. They have solicited in vain."[91]

Republicans in areas where Federalists were strong expected help in the form of patronage from the federal government. "We the Republicans in the State of Massachusetts are labouring under many incumbrances...," declared a letter addressed to Madison. "We pray your Honor's influence to the President; that he might consider our situation; knowing that we are burdened with the British Faction and no Republican can get any Lucrative Post under our State Government. Neither but a few under the Federal Government owing to the Supervisor and Post Master."[92] Another Massachusetts Republican complained of Republican difficulties in the county of Hampshire in a letter to Levi Lincoln, who passed it on to the President. Federalists in that county were "overbearing and extremely vindictive," he reported. "Priests, Judges, Jurors, Sheriffs, and the whole phalanx of Lawyers, are leagued for our destruction—the whole artillery of state patronage is leveled against us." He continued:

> Under all these circumstances, we have thought that the Republicans, in the County of Hampshire, were deserving *National Attention*. We have expected to receive, in some way, some encouragement or patronage from the federal administration.... But what is the fact? Has the fostering hand of patronage ever been extended to this County? No, it has not—but so[me] of the heads of the departments have, from *fear*, or from *affection* distributed the "loaves and fishes" among our enemies.... The Post Office in this Town, in particular, has been unreasonably, to say the least of it, kept under the control of a federalist....

And now Sir, I consider myself authorized to state, that the Republicans in this County ... wish you, if you think proper, to apply immediately to the President.... They think, that, by the aid of the general Government, they can, in one year more, neutralize this County, and, of course, completely extirpate federalism. If, however, it is of no consequence what becomes of us, or if we are beyond the reach of aid, then it behooves us, when our resources are exhausted, to yield to the law of self-preservation, and to make the best terms we can with the enemy.[93]

91. Stanton to Jefferson, Jan. 15, 1806, Jefferson Papers, Lib. Cong.
92. Date and signature torn off, endorsed by Jefferson, "Haskell to Mr. Madison," Appointment Papers, Nat. Archives.
93. Edward Upham to Levi Lincoln, May 13, 1805, Jefferson Papers, Lib. Cong. In forwarding the letter to Jefferson, Lincoln expressed the wish that its impatience might be excused by the good intentions of the writer and by his attachment to the general government. Lincoln to Jefferson, June 2, 1805, *ibid*.

The difficulties of administering the federal patronage were greatly increased by the party splits among the Republicans. Where party divisions existed, Jefferson's patronage policy could seldom satisfy all Republicans. In Pennsylvania, demands for removal of Federalists came to be coupled with similar requests to oust factional Republicans. In 1806 Thomas Leiper, an active Philadelphia leader, urged the President to dismiss all third-party men in Pennsylvania. "Turn them out," he wrote, "for a House divided against itself cannot stand. Then out with them that their influence at elections may be as small as possible."[94] A year later he wrote again that, with a few exceptions, "as for the offices of the General Government although the appointments were perfectly correct when you made them the whole are a drawback to your administration."[95] When John Shee, collector of the port of Philadelphia, died in August 1808, Leiper, writing in support of General John Steele for the office, elaborated further on the same theme. Once again he acknowledged that at the time they were made the President's appointments were "perfectly correct" and gave general satisfaction to the Republicans of Pennsylvania, but this was no longer true:

The republicans in this district want support and believe me Sir they obtain very little of it from the officers of the General government. The two last collectors did little or nothing for us whereas if they were all (I mean the officers of the General Government), they and their connexion, in our favor it would make a difference in our Ticket of some 200 to 250 votes. I have in my possession a list of the officers of the Customs. Under the Collector, the Federalists have $9250 the Quids $3050 who have heretofore been the same people, and the Democrats only $3000. In the Inspectors office they are about divided. In the naval office which MacPherson superintends from the Top to Bottom all federal. . . . The very labourers these men employ must give them great influence at our elections. It does not signify going round about the bush unless this thing is altered we may bide fairwell to the republican Ticket in this city and in time if not altered I believe it will pervade the whole state.

Leiper suggested that sentiment in favor of a general sweep of Federalists from office was still strong in Pennsylvania. "You cannot conceive what injury it has done Mr. Madison here" in keeping Federalist clerks employed in his office, he wrote, "and you may rely on it his election was a very uphill business until the republican members of Congress gave

94. Leiper to Jefferson, Mar. 23, 1806, *ibid*.
95. Leiper to Jefferson, Aug. 20, 1807, *ibid*.

the vote in his favor. Many is the time I have heard the cry Clinton was the man he would sweep from office all the old Tories and federalists." It was rumored "that Madison is all and all in the appointments at present," and an unpopular appointment to the collectorship would be "a great drawback on his Election." Leiper concluded: "After all your labours which every honest man must acknowledge merit the highest praise of your country did you ever find a Tory or a federalist but what would turn you out of office if they had it in their power, and did not make it a business to condemn every part of the Administration. Then do by them as they would do by you. Turn them out."[96]

Jefferson received other urgent pleas at this time in regard to the collectorship of Philadelphia. Matthew Lawler and six other Philadelphians, recommending Michael Leib for the post, stressed:

We have unfortunately suffered much from the want of zeal and energy on the part of some of the officers of the federal Government. We do believe that the influence and patronage attached to the office of collector, if properly cultivated would change the tone of the politics of this City, and that instead of being federal, the democratic party might become the dominant one here. Under such a conviction, and knowing how influential the politics of Pennsylvania are upon those of the union, you will pardon us for suggesting to you the expediency of appointing a man . . . competent to bring about so desirable an event.[97]

William Duane also wrote the President: "The appointment of a firm and upright character as the successor of Gen. Shee will not only be essential to the support of the public policy and law, but will in the effect of the choice, greatly influence the Elections in this district, which if something is not done by discountenancing those officers of the government of the U.S. who foment distraction . . . we shall be saddled with three malignant Federalist . . . for Congress."[98] It was evident that a number of important Philadelphia Republicans thought strictly in terms of political advantage, and they made this known to the President. Jefferson moved quickly in regard to the appointment of a new collector for Philadelphia, although Gallatin advised not being too hasty in filling the place. It was "morally impossible to make an appointment that will not displease some section of the Republicans, and of course do some injury to the Republican interest," Gallatin believed. But

96. Leiper to Jefferson, [received Aug. 18, 1808], *ibid.*
97. Lawler and others to Jefferson, Aug. 10, 1808, Appointment Papers, Nat. Archives.
98. Duane to Jefferson, Aug. 9, 1808, Jefferson Papers, Lib. Cong.

Gallatin also emphasized that the appointment was directly "connected with the existence of the Republican party in Pennsylvania," and Jefferson, as if to demonstrate clearly his concern for the Republican party in that state, speedily directed that a commission be sent to John Steele as collector of Philadelphia.[99]

Although complete and reliable statistics on appointments and removals under Jefferson are impossible to obtain, some suggestive figures can be cited. Before the President's answer to the New Haven remonstrance in July 1801, removals had not been extensive. A Federalist pamphlet, replying to Jefferson's declaration, appended "a list of removals from office and new appointments made since the Fourth of March, 1801," but could name only twenty-nine cases.[100] A detailed statement published in a Republican source in September 1801 listed the party attachments of collectors, naval officers, surveyors, supervisors, district attorneys, and marshals—the most important federal officers—and arrived at a total of 30 Republicans and 198 Federalists.[101] Under the policy announced in the President's reply to the New Haven remonstrance, removals and appointments became more frequent. Among the rare statistics on appointments and removals are two memoranda in Jefferson's private papers which furnish revealing figures for July 1803, two years after the New Haven declaration—thus covering the most important period of Jefferson's administration as far as removals were concerned. One memorandum from Gallatin to the President presented a breakdown of federal revenue officers in the different states. These included collectors, surveyors, officers of revenue cutters, and inspectors of revenue. A total of two hundred officials included 87 Republicans, 9 neutrals, and 104 Federalists. When national and territorial revenue officials were added to these state totals, the final total was 122 Republicans, 12 neutrals, and 115 Federalists.[102] The other memorandum, compiled by Jefferson at about the same time, showed the offices of district attorneys filled by 15 Republicans, 1 neutral, and 4 Federalists, and the

99. Gallatin to Jefferson, Aug. 6, 1808, Adams, ed., *Gallatin Writings*, I, 402; Jefferson to Gallatin, Aug. 11, 1808, Ford, ed., *Jefferson Writings*, IX, 203.
100. *An Examination of the President's Reply to the New-Haven Remonstrance*, Appendix, pamphlet, Hist. Soc. of Pa.
101. *A Reply to Lucius Brutus's Examination*, Appendix, pamphlet, Hist. Soc. of Pa.
102. Gallatin to Jefferson, [memorandum July 11, 1803], enclosed in Gallatin to Jefferson, [received July 11, 1803], Jefferson Papers, Lib. Cong.

marshals' offices held by 14 Republicans, 2 neutrals, and 3 Federalists.[103] Added to Gallatin's totals, these statistics show that of all the revenue officers, district attorneys, and marshals, there were 151 Republicans, 15 neutrals, and 122 Federalists. In July 1803, Jefferson also stated that "of 316 offices in all the U.S. subject to appointment and removal by me, 130 only are held by federalists."[104]

There is no accurate way to determine the actual number of political removals made. A number of Federalists lost their jobs when offices were abolished; others were moved to resign in order to avoid the embarrassment of dismissal. Joseph Habersham, after resigning as Postmaster General, an office which at that time did not carry Cabinet status, explained: "On receiving a hint too plain to be misunderstood that my services were no longer wanted I resigned to save the administration from the odium of swelling the list of removals, and myself from the mortification of being one of the proscribed."[105]

Jefferson found that he could justify most removals on grounds other than those purely political, and his endeavors to do so created a number of contradictions in the totals which he reported regarding removals. A list drawn up by Jefferson, apparently in May 1802, designated twenty-four cases as "the whole of the removals which have been made in order to give some participation in office to the Republicans previous to the close of the session of Congress." These did not include, he pointed out, replacements of midnight appointments, removals for malversation, or officers not commissioned by the President.[106] A year later, in May 1803, Jefferson drew up another list which he headed "A correct view of certain appointments arranged in classes." Under each of nine classifications he listed chronologically from March 5, 1801, to May 10, 1803, appointments and removals which he had made. The classes and totals of those listed were as follows:[107]

"I. In place of those resigned, declined, promoted or dead." 25
"II. Vacancies left unfilled when I came into office." 13
"III. Offices expired and not renewed." 6

103. Jefferson, [memorandum July 11, 1803], *ibid.* (inaccurately printed in Ford, ed., *Jefferson Writings*, VIII, 261).
104. Jefferson to William Duane, July 24, 1803 (not sent), Ford, ed., *Jefferson Writings*, VIII, 258.
105. Habersham to Abraham Baldwin, Mar. 15, 1802, Abraham Baldwin Papers, University of Georgia.
106. [List of appointments, May 1802], Jefferson Papers, CXIX, 20542, Lib. Cong.
107. "A Correct view of certain appointments," [May 1803], *ibid.*, 20545-46.

"IV. Midnight appointments. That is to say appointments made by Mr. Adams after Dec. 12, 1800, when the event of the S.C. election which decided the Presidential election was known at Washington and until Midnight of Mar. 3, 1801. These were considered as Null." 22
"V. Restorations to office of those who had been removed on principles not justifiable." 5
"VI. Attorneys and Marshals removed for high federalism, and republicans appointed as a protection to republican suitors in courts entirely federal and going all lengths in party spirit." 5
"VII. Removals on the principle of giving some participation in office to republicans, and also to disarm those who were using the weight of their official influence to oppose the order of things established." 14
"VIII. Removals on mixed grounds including delinquency or misconduct." 8
"VIIII. Removals for Misconduct or delinquency." 15
    113

The above list furnishes an interesting breakdown of the President's justification for removals and appointments. It is also significant to note that whereas a year before he had listed twenty-four removals on the grounds of giving participation in office to Republicans, he now designated only fourteen removals for such reasons. A comparison of the two lists shows that Jefferson had decided that many of the twenty-four previously listed as purely political removals could be justified on other grounds. On the 1803 list he reclassified these twenty-four cases under the following classes:

I.	1	VI.	5
II.		VII.	6
III.	2	VIII.	6
IV.		VIIII.	2
V.	2		24

Thus in listing the same appointments, only six out of twenty-four were now classed as removals solely on the basis of giving participation in offices to Republicans, while all twenty-four had been so regarded in 1802.

Such reappraisals of his patronage decisions enabled the President to reconcile his earlier less moderate position with his later more cautious policy. On whatever grounds removals might be justified, the

PROBLEMS AND PRACTICES 63

statistics cited above indicate that after two years in office Republicans had obtained slightly more than half of the principal federal offices. To some of the President's supporters, this was too sweeping, but to a much larger number of Republicans it was too moderate.

Federal patronage was not confined to appointments made by the President. Collectors, for example, appointed a number of subordinate officers subject to the approval of the Secretary of the Treasury, and Jefferson had instructed Gallatin that one-half of these offices be given to Republicans. The Post Office was also a principal source of minor federal patronage. Republicans in taking office in 1801 considered the political abuse of this office in some sections of the country as demanding extensive remedy. Ephraim Kirby, a leading Connecticut Republican, wrote the President in 1801:

The Post offices in this part of the United States have for years past been almost universally in the hands of violent political partizans—many of them insensible to the suggestions of honor and perhaps less of the obligations of official duty. This department has been a monstrous engine of private abuse, and public deception. Correspondence between persons of known Republican character has been altogether unsafe. Republican Newspapers conveyed by Mail have been either suppressed, or ridiculed at the office of delivery, in such manner as to deter many from receiving them, while other papers circulated to poison the public mind.[108]

Postmaster General Gideon Granger, assuming office in November 1801, began the process of change. He reported in August 1802 that 379 new appointments had been made in the Post Office since he had taken office and that changes were being made "as rapid as the prompt execution of the duties and the safety of the Department will admit."[109]

Patronage to printers in publishing the laws[110] and patronage to banks in depositing federal funds were other areas of federal patronage. If Gallatin had shared the President's long-standing hostility to the Bank of the United States, federal patronage to banks would have undoubtedly figured more prominently in Jefferson's administration. Jefferson judged the Bank of the United States as being "of the most deadly hostility

---

108. Kirby to Jefferson, Nov. 10, 1801, Appointment Papers, Nat. Archives.
109. Granger to Jefferson, Aug. 23, 1802, Jefferson Papers, Lib. Cong. For the operation of the Post Office, see Leonard D. White, *The Jeffersonians: A Study in Administrative History, 1801-1829* (N.Y., 1951), 299-335.
110. On patronage to printers see pp. 247-50 below.

existing, against the principle and form of our Constitution." Considering its stockholders to be mostly foreigners, he believed "we might, on a misunderstanding with a foreign power be immensely embarrassed." In a critical moment it might even "upset the government." "Now, while we are strong, it is the greatest duty we owe to the safety of our Constitution, to bring this powerful enemy to a perfect subordination under it's authorities," he wrote to Gallatin. "The first measure would be to reduce them to an equal footing only with other banks, as to the favors of the government." Jefferson also stressed the political advantages. "It is certainly for the public good to keep all the banks competitors for our favors by a judicious distribution of them," he wrote, "and thus to engage the individuals who belong to them in the support of the reformed order of things, or at least in an acquiescence under it."[111] Gallatin, however, found the Bank of the United States a useful institution, and disregarded the President's suggestions that measures be taken to weaken it.[112]

The Secretary of the Treasury, nevertheless, did make some concessions to the President's disposition to favor state Republican banks. In July 1803, Gallatin received a letter from Providence, Rhode Island, explaining that the Republicans there contemplated establishing "a Bank to be supported entirely by Individuals who are warmly attached to the present administration" and requesting that this bank be made the depository for federal funds rather than the Federalist-controlled Providence Bank.[113] Jefferson was highly sympathetic to the request. "As to the patronage of the Republican Bank at Providence," he wrote, "I am decidedly in favor of making all the banks Republican, by sharing deposits among them in proportion to the dispositions they show; if the law now forbids it, we should not permit another session of Congress to pass without amending it. It is material to the safety of Republicanism to detach the mercantile interest from its enemies and incorporate them into the body of its friends."[114]

Gallatin consulted with Rhode Island Republican Senator Christopher Ellery, who made a thorough report on the financial soundness of the

111. Jefferson to Gallatin, Oct. 7, 1802, Dec. 13, 1803, Ford, ed., *Jefferson Writings*, VIII, 172, 285.
112. Raymond Walter, Jr., *Albert Gallatin: Jeffersonian Financier and Diplomat* (N.Y., 1957), 171-73.
113. Seth Wheaton and Henry Smith to Gallatin, July 1, 1803, Gallatin Papers, N.-Y. Hist. Soc. See also Enoch Ellery to Gallatin, July 22, 1803, *ibid.*
114. Jefferson to Gallatin, July 12, 1803, Ford, ed., *Jefferson Writings*, VIII, 252.

undertaking and recommended that federal use of the bank "would be productive of advantage to the republican cause in this State, and could in no manner prove injurious to the public."[115] Additional support for the request came from Postmaster General Gideon Granger, who submitted a letter he had received from Rhode Island Republicans explaining the purposes of the newly organized Republican-backed Roger Williams Bank. "By the pecuniary accommodation we shall be able, by reason of this bank, to afford our needy and enterprizing brethren, we hope to secure them from the money influence of our adversaries, and aid effectually in their emancipation and independence," they wrote. By transferring the government's funds from the Federalist Providence Bank, "all the directors of which are and have been our bitterest adversaries. . . . a *double* advantage will be derived to the cause. Its enemies will lose, while its supporters acquire a most effectual auxiliary."[116] Gallatin did not oppose this strong pressure from his party to assist the Rhode Island Republicans. Federal funds were transferred to the Roger Williams Bank, a step which insured the flourishing of the institution and was highly gratifying to the Republican party in the state.[117]

Although Gallatin was more moderate than the President in his attitude toward banks and in his views on removals, he was not immune to political considerations. His awareness of politics can be seen in his concern over the route for the building of a federal road through western Pennsylvania. He wished to see the road pass through the town of Washington, Pennsylvania, and recommended to the President that the commissioners for the western road be instructed to make two surveys: one directly west from Brownsville, Pennsylvania, to Wheeling; the other through Washington. The President could then choose between the two routes. Finding that the survey through Washington had not been made, Gallatin wrote to the President in July 1808:

> I seriously fear the consequence at this time. Did I not believe the course which I have mentioned to be perfectly proper, I certainly would not recommend it merely on account of those consequences. Permit me, however, to state that the county of Washington, with which I am well acquainted, having represented it six years in Congress, gives a uniform majority of about 2000 votes in our favor, and that if this be thrown,

---

115. Ellery to Gallatin, Apr. 27, 1807, [referring to events of 1803-4], Gallatin Papers, N.-Y. Hist. Soc.

116. Seth Wheaton, Henry Smith, and Jonathan Russell to Gideon Granger, Dec. 20, 1803, enclosed in Granger to Gallatin, Jan. 4, 1804, *ibid*.

117. Christopher Ellery to Gallatin, Apr. 27, 1807, *ibid*.

by reason of this road, in a wrong scale, we will infallibly lose the State of Pennsylvania at the next election; for the imprudent steps taken there seem unavoidably to lead to three distinct *electoral* tickets. . . . the question, as it relates to the public interest, is in every respect so extremely insignificant, that I am very desirous that it should not be permitted to do much positive evil.

Will you have the goodness to consider the subject? And if you approve, I can write to the commissioners to make the examination of both routes for your decision.[118]

Jefferson was not very sympathetic to the pressures of towns which held up "electioneering effects, as if I were to barter away, on such motives, a public trust." Nevertheless, he sent a letter off immediately to the commissioners of the road requesting them, as far as their funds permitted, to make a study of the route through Washington and to report to him.[119] Thus the voters in Washington were provided assurance before the election that the administration was considering their interests.

Under the administration's policy of reducing the army and navy, there were few opportunities for military appointments during Jefferson's first years in office; the major problem was that of determining which officers should be discharged. Filed among the President's private papers is a revealing document, compiled from the War Office Register, listing the officers in the army, July 24, 1801. In addition to supplying name, rank, date of commission, and home state for each officer, the list contains a column labeled "Remarks." Under this heading, symbols have been added in an unknown hand describing, as far as was known, each officer's military qualifications and his political sentiments. An accompanying key, also in an unknown hand, explains the symbols which designated the following classifications:

[1] Such officers as are of the 1st Class, so esteemed from a superiority of genius and Military proficiency.
[2] Second class, respectable as Officers, but not altogether entitled to the 1st grade.
[3] Republican.
[4] Officers whose political opinions are not positively ascertained.

118. Gallatin to Jefferson, July 27, 1808, Adams, ed., *Gallatin Writings*, I, 395-96.
119. Jefferson to Commissioners of the Western Road, Aug. 6, 1808, Jefferson to Gallatin, Aug. 6, 1808, Henry A. Washington, ed., *The Writings of Thomas Jefferson*. . . , 9 vols. (Wash., 1853-54), V, 332-34. It was not until after Jefferson left the presidency that provision was made for the road to pass through the town of Washington. An act to that effect was passed in 1811. Walters, *Gallatin*, 182.

[5] Political apathy.
[6] Opposed to the Administration, otherwise respectable officers.
[7] Opposed to the Administration more decisively.
[8] Opposed most violently to the Administration and still active in its vilification.
[9] Professionally the soldier without any political creed.
[10] Unworthy of the commissions they bear.
[11] Unknown to us.[120]

This document listing the 269 officers in the army in July 1801[121] demonstrates the close attention which was given to the qualifications of officers before reductions in strength were made. It also displays that politics were taken into consideration in contemplating these changes. The policy of the Adams administration in giving preference to Federalists in army appointments had left few Republicans in service. Of the 269 officers listed, political information was recorded in regard to 145 as follows:

Republican	12
Opposed to the Administration, otherwise respectable officers	3
Opposed to the Administration more decisively	39
Opposed most violently to the Administration and still active in its vilification	9
Political opinions not positively ascertained	49
Political apathy	21
Without any political creed	12
	145

The large number of officers whose political opinions were not known makes it impossible to determine a satisfactory ratio of politics to dismissals, but a close study of the list suggests that political affiliation was not the first consideration in making dismissals. Under a congressional act of March 16, 1802, reducing the size of the army, eighty-seven of the officers on the above-mentioned list were discharged from the service on

120. Jefferson Papers, CXIV, 19697-705, Lib. Cong.
121. Secretary of War Dearborn in an official report to the House of Representatives, Dec. 24, 1801, reported 248 officers in army service, with 43 vacancies. *American State Papers: Documents, Legislative and Executive*, 38 vols. (Wash., 1832-61), *Military Affairs*, I, 154-55.

June 1, 1802.[122] Of these eighty-seven officers, twelve were opposed to the administration (four violently, eight decisively), two were Republicans, and the remainder were without political convictions or their politics were unknown. More significant than politics were military qualifications. Of the eighty-seven dismissed, thirty-five were classed as "unworthy of the commissions they bear," seventeen were second class officers, twenty-six were unknown persons, and only seven were first class officers. It is also significant to note that of the forty-four officers listed in July 1801 as unworthy of their commissions, only seven remained in service after June 1, 1802. Of the fifty-one opposed, in some degree, to the administration only fourteen had resigned or been discharged by June 1802. Nevertheless, although military qualifications were put first in discharging officers, the very fact that political sentiments were recorded reveals that they were considered of importance.

In new appointments to the army there was a decided preference given to Republicans. Secretary of War Henry Dearborn revealed this very clearly when he wrote to William Eustis, of Massachusetts, in May 1808:

Your letter in favor of Mr. Clark has been received. I wish you had added what his political standing is. We have at present a sufficient proportion of our political opponents in the Army, to render any new appointments, in the small body of additional troops, of that class, unnecessary, if not inexpedient,—and after the outragious conduct of that party within the last few months, no individual among them can pretend to any claim on the Government. If giving a Commission, is to be considered a favour conferred on the individual who receives it, ought such favours to be granted to men who have constantly mustered in the ranks of our outragious bitter and inveterate enemies. . . . I presume that about two thirds of the candidates recommended from Massachusetts, are feds. If I recommend any such to the President, it will be from the effect of deception.[123]

In a similar vein, Dearborn wrote to House Speaker Joseph B. Varnum:

I accord fully with you in sentiment, in relation to the expediency of caution in giving any appointments to such as may not be disposed to defend the best interests of our Country. I had noticed with some surprise, the undue proportion of feds. recommended for commissions from Massachusetts. . . . the Federalist party in Massachusetts, will, while in power, afford a strong example of what our conduct towards them ought

122. This figure is based on data in Francis B. Heitman, *Historical Register and Dictionary of the United States Army, from its Organization, September 29, 1789 to March 2, 1903*, 2 vols. (Wash., 1903).
123. Dearborn to Eustis, May 2, 1808, William Eustis Papers, Lib. Cong. See also Dearborn to Eustis, May 11, 1808, *ibid.*

to be, in relation to offices and appointments. We have been much more liberal towards them, than they would be towards us, and in future I think we ought to give them measure for measure.[124]

An analysis of the problems and practices relating to offices points up certain general conditions which seem to have pervaded the administering of the federal patronage. In regard to appointments, Jefferson's practice and policy were consistent and partisan: essentially only Republicans were appointed to office. On removals his practice and policy were not so clear cut. Presidential policy statements were filled with qualifying statements, and his own interpretations of his policy varied. In practice he followed a pattern of day-to-day deliberation and decision. Numerous examples can be cited to prove that removals were made on a purely partisan basis; yet other examples can be cited to show a policy of moderation. Jefferson faced each problem of removal as it came along. In each case he sought advice, frequently hearing conflicting testimony from members of his Cabinet, congressmen, or local Republican leaders; then he made his decision. He spent endless hours on appointments and removals; a large proportion of all the recommendations and applications for appointments and removals passed through his hands.[125] It was not surprising that Jefferson considered patronage decisions the heaviest burden of his office.[126]

Throughout his administration Jefferson was under conflicting pressures in regard to removal policies. In his Cabinet, Albert Gallatin exerted a persistent influence in favor of moderation; only the President's disapproval prevented him from initiating a non-partisan appointment policy for subordinate positions in the revenue service. From many quarters the demands for removals were strong and frequently convincing. These conflicting pressures are reflected in Jefferson's fluctuating actions and inconsistent explanations. Jefferson was torn between his own inclination toward moderation and the demands of many of his party for extensive removals. When cries for removals became strong, he would give in a little and dismiss some unpopular Federalists. But he never wanted the spirit of intolerance to get out of hand. Thus he met the demands of Connecticut Republicans in 1801, but when

124. Dearborn to Varnum, June 12, 1808, Henry Dearborn Papers, Lib. Cong.
125. Endorsements by the President can be found on a large proportion of the extensive collection of Appointment Papers at the National Archives.
126. "The ordinary affairs of a nation offer little difficulty to a person of any experience," he said; "but the gift of office is the dreadful burthen which oppresses him." Jefferson to James Sullivan, Mar. 3, 1808, Jefferson Papers, Lib. Cong.

they kept up their clamor, he tried to calm them down by urging moderation; he acted similarly in Pennsylvania and elsewhere. Jefferson clearly did not want to furnish grounds for charges of political intolerance, and he would more easily consent to removals if he could satisfy himself that they could be made on some other ground than politics.

When Jefferson went out of office, his followers were still debating patronage policy, but they were quick to defend the administration against charges of political intolerance. A Republican pamphlet in 1808 declared:

Under the General Government some removals have been made for malconduct in office; but not one, it is believed, for political principles, unless, indeed official influence and opportunities were abused to promote those principles, and to aid the opposition to Government. . . .

Yet notwithstanding what removals have been made it is firmly believed that more than one half of the offices under the General Government, are at this moment held by Federalists. . . . It is true that most of the *new* appointments are made from the Republican party—it is certainly natural to confide in friends in preference to enemies—but even of these, Federalists have had a considerable share—and, as already stated, it is fully believed that more offices under the General Government are held by Federalists than by Republicans, taking the Union throughout. Those in the old Army and in the Navy are almost exclusively in the hands of Federalists.[127]

In general, Jefferson tried to steer a middle-of-the-road course between Republicans who demanded a general sweep of Federalists and those who felt that the Republicans should not adopt the political intolerance of their Federalist predecessors in employing only political partisans in federal offices. This middle-of-the-road, day-to-day removal policy makes it difficult to summarize Jefferson's patronage policy. His policy and practice were partisan, yet he did not remove all Federalists from office. It is misleading to call his policy moderate, yet certainly his actions were not partisan enough to satisfy large numbers of his followers. There seems little doubt that Republican popular opinion would have supported a far more partisan policy. The Creed Taylors who were convinced that the government should "never trust one of the federal party, with any of the most unimportant offices again,"[128] were far more numerous than the Albert Gallatins who urged toleration.

127. *Plain Truth, addressed to the Independent Electors of the State of New Jersey* (Trenton, 1808), pamphlet, New Jersey Historical Society.
128. Creed Taylor to Ch. Clarke, Feb. 17, 1805, Creed Taylor Papers, Univ. of Va.

CHAPTER FOUR

The Party in Congress

When the Seventh Congress, elected in 1800-1801, met in December 1801, the Republican party had, in the President's words, "a very commanding majority in the House of Representatives, and a safe majority in the Senate."[1] In anticipation of the meeting of this first Republican-controlled Congress, editor Samuel Harrison Smith, of the Washington *National Intelligencer*, estimated party strength in the House at sixty-seven Republicans and thirty-nine Federalists.[2] After Congress assembled, Jefferson counted sixty-six Republicans and thirty-seven Federalists, with two Republicans absent and one Republican seat vacated by Thomas Sumter's election to the Senate. In the Senate had all members been present the division would have been eighteen Republicans and fourteen Federalists, but the party strength at the opening of the session was equal, causing Jefferson to delay sending his nominations to the Senate until he could be sure of a safe majority.[3]

In the Eighth Congress, with the added representation following the census of 1800 and the admission of Ohio in 1803, Republican strength increased in both houses. Party strength at the opening of the first session stood at 103 Republicans and 39 Federalists in the House, 25 Republicans and 9 Federalists in the Senate.[4] Although the party composition varied, the Republican majority increased in each of the two subsequent Congresses which met while Jefferson was President. "In short," said Representative Jacob Crowninshield summing up the Re-

1. Jefferson to Maria Eppes, Dec. 14, 1801, Jefferson Papers, Lib. Cong.
2. *National Intelligencer*, Sept. 21, 1801. On Dec. 7, 1801, Smith estimated 69 Republicans and 36 Federalists.
3. Jefferson to John W. Eppes, Jan. 1, 1802, Jefferson Papers, Univ. of Va.; Jefferson to Thomas Mann Randolph, Jan. 1, 1802, Jefferson Papers, Lib. Cong.; *National Intelligencer*, Dec. 7, 1801.
4. These are the figures listed in the *National Intelligencer*, Oct. 19, 1803; William Plumer to Daniel Plumer, Nov. 15, 1803, reports the same totals, probably obtained from the *National Intelligencer*, Plumer Papers, Lib. Cong.

publican position in Congress, "we are strong enough and have nothing to fear except from divisions among ourselves."[5]

The first Republican-controlled Congress (the Seventh Congress) began by reversing the previous Federalist Congress on a number of issues, essentially carrying out the proposals which Jefferson outlined in his first annual message to Congress in December 1801. These included the abolition of all internal taxes, the repeal of the Judiciary Act of 1801, reductions in the army and in naval expenditures, and the initiation of a program to discharge the national debt in fifteen years. The liberal naturalization law of 1795, written by Madison, was also restored.[6] Republicans sought to make their reversals of Federalist policies clear and to show that the change in parties was bringing changes of policies. That the voters were afforded visible evidence of the changes was suggested by one member who declared, on March 4, 1802: "On yesterday we passed the bill for the repeal of the judiciary system of the last session —59 to 37. On today we celebrate the anniversary of the triumph of republicanism—and on tomorrow we repeal the internal taxes. Thus, you see, this dreadful spirit—this spirit of innovation is going on."[7] Republican partisanship was reflected in the appointment by the House of Representatives in December 1801 of a Committee of Investigation authorized to inquire into expenditures of public money by the several departments under previous administrations.[8] Obviously designed to expose the misdeeds of the preceding administration, the committee carried on the investigation throughout the session, presenting shortly before adjournment its report, which John Quincy Adams denounced as "highly exceptionable to every maxim of common justice and honor. This report was hurried through the House with as little regard to decorum as it was made."[9]

5. Crowninshield to George W. Prescott, Nov. 15, 1803, Alexander C. Washburn Collection, Massachusetts Historical Society. Crowninshield reported the House membership at this time as 104 Republicans, 38 Federalists.

6. Brant, *James Madison, 1800-1809*, 84.

7. John Dawson to Alexander J. Dallas, Mar. 4, 1802, Alexander J. Dallas Papers, Hist. Soc. of Pa.

8. *The Debates and Proceedings in the Congress of the United States, 1789-1824*, 42 vols. (Wash., 1824-56), 7 Cong., 1 Sess. (Dec. 14, 1801), 319, 324. Hereafter cited as *Annals of Congress*.

9. Adams to Rufus King, Oct. 8, 1802, Ford, ed., *Writings of John Quincy Adams*, III, 8; *Annals of Congress*, 7 Cong., 1 Sess. (Apr. 29, 1802), 1251. On the operation of this committee, see Benjamin Stoddard to Joseph Nicholson, Apr. 27, 1802, Gallatin to Nicholson, Apr. 1802, Nicholson Papers, Lib. Cong. Joseph H. Nicholson was chairman of the committee.

Although the practice of party members in Congress choosing floor leaders had not yet become fixed, the role of party leaders in Congress gradually had become more and more important. In the Second, Third, and Fourth Congresses, James Madison had clearly acted as the leader of the emerging Republican party, and when he retired from Congress in 1797 his place was taken by Albert Gallatin, who fulfilled the role of a minority leader during Adams's administration.[10] When the Seventh Congress met in December 1801, with Gallatin now in the Cabinet, rivalry developed among Republican members over party leadership. As speaker of the House, the Republicans chose Nathaniel Macon, who had represented North Carolina in Congress since 1791. No aggressive leader, Macon had a consistently Jeffersonian record, no important enemies, and a certain unassuming honesty and integrity which made him a popular choice for the speakership. The speaker at this time enjoyed the extensive power of appointing standing committees, and in exercising this authority Macon played an important role in fixing the future party leadership in the House. To the chairmanship of the Ways and Means Committee, Macon appointed his close friend twenty-eight-year-old John Randolph of Roanoke, who had served but one term in Congress.[11] The fiery and erratic Randolph and the plain and stable Macon were markedly unlike, but their personal and political friendship lasted a lifetime. In view of the close friendship of Macon and Randolph, it is unlikely that Jefferson had any influence in the choice of Randolph as chairman of the Ways and Means Committee. Macon also appointed another good friend, Joseph H. Nicholson of Maryland, to the Ways and Means Committee. Passed over by Macon was William Branch Giles, who had been Madison's chief lieutenant in the early Congresses and after resigning from Congress in 1798 had returned in 1801. Giles, considered by some as "the leading member in the House of Representatives,"[12] attempted to reassert his former leadership, only to find a formidable rival in Randolph. Federalists gleefully reported considerable Republican difficulties at the opening of the session. "Randolph is ambitious of being at the head of the Virginians," observed James A. Bayard of Delaware. "It is impossible that Giles will be content to act under

10. See Cunningham, *Jeffersonian Republicans, 1789-1801*, 21-22, 51-53, 69-71, 76-78, 85, 123-24.
11. *Annals of Congress*, 7 Cong., 1 Sess. (Dec. 8, 1801), 312.
12. Caesar A. Rodney to Jefferson, Dec. 27, 1801, Jefferson Papers, Lib. Cong.

him. They have already pointedly and on principle divided on the subject of the census."[13] Connecticut's Roger Griswold also reported:

> The ruling faction in the Legislature have not yet been able to understand each other. . . . There evidently appears much rivalry and jealousy among the leaders. S[amuel] Smith thinks his experience and great address ought to give him a preponderance in all their measures, whilst Nicholson evidently looks upon these pretensions of his colleague with contempt, and Giles thinks the first representative of the Ancient Dominion ought certainly on all important occasions to take the lead, and Johnny Randolph is perfectly astonished that his great abilities should be overlooked. There is likewise a great number of other persons who are impatient of controul and disposed to revolt at any attempts at discipline.[14]

Randolph, confessing "I feel myself pre-eminently embarrassed by the station which the partiality of the Speaker has assigned me," reported the majority "somewhat unwieldly" and admitted: "There is much want of concert and even discordance of opinion in the majority."[15] As the session continued, however, workable Republican unity was established. By mid-January, Griswold, who had hopefully predicted that Federalists could profit from Republican discord, despaired. "The majority finding themselves fast sinking into contempt by their ignorance and divisions," he wrote haughtily, "have as it seems determined to remedy one difficulty if they cannot the other, they have united."[16] In March, DeWitt Clinton wrote from his seat in the Senate: "Our friends here are as well united as can be expected from so strong and so varied a majority."[17] And Jefferson was satisfied at the end of the session that Congress had "carried into execution steadily almost all the propositions submitted to them in my message at the opening of the session."[18] There is no reason to assume, however, that Randolph had as yet emerged as the party leader in Congress or as the administration's spokesman on the floor. On the other hand, the debates in the House indicated that Giles, whom one

---

13. Bayard to John Rutledge, Dec. 20, 1801, Rutledge Papers, Univ. of N.C.
14. Griswold to John Rutledge, Dec. 14, 1801, *ibid.* See also Roger Griswold to David Daggett, Jan. 1, 1802, [photostatic copy], William Griswold Lane Collection, Yale Univ.
15. Randolph to St. George Tucker, Dec. 26, 1801, Autograph Collection, Mass. Hist. Soc.
16. Roger Griswold to Matthew Griswold, Jan. 16, 1802, William Griswold Lane Collection, Yale Univ.
17. Clinton to Horatio Gates, Mar. 4, 1802, Emmett Collection, N.Y. Pub. Lib.
18. Jefferson to Joel Barlow, May 3, 1802, Ford, ed., *Jefferson Writings*, VIII, 149.

member called the "*premier* or *prime minister* of the day," acted as the principal House leader for the administration.[19]

In the second session of the Seventh Congress, which convened in December 1802, Giles, because of illness, did not appear. "Who will, in the absence of Mr. Giles, be the leader of the House is uncertain," observed New Hampshire's Senator William Plumer. "John Randolph, Samuel Smith and Joseph Hopper Nicholson, have each of them laid in their claims." Plumer saw the principal contest over "whether John Randolph or Samuel Smith is to be the ministerial leader of the House."[20] Later in the session, Federalist Representative William Barry Grove, of North Carolina, concluded: "It is very evident the majority in our House are kept together with much difficulty. Giles is much wanted to lead them. They have not a man of Business and strong talents in their party. Randolph is too infirm in health and captious in temper. Genl. Smith is too precipitate and incorrect."[21]

It was during this session that Jefferson confessed to Caesar A. Rodney the need for a leader in Congress. "We want men of business among them," he admitted. "I really wish you were here. I am convinced it is in the power of any man who understands business, and who will undertake to keep a file of the business before Congress and to press it as he would his own docket in a court, to shorten the sessions a month one year with another and to save in that way 30,000 D. a year."[22] Rodney, at Jefferson's urging, had recently successfully challenged James A. Bayard for Delaware's seat in the House, and Jefferson was anxiously awaiting his appearance in the next Congress.[23] It would hardly appear that Jefferson was satisfied with the potentialities of Randolph as the party leader in the House.

Giles did not return to the Lower House, and in 1804 he entered the Senate. In 1803, Samuel Smith also transferred to the Senate, leaving Randolph the unchallenged Republican leader in the House. When the

---

19. Dice R. Anderson, *William Branch Giles: A Study in the Politics of Virginia and the Nation from 1790 to 1830* (Menasha, Wis., 1914), 82, 85; *Annals of Congress*, 7 Cong., 1 Sess. (Feb. 23, 1802), 666.

20. Plumer to Oliver Peabody, Dec. 22, 1802; Plumer to Jeremiah Smith, Dec. 22, 1802, Plumer Papers, Lib. Cong.

21. Grove was also critical of the abilities of Joseph H. Nicholson, Samuel L. Mitchill, and William Eustis. Grove to John Steele, Feb. 25, 1803, Wagstaff, ed., *Papers of John Steele*, I, 368-69.

22. Jefferson to Rodney, Dec. 31, 1802, Jefferson Papers, Lib. Cong.

23. Jefferson to Rodney, Apr. 24, 1802, Ford, ed., *Jefferson Writings*, VIII, 147-48; Jefferson to Rodney, Nov. 28, 1802, Jefferson Papers, Lib. Cong.

Eighth Congress met in October 1803, observers for the first time agreed that Randolph was the party leader of House Republicans. Federalists referred to him as "the democratic leader," "our great premier or self created democratic Manager of the House," and "the leader of democracy in the House of Representatives."[24] Senator Plumer, who frequently attended the House debates, described in October 1803 the role of a confident leader which Randolph had assumed:

> John Randolph Jr. of Virginia is evidently the leader of the Democrats in the House. The manner in which he exercised this authority today, was very disgusting, and excited my indignation. Profuse in censuring the *motives* of his opponents—artful in evading their arguments, and peremptory in demanding the vote—sitting on his seat insolently and frequently exclaiming *I hope this motion will not prevail*—or when it suited his views, *I hope this will be adopted*.[25]

Jefferson accepted Randolph's position of party leadership in the House, took him into his confidence, and attempted to make him the administration's spokesman on the floor.[26] But Randolph's temperament hardly suited him for the role in which he was cast, and there is no evidence that he was ever popular with the President. While Randolph was at the height of his influence in Congress, Jefferson was writing to Caesar A. Rodney, who he had hoped would develop into a congressional leader, endeavoring to persuade him not to carry out his contemplated retirement after one term. The President emphasized: "I had looked to you as one of those calculated to give cohesion to our rope of sand. You now see the composition of our public bodies, and how essential system and plan are for conducting our affairs wisely with so bitter a party in opposition to us.... Talents in our public councils are at all times important; but perhaps there never was a moment when the loss of any would be more injurious than at the present."[27] Rodney yielded to the President's plea to run again, but Jefferson's hopes of his be-

---

24. Simeon Baldwin to Mrs. Baldwin, Feb. 15, 1804, Baldwin Family Papers, Yale Univ.; Thomas Dwight to John Williams, Jan. 28, 1804, Thomas Dwight Papers, Mass. Hist. Soc.; Timothy Pickering to Theodore Lyman, Feb. 11, 1804, Timothy Pickering Papers, Mass. Hist. Soc.

25. Everett S. Brown, ed., *William Plumer's Memorandum of Proceedings in the United States Senate, 1803-1807* (N.Y., 1923), entry of Oct. 24, 1803, 24-25.

26. Jefferson to Randolph, Nov. 19, 1804, Ford, ed., *Jefferson Writings*, VIII, 333-34; Jefferson to Barnabas Bidwell, July 5, 1806, Jefferson Papers, Lib. Cong.; see also pp. 89-90 below.

27. Jefferson to Rodney, Feb. 24, 1804, Ford, ed., *Jefferson Writings*, VIII, 296.

coming a congressional leader were rudely exploded when Rodney was defeated in his bid for re-election.

Although he was a favorite of Speaker Macon and a close friend of a few other congressmen, such as Joseph H. Nicholson of Maryland and Joseph Bryan of Georgia, there is no evidence that in his role as House leader Randolph was ever popular with more than a few members of the party in Congress. Congressman Simeon Baldwin of Connecticut commented: "This Randolph . . . is a thorough going Democrat, but despising the feebleness of his partisans, he attempts to manage them with so much aristocratic hauteur, that they sometimes grow unmanageable and rebel, but they have no body else who really possess the talents requisite for a leader."[28] Federalist observers reported considerable mumbling among Republicans against Randolph, as Senator Plumer noticed: "His manners are far from conciliating. Many of the party dislike him —and on trifling measures they quarrel with him, but on all measures that are really important to the party they unite with him."[29] He explained:

His ill state of health renders him fretful and peevish; his manners are haughty—and he often unnecessarily tramples on the pride and wounds the feelings of his adherents, by a constant display of his superiority. This is unpleasant to many of them, and on several occasions they have rebelled—voted down his measures—and in private conversation, some of them, say they wish to *mortify him*. But on all important measures, they tamely submit. . . . The truth is, his talents are necessary to them, and for a season he will bear rule over them.[30]

In a single week Randolph received letters from at least three members of the House demanding explanations of his conduct and climaxed the same week at a dinner where he threw a glass of wine into the face of Congressman Willis Alston, broke the glass over his head, and threw the bottle at him. There was talk of a duel, but the district judge issued a warrant charging both to keep the peace.[31]

Contemporaries wrote privately of Randolph's apparent physical disability evident in his boyish face and high-pitched voice,[32] and his

28. Simeon Baldwin to Mrs. Baldwin, Feb. 15, 1804, Baldwin Family Papers, Yale Univ.
29. Brown, ed., *Plumer's Memorandum*, entry of Jan. 26, 1804, 123.
30. William Plumer to Jeremiah Smith, Feb. 10, 1804, Plumer Papers, Lib. Cong.
31. Plumer to John Park, Feb. 15, 1804, *ibid.*
32. Samuel Taggart to Rev. John Taylor, Jan. 13, 1804, George H. Haynes, ed., "Letters of Samuel Taggart, Representative in Congress, 1803-1814," American Antiquarian Society, *Proceedings*, New Ser., 33 (1923), 125.

patterns of behavior seemed to display an effort at compensation. Although a talented speaker and fierce in debate, his insolent and overbearing manners ill suited him for a party floor leader. Sitting in on the House debates on the Yazoo lands in February 1805, Senator Plumer noted: "John Randolph has pronounced two or three very bitter and very personal phillippic's on this subject. . . . He lashed demo's and feds indiscrimately. He treated no man that was opposed to him with either respect or decency. The Speaker ought to have called him to order—for his conduct was insufferable; but the Speaker dared not offend him."[33] A colleague in the House agreed: "Mr. Randolph has abused the federalists, entreated, threatened, and lashed many of his own party."[34] And Congressman John Davenport concluded: "J. Randolph's popularity is greatly diminished. He has by his haughty and overbearing conduct given great offence to those who have been formerly his attached friends. They have forsaken him and begin to clamour against him."[35]

Randolph, in fact, came close to breaking with the administration over the Yazoo land issue. In 1802, Secretary of State Madison, Secretary of the Treasury Gallatin, and Attorney General Lincoln, acting as federal commissioners, had obtained the agreement of Georgia to the cession of her western lands, with a reservation to cover unsettled private claims. In 1804, they proposed to Congress to settle these claims by a compromise settlement to claimants, mostly the Yazoo land companies which had purchased the Yazoo lands after their sale by the 1795 Georgia legislature. The rescinding of this sale by the 1796 Georgia legislature on the grounds of bribery had left their titles to the land in dispute. Although the commissioners denied the claimants' title, they proposed to reimburse them for their average expenditures on the ground that many were innocent parties who had purchased the lands from the original speculators unaware of the corruption of the legislature.[36] To any such settlement Randolph was opposed; leading the opposition in the House to the compromise in 1804, he succeeded in postponing action until the next session. In 1805 when the matter came up again, Randolph's abusive denunciation of anyone connected with the compromise as sanctioning corruption came close to an open break with the administration. He

---

33. Brown, ed., *Plumer's Memorandum*, entry of Feb. 2, 1805, 269.
34. Silas Betton to John C. Smith, Feb. 2, 1805, John Cotton Smith Papers, Lib. Cong. See also John Davenport to John C. Smith, Feb. 2, [1805], *ibid.*
35. Davenport to John C. Smith, Mar. 13, 1805, John Cotton Smith Papers, Yale Univ.
36. For a summary of the Yazoo land question see Brant, *Madison, 1800-1809*, 230-40.

attacked Postmaster General Gideon Granger, a claimant, so bitterly that Granger addressed a letter to the House requesting an inquiry into his conduct as Postmaster General.[37] Although Randolph again succeeded in blocking the Yazoo compromise, he created much party discord. "There is a violent brakage among the Democrats," reported Representative Manasseh Cutler. "Johnny Randolph has been very much deserted by his party. . . . he has violently attacked those of his party who had left him."[38]

At the beginning of 1805, other congressmen were saying that Randolph's influence was waning. Samuel Taggart, a Federalist member from Massachusetts, noted in January: "John Randolph has . . . resigned his office of ruling the majority in Congress, for this substantial reason that he finds they will no longer be ruled by him. The candidates aiming at the honour of succeeding him are John W. Eppes, Joseph H. Nicholson, Roger Nelson, and perhaps others, none of which I think possess Randolph's abilities. One thing is certain the party at present seem broken and divided, and do not act with their usual concert."[39] But Randolph was not to abandon his position of leadership until his break with the President in 1806, and he appeared in his most partisan role at the head of the House managers who conducted the impeachment proceedings against Justice Samuel Chase, whose removal for Federalist partisanship on the bench was sought by the administration.

The Federalist domination of the judiciary had been irritating in the extreme to Republicans, who resented the fact that John Adams before going out of office had filled all the vacancies with Federalists and appointed Federalist John Marshall as Chief Justice of the United States Supreme Court. The repeal of the Judiciary Act of 1801 by the Seventh Congress, in March 1802, abolished circuit court judgeships, but it did not alter the Federalist control of the judicial branch. Marshall's pronouncement of judicial review in the *Marbury* v. *Madison* decision, handed down in February 1803, added to Republican exasperation. When Associate Justice Samuel Chase, of the United States Supreme Court, in

---

37. Silas Betton to John C. Smith, Feb. 2, 1805, John Davenport to John C. Smith, Feb. 2, [1805], John Cotton Smith Papers, Lib. Cong.

38. Cutler to Francis Low, Feb. 6, 1805, "Seven Letters written by Manasseh Cutler while representing the Essex District in Congress," Essex Institute, *Historical Collections*, 39 (1903), 331.

39. Taggart to Rev. John Taylor, Jan. 4, 1805, Haynes, ed., "Letters of Samuel Taggart," Amer. Antiq. Soc., *Proceedings*, New Ser., 33 (1923), 146; see also Taggart to Taylor, Jan. 20, 1805, *ibid.*, 150.

a charge to a Baltimore grand jury in May 1803, denounced Republican changes and tendencies in both state and national governments, Jefferson reacted promptly. "You must have heard of the extraordinary charge of Chase to the Grand Jury at Baltimore," he wrote to Maryland Congressman Joseph H. Nicholson. "Ought this seditious and official attack on the principles of our Constitution, and on the proceedings of a State, to go unpunished?"[40] At the next meeting of Congress, acting on the suggestion of John Randolph, the House appointed a committee to inquire into the official conduct of Justice Chase. This committee began hearings in January 1804 and soon amassed an unusual volume of testimony against the Justice.[41] The investigation of Chase's conduct was extended beyond his harangue before the Baltimore grand jury to include his conduct on two occasions in 1800, the treason trial of John Fries in Philadelphia and the libel trial of James Thomson Callender in Richmond.

Meanwhile impeachment proceedings against Judge John Pickering, District Judge of New Hampshire, resulted in his conviction and removal. Although the cases were dissimilar, since Pickering's misconduct in office was the product of insanity, the success in the impeachment of Pickering opened prospects of subordinating the judiciary to Republican control through the impeachment process. Before adjourning, the House voted in March 1804 to impeach Justice Chase, but the trial was not to be held until the next session. In the vote of 73 to 32 in favor of impeachment, not a Republican voted in the negative.[42] Judge Pickering had been convicted by a similar partisan vote in the Senate. Senator Timothy Pickering protested: "The *Demon* of *party* governed the decision. All who condemned were Jeffersonians—and all who pronounced the accused not guilty were federalists. Some members retired without giving any vote."[43]

The partisanship shown in the conviction of Judge Pickering convinced most Federalists that Justice Chase would be convicted by a party vote. "If a considerable majority of the House were to impeach any man

40. Jefferson to Nicholson, May 13, 1803, Washington, ed., *Writings of Thomas Jefferson*, IV, 486. See also Nathaniel Macon to Nicholson, July 26, 1803, Nicholson Papers, Lib. Cong.; Macon to Nicholson, Aug. 6, 1803, William E. Dodd, ed., "Macon Papers," *The John P. Branch Historical Papers of Randolph-Macon College*, 3 (1909), 49.

41. Caesar A. Rodney to George Read, Jan. 11, Feb. 7, 15, 1804, George Read Papers, Hist. Soc. of Pa.; William Plumer to Daniel Plumer, Jan. 13, 1804, Plumer Papers, Lib. Cong.

42. Henry Adams, *History of the United States of America during the Administrations of Thomas Jefferson and James Madison*, 9 vols. (N.Y., 1889-91), II, 159.

43. Pickering to Theodore Lyman, Mar. 14, 1804, Pickering Papers, Mass. Hist. Soc.

in the United States, he would by the Senate be found guilty," declared Senator Pickering.[44] Senator William Plumer agreed: "It seems to be understood by the *Sect,* that for a judge to be impeached, and to be convicted and removed from office, are synonymous terms. . . . The process of impeachment is to be considered in effect as a *mode of removal,* and not as a charge and conviction of high crimes and misdemeanors."[45] Senator John Quincy Adams reported in December 1804—only a few weeks before Chase's trial was scheduled to begin—that Senate Republican leader William Branch Giles had explained to the Senate that "impeachment is nothing more than an enquiry, by the two Houses of Congress, whether the office of any public man might not be better filled by another." Similar pronouncements by Giles were witnessed by others.[46]

John Randolph headed the House managers who conducted the prosecution of Chase before the Senate.[47] Although Randolph spared no efforts to obtain a conviction, he failed to win the verdict. A majority of the senators found Chase guilty on three of the eight articles of impeachment, but on no article was the two-thirds vote necessary for conviction obtained. The vote of 19 to 15 in favor of conviction on the eighth article, covering Chase's charge to the grand jury in Baltimore, was four votes short of the constitutional requirement.[48] The acquittal of Chase was a bitter disappointment to Randolph and a severe blow to his position of party leadership in the House. Jefferson too was disappointed, and he carefully recorded the votes of every senator, compiling a list classifying each member according to the number of times out of the eight roll calls that each had voted for conviction.[49]

Whether or not the deficiency of Randolph as a party leader or his conduct toward members of his own party in Congress would have led

44. *Ibid.*
45. Plumer to Isaac Lyman, Mar. 17, 1804, Plumer Papers, Lib. Cong.
46. Charles Francis Adams, ed., *Memoirs of John Quincy Adams, Comprising Portions of his Diary from 1795 to 1848,* 2 vols. (Phila., 1874-77), entry of Dec. 20, 1804, I, 321; hereafter cited as Adams, ed., *Diary of John Quincy Adams.* Timothy Pickering to James McHenry, Dec. 22, 1804, Pickering Papers, Mass. Hist. Soc.; William Plumer to Thomas W. Thompson, Dec. 23, 1804, Plumer Papers, Lib. Cong.
47. Other managers were Caesar A. Rodney, Joseph H. Nicholson, Peter Early, John Boyle, Christopher Clark, and George W. Campbell.
48. Detailed discussions of the Chase impeachment can be found in Adams, *History,* II, 147-59, 218-44; William Cabell Bruce, *John Randolph of Roanoke, 1773-1833,* 2 vols. (N.Y., 1922), I, 200-220.
49. Jefferson, [Record of the vote on 8 counts in the impeachment proceedings in the U.S. Senate, of Judge Samuel Chase, Feb. 1805], Jefferson Papers, Lib. Cong.

to the overthrow of his leadership without an open break with Jefferson can only be a matter of speculation, for in the Ninth Congress Randolph decided his own fate by deserting and denouncing the President who was also the head of the Republican party.

At the beginning of the Ninth Congress in December 1805, the President sought a secret appropriation of two million dollars for the purchase of Florida. Randolph was given a special presidential briefing,[50] but he refused to support the proposal and led an unsuccessful attack upon it in the House. "Do not be surprised when you learn that the President's measures are not approved by our leader, J. Randolph," wrote Samuel Smith, and Federalist William Plumer rejoiced that "the *Great man* cannot render Randolph subservient to all his views."[51] In January 1806, Randolph wrote privately: "The administration may do what it pleases. It favors federal principles, and, with the exception of a few great rival characters, federal men. Attack it upon this ground, and you are denounced for federalism: are told by those, who agree with you in condemning the same measures, that you are ruining the republican party—that we must keep together, etc: the *old* republican party is already ruined, past redemption. New men and new maxims are the order of the day."[52] Randolph soon was appealing to Caesar A. Rodney: "My good friend, this is the time for an 'union of all honest men,' not in Mr. Burr's acceptation of the phrase but in its plain and obvious meaning."[53] The sentiments which Randolph expressed privately were reflected in his conduct in the House. "Randolph is much more at variance, on some points with the eastern democrats, than he is with the federalists, even those from Connecticut," observed Senator Plumer, and Virginia Congressman John Smith wrote despairingly: "I am sorry to say that there is not that harmony existing among the Republicans in the House of Representatives that could be wished; some of the members of which, it is said, have gone far towards denouncing the executive."[54] Federalists

---

50. Jefferson to Gallatin, Dec. 7, 1805, Adams, ed., *Gallatin Writings*, I, 282; see also Gallatin to Joseph H. Nicholson, Dec. 7, 1805, *ibid*.
51. Samuel Smith, letter 5, Dec. 14, 1805, letter book, Samuel Smith Papers, Lib. Cong.; William Plumer to James Sheafe, Jan. 13, 1806, Plumer Papers, Lib. Cong.
52. Randolph to George Hay, Jan. 3, 1806, John Randolph of Roanoke Papers, Univ. of Va.
53. Randolph to Caesar A. Rodney, Feb. 12, 1806, Caesar A. Rodney Papers, Lib. Cong.
54. William Plumer to Bradbury Cilley, Jan. 5, 1806, Plumer Papers, Lib. Cong.; John Smith to [Wilson Cary Nicholas], Jan. 25, 1806, Nicholas Papers, Univ. of Va. See also William Paterson to Mrs. Paterson, Feb. 8, 1806, William Paterson Papers, Rutgers University.

now began to see Randolph in a more favorable light. "Randolph has behaved very handsomely upon all questions relative to our foreign affairs," said James A. Bayard. "His conduct has been candid, decided, and manly. His Party however has refused to follow him and put themselves under other Leaders. They have in consequence experienced his invective with as much severity as his former opponents ever did."[55]

Randolph's mounting hostility toward the administration reached a climax in March 1806, in the debate on the Gregg Resolution. This resolution, introduced by Pennsylvania's Andrew Gregg, proposed the suspension of the importation of British goods until England modified her policies in regard to neutral trade and impressment. Randolph began his attack on the Gregg Resolution on March 5 with a speech of two and a half hours, in which, amidst much argumentation little related to the issue, he proclaimed that the policy would lead to war and announced his own opposition to fighting for avaricious trading interests. The speech, said Senator Samuel Smith, was "replete with invective (the most severe that the English language can furnish) against the President, Mr. Madison and the Cabinet generally." Denouncing Madison's foreign policies, he read from a recent pamphlet on neutral trade by the Secretary of State and indignantly cast it on the floor. He denounced "back-stairs influence— of men who bring messages to this House, which, although they do not appear on the Journals, govern its decisions." He sneered that there was "no longer any Cabinet." "In truth," said Smith, "he astonished all his hearers, by the boldness of his animadversions on Executive conduct, the elegance of his language and the pointed and fine strokes of oratory. But he has left stings in the breasts of many, that never can be extracted."[56]

The Senate could scarcely keep a quorum while Randolph was speaking;[57] and the sensation which he created was clearly evident in all the letters written from Washington at the time. "Randolph has now come out *openly* ... against the President and the Secretary of State ... ," wrote Congressman Timothy Pitkin. "Never has the *President* been handled so severely in public debate, as by Randolph."[58] "Mr. Randolph

55. Bayard to Richard Bassett, Jan. 31, 1806, Donnan, ed., *Bayard Papers*, 165.
56. Samuel Smith, letter 13, Mar. 5, 1806, letter book, Samuel Smith Papers, Lib. Cong.; William Plumer to Daniel Plumer, Mar. 7, 1806, Plumer Papers, Lib. Cong.; *Annals of Congress*, 9 Cong., 1 Sess. (Mar. 5, 1806), 555-74.
57. Adams, ed., *Diary of John Quincy Adams*, entry of Mar. 6, 1806, I, 418.
58. Timothy Pitkin to Simeon Baldwin, Mar. 10, 1806, Baldwin Family Papers, Yale Univ.

has passed the rubicon," wrote Senator Plumer. "He can no longer be considered as the confident, the friend or advocate of Mr. Jefferson." And Plumer noted in his journal that "neither the President or Secretary of State can after this be on terms with him. He has set them and their measures at defiance."[59] New Jersey Congressman William Helms explained that "early in the session it was suspected Mr. R[andolph] would oppose the administration, but in our late debates he has flung off the mask, and abused the President, Madison and indeed all the heads of departments, Gallatin excepted."[60] To Virginia, Thomas Mann Randolph sent warning: "It may be taken for granted in the country that Mr. R[andolph] is the bitter and determined enemy of the present administration, and that he has resolved to fall himself or destroy it in the public sentiment."[61]

Randolph's break with the administration was violent, decisive, and irreparable. The reasons for his action were less clear cut. Jefferson's private secretary, William A. Burwell, in a memoir of these events wrote:

> I have always believed that Mr. R[andolph] went to C[ongress] in 1805 displeased with the administration and determined to oppose them unless he was made the sole leader in the Government. Rumors had been afloat that the Government was tired of Mr. R. and wished to substitute other men as their confidential agents in Congress. Mr. Bidwell of Massachusetts had been spoken of as his successor. This gentleman had acquired considerable eminence in his own state, and had been supposed well qualified to manage the affairs of the Government in Congress. Mr. B. was considered the leader of the New England Interest, which Mr. R. cordially hated, and which he believed Mr. J[efferson] counted on with too much ardor. Hence he appears to have hated B. with uncommon rancor and to have opposed him invariably, as the organ of the Government. . . . The secret message of the President relative to Spanish affairs first brought R. and B. in conflict.[62]

John Quincy Adams, in a similar vein, wrote in his diary at the time of Randolph's speech on the Gregg Resolution: "He has been so exasperated at the attempts to take the management of the House from his hands, and at his defeat on the secret bill, that he has poured forth all the ebullitions of his resentment on this question." But Adams also added: "It is said

---

59. William Plumer to William Plumer, Jr., Mar. 11, 1806, Plumer Papers, Lib. Cong.; Brown, ed., *Plumer's Memorandum*, entry of Mar. 6, 1806, 444.
60. William Helms to J. Rhea, Mar. 16, 1806, Simon Gratz Collection, Hist. Soc. of Pa.
61. Randolph to Major Ellis, Mar. 24, 1806, Ellis Papers, Virginia Historical Society.
62. William A. Burwell, Memoir, [1804-8], William A. Burwell Papers, Lib. Cong.

there is now very warm electioneering in the party for the next presidential election, and that Mr. Randolph's object in his present denunciation is to prevent Mr. Jefferson from consenting to serve again, and Mr. Madison from being his successor. Mr. Randolph's man is said to be Mr. Monroe."[63]

That Randolph was seeking to discredit Madison and to elevate Monroe to the presidency was widely recognized. "He is full in the spirit of electioneering for President," wrote Congressman Helms, "and to that object, in my opinion, he would sacrifice the best interests of his Country. His view is to bring in Mr. Munroe . . . perhaps he means to be Secretary of State himself the first four years, and then succeed to the Presidency."[64] The suspicions that Randolph was looking to the election of 1808 were well founded; they can be substantiated from numerous sources, but from none better than Randolph's letter to Monroe, written March 20, 1806, in which he explained:

There is no longer a doubt, but that the principles of our administration have been materially changed. The compass of a letter—(indeed a volume would be too small) cannot suffice to give you even an outline. Suffice it to say, that every thing is made a business of bargain and traffick, the ultimate object of which is to raise Mr. M[adiso]n to the presidency. To this the old republican party will never consent,—nor can N.Y. be brought into the measure. Between them and the supporters of Mr. M[adison] there is an open rupture. Need I tell you that they (the old republicans) are united in your support?—that they look to you, Sir, for the example which this nation has yet to receive—to demonstrate that the government can be conducted on open, upright principles, without intrigue or any species of disingenuous artifice.[65]

Randolph himself had, indeed, brought the election issue into the House debate on non-importation, when he declared that "all eyes were in fact fixed on the half-way house between this and Georgetown, that the question was not what we should do with France, or Spain, or England, but who should be the next President. And at this moment," he continued, "every motion that is made . . . is made with a view to the occupation of that House. And it is for this reason that certain men are to be put down, and certain men are to be put up."[66]

63. Adams, ed., *Diary of John Quincy Adams,* entry of Mar. 6, 1806, I, 418.
64. William Helms to J. Rhea, Mar. 16, 1806, Gratz Collection, Hist. Soc. of Pa. See also William Plumer to Jedediah Morse, Apr. 9, 1806, Plumer Papers, Lib. Cong.; Timothy Pickering to Fisher Ames, Mar. 11, 1806, Pickering Papers, Mass. Hist. Soc.
65. Randolph to Monroe, Mar. 20, 1806, Monroe Papers, Lib. Cong.
66. *Annals of Congress,* 9 Cong., 1 Sess. (Mar. 13, 1806), 775.

While Randolph's hatred of Madison and his preference for Monroe were apparent, the reasons for these feelings were not so evident. Randolph confessed to believe that Jefferson and Madison had deserted the true principles of the Republican party which they had affirmed when the party came to power in 1801. But it was also true that Randolph's jealousy of Madison, nourished by the Secretary of State's disinterest in cultivating Randolph's favor, had grown to exaggerated proportions. It was demonstrated in his attack on Madison as a Yazoo man, and it reached new heights in 1806 when Randolph, after intimating his availability for a foreign assignment, was not appointed minister to England.[67] "You know the man," wrote John Beckley to a friend, "and can easily see the operating motives of mortified pride and disappointed ambition."[68]

Jefferson's concern over Randolph's revolt was seen in his efforts to keep Randolph's friends from joining the opposition. To Speaker Macon, he sent a note inviting him for a private conference. "Some enemy, whom we know not, is sowing tares among us," he wrote. "Between you and myself nothing but opportunities of explanation can be necessary to defeat these endeavours. At least on my part, my confidence in you is so unqualified that nothing further is necessary for my satisfaction. I must therefore ask a conversation with you.... tomorrow evening, or the next I can be alone. I mention the evening because it is the time at which alone we can be free from interruption."[69] Meanwhile Joseph H. Nicholson, another close friend of Randolph, was offered, and accepted, a federal judgeship in Maryland. Nicholson's letter of resignation was read to the House on April 9, 1806, while Randolph, as he wrote to Nicholson, "paid it the willing tribute of my tears."[70] The President's efforts to detach Randolph's followers from him were not unsuccessful. Although Macon could not bring himself to oppose Randolph, neither would he join him in opposing Jefferson. As the inveteracy of Randolph's opposition became clear, all but a handful of his followers deserted him.

From the standpoint of party history, perhaps the most important

---

67. Brant, *Madison, 1800-1809*, 232-40, 310-22, surveys Randolph's relations with Madison and stresses that the explanation for his hatred of Madison lies in the realm of psychiatry.

68. John Beckley to John Brown, July 12, 1806, Brown Papers, Yale Univ. According to Beckley, Randolph had actually obtained from Madison his passport for a voyage to Europe.

69. Jefferson to Macon, Mar. 22, 1806, Jefferson Papers, Lib. Cong.

70. Randolph to Nicholson, Apr. 10, 1806, Nicholson Papers, Lib. Cong.; *Annals of Congress*, 9 Cong., 1 Sess. (Apr. 9, 1806), 996.

aspect of Randolph's defection was that he did not carry any significant number of Republicans into opposition with him, or, as Jefferson phrased it, "that so eminent a leader should at once and almost unanimously be abandoned." Referring to party members in the House, Jefferson explained: "The defection of so prominent a leader, threw them into dismay and confusion for a moment; but they soon rallied to their own principles, and let him go off with 5 or 6 followers only. One half of these are from Virginia. His late declaration of perpetual opposition to this administration, drew off a few others who at first had joined him, supposing his opposition occasional only, and not systematic. The alarm the House has had from this schism, has produced a rallying together and a harmony, which carelessness and security had begun to endanger."[71]

That Randolph had destroyed his leadership in the House was clear; before the session ended Randolph was being so strongly attacked by leading Republicans that Macon feared a motion to expel him. Moreover, though not adopted, a resolution was introduced to appoint all standing committees by ballot.[72] Even Randolph's closest friends expected him to be removed from the chairmanship of the Ways and Means Committee. "You have passed the Rubicon and Madison or yourself must down . . . ," wrote Joseph Bryan from Savannah. "In your fall you can only cease to be chairman of the Committee of ways and means. They can hurt you no more let them rain heaven and earth—unless indeed they choose a Dictator and literally gag you."[73]

At the second session of the Ninth Congress in December 1806, another motion, "levelled at Randolph," to change the appointment of standing committees from appointment by the speaker to selection by ballot was introduced but lost by a vote of 42 to 44.[74] Because Randolph had not yet taken his seat when the House moved the appointment of standing committees, Macon did not appoint him to the Ways and Means Committee, a decision which caused Macon great personal grief. "In the disagreeable seat of speaker . . . I have been obliged to hear the journal read, in which

71. Jefferson to Monroe, Mar. 18, 1806, Jefferson to Wilson Cary Nicholas, Apr. 13, 1806, Ford, ed., *Jefferson Writings*, VIII, 429, 435n. Jefferson wrote to Monroe, May 4, 1806: "Upon all trying questions, exclusive of the federalists, the minority of republicans voting with him has been from 4 to 6 or 8, against from 90 to 100." *Ibid.*, 447.

72. Nathaniel Macon to Joseph H. Nicholson, Apr. 21, 1806, Nicholson Papers, Lib. Cong.

73. Bryan to Randolph, Apr. 23, 1806, Bryan Family Papers, Virginia State Library.

74. William Plumer to Bradbury Cilley, Dec. 9, 1806, Plumer Papers, Lib. Cong.; *Annals of Congress*, 9 Cong., 2 Sess. (Dec. 1, 1806), 111.

the name of J. R. was not on the Committe of Ways and Means," Macon wrote sadly to Nicholson, ". . . but such was my sense of duty, that I could not act otherwise."[75] However, soon after Randolph's arrival, his close friend James M. Garnett of Virginia asked to be relieved from serving on the committee and was excused. Macon then appointed Randolph to the committee; its chairman, Joseph Clay, a friend of Randolph's, stepped aside, and the committee elected Randolph again the chairman.[76]

Nevertheless, Randolph's influence was gone, and Macon was not again to be elected to the speakership. At the opening of the Ninth Congress in 1805, it had taken three trials before Macon was re-elected; after Randolph's defection, he was certain not to be chosen again. When the Tenth Congress convened in October 1807, Macon was absent and reported sick. Thus the House could elect Joseph B. Varnum of Massachusetts as speaker without openly repudiating Macon for his friendship with Randolph, but the meaning was unmistakable.[77] The new speaker made it plain where Randolph stood when he named George W. Campbell of Tennessee to replace Randolph as chairman of the Committee of Ways and Means. Congressman John Condit summed it up when he said: "Randolph's party sings very small this session."[78]

As Randolph and others had suspected, the administration had not been satisfied with his leadership in Congress before he openly turned against the President. At the opening of the Ninth Congress in December 1805, Barnabas Bidwell, who had been an active Republican leader in New England and a member of the Massachusetts legislature, had rapidly emerged as a possible successor to Randolph. As a new member, he had made a strong impression in the House. "Mr. Bidwell is as smooth as the ocean unruffled by the slightest breeze," commented his colleague Samuel Taggart, after Bidwell's first speech from the floor in

75. Macon to Joseph H. Nicholson, Dec. 1, 1806, Nicholson Papers, Lib. Cong.; Macon to Nicholson, Dec. 2, 1806, Dodd, ed., "Macon Papers," *Branch Historical Papers*, 3 (1909), 49.
76. *Annals of Congress*, 9 Cong., 2 Sess. (Dec. 5, 1806), 115; William Plumer to Bradbury Cilley, Dec. 9, 1806, Plumer Papers, Lib. Cong. Under existing House rules the member first named on the committee was chairman unless another member was chosen by the committee, which was evidently very unusual. *Annals of Congress*, 9 Cong., 2 Sess. (Dec. 9, 1806), 130.
77. Samuel Smith, letter 1, Dec. 2, 1805, letter book, Samuel Smith Papers, Lib. Cong.; Jefferson to Thomas M. Randolph, Oct. 26, 1807, Jefferson Papers, Lib. Cong.
78. John Condit to Silas Condit, Jan. 6, 1807, Gratz Collection, Hist. Soc. of Pa.

December 1805.⁷⁹ Before long Taggart was writing home: "I believe neighbor Bidwell is now J[efferso]n's right hand man. Randolph does not spare to lash him." And Senator Plumer noted: "Mr. Bidwell ... has much of the confidence of the President."⁸⁰ Another member, reporting Randolph's irritation with Bidwell, explained: "The object of Bidwell is to be *primus inter pares,* immediately, and you may be assured, it will not be submitted to, with patience."⁸¹

Bidwell had arrived in Washington enthusiastically recommended to the President by Levi Lincoln as "a uniform and warm supporter of the measures of the existing administration" and "a very useful acquisition in the national Legislature."⁸² That he had caught the eye of the President was soon clear, and that Jefferson had picked him for his majority leader in the House can also be shown. When Bidwell considered declining to stand for re-election, Jefferson appealed to him to run again, explaining in a most unrestrained letter that "there never was a time when the services of those who possess talents, integrity, firmness and sound judgment, were more wanted in Congress. Some one of that description is particularly wanted to take the lead in the H. of R. to consider the business of the nation as his own business, to take it up as if he were singly charged with it and carry it through.... It is only speaking a truth to say that all eyes look to you. It was not perhaps expected from a new member, at his first session, ... but it would be a subject of deep regret were you to refuse yourself to the conspicuous part in the business of the house which all assign to you." Writing freely to Bidwell, Jefferson, in what is perhaps his most revealing letter on the subject of executive practices, explained his conception of, and need for, an administration spokesman and party floor leader:

I do not mean that any gentleman relinquishing his own judgment, should implicitly support all the measures of the administration; but that, where he does not disapprove of them he should not suffer them to go off in sleep, but bring them to the attention of the house and give them a fair chance. Where he disapproves, he will of course leave them to be brought forward by those who concur in the sentiment. Shall I explain

79. Taggart to Rev. John Taylor, Dec. 24, 1805, Haynes, ed., "Letters of Samuel Taggart," Amer. Antiq. Soc., *Proceedings,* New Ser., 33 (1923), 167.
80. Taggart to Rev. John Taylor, Feb. 2, 1806, *ibid.,* 174; Brown, ed., *Plumer's Memorandum,* entry of Mar. 8, 1806, 446.
81. Timothy Pitkin, Jr., to Simeon Baldwin, Jan. 2, 1806, Baldwin Family Papers, Yale Univ.
82. Lincoln to Jefferson, Nov. 6, 1805, Jefferson Papers, Lib. Cong.

my idea by example? The classification of the militia was communicated to Gen. Varnum and yourself merely as a proposition, which if you approved, it was trusted you would support.... As soon as I found it did not coincide with your sentiments, I could not wish you to support it, but using the same freedom of opinion, I procured it to be brought forward elsewhere.... When a gentleman, through zeal for the public service, undertakes to do the public business, we know that we shall hear the cant of backstairs counsellors. But we never heard this while the declaimer was himself a backstairs man as he calls it, but in the confidence and views of the administration as may more properly and respectfully be said. But if the members are to know nothing but what is important enough to be put into a public message, and indifferent enough to be made known to all the world, if the Executive is to keep all other information to himself, and the house to plunge on in the dark, it becomes a government of chance and not of design.[83]

The above letter deserves much attention, for it reveals Jefferson's concept of how the administration should function in relation to Congress. It demonstrates Jefferson's belief that the President must have a spokesman and party leader in Congress who would be kept in the confidence of the administration and in turn would see the President's measures through the legislative process. The letter also shows that Jefferson had attempted to develop this relationship with John Randolph, only to be subsequently accused by him of backstairs influence.[84]

As a result of Jefferson's appeal, Bidwell reconsidered and agreed to stand for re-election, explaining that his inclination to retire had not been due to any dissatisfaction or discouragement but because of family considerations. Obviously moved by Jefferson's flattering letter, Bidwell expressed his appreciation of the President's confidence, but pointed out the difficulties in implementing his suggestions. In a letter equally revealing as that of Jefferson, he discussed the practical operation of the party in Congress, explaining:

I am constrained to say, you appear to expect more from my exertions, as a member of the House of Representatives, than it will be in my power to perform. The cant of back-stairs influence has no terrors; but there are obstacles in my way. In every legislature, the introduction, progress and conclusion of business depend much upon committees; and,

---

83. Jefferson to Barnabas Bidwell, July 5, 1806, *ibid.*

84. This letter also refutes the statement made by White, *The Jeffersonians*, 4, that "Jefferson was not interested, indeed, in the normal process of day-by-day administration. Apart from disposing of particular cases there is hardly a reference in his public or private papers to the management of the public business."

in the House of Representatives of the U.S., more than in any other legislative body within my knowledge, the business referred to Committees, and reported on by them, is, by usage and common consent, controlled by their chairman. As the Speaker, according to the standing rules of the House, has the appointment of Committees, he has it in his power to place whom he pleases in the foreground, and whom he pleases in the back-ground, and thus, in some measure, affect their agency in the transactions of the House. From the connections and attachments of the present Speaker, I have, at least, no reason to expect to be very favourably considered, in his distribution of committee business. This circumstance, with others, of more importance, which I will forbear to mention, but of which I am deeply sensible, will prevent my acting a very conspicuous part. So far, however, as industry and moderate abilities may be relied on, I shall feel it a duty to be attentive to the business of the House; and, having had satisfaction of a cordial concurrence with the principles and measures of the Executive Administration, generally, it will be my happiness to give them the feeble aid of my support, both in and out of the House.[85]

Bidwell's frank reply in stressing the importance of committee assignments and the power of the speaker reveals much of the workings of the House. It also clearly displays why Macon's continued attachment to Randolph, after the latter's defection, was to lead to his removal from the speakership. Although Bidwell was successful in his bid for reelection, he resigned from Congress in 1807 to accept appointment as the attorney general of Massachusetts, after Republican James Sullivan won the governorship of that state. Once again Jefferson's attempt to secure a party leader in Congress collapsed.[86]

In 1807, Jefferson encouraged Wilson Cary Nicholas, who had earlier served in the Senate, to run for the House. Explaining that his son-in-law Thomas Mann Randolph had decided to retire from Congress, Jefferson wrote that "it is strongly his wish, and that of all here, that you should take his place." The President continued:

Never did the calls of patriotism more loudly assail you than at this moment. After excepting the federalists, who will be 27., and the little band of schismatics, who will be 3. or 4. (all tongue), the residue of the H of R is as well disposed a body of men as I ever saw collected. But there is no one whose talents and standing, taken together, have weight

85. Bidwell to Jefferson, July 28, 1806, Jefferson Papers, Lib. Cong.
86. Bidwell to Jefferson, June 27, 1807, *ibid.;* Jefferson to Bidwell, July 11, 1807, Ford, ed., *Jefferson Writings*, IX, 106; Bidwell to Madison, June 27, 1807, Madison Papers, Lib. Cong.

enough to give him the lead. The consequence is, that there is no one who will undertake to do the public business, and it remains undone. Were you here, the whole would rally round you in an instant, and willingly co-operate in whatever is for the public good. Nor would it require you to undertake drudgery in the House. There are enough, able and willing to do that. A rallying point is all that is wanting. Let me beseech you then to offer yourself. You never will have it so much in your power again to render such eminent service.[87]

Nicholas complied with the President's wishes by consenting to stand for election, a movement which immediately aroused the suspicions of John Randolph, who confided to Monroe: "Mr. T. M. Randolph suddenly declines a re-election, in favor of Wilson Nicholas, whose talents for intrigue you well know, I presume."[88] Nicholas was successful in his election, but, arriving as he did for the last Congress of Jefferson's tenure, he never became the kind of leader that Jefferson had in mind.

Jefferson had sought to develop a system in which the party would have an administration spokesman in a position of leadership in Congress, but various circumstances had interfered to disrupt the President's efforts. Only John Randolph effectively filled the post of floor leader, and he but for little more than two years. Although Jefferson had taken Randolph into his confidence, Randolph's position of leadership was not a result of executive influence, but rather the product of his own aggressiveness and his prominent position as chairman of the Ways and Means Committee. It is apparent that Jefferson would have preferred a sober man of business, such as Rodney or Bidwell, to the irascible Randolph, and he quietly worked to get and to keep such men in Congress. That his exertions were not more successful was not due to a lack of effort on the part of the President.

In the Senate, Virginia Republican Stevens Thomson Mason, who had been a member since 1795, appears to have been the principal party leader in that body from 1801 until his death in 1803. Senator Plumer regarded him as such,[89] and Jefferson become so greatly alarmed when Mason contemplated retiring in 1802 that he personally secured a promise from Mason that he would serve again if elected.[90] After Mason's death,

---

87. Jefferson to Nicholas, Feb. 28, 1807, Ford, ed., *Jefferson Writings*, IX, 32-33.
88. Randolph to Monroe, Mar. 24, 1807, Monroe Papers, Lib. Cong.
89. Brown, ed., *Plumer's Memorandum*, entry of Oct. 31, 1803, 29-30.
90. Jefferson to Monroe, Dec. 11, 1802, Mason to Monroe, Dec. 10, 1802, Monroe Papers, N.Y. Pub. Lib.

Senate leadership came to rest on William B. Giles, whose past experience in the House promoted him to leadership in the Senate soon after he took his seat in 1804. Senator Plumer immediately recognized him as "the Ministerial leader in the Senate," and Senator John Quincy Adams soon was writing of "our present sovereign, Mr. Giles, who rules without control as Lord of the ascendant.... His power," mused Adams, "is such that if he should move my expulsion from the Senate because he does not like my looks, he would stand a very fair chance of success. But he has nothing insolent in his *manner,* which cannot be said of all his associates."[91] Next to Giles in party leadership in the Senate was John Breckinridge of Kentucky. Adams thought it worthy of recording in his diary that in the absence of Giles, Breckinridge had called for the yeas and nays on a question, and Adams revealingly noted that later "Mr. Giles came into the Senate and took the wheel at helm from Breckinridge."[92] Breckinridge's services were lost to the Senate when he resigned to become Attorney General in August 1805.

Jefferson regarded Giles as especially important to the party in the Senate. "Giles' absence has been a most serious misfortune," the President wrote in 1806, when illness had kept the Senator at home. "A majority of the Senate means well," but Federalist Senators Uriah Tracy and James A. Bayard were "too dexterous for them, and have very much influenced their proceedings." Seven Federalists "voting always in phalanx, and joined by some discontented republicans, some oblique ones, some capricious, have so often made a majority, as to produce very serious embarrassment to the public operations; and very much do I dread the submitting to them, at the next session, any treaty which can be made with either England or Spain, when I consider that 5 joining the federalists, can defeat a friendly settlement of our affairs."[93] As in the House, the administration thus found it difficult to retain effective party leadership in the Senate for any substantial period of time.

Federalists accused Jefferson of exercising undue influence over Con-

91. William Plumer to Thomas W. Thompson, Dec. 23, 1804, Plumer Papers, Lib. Cong.; John Quincy Adams to John Adams, Dec. 24, 1804, Jan. 5, 1805, Ford, ed., *Writings of John Quincy Adams,* III, 102-3, 104.
92. Adams, ed., *Diary of John Quincy Adams,* entry of Feb. 5, 1805, I, 346.
93. Jefferson to Wilson Cary Nicholas, Apr. 13, 1806, Ford, ed., *Jefferson Writings,* VIII, 435n. Jefferson also wrote to Giles, Feb. 23, 1806, saying that his services were needed in the Senate and expressing the hope that he would be able to come to Washington before the session was over. Jefferson Papers, Lib. Cong.

gress and pictured the legislature as completely subservient to the President. "The President has only to act and the Majority will approve," wrote Archibald Henderson, North Carolina Federalist Representative, in 1802. "I do not believe that in any Country there ever was more implicit obedience paid to an administration than in this. I do not mean to say that Mr. Jefferson has this uncontrolled authority, but that when the Cabinet determines on measures they will be passed."[94] Connecticut's Senator James Hillhouse in a similar voice exclaimed that "never were a set of men more blindly devoted to the will of a *prime Mover* or *Minister* than the Majority of both Houses to the will and wishes of the Chief Magistrate,"[95] and Timothy Pickering was convinced that Jefferson "*behind the curtain,* directs the measures he wishes to have adopted; while in each house a majority of puppets move as he touches the wires."[96] Less emotionally, John Quincy Adams recorded in his diary in 1806 that the President's "whole system of administration seems founded upon this principle of carrying through the legislature measures by his personal or official influence. There is a certain proportion of the members of both Houses who on every occasion of emergency have no other enquiry but what is the President's wish."[97]

Although violent prejudices such as those displayed by Pickering colored many Federalist observations, Jefferson was a strong executive who, directly and through his Cabinet, exercised great influence over Congress. The principal legislation enacted by Congress originated in the administration: the repeal of the Judiciary Act of 1801, the financial measures, the acquisition of Louisiana and accompanying legislation, the gunboat and defense policy, and the Embargo. When Jefferson sent his annual message to Congress by his private secretary, rather than appearing in person, he had no intention of abandoning executive leadership. Yet Jefferson's influence over Congress was not so easily maintained as Federalist reports intimated. The loss of Rodney and Bidwell and the defection of Randolph greatly hampered the development of the role of a floor leader and administration spokesman. To give direction to the party's large majority demanded considerable attention, and the means

---

94. Henderson to Samuel Johnston, Dec. 16, 1802, Hayes Collection (transcript), North Carolina Department of Archives and History.

95. Hillhouse to Simeon Baldwin, Feb. 11, 1802, Baldwin Family Papers, Yale Univ.

96. Pickering to Mrs. Pickering, Jan. 31, 1806, quoted in Edward H. Phillips, "Timothy Pickering's 'Portrait' of Thomas Jefferson," Essex Institute, *Hist. Collections,* 94 (1958), 313.

97. Adams, ed., *Diary of John Quincy Adams,* entry of Feb. 7, 1806, I, 403-4.

which the President employed to this end indicate a good deal about the operation of the Republican party in Congress.

Early in his administration, Jefferson, in explaining that he rarely spoke of politics or congressional affairs with his two sons-in-law (Thomas Mann Randolph and John Wayles Eppes, both members from Virginia), suggested in a letter to John Randolph that more contact between members and the President might be helpful. "With other members, I have believed that more unreserved communications would be advantageous to the public," he wrote. "This has been, perhaps, prevented by mutual delicacy. I have been afraid to express opinions unasked, lest I should be suspected of wishing to direct the legislative action of members. They have avoided asking communications from me, probably, lest they should be suspected of wishing to fish out executive secrets."[98]

One way in which Jefferson sought to remedy this situation was to invite members to dine with him at the executive mansion. Members were asked in small groups, and generally Republican and Federalist members were invited on different days—a practice which inspired one Federalist to comment: "He is in the habit of separating the wheat from the chaff, and invites the federal members by themselves."[99] One South Carolina Republican, David R. Williams, declined the President's dinner invitation, explaining that he had regarded the entertainments formerly given by President Adams "as decoys to the representatives in Congress, and although I do not consider yours as such, still I cannot partake of that now, which I reprobated then." These remarks drew forth from Jefferson a full explanation of his practice. "The independence of the mind is one of it's best qualities, and if you suppose it could have been lessened by that kind of intercourse, you are right in declining it," replied the President, explaining, however: "I cultivate personal intercourse with the members of the legislature that we may know one another and have opportunities of little explanations of circumstances, which, not understood might produce jealousies and suspicions injurious to the public interest, which is best promoted by harmony and mutual confidence among its functionaries. I depend much on the members for the local information necessary on local matters, as well as for the means of getting

---

98. Jefferson to John Randolph, Dec. 1, 1803, Ford, ed., *Jefferson Writings*, VIII, 281-82.

99. Simeon Baldwin to Mrs. Baldwin, Jan. 5, 1804, Baldwin Family Papers, Yale Univ. See also Adams, ed., *Diary of John Quincy Adams*, entry of Feb. 25, 1806, I, 415.

at public sentiment."[100] The President must have won support for many measures at these dinners. Around the fire in the Senate Chamber, William Plumer, for example, heard Republicans admit that "the President's dinners had silenced them" in opposition to the nomination of William C. C. Claiborne to be governor of Louisiana.[101]

With party leaders in Congress and with certain members in whom he placed special confidence, Jefferson was unreserved in offering his ideas and not infrequently drafted bills for presentation to Congress by members. These activities were distinctly suggested by Senator Wilson Cary Nicholas when he wrote to the President, early in the Seventh Congress, "I have had the pleasure to receive your notes of this date, with their enclosures. The subject was not acted upon today, nor do I presume it will be for several days. In the meantime I hope to have the pleasure of conversing with you more fully upon the subject, to which your notes refer."[102] On another occasion, Joseph H. Nicholson wrote from the House:

I have this morning laid before the Committee a short sketch of the several provisions contained in the bill which you sent me. These are fully approved of, but as the business of the gun boats is likewise committed to us, I think it would be better to engraft the whole in the same bill, in order that one view of the subject may be presented. May I therefore beg the favor of you to state to me the number of boats wanted, the manner in which they are to be disposed of, how to be officered, manned and equipt; in fine such information as will enable me to meet your wishes.[103]

In another instance, at the time of the acquisition of Louisiana, the President wrote to Senator John Breckinridge, who, it may be recalled, in 1798 had introduced into the Kentucky legislature the Kentucky Resolutions secretly penned by Jefferson:

I thought I perceived in you the other day a dread of the job of preparing a constitution for the new acquisition. With more boldness than wisdom I therefore determined to prepare a canvass, give it a few daubs of outline, and send it to you to fill up. I yesterday morning

---

100. Williams to Jefferson, [received Jan. 29, 1806], Worthington C. Ford, ed., *Thomas Jefferson Correspondence Printed from the Originals in the Collection of William K. Bixby* (Boston, 1916), 128; Jefferson to Williams, Jan. 31, 1806, Jefferson Papers, Lib. Cong.

101. Brown, ed., *Plumer's Memorandum*, entry of Dec. 12, 1804, 220-21.

102. Nicholas to Jefferson, Jan. 26, 1802, Jefferson Papers, Lib. Cong.

103. Nicholson to Jefferson, Nov. 19, 1804, *ibid*. See also Nicholson to Jefferson, Jan. 28, 1805, Jefferson to Nicholson, Jan. 29, 1805, *ibid*.

took up the subject and scribbled off the inclosed. In communicating it to you I must do it in confidence that you will never let any person know that I have put pen to paper on the subject and that if you think the inclosed can be of any aid to you you will take the trouble to copy it and return me the original. I am this particular, because you know with what bloody teeth and fangs the federalists will attack any sentiment or principle known to come from me.[104]

Jefferson frequently invoked such secrecy and accompanied his suggestions with disclaimers that he had any intention of interfering in congressional affairs. Sending a draft of a bill to Virginia Congressman John Dawson, he attached a note requesting that the Congressman "will be so good as to copy the within and burn this original, as he is very unwilling to meddle personally with the details of the proceedings of the legislature."[105] On another occasion he had copies printed of a piece on the subject of the militia sent to him from West Point by Colonel Jonathan Williams and arranged to have them laid on the desks of every member of Congress "without the least indication of the quarter from whence they came."[106] In Jefferson's papers deposited at the Library of Congress are the drafts in the President's handwriting of several naval and militia measures presented to Congress.[107]

In addition to his direct contact with members of Congress, Jefferson also exerted influence and party leadership through the members of his Cabinet. Secretary of the Navy Robert Smith, for example, wrote to DeWitt Clinton, chairman of a Senate committee, in 1803: "I am charged by the President to communicate to you his opinion that provision ought to be made for procuring eight gunboats, in addition to the four vessels of war, at present contemplated by the Legislature. Should Congress concur in this opinion, it is presumed that an appropriation of 12000 Dollars, would enable the Executive to carry the measure into effect."[108]

104. Jefferson to Breckinridge, Nov. 24, 1803, Ford, ed., *Jefferson Writings*, VIII, 279-80. See also Jefferson to Breckinridge, Feb. 17, 1803, Papers of Breckinridge Family, Lib. Cong., in which Jefferson forwards a suggestion for legislative action received from Judge Harry Innes; Innes to Jefferson, Jan. 14, 1803, Jefferson Papers, Lib. Cong.
105. Jefferson to Dawson, Dec. 19, 1806, enclosing "A Bill authorizing the employment of the land or naval forces of the U.S. in cases of insurrection" [polygraph copy], Jefferson Papers, Lib. Cong.
106. Jefferson to Jonathan Williams, Nov. 23, 1808, *ibid*.
107. Jefferson Papers, CXXXVII, 23702, 23703-4, CLXXIII, 30685-86, Lib. Cong. See also Jefferson to John Randolph, Nov. 19, 1804, and draft of bill printed in Ford, ed., *Jefferson Writings*, VIII, 333-35; Gallatin to Jefferson, Nov. 25, 1807, Jefferson Papers, Lib. Cong.
108. Smith to Clinton, Feb. 16, 1803, DeWitt Clinton Papers, Columbia University.

The Secretary of the Treasury in a similar manner wrote Senator Breckinridge: "I send in the shape of a bill, the substance of what the President seems to think necessary in order to authorize him to occupy and temporarily govern Louisiana. Will you consult with your friends and decide whether the authority be necessary, and if so, what form should be given it."[109] At another time Gallatin wrote the President: "If you wish to avoid the formality of a message in relation to the Supervisor North West of the Ohio, I may write the enclosed letter to the Chairman of the Committee of Ways and Means. Please to return it, if you approve that mode."[110]

In their official capacity department heads were on occasion invited to attend committee meetings or prepare reports and recommendations.[111] Unofficially they also exerted important influence. Republican legislators frequently turned to Cabinet members for information and counsel. Georgia Senator Abraham Baldwin, for example, wrote to the Secretary of the Treasury: "The inclosed Bill has just been referred to a select committee in the Senate. Will you have the goodness to note on the bill any amendments which you think proper to recommend to their consideration."[112] To Secretary of State Madison, Senator William B. Giles sent a copy of a bill about to be passed, with a note: "If you can suggest any amendment to it in its present form be pleased to notice it in the course of the day."[113] A Senate committee in 1808 requested Madison to prepare the committee's report relating to the Embargo and submitted it with only minor changes,[114] and Albert Gallatin prepared the speech on the Embargo presented to Congress in November by George W. Campbell, chairman of the House Committee of Ways and Means.[115] In such ways, executive leadership was felt in Congress, although there is nothing to suggest that the members of the Cabinet attempted to exert any unusual or irregular influence over Congress.

109. Albert Gallatin to Breckinridge, [Oct. 1803], and draft of bill, Papers of Breckinridge Family, Lib. Cong.
110. Gallatin to Jefferson, Jan. 3, 1802, Jefferson Papers, Lib. Cong.
111. White, *The Jeffersonians*, 50.
112. Baldwin to Gallatin, Mar. 24, 1802, Gallatin Papers, N.-Y. Hist. Soc.
113. Giles to Madison, [1805], Madison Papers, Lib. Cong.
114. Brant, *Madison, 1800-1809*, 448.
115. Notes in Gallatin's hand are in the Gallatin Papers, N.-Y. Hist. Soc.; Campbell's report was published in the Washington *National Intelligencer*, Nov. 23, 1808, also printed in Adams, ed., *Gallatin Writings*, I, 435-46.

In the operation of the Republican party in Congress, the party caucus, though not formally adopted except in the nominating of candidates for president and vice-president, was irregularly employed. Since some of these caucuses were so informal that many who participated would have objected to calling them caucuses, it is impossible to establish the extent to which the caucus was adopted as a method of party procedure. According to Federalist testimony, the Republicans held frequent caucuses. Senator James Hillhouse of Connecticut protested in 1802: "In the conflict of party reason and argument are altogether unavailing, and have not the smallest influence in the decision of any question or measure that is taken up in Congress. . . . All questions are settled in private meetings, and every member composing the Majority of both houses comes pledged to support the measures so agreed on."[116] About the same time, Representative John Rutledge of South Carolina confessed on the floor of the House to be "much puzzled by the new forms of proceeding" adopted by the Republicans, when a proposal was rejected with no objections having been raised against it. It had been the practice, he said, "when measures were proposed not agreeable to the majority, for them to offer their objections to them. . . . In these days of innovation, we, it seems, are to pursue a different course." Not a voice had been raised against the resolution before the House. "This profound silence made us expect a unanimous vote; but, in consequence, he supposed, of some out-door arrangements, it was rejected by this silent majority."[117] Senator Plumer recorded several instances of Republican (and also Federalist) caucuses in his journal. "The democratic senators held a Caucus last evening in which they settled the principles of the bill—and agreed to the same in the Senate without any debate," he noted in regard to a measure affecting the Louisiana territory.[118] John Quincy Adams, likewise, referred to "consultations out of doors" determining Senate business.[119] John Randolph objected when Federalist Congressman James A. Bayard in a House debate in 1802 referred to caucuses, but the speaker decided against Randolph, and Bayard was allowed to proceed and explain: "I was not blaming these meetings, in

116. Hillhouse to Simeon Baldwin, Feb. 18, 1802, Baldwin Family Papers, Yale Univ.
117. *Annals of Congress*, 7 Cong., 1 Sess. (Jan. 25, 1802), 455.
118. Brown, ed., *Plumer's Memorandum*, entry of Feb. 8, 1804, 140-41. See also entries for Oct. 27, 1803, Dec. 12, 1804, Dec. 1, 1805, *ibid.*, 28, 220-21, 337.
119. Adams, ed., *Diary of John Quincy Adams*, entry of Feb. 5, 1805, I, 346.

what are called caucuses. I do not see why thirty or forty members may not meet together to talk politics, or any other more entertaining subject, as well as a smaller number."[120] Few Federalists, however, were willing to be so generous to Republicans, and not many members of either party were inclined to discuss their caucuses openly. Of the few Republicans who mentioned their caucuses, John Taylor of Caroline, who filled a vacancy in the Senate for two months in 1803, was unusually informative. In answering charges of Virginia influence in the Senate, he wrote:

> I do not recollect what is called a caucus, or any other meeting, to determine what should come before the Senate; or to consider any depending political subject or question, in a single case; except what I shall relate, should be considered in that light.
> The evening before the Senate met, several members (whether designedly or accidentally I know not) fell in company, and consulted as to a fit person for president pro tempore; it being understood that the vice president was absent. Soon after a house was formed, a proposal was made to choose a clerk, and I believe a member did procure a meeting of several other members, to lay before them the pretensions of a candidate he intended to propose; knowing nothing of the gentleman's qualifications, I attended. And there was a general meeting of the friends to the discriminating amendment (with a few exceptions) an evening or two before its passage, to consider a proposition for enabling a vice president to act as president, in every case of no existing president. I speak from memory, but this I believe was its object. This meeting was made no secret of, and the subject was discussed with great talents.[121]

Although hesitant to admit that these were party caucuses because of the common belief that caucuses were improper, Taylor revealed much about how the party operated in Congress. Since Taylor was accounting for a period of only two months, his comments suggest that party caucuses were not infrequent.

---

120. *Annals of Congress*, 7 Cong., 1 Sess. (Feb. 4, 1802), 480. Wilfred E. Binkley, *President and Congress* (N.Y., 1947), 54, says that Bayard was called to order for using the word caucus on the House floor, and cites the above source. The record of the debate, however, does not support that conclusion. In fact, Bayard used the term *caucuses* again after the speaker decided against Randolph.

121. Taylor to Wilson C. Nicholas, June 23, 1804, Edgehill-Randolph Papers, Univ. of Va.

CHAPTER FIVE

National Party Machinery

The Republican members of Congress provided the national party organization of the Jeffersonian party. They maintained close touch with their state party organizations and through their informal association in Washington supplied the leadership of a national party committee. The administration relied heavily on Republicans in Congress for contact with state organizations, for patronage recommendations, and for communicating the accomplishments of the administration to the voters.

The private and circular letters which congressmen sent to their constituents provided an important medium of communication between national party leaders and the voters. Senator John Breckinridge of Kentucky kept a list, arranged by counties, of persons with whom he corresponded while in Washington. A manuscript draft of a review of the proceedings of Congress, in the Breckinridge Papers, is endorsed by Breckinridge: "Original letter—12th Feb. 1802—23 copies sent to the persons marked thus √ in the list."[1] Congressman Joseph B. Varnum of Massachusetts in 1808 transmitted by mail to each town in the district which he represented "a full set of all the public documents calculated to exhibit a full and correct view of the real situation of our country," explaining: "I have impressed by letter to each gentleman to whom the documents have been directed, the importance of promulgating them in their respective towns."[2]

A number of congressmen, primarily southern and western members, sent printed circular letters to their constituents. These letters appeared most frequently just before congressional elections. John Clopton, a Virginian who reported regularly through circular letters, scribbled on a copy which he sent to his wife, in April 1806: "I have been so closely engaged in getting circular letters ready to go by this mail to be in time

---

1. Papers of Breckinridge Family, XXI, 3564a, 3653a, Lib. Cong.
2. Varnum to William Eustis, Dec. 5, 1808, Eustis Papers, Lib. Cong.

to arrive at the election for New Kent next Thursday that I have barely time to drop you a few lines on this to let you know that I am well."[3] Thomas T. Davis, seeking re-election from Kentucky in 1801, revealed both the manners and the motives of communicating with the voters when he asked: "Have I not taken pains, as well by distributing newspapers, as by written and printed letters, to show the part I had acted, and the general proceeding of Congress?"[4] Concluding a circular to his Tennessee constituents, Representative William Dickson suggested that "having thus given you an account of the principal measures which have engaged the attention of Congress during the present session, I take the liberty to observe, that my fellow-citizens may, if they think proper, again command my services."[5] Congressmen generally had their own elections in view when they reported to their constituents, but their reviews of the proceedings of Congress and of the administration were an important factor in molding public opinion and in maintaining popular support for the party.

In the new capital, where many members lived with their political friends in boarding houses and took their meals among little groups of political associates, the party role of members of Congress was unusually important. "You may suppose that being thrown together in a few boarding houses, without any other society than ourselves, we are not likely to be either very moderate politicians or to think of any thing but politics," wrote Albert Gallatin in 1801.[6] Congressional society was highly partisan throughout Jefferson's administration. "The men of the different parties do not associate intimately," observed Congressman Simeon Baldwin, and Senator William Plumer explained: "The two parties board separately, and visit each other but seldom."[7] Baldwin reported thirteen Federalists at his table where "we make ourselves some sport at the expence of the blunders as we conceive them, of the great folks in power."[8] Republican Senator John Breckinridge dined with "a Club of 17 members, most of them my old acquaintances, six of whom

---

3. John Clopton, [circular], Washington, Apr. 4, 1806, addressed to Mrs. Sarah Clopton, Apr. 6, 1806, John Clopton Papers, Duke Univ.
4. Lexington *Kentucky Gazette,* Apr. 27, 1801.
5. William Dickson, [circular], Washington, Mar. 3, 1803, broadside, Amer. Antiq. Soc.
6. Gallatin to Mrs. Gallatin, Jan. 22, [1801], quoted in Walters, *Albert Gallatin,* 127.
7. Baldwin to Mrs. Baldwin, Dec. 20, 1803, Baldwin Family Papers, Yale Univ.; Plumer to Oliver Peabody, Dec. 22, 1802, Plumer Papers, Lib. Cong.
8. Simeon Baldwin to Mrs. Baldwin, Dec. 20, 1803, Baldwin Family Papers, Yale Univ.

are senators."⁹ Another contemporary concluded that "no Tavern or boarding house contains two members of opposite sentiments."¹⁰

Much party business of which the historian will ever remain unaware was undoubtedly transacted at the dinner tables and in the private quarters of members. This close association of party leaders during the sessions of Congress gave them a commanding voice in party affairs and supplied vital national party organization. The best evidence of the important role of the party members in Congress in providing national party machinery was the congressional nominating caucus. Experimented with in 1796, the caucus was used by both Republicans and Federalists in 1800¹¹ and was successfully employed by Republicans until 1824. Its role in the party organization can be seen in the caucuses of 1804 and 1808.

As the election of 1804 approached, Republicans directed their attention toward the vice-presidential nomination. That Jefferson would receive the unanimous nomination of his party for re-election was unquestioned; that Burr would not obtain the party's nomination for vice-president seemed equally certain.¹² New York Republicans who wished to undermine Burr's ambitions for the governorship of New York were impatient for the congressional nominating caucus to meet. "The republicans here are anxiously looking to our friends at Washington for a nomination of President and Vice President," wrote Brockholst Livingston to Gallatin, in December 1803. "This ought not to be delayed. It is the only thing necessary completely to prostrate a very wicked but important faction which exists among us here. Rely on it, that the sooner our friends in Congress designate their candidates for their offices the better."¹³

There was no obvious candidate to be substituted for Burr on the Republican ticket. In the fall of 1803, party leaders had sounded out Pennsylvania's Governor Thomas McKean about accepting the nomination, but he had declined.¹⁴ New York's Governor George Clinton was

9. Breckinridge to Mrs. Breckinridge, Dec. 19, 1804, Papers of Breckinridge Family, Lib. Cong.
10. Benjamin G. Orr to John Steele, Feb. 13, 1803, Wagstaff, ed., *Papers of John Steele*, I, 361.
11. See Cunningham, *Jeffersonian Republicans, 1789-1801,* 91, 162-66.
12. In regard to Burr's position in the party see pp. 203-12 below.
13. Livingston to Gallatin, Dec. 17, 1803, Gallatin Papers, N.-Y. Hist. Soc.
14. Alexander J. Dallas to McKean, Oct. 14, 27, 1803, Thomas McKean Papers, Hist. Soc. of Pa.; McKean to Gallatin, Oct. 16, 1803, Gallatin Papers, N.-Y. Hist. Soc.

prominently mentioned, and there was strong western support for Senator John Breckinridge of Kentucky. Others thought a New Englander would add the proper balance to the ticket, and John Langdon of New Hampshire was widely spoken of. The day before the caucus met, Breckinridge reported "much talk about the person to be voted for as the next vice president," and concluded: "Langdon and Clinton are the most prominent characters held up by the Republicans. I have no doubt the latter will be the most strongly supported here."[15]

The Republican caucus met on Saturday evening, February 25, 1804. There were 108 members present and Senator Stephen R. Bradley of Vermont was chosen as chairman. Jefferson was unanimously nominated for president, but there was no unanimity of sentiment in regard to the second office. "To avoid unpleasant discussions," as John Randolph expressed it, "a ballot without any previous nomination was resolved on."[16] The result of the first ballot was as follows:[17]

George Clinton, of New York	67
John Breckinridge, of Kentucky	20
Levi Lincoln, of Massachusetts	9
John Langdon, of New Hampshire	7
Gideon Granger, of Connecticut	4
Samuel Maclay, of Pennsylvania	1
	108

Clinton's nomination by a majority on the first ballot was not unanimously applauded. It was reported that "some Western and Jersey members refused to stand pledged at first but there was a tacit acquiescence understood to be given by the act of balloting."[18] The repudiation of Burr by the national party was markedly demonstrated. "Mr. Burr had not one single vote, and not a word was lisped in his favor at the meeting," noted Congressman Jacob Crowninshield of Massachusetts.[19]

A committee was appointed by the caucus "for the purpose of devising measures to promote the success of the republican nominations." It was

15. John Breckinridge to James Beckinridge, Feb. 24, 1804, John Breckinridge Papers, Filson Club.
16. Randolph to James Monroe, Feb. 28, 1804, Monroe Papers, Lib. Cong.
17. Philadelphia *Aurora*, Mar. 6, 1804; Richmond *Virginia Argus*, Mar. 3, 1804.
18. "Caucus of republicans, Washington, February 25, 1804," Jefferson Papers, Lib. Cong.
19. Crowninshield to Barnabas Bidwell, Feb. 26, 1804, Henry W. Taft Collection, Mass. Hist. Soc.

composed of the following members, listed below in the order in which the names were published:

> Wilson C. Nicholas, Senator from Virginia
> Abraham Baldwin, Senator from Georgia
> John Breckinridge, Senator from Kentucky
> Thomas Sumter, Senator from South Carolina
> William Cocke, Senator from Tennessee
> Samuel Smith, Senator from Maryland
> John Condit, Senator from New Jersey
> Andrew Gregg, Representative from Pennsylvania
> Samuel L. Mitchill, Representative from New York
> Nathaniel Macon, Representative from North Carolina
> Caesar A. Rodney, Representative from Delaware
> Joseph Stanton, Jr., Representative from Rhode Island
> Gideon Olin, Representative from Vermont[20]

This was the first time that the nominating caucus had appointed such a committee. This committee, which has attracted little historical notice, may properly be considered the central committee of the Republican national party organization, at least for the presidential campaign. The principal duty assigned by the caucus to the committee was to provide for the support of George Clinton for vice-president "in such manner . . . as not to endanger the election of Mr. Jefferson."[21] This instruction was due to the fact that the Twelfth Amendment had not yet been ratified, and there was no assurance that it would be before the election. Until this amendment was adopted, presidential electors would continue to cast two ballots without distinguishing between presidential and vice-presidential choices. Republicans were taking steps to ensure that there would not be another outcome such as the Jefferson-Burr tie in 1800, though, as it turned out, the amendment did go into force before the electoral vote was cast.

Unlike 1800, when Republicans had tried to keep their nominating caucus a secret, there was nothing secretive about the Republican caucus of 1804. Congressmen discussed it freely in their letters from Washington, and the caucus was reported in newspapers throughout the country. Some papers published the proceedings showing the result of the ballot for the vice-presidential nomination. Other papers simply announced

20. Philadelphia *Aurora*, Mar. 6, 1804; Fredericksburg *Virginia Express*, Mar. 15, 1804.
21. John Randolph to Littleton W. Tazewell, Feb. 26, 1804, Tazewell Family Papers, Va. State Lib.

that Thomas Jefferson was unanimously nominated as the next president and that George Clinton was "by a very large majority" nominated as the next vice-president. It was also widely reported, though not quite correctly, that a "respectable committee, consisting of a member from each state was appointed to make proper arrangements." More accurately, other papers listed the names and the states of the committee members, thus showing that three New England states (Massachusetts, Connecticut, New Hampshire) and the newly admitted state of Ohio were not represented on the committee.[22]

There was less protest against the caucus procedure in 1804 than there had been in 1800. Federalists wrote cynically of "the Friends of the People" deciding the election of the president and the vice-president for them,[23] and the former Federalist Congressman William B. Grove murmured: "I suppose it will become fashionable for the Members of Congress to Nominate all the Officers of the General and State Government by and by."[24] There was an occasional Republican dissent. Virginia Republican Littleton W. Tazewell, who had not been convinced that Burr should be abandoned, protested strongly to John Randolph:

> How fast is this government of ours settling into aristocracy; and into an aristocracy of the worst kind, the aristocracy supported by Intrigue. The people although nominally still possessed of the authority and power of the government, in fact have no interest whatever, except in Congressional elections. When these are made, they become a mere tool in the hands of their Representatives, compelled to execute whatever they decide. The manner of your late proceedings conclusively proves these positions. An unauthorized meeting undertake to decide, that one of the old Servants of the people is no longer worthy of their confidence. Without specifying any charge against him, or offering any proofs to support it, they offer to the public choice a new candidate of their own selection. What is the consequence? The people are compelled to elect this candidate so thrust upon them, or run the risk of splitting among themselves, and thereby permitting the election of a man whose political tenets differ altogether from their own. An intriguing character has

---

22. Washington *National Intelligencer*, Feb. 29, 1804; Richmond *Virginia Argus*, Mar. 3, 7, 1804; Norfolk *Herald*, Mar. 7, 1804; Hartford *American Mercury*, Mar. 15, 22, 1804; Boston *Independent Chronicle*, Mar. 12, 1804; Sparta (Ga.) *Farmer's Gazette*, Mar. 31, 1804; Louisville (Ga.) *Gazette and Republican Trumpet*, Mar. 28, 1804; Elizabeth-Town *New-Jersey Journal*, Mar. 13, 1804; Charleston *Carolina Gazette*, Nov. 23, 1804.

23. Samuel Tenney to Winthrop Sargent, Feb. 27, 1804, Winthrop Sargent Papers, Mass. Hist. Soc.; William Plumer to Jeremiah Smith, Feb. 28, 1804, Plumer Papers, Lib. Cong.

24. Grove to William Gaston, Mar. 12, 1804, William Gaston Papers, Univ. of N. C.

nothing therefore to perform, but to secure the good will of a majority of the majority of the members of Congress, and his success is inevitable. Nay the Intrigue becomes more dangerous from the manner in which it is conducted. If the proceedings of this Caucus were open, and the sentiments of each of its members necessarily known, there would be a degree of responsibility attached to their actions, which would render them liable to fewer objections. But instead of this, they decide without debate, and nothing is known but the result of their decision even to themselves; burying thus all sort of responsibility in the secrecy and confusion of a ballot box.[25]

To Tazewell's objections, John Randolph replied: "Your remarks on the mode in which men are brought forward to public notice are forcibly striking. Yet, as you cannot devise a remedy, it appears to be one of those inherent evils of our system (for what system is without them) to which we must submit. Instead of railing at the thing, I wish you would come and participate in it. . . . cabal is the necessary effect of freedom. When men are left free to act, we must calculate on their being governed by their interests and passions."[26] Randolph's suggestion that until a better method was devised the caucus should be submitted to seems to have been widely accepted among Republicans by 1804. Urging support for the caucus nominations, the Philadelphia *Aurora* explained:

It is well known that on great national occasions the representatives of the people in congress, have undertaken to *recommend* to their constituents the pursuit of a particular line of conduct. Previous to the election of president and vice-president on former occasions, the republican members of the senate and house of representatives, convened, for *deliberation*; the names of persons to be supported as president and vice-president were mentioned, respective merits considered, and it was finally decided by a plurality of votes who should be *recommended* to the electors.

A particular plan was necessary to ultimate success, its adoption by the electors was equally necessary. The *recommendation* by the representatives in congress had been considered useful and necessary by the people, and custom has sanctioned the procedure.

In our representatives to congress, then, the republicans had been willing to entrust the *initiation* of the important choice of president and vice-president. Experience had shewn the utility of the measure, the persons recommended had in every instance been *cheerfully supported* by the *electors*, and we must continue in the same course if we desire

25. Tazewell to Randolph, Mar. 4, 1804, Tazewell Family Papers, Va. State Lib.
26. Randolph to Tazewell, Apr. 21, 1804, *ibid.*

to triumph; we must respect the *recommendation,* as long as we can discover no sinister motives in the conduct of those who recommend."[27]

Shortly after the caucus had met, the *National Intelligencer* had declared: "We may anticipate without much presumption, that the nominations of President and Vice-President, made by the Republican members of Congress, will be universally acceptable to the friends of liberty throughout the union." As Republican printers throughout the country echoed this verdict, it was clear that the congressional nominating caucus had become an accepted part of Republican party machinery.[28] In Kentucky an abortive attempt to challenge the caucus decision by supporting Breckinridge for vice-president collapsed when Breckinridge publicly disclaimed any candidacy for the office and urged united support for Clinton.[29] Amidst the controversy, the editor of the *Kentucky Gazette* significantly reminded Kentucky Republicans that the nomination of a vice-presidential candidate "was, by general consent, confided to the members of Congress.... The nomination has been made, and, by the real Republicans, universally approved."[30] All Kentucky electors, along with all other Republican electors throughout the nation, cast their electoral votes for Jefferson and Clinton. Thus in 1804, as in 1800, the Republican caucus nominations prevailed.

So decisive had the caucus choice become by 1808 that political maneuvering and competition for the caucus nomination was one of the most keenly contested aspects of the presidential campaign. Nathaniel Macon in December 1807 voiced an opinion shared by others that "whoever that caucus shall recommend will it is believed be elected."[31] The question of the caucus nomination in 1808 reflected the internal rivalries within the Republican party over the presidency. Three principal contenders vied for the Republican nomination as Jefferson's successor: Secretary of State James Madison, who was believed to have the President's blessing; Vice-

27. Charleston *Carolina Gazette,* Nov. 23, 1804, from the *Aurora.*
28. Washington *National Intelligencer,* Mar. 2, 1804; Morristown *Genius of Liberty,* Mar. 16, 1804; Newport *Rhode-Island Republican,* Mar. 22, 1804; Boston *Independent Chronicle,* Mar. 13, 1804; Philadelphia *Aurora,* Mar. 1, 1804; New York *American Citizen,* Mar. 3, 1804.
29. Lexington *Kentucky Gazette,* July 10, 1804; Lowell H. Harrison, "John Breckinridge and the Vice-Presidency, 1804: A Political Episode," Filson Club, *History Quarterly,* 26 (1952), 155-65.
30. Lexington *Kentucky Gazette,* July 3, 1804, extra.
31. Macon to Joseph H. Nicholson, Dec. 2, 1807, Nicholson Papers, Lib. Cong.; William Short to Jefferson, Dec. 29, 1807, Jefferson Papers, Lib. Cong.

President George Clinton, who had strong support in New York and Pennsylvania; and James Monroe, backed by John Randolph and enjoying loyal support in Virginia. The election of 1808 was the first time, in fact, that there had been a contest for the Republican nomination for President. Jefferson had been the unanimous party choice in 1796, 1800, and 1804; the principal caucus decision in 1800 and 1804 had been the vice-presidential nomination.

There had been a strong movement to persuade Jefferson to seek a third term. In addition to the generally voiced opinion that no other leader could serve the nation so well in critical times, it was also emphasized that Jefferson's agreement to run would prevent a division in the party over the choice of a candidate. A committee appointed by a special meeting of Republicans of Kent County, Delaware, in December 1806, pointed to a reason which "calls strongly for a continuance of your services to our common country. We allude, with peculiar reluctance, to the schism which unhappily exists, or has existed, amongst some of the principal friends of the republican party. This schism, we are induced to believe, will burst out into a dangerous flame at the election of a new chief magistrate, should you absolutely determine to retire."[32] The same fear was also expressed in private letters to Jefferson urging him to seek re-election in 1808.[33] But Jefferson did not alter his resolve to retire at the end of his second term, and the anticipated conflict over the party's nomination developed, although it did not produce so disastrous a party split as many had feared.

As the election of 1808 approached, Madison's strong support among the Republican members of Congress appeared to assure him of the caucus nomination. Madison proponents were thus anxious to use the caucus to promote Madison's candidacy, while the supporters of Clinton and of Monroe, who had no hope of winning the caucus recommendation, were equally anxious to prevent the caucus from making a nomination, or at least to delay the meeting of the caucus. In both 1800 and 1804, the caucus had been held toward the end of the session. In 1800, it met in May shortly before adjournment; in 1804, the caucus met on February 25 with Con-

---

32. Address by committee appointed Dec. 9, 1806, signed Peter Lowber, chairman, John Hamm, secretary, Dover, Jan. 13, 1807, Jefferson Papers, Lib. Cong. Jefferson's papers between November 1806 and March 1807 are filled with addresses urging him to seek re-election; there are other similar addresses in December 1807.

33. See Thomas Leiper to Jefferson, Nov. 21, 1806, Robert R. Livingston to Jefferson, Dec. 20, 1807, Jefferson Papers, Lib. Cong.

gress adjourning on March 27. In 1808, the caucus was called for January 23, when Congress was nowhere near adjournment (the session ended on April 25). This early action can be explained only as the product of fierce political maneuvering between the supporters of Madison and Monroe.

Pressure for an early meeting of the caucus had come from Madison supporters in Virginia, where Monroe's candidacy was being pushed with enthusiasm following his return from service as minister to England in December 1807. "Many here believe Col. Monroe can be elected President, if his friends will take a firm ground," wrote Creed Taylor from Richmond, where the Virginia legislature was in session. "At this time I have no doubt from what I hear and see, but he will be supported by a majority in Virginia.... This day in the house of delegates ... by a very large majority a very handsome complimentary address was voted to Col. Monroe—designed as an entering wedge and so understood. I believe the majority here wish him their candidate. They seem to be opposed to a *caucus* at Washington fixing a President and Vice President upon the States. And it is not wrong upon principle."[34] Another Monroe supporter, Alexander McRae, about the same time wrote to Monroe: "I hope there will be no Caucus in Washington, and if there should be, Let their decision be what it may, you will I hope, obey the voice of your Country, if the people call you to the Presidential Chair."[35] Monroe's friends in Virginia were thus opposed to a caucus nomination because they feared that it would support Madison.

Conversely, Madison's Virginia friends wanted the caucus to announce a choice in order to weaken the Monroe movement in Virginia. On January 8, 1808, Governor William H. Cabell wrote from Richmond to Senator Wilson C. Nicholas:

It is very important that the nomination at Washington shall be speedily made; for the Legislature of Virginia will have to act on the subject before they rise, the former General ticket laws having all of them been temporary; and there must be a meeting to fix on the persons to be run as Electors. The friends of Col. Monroe here are very numerous; and many of them are very violent; and I fear will attempt to run him at all events. The opposition of many of them to Mr. Madison is virulent in the extreme; and confident in their supposed strength in this State, they talk of bringing forward Col. Monroe, at once, without waiting for the meeting in Washington.... I hope therefore you will soon have a meet-

---

34. Taylor to ————, Dec. 21, 1807, Creed Taylor Papers, Univ. of Va. On Monroe's candidacy in Virginia see pp. 232-35 below.

35. McRae to Monroe, Dec. 31, 1807, Monroe Papers, N. Y. Pub. Lib.

ing at Congress, and ascertain, in a way which cannot be mistaken, the sentiments of the other republican States. A Declaration of such a meeting, in favor of Mr. Madison, would certainly defeat the attempt which *might* otherwise be successfully made here to bring forward Col. Monroe; an attempt which would ultimately produce the most unhappy consequences.[36]

This confidential letter confirms the suspicions voiced by John Quincy Adams, who after attending the caucus recorded in his diary: "From the appearances at the meeting I judged it to be called in concert, and probably at the instigation of the Virginian Madisonians and particularly Messrs. Giles and Nicholas. I suppose their particular object to be to aid the canvass of Mr. Madison's friends for electors of President and Vice-President, which is now going on in the Virginia Legislature."[37]

The friends of Madison thus sought an early meeting of the congressional caucus in order to influence the Virginia state caucus in making its choice of an electoral ticket. At the same time, the friends of Monroe were working to nominate him in Virginia before the Washington caucus met, in the hope of influencing its choice. On January 16 the Richmond *Enquirer* carried an announcement calling a caucus of Virginia Republican legislators to meet on January 28 to recommend presidential electors. On January 19 the call was issued for the Washington caucus to convene January 23. Then suddenly on January 21, two Republican caucuses were held in Richmond; the friends of Madison met and formed an electoral ticket pledged to him, while Monroe's friends in a separate meeting took similar action in support of their candidate. The majority of Republican members attended the caucus in support of Madison.[38] The hurried meeting of the Virginia caucuses, a week before the scheduled date, led to charges that Madison supporters had tried to influence the Washington caucus. Madisonians replied that their caucus had been called because they were convinced that Monroe's friends were planning to call a caucus to influence the Washington nomination.[39] In view of the fact that Monroe's strength was concentrated in the Virginia legislature rather than in Congress, the advantage of an early nomination

36. Cabell to Nicholas, Jan. 9, 1808, William H. Cabell Personal Papers Miscellaneous, Lib. Cong.
37. Adams, ed., *Diary of John Quincy Adams*, entry of Jan. 23, 1808, I, 507; similar recollections were recorded by William A. Burwell, Memoir, [1804-08], Burwell Papers, Lib. Cong.
38. Richmond *Enquirer*, Jan. 16, 21, 23, 26, 30, 1808; Richmond *Virginia Argus*, Jan. 26, 1808. On the operation of the Virginia caucus see pp. 180-84 below.
39. Richmond *Enquirer*, Feb. 13, 1808.

in Virginia appeared to favor Monroe, while an early Washington nomination could be expected to favor Madison.

That each side was maneuvering for political advantage and that these considerations influenced the calling of caucuses in both Richmond and Washington is clear. But, as it turned out, the caucuses met so nearly at the same time that no influence appears to have been exerted either way. The Richmond caucuses met on Thursday evening, January 21; the Washington caucus, on Saturday evening, January 23. Editor Thomas Ritchie, of the Richmond *Enquirer,* affirmed that there was no express from Richmond to Washington and that the mail which went on Friday could not have arrived at Washington by Saturday night.[40] No evidence has been uncovered to discredit Ritchie's assertion; there is no indication that the Virginia action was known when the Washington caucus met. All evidence points to the Washington caucus being held in an effort to influence the Virginia proceedings in favor of Madison.

The Washington caucus in 1808 was called by Senator Stephen R. Bradley of Vermont, who based his authority to act on the fact that he had been the chairman of the Republican caucus in 1804. On January 19, Bradley circulated a printed notice announcing:

> In pursuance of the power vested in me as president of the late convention of the Republican members of both houses of Congress, I deem it expedient; for the purpose of nominating suitable and proper characters for President and Vice President of the United States for the next Presidential election; to call a convention of the said Republican members, to meet at the Senate chamber on Saturday the 23d instant at 6 o'clock P.M. at which time and place your personal attendance is requested, to aid the meeting with your influence, information and talents.[41]

The circular invitation was sent to every Republican member of both Houses and to some nominal Federalists such as John Quincy Adams. Bradley claimed to have issued invitations to all but five members of the Senate and all but twenty-two members of the House.[42] A copy of the notice was also posted in the Senate chamber. This was the first time that a formal notice had been issued for the nominating caucus; and Bradley's authority to call the meeting was challenged. Josiah

---

40. *Ibid.,* June 14, 1808.
41. One of the original notices is in the Edwin Gray Papers, Duke Univ., and is reproduced on p. 113.
42. Adams, ed., *Diary of John Quincy Adams,* entry of Jan. 23, 1808, I, 506.

SIR,

 IN pursuance of the power vested in me as president of the late convention of the Republican members of both houses of Congress, I deem it expedient; for the purpose of nominating suitable and proper characters for President and Vice President of the United States for the next Presidential election; to call a convention of the said Republican members, to meet at the Senate chamber on Saturday the 23d instant at 6 o'clock P. M. at which time and place your personal attendance is requested, to aid the meeting with your influence, information and talents.

 Dated at Washington, this 19th day of January, A. D. 1808.

S. R. BRADLEY.

Invitation to the Republican Nominating Caucus of *1808*
(Courtesy of the Duke University Library)

Masters, a New York Republican supporter of Clinton, posted another notice denouncing Bradley's action and calling on Republicans not to attend.[43] Congressman Edwin Gray, a Randolph follower, replied to Bradley in a strongly worded letter declaring his "abhorrence of the usurpation of power declared to be vested in you—the mandatory style —and the object contemplated therein." He continued:

 I deny that you possess the right of calling upon the Republican Members of Congress, or others at this time and place, to attend a Caucus for the Presidential election.

 You must permit me to remind you Sir, that it was a far different purpose for which my Constituents reposed their confidence in me. I will not consent either in an individual or representative capacity, to countenance by my presence, the midnight intrigues of any set of men, who may arrogate to themselves the right, which belongs alone to the people, of selecting proper persons to fill the important offices of President and Vice President—nor do I suppose that the honest and unsuspecting people of these United States, can, much longer suffer in silence, so direct

---

43. James A. Bayard to Andrew Bayard, Jan. 21, 1808, Donnan, ed., *Bayard Papers*, 173-74; Samuel Taggart to Rev. John Taylor, Jan. 27, 1808, Haynes, ed., "Letters of Samuel Taggart," Amer. Antiq. Soc., *Proceedings*, New Ser., 33 (1923), 303.

and palpable an innovation upon an important and sacred right, belonging exclusive to them.⁴⁴

Despite the opposition to Bradley's action, the caucus met as summoned on January 23. When the meeting convened, Bradley announced that his authority was at an end, but upon the motion of Senator William B. Giles he was returned to the chair. As in the 1804 caucus, votes were taken by ballot without previous nomination.⁴⁵ Eighty-nine members⁴⁶ voted as follows:

For President		For Vice-President	
James Madison	83	George Clinton	79
George Clinton	3	John Langdon	5
James Monroe	3	Henry Dearborn	3
		John Quincy Adams	1

Madison was thus recommended for president and Clinton for vice-president. Following the 1804 precedent, "a committee of correspondence and arrangement was appointed," now empowered to act in case of the death or resignation of the persons recommended. The following members were placed on the committee:

> John Milledge, Senator from Georgia
> John Taylor, Representative from South Carolina
> Jesse Franklin, Senator from North Carolina
> William B. Giles, Senator from Virginia
> John Montgomery, Representative from Maryland
> John Smilie, Representative from Pennsylvania
> Aaron Kitchell, Senator from New Jersey
> William Kirkpatrick, Representative from New York
> Benjamin Howland, Senator from Rhode Island
> Joseph B. Varnum, Representative from Massachusetts
> Nahum Parker, Senator from New Hampshire
> Stephen R. Bradley, Senator from Vermont
> Edwin Tiffin, Senator from Ohio
> John Pope, Senator from Kentucky
> Joseph Anderson, Senator from Tennessee

44. Gray to Stephen R. Bradley, Jan. 21, 1808, Edwin Gray Papers, Duke Univ.
45. Adams, ed., *Diary of John Quincy Adams*, entry of Jan. 23, 1808, I, 505-7.
46. John Q. Adams recorded in his diary that the number attending was counted and 89 were present, *ibid.*, 506. Later Richard M. Johnson, who had served as secretary to the caucus, drew up a list of those present which numbered 94. No list was made at the meeting; Johnson's list, dated Mar. 12, 1808, was published in Washington *National Intelligencer*, Mar. 16, 1808, and in Philadelphia *Aurora*, Mar. 22, 1808.

The only states not represented on this committee were Connecticut and Delaware, neither of which had Republican members in Congress. Anticipating opposition to the caucus nomination, it was resolved that "the members of this meeting have acted only in their individual characters as citizens; that they have been induced to adopt this measure from the necessity of the case; from a deep conviction of the importance of union to the Republicans throughout all parts of the United States, in the present crisis of both our external and internal affairs; and as being the most practicable mode of consulting and respecting the interest and wishes of all."[47]

The Washington caucus, although representing a majority of the Republican membership of the two houses of Congress, was not a full meeting of Republican members. The supporters of Monroe and of Clinton almost entirely refused to attend. John Randolph and his adherents stayed away, and there was only one member from New York present.[48] Ten Republicans were reported to be out of town. "It was a pretty general understanding among those who did not wish to support Madison not to attend the meeting," declared a Federalist representative.[49] The membership of both houses numbered 176; of these Bradley considered 27 as inflexible Federalists, thus inviting to the Republican caucus 149 members.[50] Since only 89 of these registered their vote at the caucus, a large Republican absence is evident. However, the vote of 83 members which Madison received at the caucus made it clear that he had the support of a majority of the Republican congressional membership.

Clinton and Randolph forces, however, were unwilling to accept the caucus decision; having failed to stop the caucus, they turned to denounce it. Clinton issued a letter disassociating himself from the caucus which had nominated him as vice-president. He declared that he had not attended the caucus, that he had not been consulted on the subject,

47. Washington *National Intelligencer*, Jan. 25, 1808. Reports of the caucus were published throughout the country. See Richmond *Enquirer*, Jan. 28, 1808; Philadelphia *Aurora*, Feb. 1, 1808; Windsor *Spooner's Vermont Journal*, Feb. 8, 1808; *Raleigh Register*, Feb. 4, 1808; Edenton (N. C.) *Gazette*, Feb. 10, 1808; Savannah *Republican*, Feb. 13, 1808; *Augusta Chronicle*, Feb. 20, 1808; Frankfort *Western World*, Feb. 18, 1808; Newark *Centinel of Freedom*, Feb. 2, 1808; Charleston *Carolina Gazette*, Feb. 12, 1808.
48. Richmond *Enquirer*, Jan. 28, 1808; James Hillhouse to Simeon Baldwin, Jan. 27, 1808, Baldwin Family Papers, Yale Univ.
49. Samuel Taggart to Rev. John Taylor, Jan. 27, 1808, Haynes, ed., "Letters of Samuel Taggart," Amer. Antiq. Soc., *Proceedings*, New Ser., 33 (1923), 303.
50. Adams, ed., *Diary of John Quincy Adams*, entry of Jan. 23, 1808, I, 505-6.

and that it should not be inferred that the proceedings had his approbation.[51] John Randolph and sixteen other members of Congress published a formal protest against the caucus which concluded:

> We do therefore in the most solemn manner protest against the proceedings of the meeting held in the Senate Chamber on the twenty-third day of January last, because we consider them—
> As being in direct hostility to the principle of the constitution:
> As a gross assumption of power not delegated by the people, and not justified or extenuated by any actual necessity:
> As an attempt to produce an undue bias in the ensuing election of President and Vice-President, and virtually to transfer the appointment of those officers from the people, to a majority of the two Houses of Congress.
> And we do in the same manner protest against the nomination of James Madison, as we believe him to be unfit to fill the office of President in the present juncture of our affairs.[52]

The signers of this protest included supporters of George Clinton and Randolph adherents who supported Monroe.[53] Their opposition to the caucus was political; it was not based upon abstract principles. Randolph's remarks in reference to the Republican caucus of 1804 demonstrated that he had no objection to the caucus when he approved of its nomination.[54]

On the other hand, Republicans who approved of the nomination of Madison defended the caucus. Editor Thomas Ritchie of the Richmond *Enquirer* wrote in a column labeled "My Own Opinions":

> Some objections have been made to the recommendations of the caucus at Washington. . . . I believe, for my own part, that this system is not absolutely destitute of objections; but the only reasonable question is, where is there a *better* plan? The members of Congress have just as much right (as citizens) to recommend a President and Vice-President, as the republican delegates of Virginia have to frame an electoral ticket. There *must* be some plan to produce a concert and harmony of operations

---

51. George Clinton letter dated Mar. 5, 1808, publ. in New York *American Citizen*, Mar. 10, 1808.

52. Washington *National Intelligencer*, Mar. 7, 1808. The protest was dated Washington, Feb. 27, 1808, and was printed in newspapers throughout the country.

53. The signers were: from New York, John Russell, Josiah Masters, George Clinton, Jr., Gurdon S. Mumford, John Thompson, Peter Swart, and John Harris; from Pennsylvania, Joseph Clay, William Hoge, Daniel Montgomery, Samuel Smith, and Samuel Maclay; from Virginia, John Randolph, Abram Trigg, Edwin Gray, and James M. Garnett; and from South Carolina, David R. Williams.

54. See pp. 106-7 above.

between men of the same party, or else their influence will be *lost by division,* and their enemies will *conquer* by superior prudence.

The Representatives of the people may be presumed to carry with them the wishes of the different quarters of the union. . . . In what better way can this nomination be accomplished?[55]

A meeting of "Democratic Republican Citizens" of New Castle County, Delaware, resolved:

That the mode of selection of proposed candidates for the Presidency and Vice-Presidency of the United States, is less exceptionable, and liable to fewer objections, than any other that has suggested itself to us. The circumstance of the men, who advised together and determined on the measure, being members of Congress, cannot certainly diminish the weight of their recommendation, or lessen its claim to public attention; although to be viewed as private citizens on the occasion, they were entitled to all the confidence, which individual merit, distinguished by public favor could confer; and we esteem it essential to the due exercise of the right of suffrage, connected with this subject, that a recommendation to a nomination should take place previous to the election, in order that improper characters should not be foisted into office. . . . we do therefore most explicitly and unreservedly approve of the mode of selection adopted by the Republican meeting at Washington City last winter.[56]

Thus Republicans who a few years before had debated the merits of the nominating caucus with the Federalists now argued the same issues among themselves. Now, as earlier, each side thought in terms of immediate political advantage.

From the point of view of institutional party history, perhaps the most reflective evaluation of the caucus system was found in the *Address of the General Committee of Republican Young Men, of the City and County of New-York,* concurring in the approval of the caucus nomination. The address said, in part:

That objections should at this day be urged against a mode of nomination which has so long met the concurrence and approbation of the people—which has always appeared to them the *best* means of securing a judicious selection, and which experience proves to have been attended with such beneficial consequences to the union and safety of the Republican party, did at first surprise us not a little. . . .

That no party can long exist without concert among its members,

55. Richmond *Enquirer,* Feb. 2, 1808.
56. *At a Very Numerous and Respectable Meeting of the Democratic Republican Citizens of New-Castle County in the State of Delaware, on the 3d of September, 1808,* broadside, Lib. Cong.

and an unity of object and pursuit; and that these are to be obtained only by a ready submission of *private opinion,* to the will of the MAJORITY, are truths universally admitted. . . .

In the REPUBLICAN PARTY, the necessity of selecting a *single* candidate for each of these offices [president and vice-president], to whom the PEOPLE may be directed in their choice, has never yet been disputed. *How* this selection is to be made, whether by *committees appointed specially for the purposes,* or by the *Representatives of the People in Congress,* PROVIDED THE WILL OF THE MAJORITY BE KNOWN AND PURSUED, cannot, we think, be in any wise material. In every instance hitherto, that trust has been reposed in *Representatives* as the most convenient mode, and least liable to unnecessary expence and delay.[57]

The caucus faced the severest test yet experienced in its stormy history when the supporters of Clinton and Monroe refused to give up their candidates and to accept the caucus nomination. In Virginia, supporters of Monroe declined not only to acknowledge the decision of the congressional nominating caucus but also rejected the action of the state legislative party caucus which nominated Madison electors. Encouraged by Monroe's refusal to withdraw from the contest, his Virginia friends organized a rival state party organization, nominated electors pledged to Monroe, and waged a campaign in his behalf. The defeat of these efforts and the triumph of the Madisonian ticket in Virginia was to result in the strengthening of the caucus system.

Strong support for George Clinton persisted in both New York and Pennsylvania after the caucus nomination. In Philadelphia William Duane, editor of the influential *Aurora,* admitted that Clinton was his first choice and Monroe his second.[58] But he reluctantly affirmed his willingness to abide by the caucus decision: "It is certainly not a period to bicker about men; and if we can only ensure the pursuit of the same system of policy that has been pursued under *Jefferson,* it is a very subordinate consideration at this moment which is the man. The democracy will not divide—they will support the choice made in the usual manner, since no other or better manner had been provided by the constitution."[59] This was not a very strong endorsement of the caucus candidate, however, and Duane's reluctance reflected the strong support for Clinton in Pennsylvania. This was also demonstrated in the "Demo-

57. *Address of the General Committee of Republican Young Men, of the City and County of New-York* (N. Y., 1808), pamphlet, N.-Y. Hist. Soc.
58. *Aurora,* Mar. 28, 1808.
59. *Ibid.,* Jan. 28, 1808.

cratic Conference" which convened at Lancaster in March 1808.[60] Although this conference met six weeks after the Washington caucus had named Madison the party's presidential candidate, the slate of presidential electors nominated was not pledged to any candidate. The compromise ticket adopted was composed of both Clinton and Madison supporters, designated only as "the friends of Jefferson, and of democratic principles."[61] Subsequently the *Aurora* and the state Republican general committee, of which Duane was a member, came out strongly for Madison;[62] and when the Pennsylvania Republican electors met, the state's twenty electoral votes went to Madison for president and Clinton for vice-president. The fact that the caucus decision had not been immediately and enthusiastically accepted in Pennsylvania, however, had posed a serious threat to the caucus system. Thus Madison's success in Pennsylvania as in Virginia was a victory for the caucus system.

In New York, James Cheetham, editor of the Republican *American Citizen*, denounced the "Grand Caucus" as produced by "many precious intrigues, of which Mr. Burr would not be ashamed, and cabals, which would do honour to the sublimest projector of political necromancy."[63] Seeking to arouse support for Clinton by stressing Secretary of State Madison's responsibility in regard to the Embargo policy, Cheetham boldly declared his opinion "that if Mr. Madison, who by surprise if not by collusion has been nominated for the Presidency, be elected, the external commerce of the United States will be annihilated, and that nothing short of a miracle can save the republican party from destruction—I AM THEREFORE OPPOSED TO HIS ELECTION." The *American Citizen*, he affirmed, "shall be devoted to the election of the venerable GEORGE CLINTON, of New York, for the next President, and of the patriotic JAMES MONROE, of Virginia, for the next Vice-President of the United States."[64] In an effective answer to Cheetham, the New York *Public Advertiser* defended the caucus as "fixed by former precedent," and announced: "In declaring ourselves in favor of JAMES MADISON for the next president of the United States, we are guided by the opinion of the majority. However our personal partiality may extend to the venerable CLINTON; yet that partiality must give way to the general will—to a free and unbiased

60. See pp. 164-65 below.
61. *Aurora*, Mar. 10, 1808.
62. *Ibid.*, May 5, 1808.
63. New York *American Citizen*, Jan. 27, 1808.
64. *Ibid.*, May 30, 1808.

declaration of a large majority of congress. It is a duty we owe to ourselves and posterity, to support the nomination."[65]

Cheetham refused to give up Clinton, however, and kept the political waters churning in New York down to the casting of the electoral vote.[66] In trying to counteract the argument that Madison was the regular party nominee, Cheetham discovered that the Richmond caucus met previous to the congressional caucus. He thus devoted considerable newspaper space to efforts to prove that the Washington caucus merely echoed the nomination of Madison previously made at Richmond. Cheetham insisted that the unprecedented attempt of a state to arrogate to itself the right of making nominations destroyed the argument that the Washington nomination had been made according to the previous practices of the Republican party. "Is then," he asked, "a nomination made at Richmond by a caucus *partially* selected, obligatory on the Republican party throughout the United States?"[67]

The support for Clinton in New York represented by the *American Citizen's* belligerent advocacy of his candidacy produced considerable party divisions, particularly in New York City. In the summer of 1808, Madison Republicans organized meetings to express approval of the caucus nomination and to affirm their confidence in Madison. The following resolutions passed by a Republican meeting in the seventh ward illustrate the proceedings of a number of other wards:

WHEREAS it is the opinion of this meeting, that harmony among republicans is at all times necessary and desirable, and particularly so at the present important crisis in our national affairs; therefore it has, for a number of years, *been the uniform practice in this state, for the republican members of our legislature to nominate and recommend candidates for the office of Governor and lieutenant Governor.* The same system was adopted in the year 1800 and 1804, by the republican members of congress nominating candidates for President and Vice President of the United States; and whereas a large majority of the republican members of Congress have recently, and in conformity with the usual practice, nominated and recommended James Madison for the office of President, and George Clinton for the office of Vice President; and *we having full confidence in the integrity of the republican members of Congress,* and having no reason to doubt, but in making said nomina-

65. New York *Public Advertiser*, Jan. 30, May 30, 1808.
66. Cheetham published a state-by-state survey of election prospects to show that "Mr. Madison cannot possibly succeed in his pretensions to the Presidency." *American Citizen*, May 31, 1808.
67. *Ibid.*, June 8, 20, 1808.

tion, that they were actuated by the most laudable and patriotic motives, and we, knowing no mode better calculated to ascertain the sentiments of, give satisfaction to, and promote harmony among, the republicans throughout the United States:—Therefore,

Resolved, That we cordially acquiesce in the nomination of JAMES MADISON, for the office of PRESIDENT, and GEO: CLINTON for the office of VICE-PRESIDENT of the United States.[68]

The meeting also resolved that the papers edited by Cheetham, "the *American Citizen* and *Republican Watch Tower,* are not any longer considered by us as republican papers, and that they ought not to be any longer esteemed as organs of republican opinions."[69] In addition to meetings in other wards where similar resolutions were adopted, a general Republican meeting was held in New York City in September 1808. Here resolutions were passed approving the caucus nomination of Madison for president and Clinton for vice-president and endorsing the policy of the Embargo, which had become the most prominent issue of the election.[70]

New York's presidential electors were chosen by the Republican-controlled state legislature in November, yet even after the electors were named it was not clear how many of them would support Clinton. The *American Citizen* announced that sixteen would vote for Clinton and three for Madison, but the prediction was far from accurate. The actual electoral vote gave Madison thirteen and Clinton six for president. For vice-president, Clinton received thirteen votes, Madison, three, and Monroe, three.[71] Thus, although Madison received the majority of New York's electoral votes, six Republican electors failed to vote for the regular party nominee. Since these were the only Republican electors in the nation who did not vote for Madison, the caucus nominations, though seriously challenged, prevailed.

Retaliation against Clinton by withholding vice-presidential votes from him was considered by Madison electors in Virginia. At least two of these electors, John Preston and Philip Norborne Nicholas, wrote to Senator Wilson Cary Nicholas seeking his advice before the casting of the electoral vote. Preston explained: "Some doubts are entertained with

68. New York *Public Advertiser,* July 2, 1808.
69. *Ibid.;* for similar meetings and resolutions see *ibid.,* July 16, 19, 26, 29, 30, August 4, 5, 1808.
70. *Ibid.,* Sept. 14, 16, 17, 22, 1808.
71. *American Citizen,* Nov. 8, Dec. 12, 1808; *Public Advertiser,* Dec. 10, 1808.

respect to the course the Virginia Electors ought to pursue towards New-York. We do not feel ourselves as yet pledged for any thing but to vote for Mr. Madison, but on the contrary entirely at liberty to do as we may think best with respect to the Vice President. It is highly to be desired that we may be well informed on this head before the day of our meeting, that we may act in perfect concert and give compleat efficacy to our vote."[72]

Senator Nicholas's reply, weighing numerous circumstances which might affect the future of the party and the party's nominating caucus, advised that Virginia's vote for vice-president be given to Clinton. He admitted:

> At the same time I can not conceal from you, its being the wish of a number of our friends that he should be set aside. This proceeds from dissatisfaction at Mr. Clinton's conduct. It is believed he should have acquiesced in the nomination of Mr. Madison, that he should have declared whether he would accept of the office of Vice President or not. It is suspected he is alienated from the republicans. This is believed from his own deportment, and from the conduct of his friends and the editors of papers that are supposed to be under the direction of D[eWitt] Clinton. Among the warm friends of Mr. Clinton are to be found the bitterest enemies of the administration and its measures. The reasons that induce me to think that he ought to be elected are, that he was nominated by the caucus at this place, and that nomination not having been revoked, if he is not elected there will not in future be any reliance upon such nominations, all confidence will be lost and there can not be the necessary concert.

Nicholas also explained that he was convinced that Clinton could not fail to be elected vice-president unless the vote of Virginia were against him. If Clinton lost, therefore, it would be ascribed to the intrigues of Virginia and would increase the jealousies toward Republicans in that state. Nicholas also felt that it would give serious offense to the Republicans of Pennsylvania where Clinton had enjoyed a vast popularity. That state "has peculiar and strong claims upon us," he wrote, "not only on account of its great weight in the union, of its importance to the republican party (which is very much increased by the ticklish state in which New York stands), but for sacrificing a preference that I believe they felt for Mr. Clinton for the office of president to their attachment to the republican cause and for their prodigious exertions to support that

---

72. Preston to Wilson C. Nicholas, Nov. 15, 1808, Nicholas Papers, Lib. Cong.

cause." Nicholas believed the caucus nominations would be respected in other states and hoped that Virginia would act with them in good faith.[73]

Confidentially revealing the deliberations of the Virginia electors, Philip Norborne Nicholas soon reported: "The general sentiment which prevailed when the electors met was unfriendly to Mr. Clinton on account of his conduct since the nomination at Washington, but there was also a general impression entertained that under circumstances it was difficult to drop him without injury to the Republican cause. There were some of the electors who expressed a strong objection to voting for him and even indicated a determination not to do so." In the course of a full discussion of the subject, reference was made to a letter written by Wilson Cary Nicholas to Philip Norborne Nicholas, and the letter, which had been privately shown to some of the electors, was introduced for all to consider. Wilson Cary Nicholas's arguments apparently carried considerable weight, for after much deliberation it was agreed to cast a unanimous Virginia electoral vote for Clinton for vice-president.[74] All Virginia electors were committed to vote for Madison for president, and there was never any question about carrying out this obligation.

The party considerations which largely determined the casting of the Virginia electoral vote for vice-president in 1808 displayed much of the nature of the national party machinery: (1) the importance of the congressional nominating caucus and of party members in Congress in maintaining national party organization and unity, and (2) the necessity of interstate party co-operation and mutual concessions for the sake of the party.

The election of 1808 proved the strength of national party unity under the difficult circumstances engendered by the unpopularity of the Embargo. Madison's electoral vote for president totaled 122, Clinton's, 6, while Federalist Charles C. Pinckney won 47 electoral votes. For vice-president, Clinton received 113 votes. The Clintonian electors in New York cast three votes for Madison for vice-president and three for Monroe; John Langdon, of New Hampshire, received the six vice-presidential votes of Vermont's Republican electors and the three votes of Ohio's Republican electors. The party unity of 1800 and 1804,

---

73. Wilson C. Nicholas to ———, Washington, Dec. 3, 1808, draft, probably to Philip N. Nicholas (see Philip N. Nicholas to Wilson C. Nicholas, Dec. 17, 1808), *ibid.*

74. Philip N. Nicholas to Wilson C. Nicholas, Dec. 17, 1808, Spencer Roane to Wilson C. Nicholas, Dec. 8, 1808, *ibid.*

which had produced the same number of votes for both Republican presidential and vice-presidential candidates, was not equaled in the election of 1808. But the damage to the party was not sufficient to endanger the stability of the national party machinery which had successfully served the Republicans through three national elections. The caucus decision prevailed in 1808 as it had in 1800 and in 1804; and the Republican majority in Congress remained the dominant influence in national party decisions. As long as the congressional nominating caucus survived, national party organization could be expected to remain where it had rested since the emergence of the party—in the hands of the party members of Congress.[75]

75. The influence of Jefferson's administration on this leadership has been treated in the preceding chapter.

CHAPTER SIX

Party Machinery in New England

The structure of party machinery throughout the country reflected regional patterns of electoral procedures, campaign customs, and party attachments. The sectional distinctiveness of New England, the middle states, the South, and the West was thus visible in the operation of parties. Yet, although regional patterns can be discerned, there were so many variations from state to state within any given area that each state must be examined separately if a full view of the structure of the party system is to be obtained.

During Jefferson's administration there was more extensive development of Republican state party machinery in New England than in any other part of the country. Before 1800, Federalist domination of New England had successfully limited the growth of formal party organization; in the campaign of 1800 the Republicans had been active, but little definite party machinery had been instituted. The national triumph of the Jeffersonians in 1800 stimulated such a rapid growth of Republican machinery in areas where Federalist resistance was most vigorous that New England, the stronghold of Federalism, soon became the region where Republican organizational efforts were most concentrated.

In Connecticut, informal Republican organization in the election of 1800 had produced party tickets, concerted action, and a spirited campaign, but more definite party machinery was needed to contest the entrenched Federalist control of the state. The enthusiasm generated by the victory celebrations of Jefferson's election inspired Connecticut Republicans to project a scheme for creating formal party machinery. In June 1801, a group of twenty-four Connecticut Republicans, headed by Pierpont Edwards, Jared Potter, and Ephraim Kirby, explained the plans for improving their party machinery to Jefferson's new Attorney General, New Englander Levi Lincoln. "The season has now arrived, when it is necessary for us to organize," they wrote, "and to adopt measures for conveying to our people just sentiments respecting the motives, measures and objects of the present administration and to obviate the false impressions which the federalists and federal papers have made and are making upon their minds. This organization will consist of a General Committee, of County Committees and of Subcommittees in the Towns of the State, and must be conducted with great fortitude and perseverance, through much labor and expense, to an end difficult to be attained but highly important to a republican administration."[1]

This plan was soon being put into operation. A printed circular of instructions, issued in October 1801, directed county committees to instruct the town committees, as early as possible after such committees were appointed and organized, to make out a list of all the freemen in their respective towns, to divide the names on this list among the committee members, and to determine those who were "decidedly of the republican party." After the Republicans had been thus classified, each committeeman was advised to convene "in as private a manner as possible" all the Republicans on his list and "to instruct them as to the mode of operating for the purpose of diffusing Republican principles." Each committeeman was also charged with seeing that Republicans on his list attended the freemen's meetings and stayed until the business was finished; and each town committee was urged to make every exertion to procure a general circulation of republican newspapers.[2] Additional instructions, issued in October 1802, directed each town committee to divide its town into districts and to appoint committeemen for each district. The district committees were to proceed as town committees had in the past and were to report monthly their "doings and operations" to the town committee. In addition, a system of inspection was outlined. The town committees were to appoint members to examine the proceedings of district committees; and the county committees, likewise, were advised to appoint members to examine the proceedings of town committees. Final reports were to be sent by the county chairmen to the secretary of the general committee.[3]

As Republican plans matured, the direction of party affairs in Con-

1. Pierpont Edwards and others to Levi Lincoln, June 4, 1801, Jefferson Papers, Lib. Cong.

2. [Circular], Oct. 1801, printed in Boston *New-England Palladium,* May 10, 1803. Acknowledgements of local committee appointments are found in S. S. Porter to Ephraim Kirby, Sept. 24, 1801, and Jeremiah Dauchy to Kirby, Oct. 19, 1801, Ephraim Kirby Papers, Duke Univ.

3. [Circular], Oct. 1802, printed in Boston *New-England Palladium,* May 10, 1803.

necticut centered in the hands of the Republican general committee. Information regarding this committee is limited. Although Federalists on occasion attempted to goad Republicans into publishing the names of committee members,[4] this was apparently never done. Circulars signed by the chairman of the general committee reveal that Abraham Bishop was chairman in 1803 and Pierpont Edwards in 1804,[5] but party literature published by the committee was generally printed "by order of the General Committee" and signed by a clerk. The general committee appointed county committees, but it is not entirely clear how the general committee was chosen. Apparently it was appointed by a caucus of party leaders and Republican members of the state legislature. A party circular in 1804 referred to "the semi-annual Meeting of the Republicans of the state Legislature, and others from different parts of the State." This meeting transacted a variety of party business, including the arranging of party tickets, the appointment of county committees to solicit funds "to defray the expences of the Committee of publications," and the establishment of a committee of correspondence (consisting of the Republican members of the Connecticut House of Representatives) which was instructed to communicate with county subscription committees.[6] It appears that the general committee was responsible to this general caucus of party leaders and Republican members of the legislature. Before 1804, party nominations seem to have largely originated with the general committee. After 1804 Republican tickets for nominations in state-wide elections were decided by the general caucus or a "General meeting of Republicans."[7]

Although popular control of the party machinery was limited in this centralized structure, party leaders gave attention to public participation and support. Federalists noticed:

It has been fashionable ever since the organization of the democratic party, for their leaders to appoint public meetings and festivals, which all are invited to attend, and on which great numbers constantly do attend.

4. Uriah Tracy, *To the Freemen of Connecticut* (Litchfield, 1803), pamphlet, Duke Univ.

5. *Republican Address to the Freemen of Connecticut*, by order of the General Committee, Levi Ives, Jun., clerk, Aug. 30, 1803 (n.p., 1803), pamphlet, Amer. Antiq. Soc.; circulars dated Feb. 11, 1803, and July 30, 1804, printed in Hartford *Connecticut Courant*, Aug. 1, 22, 1804.

6. [Circular], 1804, printed in Hartford *Connecticut Courant*, July 4, 1804.

7. *Republican Address to the Freemen of Connecticut*, by order of the General Committee, Aug. 30, 1803; Hartford *American Mercury*, Mar. 7, Aug. 22, 1805; Norman L. Stamps, Political Parties in Connecticut, 1789-1819 (unpubl. Ph.D. diss., Yale Univ., 1950), 87-88.

Thus in March 1801, a festival in honor of the election of Mr. Jefferson as President and Mr. Burr as Vice-President, was holden at Wallingford—in 1802, a like festival was holden also at Wallingford—in 1803, at New Haven—in 1804, at Hartford to celebrate the purchase of Louisiana—in 1806, at Litchfield to celebrate the independence of the United States. . . .

In the last six years then, the leaders of democracy have collected together from all parts of the State, their followers once in each year."[8]

These occasions were indeed used for party organizing work. A circular announcing plans for a Republican festival on March 9, 1803, carried a notice that "the members of the general committee throughout the State are respectfully invited to attend a general meeting, at Mr. Isaac's Assembly Hall in New-Haven, on the day previous to the Festival, at 4 o'clock, P.M." The same circular outlined local party preparations which might be pursued "because we are desirous of connecting, with our festivity for the blessings of the general government, some well founded calculations of the triumph of republicanism in this State." Among the suggestions, it was urged "that Babcock's *Mercury* be most extensively circulated without delay," that preparations be made to get every Republican to the freemen's meeting ("those, who live distant from the place of meeting, should be assisted, if they need it, in getting to meeting"), and that "no one permit himself or others to express a doubt of success. . . . One doubt expressed will lose for us 10 votes."[9]

Considerable public interest and participation was created by the Republican proposal for a state constitutional convention to provide Connecticut with a written constitution. In August 1804, Republican delegates from ninety-seven towns in the state met in a convention in New Haven and passed resolutions calling for a constitutional convention. Although the movement failed at this time, the question remained a leading party issue until a written constitution was adopted in 1818.[10]

In 1805, Republican party machinery in Connecticut was revamped to include a state manager and a system of county managers, replacing the chairman of the general committee and the county chairmen. Following this reorganization, Alexander Wolcott, the new state manager, issued a

8. *The Sixth of August; or the Litchfield Festival: An Address to the People of Connecticut* (Hartford, 1806), pamphlet, Lib. Cong. On celebrations, see pp. 284-86 below.
9. "Circular, New Haven, February 1, 1803," printed in New Haven *Connecticut Journal*, Feb. 24, 1803.
10. Hartford *Connecticut Courant*, Aug. 22, 29, 1804. See Richard J. Purcell, *Connecticut in Transition, 1775-1818* (Wash., 1918), 254-55; Stamps, Political Parties in Connecticut, 102-12.

circular letter on November 1, outlining the procedures for the operation of the party machinery. This circular—which the Federalists promptly obtained and printed in their press[11]—provides an unusually full picture of the party organization and its operation throughout the state. Addressed to each county leader who had been "appointed, by the general meeting of Republicans, sole manager for the county," the circular instructed the county manager *"immediately after the receipt of this,* to appoint in each town of your county, an active, influential, republican manager, who will assure you verbally or in writing, that he will faithfully discharge his trust."

The first duty of the town manager was "to appoint a district manager in each district or section of his town, obtaining from each an assurance that he will faithfully do his duty." With the assistance of his district managers, the town manager was to prepare a report listing the following information about his town: (1) the total number of male inhabitants who were taxed, (2) the number of freemen, (3) the number of freemen who were "decided republicans," "decided federalists," or "doubtful," and (4) the number of Republicans who were not freemen, but who might be qualified at the next election. This return was to be in the hands of the county manager on or before November 25; from the reports of the town managers, the county manager was to make a comprehensive summary of county totals to be sent to the state manager on or before December 1.

The town and district managers were charged with getting all eligible Republicans to the freemen's meetings and assisting young Republicans in qualifying to vote. "They shall also notice what republicans are present, and see that each stays and votes till the whole business is ended. And each District-Manager shall report to the Town-Manager the names of all republicans absent, and the cause of absence, if known to him." The managers also were to see that the Republican ticket was circulated. "The list of candidates, as agreed on at the general meeting, will be sent seasonably into every town," the circular pointed out. "The representatives, to be set up in each town, and other town officers will be nominated in such way, as the town and district managers shall agree."

County managers were informed that they would be supplied with newspapers for each town for distribution by town and district managers. The town manager was also charged with forwarding to the county

11. Hartford *Connecticut Courant,* Nov. 27, 1805, Mar. 12, 1806.

manager within twenty-four hours after an election a summary of election returns, from which the county returns would be sent to the state manager and to Republican newspapers.

The state manager explained in his circular letter that it would be his duty to report to a general meeting of Republicans in May the information received from the county managers and to relate "what hindrances have been given to our cause in any part of the state, either by false reports, by political sermons, by official influence, by refusals to admit freemen, by federal tricks at elections, or *by negligence of republicans.*" He would also be required to report the conduct of each class of managers.

The wide powers of the Republican state manager are indicated by his power to remove county managers and to supply vacancies. County managers in turn had the same authority with respect to town managers, and the latter, in respect to district managers. It was thus a highly centralized party structure. "Formerly responsibility was too much divided," wrote State Manager Wolcott; "now each one knows the part assigned to him, and if he has the least idea of neglecting it, he must refuse his appointment at once."[12]

The new Republican party machinery was loudly denounced by the Federalists as "singular for its effrontery, and destructive of the freedom of election." A Federalist tract warned:

A State-Manager has been appointed by the leaders of our opponents, and to him ... is committed the management of the future elections in this State. He, and his numerous agents, spread over every part of the community, are to bear supreme controul in all our freemen's meetings. In violation of our ancient and fundamental laws, these men are to furnish the freemen with votes, to name the representatives in the several towns, and to become a Council of Appointments for the State. ... Let it be forever remembered that if the people will suffer their elections to be governed by one who assumes the name of a State-Manager, they will be compelled to surrender all their rights into the hands of a usurper.[13]

Another writer protested: "Freemen are to be made—candidates for office held up, and offices filled entirely at the nod of these various juntos, and they all subjected to their chief consul Alexander Wolcott."[14] When Federalist newspapers printed a copy of Wolcott's circular, former

12. *Ibid.*
13. *An Address to the Freemen of Connecticut* (Hartford, 1806), pamphlet, Univ. of Va.
14. *The Sixth of August; or the Litchfield Festival: An Address to the People of Connecticut.* See also Hartford *Connecticut Courant*, Mar. 12, 1806.

Congressman Simeon Baldwin suggested that extra copies of the paper be run off, voicing his hope that "the attention of the public will be kept alive on this subject 'till it is thoroughly understood and deeply felt—It will be a useful and a fruitful subject for frequent communications."[15]

While strongly condemning Republican methods, Federalists in practice were adopting similar organization but were more successful in keeping their confidential circulars out of the newspapers. Federalist circulars reveal that the party had state, county, and town committees and that they issued instructions which were very similar to those found in Alexander Wolcott's circular of 1805.[16] Indeed, much of the Federalist organization seems to have been inspired by the success of the Republican machinery in increasing Republican support in the state. "The effects of the thorough organization of the State by the Democratic party," a Federalist confidential circular pointed out in August 1806, "were proved last spring, by the addition of more than twelve hundred votes for their candidate for Governor." Consequently, additional instructions were sent to Federalist county committees to assist them in increasing their activities in maintaining Federalist support and in counteracting Republican methods.[17]

Republican party machinery labored under great difficulty in Connecticut, staunchest of the Federalist states. "The work of reformation will be slow," warned Ephraim Kirby in 1801. "The priest-hood are armed against us with all the powers of their order."[18] Gideon Granger confessed in 1802 that Republicans "have a hard time—their perseverance is wonderful," while Pierpont Edwards wrote more hopefully: "We are looking for the day of retribution for the feds; we hope it is not far off."[19] But in 1804, Republicans were still reporting: "Republicanism in this State progresses; but rather slow ... such a host of Priests, Lawyers and Political Hypocrites it is hard combating."[20] And in 1806, Granger

15. Baldwin to Matthew B. Whittlesey, Nov. 25, 1805, Baldwin Family Papers, Yale Univ.

16. The Baldwin Family Papers, 1804-1806, in the Yale University Library contain a long series of Federalist party circulars. For an analysis of Federalist organization in Connecticut, see Stamps, Political Parties in Connecticut, 116-61.

17. [Circular], enclosed in Timothy Dwight to Simeon Baldwin, Aug. 21, 1806, Baldwin Family Papers, Yale Univ.

18. Kirby to Jefferson, Aug. 17, 1801, Jefferson Papers, Lib. Cong.

19. Granger to Jefferson, May 23, 1802, *ibid.;* Edwards to Granger, Dec. 30, 1802, Papers of Gideon and Francis Granger, Lib. Cong.

20. Elisha Tracy to Samuel Huntington, July 3, 1804, "Letters from the Samuel Huntington Correspondence, 1800-1812," Western Reserve Historical Society, *Tracts*, 95 (1915), 91.

lamented: "The Fall Elections in this state have gone much against the Republican party. I left them in October 1801 with 67 members in the legislature, the coming session will exhibit only 61, yet there has been a great increase of Republicanism through the state, and it is my firm belief that the party is equal or nearly so to the Federal party."[21] When Jefferson went out of office in 1809, Connecticut was still under Federalist control; it was represented in Congress by Federalists, and it had yet to cast a Republican electoral vote.

Republicans tended to blame official influence and the clergy for their failure to win control of the state. Eldred Simkins, a young southern Republican attending Yale College, expressed the feelings of many when he protested: "The clergy so far from being the meek and lowly followers of Christ . . . are the most violent partizans, the most busy electioneerers, the source of violent animosities and discussions and the very essence of political wrangling and disturbance! . . . Their situation and importance here give them an influence but little thought of in states southwardly of this. . . . They tell their charge that they must vote for such and such men to represent them, or their religion and peace will be in danger. These very men when elected would naturally resound the praises of the clergy and say *they* must be supported."[22] At a Republican celebration in 1804, Abraham Bishop exclaimed: "It is astonishing that against such a system of impediments, and against such a host of excellencies and honorables, as are constantly paraded before the people, our cause and our untitled candidates should have made any progress."[23]

Federalist strength in Connecticut rested upon their control of the state government, the virtual exclusion of Republicans from all state offices, and the influence of the clergy. In addition, the Federalists successfully operated party machinery as well organized as, and better concealed than, the Republican party machinery. Together the strength of the informal and formal Federalist machinery kept the Republicans, despite their well-organized efforts, from power.

21. Gideon Granger to Jefferson, Oct. 9, 1806, Jefferson Papers, Lib. Cong.
22. Simkins to Creed Taylor, May 17, 1803, Creed Taylor Papers, Univ. of Va.
23. Abraham Bishop, *Oration, in Honor of the Election of President Jefferson and the Peaceful Acquisition of Louisiana, delivered at the National Festival in Hartford on the 11th of May, 1804* (n.p., printed for the General Committee of Republicans, 1804), 13-14, pamphlet, Lib. Cong.

Republican party machinery in Massachusetts developed extensively during the years from 1801 to 1809, both in state-wide organization and in county operation. The state party organization was headed by the Republican caucus composed of the Republican members of the legislature and "other respectable citizens."[24] The caucus made nominations for governor and lieutenant governor and, as early as 1804, established a committee system, consisting of a central committee with headquarters in Boston and county and town committees throughout the state.[25] The size of the central committee appears to have varied. It was reported to number five members in 1804;[26] and Dr. Nathaniel Ames listed five members in a diary entry in 1808.[27] But a circular sent out by the committee in 1806 was signed by eight members.[28] County committees also differed in the number of members; examples have been found of committees ranging in size from five to seventeen.[29] The general intent was that the county committee should consist of one member from each town.[30]

The central committee was appointed by, and acted under the direction of, the Republican caucus.[31] County committees appear generally to

24. Reports on caucuses can be found in Boston *Independent Chronicle*, Mar. 1, 1804, Feb. 11, 1805, Feb. 12, 1807; Philadelphia *Aurora*, Apr. 2, 1804; Boston *Democrat*, Feb. 13, 1805; Boston *Columbian Centinel*, Feb. 27, 1808.

25. A circular in 1805 refers to the reappointment of the central committee and of district committees. Worcester *Massachusetts Spy*, May 15, 1805; Boston *New-England Palladium*, May 7, 1805. The attention given by Federalist editors to the discovery of this Republican circular suggests that the Republican system was of recent origin. No evidence of a central committee before 1804 has been found.

26. Thompson J. Skinner, Charles P. Sumner, N. Fellows, C. Brazier, and James Prince. Boston *New-England Palladium*, May 7, 1805; Worcester *Massachusetts Spy*, May 15, 1805.

27. Aaron Hill, Perez Morton, Samuel Brown, Charles P. Sumner, and William Jarvis. Diary of Dr. Nathaniel Ames, Aug. 28, 1808; Charles Warren, *Jacobin and Junto; or Early American Politics as Viewed in the Diary of Dr. Nathaniel Ames, 1758-1822* (Cambridge, Mass., 1931), 226.

28. Thompson J. Skinner, Aaron Hill, John Howe, Thomas Harris, Perez Morton, Benjamin Austin, Jr., James Prince, and Nathaniel Ruggles. [Circular], Boston, Feb. 20, 1806, broadside, Amer. Antiq. Soc.

29. [Circular], Worcester, Mar. 12, 1806, signed by Samuel Flagg and seven others, broadside, Amer. Antiq. Soc.; [Circular], Mar. 23, 1807, signed by Simon Larned and nine others, broadside, N. Y. Pub. Lib.; Diary of Dr. Nathaniel Ames, Aug. 28, 1808, Warren, *Jacobin and Junto*, 226; [Circular], Hallowell, Oct. 10, 1808, signed by John Chandler and four others, broadside, N. Y. Pub. Lib.; [Circular], Worcester, Oct. 15, 1808, signed by Abraham Lincoln and sixteen others, broadside, Amer. Antiq. Soc.

30. Boston *Columbian Centinel*, Aug. 3, 1808.

31. Boston *New-England Palladium*, May 7, 1805; Worcester *Massachusetts Spy*, May 15, 1805; [Circular], Boston, Feb. 20, 1806, signed by Thompson J. Skinner and other members of central committee, broadside, Amer. Antiq. Soc.

have been appointed by the direction of the caucus, presumably the central committee arranging the appointments.[32] However, some of the county committees came to be chosen locally. Dr. Nathaniel Ames recorded in his diary in 1808 that "at a convention of Republicans from all the towns in the county of Norfolk, Cohassett excepted," seven men "were appointed a County Committee to communicate with the Central Committee of the State." "Town or sub-committees" were also appointed at this meeting.[33] In another instance a circular sent out by the Worcester County committee, in October 1808, announced "the honor of being constituted a County Committee, at a Meeting of their Republican Brethren."[34]

The few party circulars which have survived and the occasional Republican documents which fell into Federalist hands and were published in the newspapers reveal how the committee system operated. Communications between the committees show a centralized organization; instructions were sent by the central committee in Boston to the county committees, which in turn sent directions to the town committees. A circular dispatched by the central committee to county committees in 1805 advised:

By direction of a great number of our Fellow Citizens, lately assembled at Boston, from all parts of the Commonwealth, the Central Committee have the pleasure to announce your reappointment as a Committee for the District to which you belong. It would be altogether superfluous to enter into a minute exposition of the important duties involved in this appointment, or to express to you the precise wishes and expectations of the meeting from which it emanated. Suffice it to say, that the services which you have lately rendered to the Republican Cause . . . have been highly appreciated by your Fellow Citizens; and a repetition of those at the approaching Elections, is what they earnestly ask of you. . . . It is to be hoped that no labor will be deemed irksome, no effort excessive. . . . Among the means tending to ensure success to our efforts, the correction of error, and the diffusion of sound political information we consider not only the most honorable but the most efficient; we therefore earnestly recommend a seasonable distribution of the *Address,* which has been submitted to the General Meeting, and received their cordial approbation.

In the course of your preparations . . . we beseech you, Gentlemen,

---

32. Boston *New-England Palladium,* May 7, 1805; Worcester *Massachusetts Spy,* May 15, June 12, 1805; Boston *Columbian Centinel,* May 29, 1805, Aug. 3, 1808.

33. Diary of Dr. Nathaniel Ames, Aug. 28, 1808, Warren, *Jacobin or Junto,* 226.

34. [Circular], Worcester, Oct. 15, 1808, signed by Abraham Lincoln and sixteen others, broadside, Amer. Antiq. Soc.

strenously to enforce the necessity of union, and mutual concession. . . . Local interests and individual opinions should be persuaded to yield to the sense of the majority, and . . . we should adopt it as an axiom *"United we stand; divided we fall."*[35]

In another circular the central committee announced that "the Duty has been enjoined on us to forward to the several Counties the enclosed Address on the subject of the approaching Election, to be distributed among the People by the County Committees, to correspond with them, and to receive any Communications from them, which they may think it expedient to make."[36] Through the addresses furnished to the county committees, the central committee supplied the party line to be followed in elections. For example, in the gubernatorial race in 1806, the strategy was not to attack the private character of the Federalist candidate (the incumbent Governor Caleb Strong) but to emphasize that neither he nor his supporters would harmonize with the national administration and that in time of crisis it was "most essentially necessary" that every state government unite in support of the national administration.[37] In 1808, the central committee supplied the county committees with a defense of the Embargo, which had become a dominant campaign issue.[38] The central committee regularly exhorted the local committees to be active, writing in 1808: "In consideration of the indefatigable exertions of our federal opponents, the Central Committee of the republicans earnestly request you to communicate immediately with the republicans of the respective towns in your county, and to take all honorable and reasonable measures to draw forth, at the approaching election, the whole strength of the republican interest."[39]

Dr. Nathaniel Ames, a member of the Norfolk County committee in 1808, described the functions of the Republican committee system as designed "to watch over the Republican interest both in State and National Governments, especially as to elections and appointments—convey intelligence—confute false rumors—confirm the wavering in

---

35. [Circular], 1805, printed in Worcester *Massachusetts Spy*, May 15, 1805; Boston *New-England Palladium*, May 7, 1805. Address referred to was published in Boston *Democrat*, Feb. 23, 1805.
36. [Circular], Boston, Feb. 20, 1806, signed by Thompson J. Skinner and other members of the central committee, broadside, Amer. Antiq. Soc.
37. *Ibid*. A similar line was followed in 1807; see *United We Stand—Divided We Fall*, Boston, Feb. 20, 1807, signed "The Central Committee," broadside, Hist. Soc. of Pa.
38. Boston *Democrat*, Mar. 26, 1808.
39. *Ibid*.

right principles—prevent delusion of weak brethren—and fight that most formidable enemy of civilized men, political ignorance."[40]

The county committees, receiving instructions and communications from the central committee, passed them on to town committees with additional words of advice and encouragement. The Worcester County committee, in 1806, had copies printed of a letter received from the central committee and sent a copy to Republican committees in each town of the county, together with a printed circular of its own.[41] In its circular, the Worcester committee listed the Republican candidates to be supported and explained how it proposed to proceed in their behalf: "In this town, we mean to have a meeting of as many Republicans as we can call together; and there pledge ourselves, and endeavor to induce others, to give up private interest on the day of Election and devote their time to the good of our country. We shall also choose one Republican in each School district, whose particular duty it will be, to induce all those within the district, to come forth and give their votes. We shall be particularly careful to have ready, written votes, with persons appointed to distribute them." After these suggestions as to what town committees might do, the county committee concluded: "We mean not to dictate to you. You will use your own discretion, in adopting this, or any other mode, best calculated to ensure the Election, which rightly belongs to the Republicans, as the majority."[42]

Other county committees were more commanding in their suggestions. The Republican committee in Hallowell, in Massachusetts's Maine district, advised in a circular to town committees in 1808: "Your republican friends have great confidence in you as a committee; your duty is important—your greatest industry and active vigilance among your townsmen, is indispensably requisite. By the number of republican votes which will be returned from your town, your exertions will be estimated. To give the utmost power and efficacy to your labours, we recommend that the whole town committee meet previous to the day of election, and assign to each member a particular part of the town as his circle of

40. Diary of Dr. Nathaniel Ames, Aug. 28, 1808, Warren, *Jacobin and Junto,* 226.
41. [Circular], Boston, Feb. 20, 1806, signed by Thompson J. Skinner and other members of the central committee, broadside, Amer. Antiq. Soc.; [Circular], Worcester, Mar. 12, 1806, signed by Samuel Flagg and other members of the Worcester committee, broadside, Amer. Antiq. Soc.
42. [Circular], Worcester, Mar. 12, 1806, signed by Samuel Flagg and other members of the Worcester committee, broadside, Amer. Antiq. Soc.

immediate action; extending however, *a general influence,* as time and opportunity will admit."⁴³

County and town committees encouraged the holding of party meetings and the arousing of public interest and participation in elections; much attention was given to getting out the vote.⁴⁴ "We conjure you by every thing dear to freemen, to be active and vigilant," exhorted the Republican committee of Hallowell; "let no man remain at home on the day of election who will give a republican vote." The Worcester committee urged "the earliest attention to the polls; that every confirmed Republican be called upon to attend on the day of election."⁴⁵ Much time also was occupied in refuting Federalist attacks. The Hallowell committee sent copies of an affidavit signed by Gabriel Duvall, the Comptroller of the Treasury, certifying that the two million dollars appropriated by Congress in 1806 to purchase Florida had not been drawn from the Treasury. The purpose was "to disprove an atrocious and wicked lie, circulated by the federalists, in relation to two millions of dollars, stated by them to be given by our government as tribute to France."⁴⁶ Various other materials were sent to aid local committees in support of Republican campaigns, as was indicated by a circular of 1807 which advised: "As an exposition of the principles by which we are governed, . . . as a designation of the Candidates in whose support a general union of sentiment appears to exist among our Republican friends; and as furnishing the means of general information to our fellow-citizens, both as to the principles and characters for whom their suffrages are requested, we enclose the accompanying Papers, to be used in such manner as your judgment may dictate."⁴⁷

In Massachusetts the Republican caucus nominated only candidates for governor and lieutenant governor, while in all other New England states, party caucuses made more extensive nominations.⁴⁸ With nomi-

43. [Circular], Hallowell, Oct. 10, 1808, signed by John Chandler and other members of the committee, broadside, N. Y. Pub. Lib.

44. [Circular], Worcester, Mar. 12, 1806, signed by Samuel Flagg and others, broadside, Amer. Antiq. Soc.

45. [Circular], Hallowell, Oct. 10, 1808, signed by John Chandler and other members of committee, broadside, N. Y. Pub. Lib.; [Circular], Worcester, Oct. 15, 1808, signed by Abraham Lincoln and other members of committee, broadside, Amer. Antiq. Soc.

46. [Circular], Hallowell, Oct. 10, 1808, signed by John Chandler and other members of committee, broadside, N. Y. Pub. Lib.

47. [Circular], Mar. 23, 1807, signed by Simon Larned and others, probably the committee of Berkshire County, broadside, N. Y. Pub. Lib.

48. William A. Robinson, *Jeffersonian Democracy in New England* (New Haven, 1916), 59.

nations for members of both houses of the legislature and for representatives to Congress being made on the local, county, or district level, local initiative in party organizing was more important in Massachusetts than in any other New England state. Newspapers, from time to time, reported Republican county meetings and party "conventions" where nominations for state senators and congressmen were agreed upon. In addition to the state-wide system of committees, certain local party machinery operated sporadically within the state, both before and after the committee system came to dominate the Republican party in the state. When some two hundred Republicans gathered at Kennebunk in York County on March 5, 1804, to celebrate the anniversary of Jefferson's inauguration, "the exercises of the day being over a special meeting was held, to take into consideration the subject of ensuing County Elections." Candidates for state senators were nominated and a committee appointed "to confer with gentlemen in any part of the County, who may have thought of different Candidates." Approval was also expressed of the Republican nominees for governor and lieutenant governor.[49]

One of the best examples of well-developed local organization was found in the Essex South District in 1802, when "a Convention of Delegates" was held at Danvers to nominate a Republican candidate for the Eighth Congress. Delegates were present from Salem, Marblehead, Beverly, Danvers, Lynn, and Wenham, but "Gloucester was unrepresented by local circumstances—Lynnfield by accident—and Manchester by not being notified." There is no record as to how the delegates were chosen. After voting unanimously by ballot for Jacob Crowninshield as the Republican nominee, the convention resolved itself into a committee and passed the following recommendations, revealing the attention given to election preparations and to the press.

1st. Resolved, That previous to the election the list of voters be inspected by the Republicans of every town, and care be taken that no legal voter be excluded from the list, and no illegal one admitted on the list.

2d. Resolved, That every exertion be made to support the Republican candidate, by appointing committees, by distributing newspapers, by refuting objections, and by supplying with votes the various wards of every town.

3d. And for the purposes of giving information to the people, as well

49. Portland *Eastern Argus*, Mar. 9, 1804. A convention of Republicans of Bristol County was reported in Boston *Independent Chronicle*, Mar. 15, 1804.

as counteracting the arts of imposture—Resolved, That the Printer of the SALEM REGISTER be requested to print an extra number of papers from this time to the time of election, to be distributed GRATIS among the people by the committees of the various towns, and that these committees be EARNESTLY REQUESTED to send by all opportunities to Salem for the same, in as great a number as they can use advantageously, and that the same be delivered to said committees FREE OF EXPENCE.

4th. Resolved, That it be most seriously recommended to all Republicans to exert themselves to obtain subscriptions for THE SALEM REGISTER, as a free and well conducted paper, devoted to the republican cause—and particularly that the committees interest themselves in this behalf.[50]

The circular sent out by the chairman of the convention announced that the printer had already been engaged to carry out the third resolution and urged that the freest use be made of the arrangement as "highly important to the cause." It is also significant to note that this circular concluded with a summary of the party platform to be secured, it was affirmed, by the election of a Republican member to Congress. This platform declared: "We hold as the creed of Republicans—Freedom of speech—freedom of the press—the right of trial by jury—the union of our states—the right to elect all officers—inviolability to the constitution—just confidence in government—equal privileges, and equal laws—no expenditures but by appropriations of law—no summary tribunals—no nobility—no powers independent of the people—In one word, we hold that liberty is the birthright of mankind, and a Democracy its only sure preservative."[51]

The above details display well-developed party methods and organization, but most reports of county party meetings or conventions are not so full and do not reveal such elaborate arrangements. The newspaper accounts of county meetings and conventions seldom disclose how the delegates were chosen, and in many cases the gatherings were apparently party caucuses. The Boston *Independent Chronicle* in 1804 reported a "Democratic-Republican Meeting ... of between forty and fifty Republican Citizens, from 24 towns in the District of Middlesex, held at the house of Noah Brooks, in Lincoln," at which a candidate for Congress was nominated and support pledged to the Republican ticket of

50. [Circular], Salem, Sept. 24, 1802, signed by John Hathorne, chairman, broadside, Amer. Antiq. Soc.
51. *Ibid.*

presidential electors.⁵² Noticing the gathering, a Federalist writing in the *Columbian Centinel* referred to "the caucus, *alias* County Convention, *alias* Jacobin Club" which met "at *Noah Brooks'* tavern in *Lincoln*," and commented: "As these Conventioners were all men *picked* by the authors of the meeting from 24 out of 42 towns, and chosen the Lord only knows how, or whom by;—and as 'Squire Dana, had the Resolutions already *cut and dried,* at hand; there was a wonderful *unanimity.*"⁵³ Some credence should be given to such Federalist outbursts in assessing the party conventions in Massachusetts, for it is doubtful that they were ever so democratic as they appeared to be.⁵⁴

A trend toward more democratic party procedures, however, did appear to develop in Republican activities. For example, in Boston in 1804, agreement to support the re-election of William Eustis to Congress was reached at Republican caucuses, while in 1808, Boston Republicans were invited to assemble to choose delegates to confer with delegates from other towns in the district in nominating a candidate for Congress.⁵⁵ More conventions attended by Republican delegates were reported in 1808 than ever before,⁵⁶ and the area of activity of these conventions tended to widen. A meeting of "Republican Delegates, from every Town in the County of Essex, except Manchester and Lynnfield, convened at Ipswich" in the fall of 1808 to nominate candidates for Congress and to perform "such other business as might be deemed necessary for the support of the Republican cause." This other business included the passage of resolutions expressing confidence in Thomas Jefferson, approving the Embargo, commending the disinterested conduct of John Quincy Adams, disapproving the conduct of Timothy Pickering, denouncing the action of the Massachusetts legislature in regard to the method of choosing presidential electors, approving and pledging to support the nomination of James Madison for president and George Clinton for vice-president, and authorizing the publication of a lengthy campaign address.⁵⁷

Massachusetts Federalists were severely critical of all Republican party

---

52. *Independent Chronicle,* Oct. 29, 1804.
53. Boston *Columbian Centinel,* Oct. 27, 1804.
54. See also *ibid.,* Aug. 3, 1808.
55. Boston *Independent Chronicle,* Nov. 5, 1804, extra, May 9, Sept. 26, 29, 1808.
56. Boston *Democrat,* Feb. 27, Mar. 9, 1808; Boston *Independent Chronicle,* Feb. 29, Mar. 7, May 19, Sept. 26, 29, Oct. 6, 13, 20, 24, 1808.
57. *Republican Convention,* Essex County, Massachusetts, [1808], pamphlet, Amer. Antiq. Soc. See also report of Essex Convention, Feb. 24, 1808, in Boston *Independent Chronicle,* Feb. 29, 1808.

organizing efforts, especially the committee system. The Boston *Columbian Centinel* protested that "the democratic senators and representatives, *whom you have chosen,* have appointed a committee in each county to direct you *whom you shall choose.* To these wicked exertions of wicked men, these encroachments on your elective rights, this profanation of the temple of freedom, are owing all the misfortunes of your suffering country and still greater misfortunes which will inevitably follow. . . . Time was when such a committee would be held up as objects of public detestation."[58] Nevertheless, the Federalists in Massachusetts had a party organization which closely resembled the Republican machinery with one significant exception—the Federalists apparently made no efforts to organize mass meetings or conventions of its party supporters. They depended on party caucuses, headed by a legislative caucus, and on a well-organized committee system. The Federalist committee machinery, which seems to have appeared almost simultaneously with the Republican organization in 1804, was headed by a central committee and included county and town committees and subcommittees within towns throughout the state.[59] The circulars sent out by the Federalist committees contained many instructions similar to those found in Republican circulars,[60] though frequently accompanied by apologies for suggesting such methods. "We regret," declared a Federalist circular of 1805, "that we are compelled, by necessity, to resort to any measures to preserve the Commonwealth from the dangers and confusion of innovation, besides those, which result from the natural and unsolicited exercise of the right of suffrage. . . . But the intrigues, the arts, the falsehoods, and the perseverance of our opponents leave us no choice. They are drilled and disciplined with the regularity of an army, and their plans can be counteracted only by equal organization."[61]

The Federalists were also more secretive about their actions than the Republicans, instructing: "As the success of these exertions, for the public good, in some measure, depend upon secrecy, we therefore recommend to the town Committee, to be silent even with federalists, and with the

58. *Columbian Centinel,* Aug. 3, 1808; see also *ibid.,* May 29, 1805; Worcester *Massachusetts Spy,* June 12, 1805.
59. [Circular, Massachusetts, 1804], broadside, Lib. Cong.; Boston *Independent Chronicle,* Mar. 28, 1805.
60. [Circular], Boston, June 13, 1805, signed by Samuel Dexter and others, broadside, Amer. Antiq. Soc.; [Circular], Boston, Feb. 1806, broadside, Amer. Antiq. Soc.; [Circular], Boston, Apr. 14, 1806, broadside, Amer. Antiq. Soc.
61. [Circular], signed by Ebenezer Bacon and others, [1805], broadside, Mass. Hist. Soc.

sub-Committees on the subject of their connexion with us, the county Committee; in order that the exertions, in every town, may appear to originate in said town."[62] But Federalist efforts at secrecy were not always successful, and when one of their circulars fell into Republican hands it was gleefully published in Republican newspapers.[63] "The Cat out of the Bag!" cried the editor of the Portland *Eastern Argus* in publishing extracts from the circular and recalling that "our *self-righteous Federalists* have always professed to abhor every kind of *Secrecy* and *improper Influence* at *Elections*." "These are the men who exclaim so loudly against Party Measures, Secret Caucuses, and pretend to be all fairness, while they are deep in midnight plots, and practicing the most insulting conduct!" "Are you thus to be organized and maneuvered ... ?" he asked. "Are you willing to be *counted, sorted* and *maneuvered* by a few designing men, in the same manner that a Nabob would his slaves?"[64] The editor boldly ignored, or was unaware of, the fact that Federalist papers had exposed the Republican system.

In New Hampshire, Republican party organization was directed by a general caucus of Republican members of the legislature and other party leaders, commonly referred to as a "convention."[65] A "General Convention of the Republican members of the general court of New Hampshire and of a large number of respectable citizens from distant parts of the state" gathered at Concord in December 1803 to nominate candidates for state offices and to adopt "a system of measures ... to promote *union* and *harmony* among the Republicans."[66] This caucus appointed a "Grand Committee of Election and Correspondence," consisting of six persons from each county, with John Goddard as chairman of the grand committee. County election committees, composed of one or more Republicans in each town, were also designated to assist the grand committee in promoting the Republican ticket.[67] A printed letter,

---

62. *Ibid.*
63. Boston *Independent Chronicle,* Mar. 28, 1805.
64. Portland *Eastern Argus,* Mar. 21, 28, 1806.
65. Boston *Independent Chronicle,* Feb. 23, 1804; Portsmouth *New Hampshire Gazette,* Aug. 7, 1804.
66. Boston *Independent Chronicle,* Feb. 23, 1804.
67. Boston *Columbian Centinel,* Feb. 29, 1804; Jeremiah Smith to William Plumer, Feb. 22, 1804, Plumer Papers, Lib. Cong. Smith's information regarding the Republican organization agreed with that in the *Columbian Centinel* except that he reported the grand committee was composed of five members from each county.

signed by order of the Republican "convention," was sent to committee members, outlining the party organization, informing them of their appointment, and exhorting them to labor in promoting the cause of Republicanism. "What think you of these things?" exclaimed a shocked Federalist. "Did you believe 15 years ago that a thing of this kind would happen in New England?"[68]

This system seems to have attained firm control over Republican nominations. Dissatisfied Republicans were repulsed when they attempted to make a substitution on the list of candidates nominated for Congress by the caucus held at Concord in July 1804. This caucus was referred to in the press as "a convention of the majority of the members of the Legislature and a large number of gentlemen from various parts of the State."[69] An address explained: "It was . . . for the purpose of uniting the free suffrages of all the friends of union, peace and republicanism in some ticket, that it was thought expedient to adopt this mode, which it is hoped will be satisfactory. The convention do not presume to *dictate* this or any other ticket to you—they recommend it to your attention, and hope it will meet with your approbation."[70] Shortly thereafter, it was announced that the insurgent candidate "positively declines being considered a candidate" and would give his support to the Republican ticket nominated by the "convention."[71]

The central Republican organization directed all of the state-wide campaigns, which under the general ticket system included congressional elections. An example of the methods employed can be found in a printed letter sent to party leaders throughout the state during the election of 1808. Signed by Richard Evans, "Chairman of the Conventional Committee," the circular reported the meeting of the Republican caucus at Concord during the session of the legislature.[72] It explained that the members of the convention "were conscious that their constituents looked

68. Jeremiah Smith to William Plumer, Feb. 22, 1804, Plumer Papers, Lib. Cong. One of the Republican circulars had fallen into Federalist hands. By July 1804, New Hampshire Federalists were likewise establishing party machinery, including county committees, town agents, and lieutenants for each school district. For a summary of the Federalist organizational efforts see Lynn W. Turner, *William Plumer of New Hampshire, 1759-1850* (Chapel Hill, 1962), 144.

69. Portsmouth *New Hampshire Gazette,* July 24, 31, Aug. 7, 1804.

70. *Ibid.,* Aug. 7, 1804. This same caucus also nominated the Republican ticket for presidential electors, *ibid.,* Aug. 7, Sept. 18, 1804.

71. *Ibid.,* Aug. 14, 1804.

72. [Circular], State of New-Hampshire, July 4, 1808, signed by Richard Evans, addressed to Israel Hunt, broadside, N.-Y. Hist. Soc.; copy of circular also printed in Portsmouth *New-Hampshire Gazette,* Aug. 23, 1808.

to them for information in an hour of peril, and had a right to expect such advice as might combine their powers, and direct their exertions in defence of the public weal." Therefore, they "were induced to recommend a list of candidates for Representatives to Congress, ascertained by a general ballot, and composed of men whose political opinions are in union with their own." After supplying arguments for the defense of the national administration, the circular concluded by notifying the recipient that he had been selected as a "friend of man" and explaining that the enclosed list of Republican nominations was sent according to the wishes of the convention and "in the belief that your exertions will be productive of happy effects." "The cause of liberty is a glorious cause!—let us rally its defenders, and join *heart* and *hand* in support of men, who are determined to maintain the Government of the People."[73]

An example of the methods employed by the county committees and town organizations can be found in a circular sent to local leaders in 1805, a copy of which was obtained by the Federalists and published in the press. It advised:

> The Committee, appointed by the Convention of a majority of the Members of both branches of the Legislature of this State, to promote in the county of ———— the election of such men to fill the offices of State Government, as wish a continuance of the union of the States, and are not inimical to the present administration of our Federal Government—in pursuance of the regulations made by the said Convention, hereby inform you, that you are requested particularly to attend to the affairs of the next election in the town of ————. And it is earnestly recommended to you to use all your influence and exertions upon this occasion.
>
> The mode pointed out by the Convention as the most adviseable for you to pursue, is—that on some short time before election day, you assemble the most active republicans in your town, and cause the town to be divided into districts, assigning to each man his district, whose duty it shall be to see that every republican in the district be furnished with a vote, and attend the town meeting.
>
> That you be careful that there be provided a sufficient number of votes for all the republican voters in your town.
>
> That such political information and writings as you may from time to time receive, be distributed among your fellow-citizens in such manner as will best promote the republican cause.
>
> That you endeavor to have a firm republican chosen to represent your town in the General Court.

73. *Ibid.*

That if there should be a majority of republican votes in your town, you be careful that the certificate thereof be legally made and seasonably returned.[74]

New Hampshire Republican machinery was thus organized from the state level downward, with the legislative caucus appointing and instructing the county committees and the county committees in turn instructing the local party leaders. If all instructions, down to the dividing of towns into districts for campaign purposes, were carried out, the New Hampshire Republicans were thoroughly organized.

While Republican machinery in New Hampshire was similar to that found in Connecticut and in Massachusetts, Republicans in Vermont were not so well organized. In that state, Federalism was less powerful than in most of New England. The fall elections of 1801 gave Republicans a majority in both houses of the Vermont legislature—a success "beyond our highest expectations," rejoiced one jubilant Republican.[75] With the threat of Federalism weakening, Republican party machinery in Vermont was less elaborate than in any other New England state. Republican organization consisted basically of party caucuses headed by a legislative caucus which decided on state-wide party nominations and served to unite Republican efforts in elections. Although not all caucuses appear to have been publicized, the legislative caucus was publicly reported. A party ticket for state offices in 1805, for example, published in the press as the "Vermont Republican Nomination," openly announced that the nominations had been made at "a general meeting of the Republican members of the legislature, at Rutland."[76]

As in other states, the Vermont caucus system was subjected to frequent attacks. "Of late the people are supposed to have nothing to do but to *confirm* the doings of the *Caucus*," protested one writer. "It was *formerly* the case, that the freemen, *proud of their privileges*, claimed and exercised the right of *thinking and acting for themselves*."[77] Against Federalist criticism, Republicans defended their caucuses "because they are not very frequent, and are open to all comers, and to discussion, and because their results are submitted to the public." At the same time they

74. Circular printed in *Portsmouth Oracle*, Mar. 2, 1805.
75. Moses Robinson to Jefferson, Nov. 17, 1801, Jefferson Papers, Lib. Cong.
76. Walpole (N. H.) *Political Observatory*, Aug. 10, 1805; Windsor *Spooner's Vermont Journal*, Nov. 28, 1808; Robinson, *Jeffersonian Democracy in New England*, 57-59.
77. Windsor *Spooner's Vermont Journal*, Nov. 28, 1808.

accused the Federalists of holding numerous caucuses as "*secret* as the midnight meetings of Burr, Martin, Blennerhasset, and their associates."[78]

Republican party organization in Rhode Island was unique among New England states in the introduction of a state party convention composed of delegates chosen by localities. Such a system was used in 1808 to nominate candidates for Congress and for presidential electors. The legislative caucus system of deciding state nominations and directing state-wide elections predominated, however, during the years from 1801 to 1808. Both congressional candidates and presidential electors, for example, were nominated by the Republican members of the legislature in 1804.[79] In 1808, the governor and lieutenant governor were nominated by "a conference holden in Providence during the session of the General Assembly," as the newspapers reported, avoiding, as usual, the use of the term caucus.[80]

While caucuses were thus being employed, conventions were also making their appearance. In 1807, the press announced the nomination of James Fenner for re-election as governor by "a republican Convention" at East-Greenwich.[81] The composition of this convention or the manner in which its members were chosen was not revealed, however, leaving doubts as to its exact character. But more information is available regarding the convention in 1808. At a meeting in Newport, on June 24, 1808, "a number of republicans, from different parts of the State" voted that "a general convention be held at East-Greenwich, on the second Tuesday in August." A committee of five, consisting of one member from each county, was appointed "to give information to the republican freemen, respecting the convention," and notices were ordered published in the press.[82] This "general Convention of the Republicans of the State of Rhode-Island" met according to arrangements on August 9, with sixty-two "delegates from the several towns" in attendance.[83] It is not clear how all the delegates were chosen, but a Providence newspaper notice had summoned the Republicans in that town to a meeting "to choose four delegates to represent them in the General Convention of the Republicans of the State."[84] Thus, the Republican convention demonstrated a trend

78. *Rutland Vermont Herald*, Aug. 13, 1808; Bennington *World*, Aug. 8, 1808.
79. Newport *Rhode-Island Republican*, June 21, 1804.
80. Providence *Columbian Phenix*, Apr. 9, 1808; *Newport Mercury*, Apr. 16, 1808.
81. *Newport Mercury*, Mar. 28, 1807.
82. Providence *Columbian Phenix*, July 9, 1808.
83. *Ibid.*, Aug. 13, 1808; Boston *Independent Chronicle*, Aug. 18, 1808.
84. Providence *Columbian Phenix*, July 9, 1808.

toward more democratic procedure within the party structure than was afforded by the caucus system; at least some of the delegates to this convention were elected by the local party members whom they represented.

The Rhode Island convention of 1808 nominated candidates for Congress and for presidential electors, voted unanimous approval of the nomination of James Madison for president and George Clinton for vice-president made by the Republican members of Congress at Washington,[85] and issued an address signed by all sixty-two delegates urging support for the Republican ticket and defending the policies of the national administration.[86] In contrast to the Republican method of nominating congressional candidates, Rhode Island Federalists announced that their nominations came only as "the result of free consultation and extensive communication throughout the State . . . the unsolicited dictates of public opinion."[87]

The extensive organizational efforts of the Republicans in New England during Jefferson's presidency left little of the region unaffected by party activities. The extent and the tightness of party machinery varied considerably from the well-organized system of Connecticut Republicans to the less formal caucus-run organization in Vermont. Viewing the region as a whole, the Republican party machinery of the New England states was predominantly characterized by highly centralized state party organizations controlled by state caucuses and committee systems directed from the top. This was most plainly displayed in Connecticut where the state party manager had wide powers and nearly all party directions emanated from the top downward. A state caucus and central committee also dominated in Massachusetts and in New Hampshire, but there was noticeably more local party activity in Massachusetts than elsewhere in New England. Although the state caucus was supreme in Rhode Island in most of the years down to 1808, the initiation of the party convention introduced a more democratic process into the party machinery. This innovation in Rhode Island and such locally developed organizations as appeared in Massachusetts indicated that party machinery had not become fully stabilized, but there could be little doubt that party machinery had come to stay in New England.

85. *Ibid.*, Aug. 13, 1808.
86. *Ibid.*, Aug. 20, 1808; New York *Public Advertiser*, Aug. 27, 1808.
87. *Newport Mercury*, July 9, 23, 1808.

CHAPTER SEVEN

Party Machinery in the Middle States

While in the New England states Republicans were extensively engaged in the initial stages of establishing party machinery, Republicans in the middle states could build upon much basic machinery which had already been constructed before Jefferson took office in 1801. As parties had formed in the 1790's, New York and Pennsylvania had been the areas of the most extensive building of party machinery in the nation, and in the neighboring states of New Jersey and Delaware the Jeffersonians, by 1800, had likewise become actively engaged in party organizational efforts. Although party machinery was to develop in its own peculiar way in each state of the region, the middle states in the early 1800's furnish some of the most significant examples of the developing maturity of party machinery in the United States. At the same time, Republican divisions in these states created some of the party's most difficult problems.

In New York, party machinery which had become well established in that state by 1800 was not greatly altered in structure during the period 1801 to 1809, and the problem of controlling existing organizations rather than innovating new systems mainly engaged the attention of Republican leaders. But at the same time, there was an increase of party organization by local initiative and an enlarging of the opportunities for public participation in party affairs.

The legislative caucus, which was open also to party leaders from throughout the state, supplied the basic framework of the New York state-wide Republican organization. The caucus in 1801, 1804, and 1807 nominated the successful Republican candidates for governor and lieutenant governor. It also appointed a Republican corresponding committee which directed the state-wide gubernatorial campaigns. Because of divisions within the Republican party in New York, only in 1801 did the regular caucus nomination go unchallenged. In both 1804 and 1807, rival candidates were sponsored by dissident Republican factions.

The activities of the Republicans in 1804 may be taken as an example of the operation of party machinery in New York. Reports of the caucus nomination, published in the newspapers and in handbills, announced: "At a Meeting of the Republican Members of the Legislature of this state, and a number of other respectable citizens from different parts cf the state, held at the Assembly Chamber, in the city of Albany, on the evening of the 20th of February, 1804," it was resolved unanimously to support Morgan Lewis for governor and John Broome for lieutenant governor. A committee of five was appointed to draft an address to the voters and to report on February 22. When the caucus reconvened, the address in support of the ticket was approved and ordered printed. Signed by all persons present, it revealed the exact composition of the caucus. In attendance were 104 members of both houses of the legislature and 53 Republicans from different parts of the state, including fourteen from Albany and a delegation of thirteen, headed by Brockholst Livingston and DeWitt Clinton, from New York City. Before adjourning, a committee of publication and correspondence, composed of four members of the Senate, four members of the Assembly, and four from outside the legislature, was appointed.[1]

The committee prepared a circular which was mailed to Republican leaders throughout the state. Signed by all twelve members of the committee, it announced:

We take the liberty to enclose you several copies of the Republican Nomination for GOVERNOR and LIEUTENANT-GOVERNOR of this state, together with the Address of the members of the Legislature, and respectable Citizens from various parts of the state, which composed the Republican meeting at this place: And to request that you will take the earliest opportunity of distributing them in your county in such manner as shall best promote the Election of the Candidates. We deem it unnecessary on this occasion to make any other remark than that as these Candidates have been unanimously nominated by a very large and respectable Meeting of our Fellow-Citizens from every part of the state, it is expected they will receive the cordial and active support of every real friend to the prosperity and happiness of his country.[2]

---

1. *Republican Nomination*, Albany, Feb. 20, 1804, Ebenezer Purdy, chairman, broadside, Lib. Cong.; New York *American Citizen*, Mar. 3, 1804; *Albany Gazette*, Mar. 5, 1804; *Genuine Republican Nomination*, Albany, Feb. 20, 1804, broadside, N.-Y. Hist. Soc. It should be noted that John Lansing had been nominated by an earlier Republican caucus but had declined the nomination. New York *American Citizen*, Feb. 21, 1804; George Clinton to Pierre Van Cortlandt, Jr., Feb. 25, 1804, Papers of Pierre Van Cortlandt, Jr., N. Y. Pub. Lib.

2. [Circular], Albany, Feb. 28, 1804, signed by John Tayler and others, committee of correspondence and publication, broadside, N. Y. Pub. Lib.

A second address, prepared by the committee of publication and correspondence, was also sent out during the campaign.[3]

Meanwhile, on February 23, the day after the caucus adjourned, a "numerous meeting of the Republican citizens" of Albany met at Skinner's Albany Coffee-House, with George Merchant, who had been one of the Albany members of the caucus, as chairman. Resolutions were passed highly approving the nomination of Lewis and Broome made by the caucus, and a general committee was appointed, which in turn named a corresponding committee.[4]

On February 28, similar action in approving the Republican nominations was taken at a "General Meeting of Republican Citizens" in New York City. It was also "recommended to our Republican Fellow Citizens that they take immediate measures for the purpose of calling meetings in the different wards in this city, in order to choose a Committee to consist of seven persons for each ward," to make arrangements for promoting the election of Lewis and Broome. The committees chosen were to meet together the following week. Notices calling the ward meetings appeared in the newspapers; ward meetings were held, resolutions passed in support of Lewis and Broome, and committees chosen as suggested by the general meeting.[5] Subsequently, sixty-four "delegates from the respective wards of the City and County of New-York" met as the "General Republican Committee" to make plans to promote the party ticket. Their first step was to issue an address urging support for Lewis and Broome.[6] The meetings in Albany and in New York to support the nomination of Lewis and Broome were followed by similar Republican meetings in other parts of the state, approving the caucus nomination and appointing campaign committees. At some of these meetings nominations were also made for members of the state senate and assembly.[7]

The "General Committee of Republicans" in New York City also appointed a five-member corresponding committee headed by DeWitt

3. Published in New York *American Citizen*, Apr. 14, 1804.
4. *Republican Nomination*, Albany, Feb. 23, 1804, George Merchant, chairman, broadside, N.-Y. Hist. Soc.
5. New York *American Citizen*, Mar. 1, 2, 3, 1804.
6. *New York Address: To the Republican Electors for Governor and Lieutenant Governor of the State of New-York*, [1804], broadside, N.-Y. Hist. Soc.; New York *American Citizen*, Mar. 19, 1804.
7. *Ibid.*, Mar. 19, 22, Apr. 5, 9, 11, 1804.

Clinton.⁸ A printed circular was sent out by this committee to Republican leaders throughout the state. Written by DeWitt Clinton, the communication assured Republicans in other parts of the state that the city of New York was strongly in support of Lewis and Broome, despite contrary reports circulated by their opponents. "We will thank you to inform us by the mail, or other safe conveyance, of the state of public sentiment in your county . . . ," the New York committee wrote. "The more you go into detail, the more gratifying it will be. If you can furnish us with a conjectural statement of the interest in each town of your county of the republican and federal parties, and of the adherents of Mr. Burr, it may be productive of benefit, and will be esteemed a favour." The committee also requested communications on "the artifices and misrepresentations employed by our adversaries in your quarter, and the best means in your opinion of counteracting them." Promising to communicate anything of moment that should occur previous to the election, the committee suggested that "we shall be happy to receive such information and advice from you as may in your opinion be useful to the republican party."⁹ This circular clearly revealed that the New York committee of correspondence did not limit its activities to the city, but under the direction of DeWitt Clinton was active throughout the state.

These activities of what may be termed the regular Republican organization, combining at this time the Clinton and Livingston factions, were resisted by the rival Burr faction within the New York Republican party. At what was reported to be "a respectable meeting of Republican Citizens, from different parts of the state of New-York," convened at the Tontine Coffee-House in Albany on February 18, Aaron Burr had been nominated as a candidate for governor.¹⁰ This nomination was followed on February 20 by a meeting in New York City where Republicans comprising committees from various wards pledged to

8. See Henry Rutgers to DeWitt Clinton, James Fairlie, John R. Livingston, A[drian] C. Van Slyck, and John R. B. Rodgers, committee of correspondence, Apr. 30, 1804, DeWitt Clinton Papers, Columbia Univ.

9. *CIRCULAR*, New York, Mar. 14, 1804, with signatures of DeWitt Clinton, James Fairlie, J[ohn] R. B. Rodgers, and A[drian] C. Van Slyck, broadside, Lib. Cong.; another copy with the additional signature of J[ohn] R. Livingston is in the N. Y. Pub. Lib. The draft of the circular in the handwriting of DeWitt Clinton is in the DeWitt Clinton Papers, Columbia Univ.

10. *Albany Gazette*, Mar. 5, 1804; *NOMINATION*, Albany, Feb. 18, 1804, William Tabor, chairman, broadside, N. Y. Pub. Lib. William Tabor, chairman of the meeting, was a member of the Assembly, and Joseph Annin, secretary of the meeting, a member of the Senate.

support Burr.[11] This rival faction, denounced by the regular organization as "the *Little* Band,"[12] created a committee of correspondence, which in turn organized a "Committee of 100 Republican Freeholders" of New York to promote Burr's election. When the names of this "Committee of 100" were published in an address supporting Burr's candidacy,[13] the character of the committee was challenged by Republican supporters of Lewis and Broome. They claimed the list of names contained many persons wholly unknown, many generally believed to be without the freehold, and others known to have been uniformly hostile to the Republican cause.[14] Taking their cues from Albany and New York, "Republican Citizens" held meetings in various parts of the state and pledged support to Burr.[15] But Burr's opponents reminded the voters that "the same men and the same party who supported Mr. Jefferson and Governor Clinton, now support Morgan Lewis," and argued: "Morgan Lewis, Esq. is certainly the republican candidate. Has he not been nominated by the almost unanimous voice of the members of the legislature convened from every county in the state? Can any better method be devised to collect the expression of the general will? Is it not our duty as good and faithful men to be governed by the voice of the majority fairly expressed?"[16] Although the bitterly waged contest between Burr and Lewis thus divided the Republican party in New York in 1804, the election of Lewis was accomplished by the Republicans who were able to keep control of the caucus and the regular party organization.[17]

Party machinery in New York was again disrupted by Republican divisions in the gubernatorial race in 1807. This contest once more displayed the influence in state politics of the New York City Republican organization loyal to DeWitt Clinton, now aligned against Governor Lewis. A struggle for control of the Republican party in the state was signaled when a general meeting of Republicans in New York in December 1806 proclaimed that Governor Lewis by forming coalitions with Federalists had forfeited the confidence of Republicans. This

11. *Albany Gazette*, Mar. 5, 1804. Marinus Willett was chairman of this meeting.
12. New York *American Citizen*, Feb. 21, 1804.
13. *To the Republican Electors of the State*, New York, [1804], broadside, N. Y. Pub. Lib.; *Albany Gazette*, Mar. 29, 1804.
14. *To the Republican Electors of Governor and Lieutenant-Governor of the State of New-York*, New York, Apr. 6, 1804, broadside, N.-Y. Hist. Soc.
15. *Albany Gazette*, Mar. 29, Apr. 12, 1804.
16. *To the Independent and True Republican Electors of the State of New-York*, [1804], broadside, N. Y. Pub. Lib.
17. On New York election in 1804 see pp. 209-13 below.

meeting also announced that, in the future, support would be given only to such Republican candidates for governor as should be nominated "by a fair majority of the republican representation of this state, *separately from the federalists.*" These sentiments were circulated through the state in a circular prepared by the "Committee of Correspondence appointed in behalf of the Republicans of the City of New York." The New York Republicans pledged their willingness "to acquiesce in the determination of a fair majority of our republican fellow citizens throughout the state, upon every political occasion," and urged all minorities in the party to yield to the opinions of the majority in order to end the "unhappy divisions which exist among us."[18] On February 16, 1807, two Republican caucuses met in Albany. One, reported to be "a numerous and respectable meeting of Republican members of the Legislature, and Republican Citizens from different parts of this state," nominated Morgan Lewis for re-election as governor and Thomas Storm for lieutenant governor.[19] The other caucus, described as "a numerous meeting of a large majority of the Republican members of the Legislature, and of Republican Citizens from various parts of the state," nominated Daniel D. Tompkins for governor and John Broome for re-election as lieutenant governor.[20] The address published by the caucus favoring Tompkins was signed by 65 members of the legislature and 26 Republican citizens; the address issued by the caucus nominating Lewis carried the names of 105 undesignated participants.

Thus in 1807, as in 1804, rival factions within the Republican party faced each other in a state-wide contest; both groups used the same methods of organization and sought control over the party in the state. If the caucus which nominated Tompkins, can, by virtue of the support of a majority of the Republican members of the legislature, be called the regular party machinery, then once again, with the success of Tompkins in the election, control of the regular party organization led to victory at the polls.

John Nicholas, a Republican supporter of Governor Lewis, credited Tompkins's victory to the superior organizational efforts and influence of

18. [Circular], New York, Dec. 23, 1806, broadside, N.-Y. Hist. Soc.
19. *Republican Nomination, For Governor & Lieut. Governor,* Albany, Feb. 16, 1807, Abraham G. Lansing, chairman, broadside, N.-Y. Hist. Soc.
20. *Republican Nomination,* Albany, Feb. 19, 1807, broadside, N. Y. Pub. Lib. This caucus which met on February 16 reconvened on February 19 to approve an address to the electorate. See also *Supplement to the Albany Register,* Mar. 9, 1807, broadside, N. Y. Pub. Lib.

DeWitt Clinton and his followers. "The organization of their party must have been a most laboured one," he wrote to Secretary of the Navy Robert Smith. He explained:

> Judging from appearance we must believe that every neighborhood had its' committee of correspondence. . . . The sums of money which have been sent to all parts of the state for necessary expences and for securing men of influence must have been immense. . . . There have been 10 papers printed in this state which had no law but DeWitt Clinton's will. There is a complete organization for conveying and enforcing any impressions he wishes to make and he can command any sum of money he pleases. The offices in the City of New York are very lucrative and there are several very rich men over whom he has absolute command and it is his custom I am informed and believe to tax them according to his ideas of their ability and emoluments whenever money is wanted for political purposes. It is said that the election has cost them 60,000 dollars and I can readily believe it.[21]

Since only the governor and lieutenant governor were elected on a state-wide basis in New York, the nomination of candidates for the legislature and for Congress remained in the hands of local and district party organizations. In New York City, party committees chosen in each ward formed the "General Republican Committee" of the city. This committee made nominations, appointed campaign committees, and in general managed party affairs. In the counties throughout the state, party organization varied. In some counties, nominations were made at general party meetings; in others, party committees were appointed to make nominations or to confer with committees from neighboring counties in the legislative or congressional district to agree upon Republican candidates. The appointment of committees, usually called committees of correspondence, to promote the party cause in elections was a common feature of nearly all organizations.[22]

21. John Nicholas to Robert Smith, June 6, 1807, Carter-Smith Family Papers, Univ. of Va. Similar comments on DeWitt Clinton's methods and influence are in John Nicholas to Wilson C. Nicholas, Apr. 2, [1806], Nicholas Papers, Univ. of Va. John Nicholas, a brother of Wilson Cary Nicholas and of Philip Norborne Nicholas, had served in Congress from Virginia from 1793 to 1801 and in 1807 was a member of the New York Senate and of the Council of Appointment. See Philip N. Nicholas to Wilson C. Nicholas, Feb. 24, 1807, Wilson Cary Nicholas Papers, Lib. Cong.

22. New York *American Citizen*, Mar. 1, 2, 3, Apr. 11, Dec. 24, 1804, Apr. 2, 7, 9, 14, 20, 1808; *At a Numerous and Respectable Meeting of Republican Electors of the County of West Chester*, Apr. 9, 1804, broadside, N.-Y. Hist. Soc.; New York *Public Advertiser*, Apr. 20, 1808; Peter Townsend to William P. Van Ness, Apr. 20, 1802, Van Ness Papers, N. Y. Pub. Lib.; *Circular*, New York, Apr. 25, 1805, signed by Theodorus Bailey, chairman, broadside, N. Y. Pub. Lib.

An example of party operations on the county level is furnished by an unusually revealing circular prepared by Republican leaders in Canandaigua in 1808. Anticipating changes in representation under a new census and an end to a joint ticket with neighboring Genesee County, a plan for Republican machinery in Ontario County was proposed. On the subject of nomination, the Canandaigua Republicans explained: "We conceive the most just and efficacious method to be, *the nomination of the Candidates by a County Meeting, composed of town Delegates.* It is *more just,* as the Delegates by their election from the Republicans of each town, will give a fairer expression of their sentiments than if the Delegates were desultory and self-nominated—less subject to intrigue; and by this *double election,* a more correct wish and will of the people is carried into our Legislatures." Suggesting further details, the circular continued:

It is probable that the Republicans can be more conveniently and generally collected on Town-Meeting day than at any other time—to retire after the business of the day is over, and form a meeting—choose a chairman and clerk—discuss the subject, and choose the Delegates—furnish each Delegate with a certificate, signed by the chairman and clerk, as vouchers of their election, and prevent altercations on admitting them to a full vote in nominating the Candidates; from which dissentions have sometimes arisen—to give your Delegates the best information on the probable number of votes your town will give to each party—this will enable the county meeting to calculate on the probable result of the Election. By being somewhat reserved, will prevent the Federalists from knowing the whole of our exertions, and leave them less disposed to exertions on their part.

We suggest that two Delegates from each town will be a competent number, which will make forty for the county. We also think advisable to hold the county meeting on Thursday the 14th of April next, at Phinehas P. Bates' Tavern, punctually at two o'clock, P.M., of which no public notice will be given. The towns which neglect to send Delegates will be unrepresented.

The circular also urged support of the Republican press, particularly the *Genesee Messenger.* To provide for party expenses in printing nominations and handbills, paying for dispatches and expresses, and meeting other expenditures which the Republican interest might require, it was proposed that at the time of electing town delegates each man present pay one shilling. This money was to be sent to the county meeting which would appoint a treasurer and a committee of elections to supervise its expenditures, make arrangements for printing, and handle other details.[23]

This circular reveals the type of party organizing activity found on the county level. It also suggests some of the problems faced: the selection and accreditation of delegates, the support of the party press, and the task of meeting the expenses of the party campaigns. Finally, it indicates an increasing local initiative in party organization and a trend toward more democratic procedures in party operations.

Pennsylvania had been the scene of considerable party activities in the 1790's, and party machinery had early been put into operation in that state. Voters by 1801 were thoroughly familiar with party meetings and corresponding committees, and an unusual amount of popular participation characterized the politics of the state.

In Philadelphia, Republican party machinery was extensive. Its principal feature was a general ward committee composed of five delegates from each of the fourteen wards. The delegates from the wards were appointed at general party meetings, called by public notices and held in the respective wards. The general ward committee made the Republican nominations for the city and appointed conferees to meet with delegates from counties in the senatorial and congressional district to agree on candidates for the state Senate and for Congress. "Committees of vigilance" were also appointed in each ward to distribute tickets and supervise the conduct of elections. In addition, the general ward committee appointed an election committee to act as a general committee of superintendence.[24]

Throughout the state by the early 1800's, the system of general party meetings which had made nominations and appointed committees was being replaced by party machinery based on the participation of delegates chosen by townships, counties, or other electoral units. The procedures adopted by Republicans in most counties rested upon the appointment of delegates by township party meetings to compose a county committee or to attend a county nominating convention. The county committee or

---

23. (*Circular*), Canandaigua, Mar. 23, 1808, signed by Hugh Jameson, Reuben Hart, Michael Brooks, Stephen Bates, broadside, N.-Y. Hist. Soc.

24. Philadelphia *Aurora*, Sept. 4, 1801, May 15, 17, 24, June 4, 6, Aug. 11, Sept. 7, Oct. 1, 9, 26, 1804, July 21, Sept. 8, 1808; Higginbotham, *Keystone in the Democratic Arch*, 36, 45. Election inspectors and assessors were also nominated at ward meetings. *Ibid.*, 36.

the convention nominated candidates for the state House of Representatives and appointed conferees to meet with similar delegates from other counties in the senatorial or congressional district to nominate a candidate for the state Senate or for Congress. In smaller or newly organized counties which shared a state representative with one or more other counties, conferees might make nominations for the state's lower house also. The county committees or conventions appointed sub-committees for specific party activities, published addresses, and, in general, directed the party efforts in elections.[25]

Township committees acted on the local level as campaign committees. A meeting of Chester County Republican delegates in 1804 instructed that "the permanent committee of two in each township be earnestly requested to use every honorable means in their power to promote the election of the candidates named on the . . . ticket, and also to see that none of the republicans remains at home on the day of the election."[26] In time, it became a common practice for county committees to appoint "committees of vigilance" in the various townships "to organize a system of energetic measures." These committees were instructed to distribute party tickets, to get out the vote, and "to use every laudable exertion in their power to promote and secure the democratic interest at the approaching election."[27]

Republicans were much better organized in some counties than in others. A Northampton County Republican leader, Thomas J. Rogers, wrote from Easton in 1803: "With respect to the proper person to whom the Committee of correspondence of Montgomery ought to address their communications to, it is difficult to ascertain. We have no society or even a standing committee of correspondence in this county; indeed those Democrats in the county who might be useful to the cause are not active, which I am sorry to mention." Rogers volunteered to make known any communications addressed to him, explaining that he was generally visited by Democrats from the county whenever they came to Easton.[28]

25. *Montgomery County . . . Republican Committee*, Sept. 25, 1802, Samuel Miles, chairman, broadside, Hist. Soc. of Pa.; Philadelphia *Aurora*, Aug. 16, 1804; John Israel to Albert Gallatin, Aug. 12, 1801, Gallatin Papers, N.-Y. Hist. Soc.; Higginbotham, *Keystone in the Democratic Arch*, 21-22.
26. Philadelphia *Aurora*, Aug. 16, 1804.
27. *Ibid.*, May 7, June 2, 22, Aug. 12, 1808.
28. Thomas J. Rogers to Jonathan Roberts, Jr., Jan. 3, 1803, Jonathan Roberts Papers, Hist. Soc. of Pa. Republicans later became better organized in Northampton County. Philadelphia *Aurora*, May 14, 1808.

In contrast, at about the same time, Republicans in neighboring Bucks County were taking measures to improve the party machinery of that county. An address from the Republican committee of Bucks County explained that in the recent decline of Federalist strength "the appointment of committees to diffuse information, and unite the votes of honest men had a principal effect," and only by a perseverance in the same system could Republicanism be maintained. The committee continued: "Time was in this county, when a few men met at a court, erected themselves into a committee, and assumed the power of forming a ticket for the county." Now Republicans formed their tickets "agreeably to the representative system; by men elected and specially appointed to the service." However, the address suggested, due attention had not been given to the selection of delegates to form the county committee, and symptoms of disunion among Republicans had appeared. Republicans had dissented from the tickets thus proposed, because "these tickets were formed by committees, chosen in such a manner, as to render it doubtful, whether they spoke the sense of the majority. The members in some townships were chosen by a very few votes; and these perhaps given by a candidate and his friends."

Proposing to remedy these evils, the Bucks County committee recommended a detailed plan, the main provisions of which may be viewed as an example of well-organized county party machinery. The committee agreed that "the republican committee of Bucks County shall hereafter be chosen, at the same places, and on the same day, as township officers are chosen" (the third Saturday in March), and that the election shall be conducted in the following manner: (1) the secretary of the committee shall publish notices ten days in advance of the election in one or more newspapers which circulate generally in the county; (2) members of the committee for each township shall see that notices are posted in four or more public places in each township; (3) two judges of the election and a secretary shall be chosen to decide the qualifications of electors, to see that the election is fairly conducted, and to certify the names of the delegates chosen; (4) each township shall elect from one to three delegates but shall have only one vote in the county committee in determining the ticket for the general election; if members for any township are equally divided or cannot agree, the township shall lose its vote; (5) every elector shall have the right to propose nominations and election shall be by ballot; (6) every qualified elector shall have a right to elect or be elected "provided he professes to be a democratic republican and has supported the character for at least six months."

The resolutions further provided that the powers of the previous county committee should cease with the election of the new committee which should hold its first stated meeting on the first Tuesday of September. At this meeting the committee was to propose nominations for county offices, members of the state legislature, and, when required, representatives to Congress. The committee was charged with publishing these proposed nominations in one or more newspapers and was to reconvene on the third Tuesday of September to choose by ballot, from those candidates proposed at the previous meeting, the county Republican ticket. When members of Congress were to be chosen, the county committee was to appoint conferees to meet with those of other counties in the district to agree on a nomination. Extra meetings of the county committee could be held when six members from three townships thought it expedient, provided ample public notice was given.[29] These detailed provisions displayed the attention which was given to party machinery on the county level, and subsequent newspaper reports showed that the Bucks County organization was put into operation.[30] It should be noted, however, that the Bucks County organization was more elaborate than that found in most counties and thus represented the best organized rather than the most typical county machinery.

Persuading Republicans to adhere to the decisions of their delegates was a difficult problem. The Bucks County committee warned that "no committee, however perfectly constituted, can form a ticket to please you all" and urged all Republicans to bow to the will of the majority by supporting the party nominations. "Make your Committees a just representation of the Republican interest—support by your votes the ticket they recommend—and take for your pole star that political maxim, *United We Stand, Divided We Fall*."[31] At times, political aspirants refused to accept the party's nominating decisions. Such a circumstance developed in York County in 1803. Here a meeting of township delegates appointed six delegates to meet with the deputation from neighboring Adams County to agree on a candidate for the state Senate.

29. Resolutions adopted by Republican committee of Bucks County, Newton, Feb. 8, 1803, in Philadelphia *Aurora*, Feb. 23, 1803. The organization of the Chester County committee system is explained in *ibid.*, June 11, Aug. 16, 1804.
30. *Ibid.*, Apr. 19, 1804.
31. *Ibid.*, Feb. 23, 1803.

The candidate of the York delegation, Frederick Eichelberger, proved unacceptable to the Adams County delegates, and another candidate was agreed upon.[32] However, Eichelberger refused to recognize the decision of the conference and announced that he was still a candidate on the basis of having been nominated by the delegates of York County. "It might certainly be considered contrary to the principles heretofore established by the Republicans, to come forward as a Candidate, after a Ticket had been settled," he admitted, but he felt he was a proper candidate "as the Delegates of this county had fixed upon a Ticket, by which I was nominated." Eichelberger's actions were denounced as improper efforts "to innovate upon the established usage of York and Adams Counties," and he was criticized for soliciting support for his own election. Eichelberger refused to withdraw, but he was defeated in the election.[33] Such difficulties led to the practice of delegates being required to affirm their loyalty to the party ticket. For example, at a meeting of Republican delegates from the several townships of Chester County, in August 1804, to nominate a ticket to be supported at the next election, it was resolved that "the delegates present do pledge their words and their sacred honors, that they will support the ticket which shall be formed this day."[34]

Because of divisions among Pennsylvania Republicans,[35] the party machinery did not always operate smoothly. When Republican divisions arose, party factions commonly resorted to factional caucuses to make their plans and decisions, and then they attempted to gain control over the regular party machinery. Thomas Leiper reported in 1804 that a meeting of the general ward committee in Philadelphia broke up because it was impossible to keep order between opposing groups attempting to win control of the party machinery.[36] In Philadelphia County in 1804, two rival delegations sought the right to confer with the delegates from Philadelphia and Delaware County to nominate a congressional candidate for the district. One group of delegates, opposed to the nomination of

32. *Fellow-Citizens of York County*, York, Oct. 5, 1803, broadside, Amer. Antiq. Soc.
33. *To the Public, and to Frederick Eichelberger, the Man who wishes to introduce a new mode of Senatorial Electioneering*, [1803], *A Caution! To the Free & Independent Electors of York County*, [1803], *To the Independent Electors of York and Adams Counties*, [1803], broadsides, Amer. Antiq. Soc.
34. Philadelphia *Aurora*, Aug. 16, 1804; for similar examples see *ibid.*, June 23, 1804, Sept. 8, 1808.
35. See pp. 214-20 below.
36. Leiper to Jefferson, Aug. 16, 1804, Jefferson Papers, Lib. Cong.

Dr. Michael Leib, was appointed by meetings held in districts. The other delegation, supporting Leib, was chosen at a general county meeting of "Democratic Citizens." Faced with deciding between the two groups, the Philadelphia city conferees at first proposed to double their own representation and meet with both delegations, but when the district delegates rejected this plan, the city conferees met with the delegates chosen by the county meeting, and the nomination of Leib was agreed upon.[37]

Republican state party machinery was not so well organized as most county systems. In 1802, Governor Thomas McKean was renominated by a Republican legislative caucus.[38] But the "State Committee of Republicans" was appointed by a meeting of Republicans of the city and county of Philadelphia. Established "to correspond with the committees of the several counties of the State," and composed of eight prominent Republicans,[39] this committee directed the state-wide campaign. The election address issued by this committee was the most important Republican campaign leaflet to appear during the campaign.[40]

In the presidential election of 1804, "under an impression that it would be acceptable to their fellow-citizens, the republican members of the legislature of Pennsylvania convened in the chamber of the Senate" on March 22 to nominate the Republican list of electors to be popularly chosen on a general ticket. A committee appointed to prepare an address in support of the party slate reported to a second meeting of the caucus on March 31, and its address was adopted and published.[41] Various party meetings, particularly in Philadelphia, adopted resolutions approving of the caucus nominations, but in view of the feebleness of Federalist opposition there was a minimum of party activity relating to the presidential contest.[42]

37. Philadelphia *Aurora*, June 23, Aug. 17, 22, Sept. 7, 1804. See also Higginbotham, *Keystone in the Democratic Arch*, 70.
38. *Ibid.*, 41.
39. Peter Muhlenberg, Richard Bache, Samuel Miles, Alexander J. Dallas, William Jones, Matthew Lawler, Michael Leib, and Thomas Leiper.
40. *Address of the State Committee of Republicans*, Philadelphia, Sept. 21, 1802 (Phila., 1802), pamphlet, Hist. Soc. of Pa.; also published in Washington *National Intelligencer*, Oct. 4, 1802.
41. Philadelphia *Aurora*, Apr. 4, July 9, Oct. 3, 25, Nov. 2, 1804; New York *American Citizen*, Apr. 6, 1804.
42. Philadelphia *Aurora*, Oct. 19, 26, 27, Nov. 4, 1804; *To the Democratic Republican Electors, of the State of Pennsylvania*, [1804], signed Benjamin Franklin Bache [pseud.], broadside, Lib. Cong.

The party machinery employed in the gubernatorial race of 1805 markedly displayed Republican divisions in Pennsylvania. A caucus of fifty Republican members of the legislature rejected Governor McKean and nominated Simon Snyder as the Republican candidate for governor. Then twenty-six other Republican members of the legislature, joined by eight Federalists, recommended the re-election of Governor McKean.[43] The direction of McKean's campaign was assumed by the recently organized Society of Constitutional Republicans (also known as Quids), which had been formed in March 1805 to marshal opposition to demands for a constitutional convention to revise the state constitution. Of the ten leaders who sponsored the organization of this society, five had been members of the state committee of Republicans in 1802.[44] Led by Alexander James Dallas, William Jones, and George Logan, the society appointed a corresponding committee, issued an address in support of McKean, and organized supporters throughout the state.[45]

To counteract the influence of this organization, the Republican supporters of Snyder organized the "Democratic Society of Friends of the People." Officers of the society included three members of the state committee of Republicans in 1802: Matthew Lawler, president; Thomas Leiper, one of two vice-presidents; and Michael Leib, one of the five members of the committee of correspondence, which also included William Duane and Joseph Clay.[46] All eight members of the 1802 committee were thus actively engaged in the organization of one or the other of the two Republican factions in 1805.

The Democratic Society of Friends of the People drew up a constitution to be subscribed to by branches of the society in counties throughout the state. It provided that in joining the society members must affirm their belief in the principles of the Declaration of Independence and the

43. *The Address of the Members of the General Assembly agreed upon at a Numerous Meeting held after a General Notice at Lancaster on April 3d, 1805* [n.p., 1805], pamphlet, Lib. Cong.; Higginbotham, *Keystone in the Democratic Arch*, 87, 89.

44. Alexander J. Dallas, William Jones, Richard Bache, Peter Muhlenberg, and Samuel Miles; other sponsors were George Logan, Samuel Wetherill, Guy Bryan, Chandler Price, and Manuel Eyre. *The Society of Constitutional Republicans*, Philadelphia, Mar. 16, 1805, signed by Alexander J. Dallas and others, broadside, Amer. Antiq. Soc.

45. A manuscript "List of Signers of the 'Society of Constitutional Republicans,'" in the Gallatin Papers, N.-Y. Hist. Soc., contains 110 names. See also *The Address of the Society of Constitutional Republicans, established in the City and County of Philadelphia, to the Republicans of Pennsylvania, . . . 10th of June, 1805* (Phila., 1805), pamphlet, Lib. Cong.; Higginbotham, *Keystone in the Democratic Arch*, 82-83, 89-90.

46. *Constitution of the Democratic Society of Friends of the People*, Philadelphia, Apr. 13, 1805 (Phila., 1805), pamphlet, Hist. Soc. of Pa.

right of the majority of the people, by duly chosen representatives, to amend their state constitution. New members also had to pledge "to support and promote the harmony and prosperity" of the society by at all times conforming to the "determinations of the majority of the Democratic party, expressed by them in general meeting or by their delegates convened by public notice." The constitution further provided that any member who should violate the principles of the society's constitution or "oppose himself to the democratic interest of the State, shall be expelled [from] the Society." Tickets of membership, costing fifty cents, were necessary for admission to all meetings.[47]

Existing county committee systems were temporarily replaced by county societies of Constitutional Republicans or of Democratic Friends of the People. A manuscript letter from "The General Committee of Correspondence of the Chester County Society of Friends of the People, To the Corresponding Committee of Montgomery County," July 16, 1805, reveals that the county organizations operated in much the same way as previous county committees. The Chester County committee sought communications from neighboring counties and stressed that the activities of Governor McKean's supporters had made it necessary "to adopt such a system of organization as might at once enable us to conduct our proceedings with regularity and order and give to our operations the greatest energy and effect."[48]

The supporters of Simon Snyder represented the majority of Pennsylvania Republicans and made extensive efforts to obtain the election of their candidate through the established party machinery which they controlled as well as through the new devices of the Democratic Society of Friends of the People. But the Constitutional Republicans, though less well organized than their opponents,[49] were able, by attracting the support of the Federalists, to re-elect Governor McKean. The Society of Constitutional Republicans and the Democratic Society of Friends of the People displayed the critical schism within the Republican party. Each group was forced to provide temporary devices for party operations under such circumstances, but neither organization introduced changes which substantially altered the structure of party machinery in the state.

The election of 1808 brought significant developments in the operation

47. *Ibid.*
48. Letter signed by John E. Porter, secretary, July 16, 1805, in Jonathan Roberts Papers, Hist. Soc. of Pa.
49. William Barton to Alexander J. Dallas, Nov. 19, 1805, Dallas Papers, Hist. Soc. of Pa.

of party machinery in Pennsylvania. "Feuds among the republican party seem to be wearing away," observed one active political figure at the beginning of 1808,[50] and, as the year continued, an increasing harmony and unity among Republicans became more and more evident. Although party division did not entirely disappear, the reuniting of Republicans was reflected in the party machinery.

On January 6, 1808, the "democratic members of the senate and house of representatives" met in caucus in Lancaster and agreed that it was "consistent with sound democratic principles, that the members of the democratic party, should have the opportunity, either by themselves or their representatives, to participate in the selection of all public functionaries, who are to represent them." It was further resolved that "in the present momentous crisis of our affairs, every rational and just expedient should be employed, to harmonize and consolidate the democratic party, to the end that success might attend their patriotic efforts." It was therefore agreed "that the democratic citizens of those counties or districts in the state, who have not a democratic representation in the general assembly, be invited to nominate delegates, in proportion to the number of representatives each of said counties or districts has in the house of representatives, for the purpose of fixing upon candidates, for the office of governor; and electors of a president and vice president of the United States." The delegates so nominated were requested to meet at Lancaster on the first Monday in March.[51]

This decision to replace the legislative caucus with a combination caucus-convention was in part the result of a movement which had been started in the state to hold a state nominating convention. Apparently originating with a faction which hoped thereby to block the nomination of Simon Snyder as governor, the proposal had been made that the nominations for governor and presidential electors be made by delegates specifically chosen for that purpose. Although approved by a Philadelphia meeting in September 1807, the plan, regarded as a scheme to defeat Snyder, did not win wide support in the state at large.[52] Nevertheless, the invitation to counties without representation in the party caucus to participate in the nominations was designed to allay criticism of the

50. Jonathan Roberts, Jr., to Jonathan Roberts, Sr., Jan. 8, 1808, Jonathan Roberts Papers, Hist. Soc. of Pa.
51. Philadelphia *Aurora*, Jan. 11, 1808; Jonathan Roberts, Jr., to Jonathan Roberts, Sr., Jan. 8, 1808, Jonathan Roberts Papers, Hist. Soc. of Pa.
52. Higginbotham, *Keystone in the Democratic Arch*, 142-43, 151.

caucus nominating procedure. The invitation to send delegates to the "conference," or "convention" (both terms were used), was speedily acted upon in a number of localities.[53] In Philadelphia, ward meetings appointed delegates to the general ward committee which convened and chose a delegation of five members, including Thomas Leiper and William Duane, to attend the conference.[54]

The "Democratic Conference" met at Lancaster on March 7. Thomas Leiper was chosen chairman, and Michael Leib was appointed one of the two secretaries. Before nominations were proposed, it was resolved: "That every member of this conference will consider himself bound, and hereby pledges himself to support by every honorable means in his power, the nominations that shall have been agreed upon." Simon Snyder was then nominated as the candidate for governor, and a ticket of presidential electors was agreed upon. Because Republican sympathies were divided between George Clinton and James Madison for the presidency, the electoral ticket was a compromise slate which was not pledged to either candidate but was presented as composed of "the friends of Jefferson, and of democratic principles." A "committee of general correspondence" was appointed with Leib, Duane, and Leiper among its seven members. The conference, reconvening on the second day, adopted an address in support of the nominations to which eighty-three delegates affixed their signatures.[55]

A subsequent meeting of Constitutional Republicans, composed of thirty-eight members of the legislature, placed in nomination for governor John Spayd and formed an electoral ticket pledged to support Madison for president and Clinton for vice-president. But in the course of the campaign, as more and more Constitutional Republicans became reconciled with the majority Republicans, the Constitutional Republican faction disintegrated. Its remnants ultimately accepted the electoral ticket nominated by the Democratic Conference with the substitution of one name.[56]

The state committee of correspondence appointed by the Democratic Conference took charge of the Republican campaign. Letters which the

53. Philadelphia *Aurora*, Feb. 8, 19, 27, 1808.
54. *Ibid.*, Feb. 4, 12, 16, 19, 22, 1808.
55. *Ibid.*, Mar. 10, 1808; see also Jefferson to Thomas Mann Randolph, Mar. 15, 1808, Jefferson Papers, Univ. of Va.
56. Higginbotham, *Keystone in the Democratic Arch*, 154-55, 170-74; Richmond *Enquirer*, Apr. 8, 1808.

committee sent to county committees throughout the state were followed by considerable local activity, particularly in holding meetings at which resolutions were passed in support of the nominations made at the Lancaster Democratic Conference. At a number of meetings resolutions were also passed supporting the congressional caucus nomination of Madison for president and Clinton for vice-president and expressing confidence in Jefferson and the Embargo policy.[57] The addresses issued by the state committee set the tone for the campaign, and, when the committee came out in full support of Madison, all hope of the supporters of Clinton vanished.[58]

The revival of Federalist activity, encouraged by discontent with the Embargo, played an important role in promoting Republican co-operation in Pennsylvania in 1808; rival party organizations could not be tolerated at the risk of inviting a Federalist resurgence. The sweeping victory of Snyder in the gubernatorial race and of Republican electors in the presidential contest was proof of the re-emergence of Republican unity in the state.

Republicans in New Jersey in 1800 had organized an extensive system of committees which included township and county committees, and a general meeting of deputies from the counties met in 1800 to nominate the Republican ticket of presidential electors.[59] In 1801, Democratic associations were organized in several counties, introducing a plan of party organization which soon was adopted in a number of counties. "At a meeting of a large number of the Republican Citizens of Cumberland County," early in February 1801, it was agreed "to form an Association in the County," and a committee of three was appointed to draft a plan and to report on March 4, when Republicans would gather to celebrate the election of Jefferson. As instructed, the committee presented at

---

57. Philadelphia *Aurora*, May 7, 14, 16, 17, June 1, 2, 22, July 9, Aug. 9, 12, 1808.
58. *Address of the State Committee of Correspondence, to the Citizens of Pennsylvania, July 25, 1808* [Phila., 1808], pamphlet, Hist. Soc. of Pa.; also published in Philadelphia *Aurora*, Aug. 8, 1808. For other addresses see *Aurora*, June 7, 23, 1808.
59. For details of this organization see Cunningham, *Jeffersonian Republicans, 1789-1801*, 154-58; for election machinery see Richard P. McCormick, *The History of Voting in New Jersey: A Study of the Development of Election Machinery, 1664-1911* (New Brunswick, 1953), 111-15, and J. R. Pole, "Jeffersonian Democracy and the Federalist Dilemma in New Jersey, 1798-1812," New Jersey Historical Society, *Proceedings*, 74 (1956), 260-92. For treatment of issues in the state politics of New Jersey see Walter R. Fee, *The Transition from Aristocracy to Democracy in New Jersey, 1789-1829* (Somerville, 1933), 100-69.

the March 4 gathering a "Declaration and Form of Association," which was approved, and the committee was directed to send a copy to each township in the county. Republicans carried out the proposals by appointing township committees, which then appointed representatives to a county committee. This committee met in June, corrected and approved the "Declaration and Form of the Association," and ordered three hundred copies of it printed. A corresponding committee of three members was also appointed. The "Form of the Association," as approved by the county committee, provided that members of the association should assemble in their respective townships on the third Tuesday of February to appoint a township committee consisting of nine members. In turn, the township committee was to elect three persons to represent it in the county committee. Subsequent meetings of the township committees were to be held on specified days in May, September, and November and at such other times as the county committee should direct. The duties of the township committees were: to receive all communications from the corresponding and county committees, to procure and disseminate information, and to communicate to the county committee the views and wishes of the township. The county committee was to meet on designated days in February, June, September, and November and "at such other times as a majority of them may think proper, or as the Corresponding-Committee may judge necessary." The corresponding committee of three members appointed by the county committee was to meet on the third Wednesday of every month and "at such other times as they may think expedient."[60]

In Gloucester County, a "Constitution of Association" was presented at a Republican meeting on March 4, 1801, signed by a number of new members, and three hundred copies were ordered printed. It provided that general meetings of the association be held on March 4 and on designated days in August, October, and January. At the March meeting a president, vice-president, treasurer, and committee of correspondence were to be elected. The committee of correspondence was to consist of two or more members in each township and was instructed to "collect such political or other information as may be beneficial to the institution; to correspond with similar societies that are or may be formed in this

60. *A Declaration of the Principles and Views of the Democratic-Federalists, in the County of Cumberland, and State of New-Jersey, with their Form of Association* (Phila., 1801), pamphlet, Lib. Cong.

state or elsewhere, . . . and in case of a state meeting to appoint delegates to attend the same." The president was authorized to call special meetings of the association. Members were to pay fifty cents upon joining and twenty-five cents per year to support the activities of the society. After March 4, 1801, no person was to be admitted as a member except upon recommendation of a majority of the committee of correspondence in the township in which he resided and by a majority of members present at a general meeting. Members could be expelled for disorderly conduct or for "holding sentiments contrary to the principles of this constitution" by a plurality of votes of members present.[61] The dues paid by the members of the Gloucester association permitted the publication of proceedings and of political addresses. Five hundred copies of one address were printed and distributed.[62]

The Hunterdon County association provided that Republican meetings in each township should elect a standing committee, of as many members as thought proper, and that the chairmen of the several township committees were to constitute the county committee of correspondence.[63] The constitutions of these Democratic associations thus differed in details. Their activities, however, were similar. They nominated party tickets, supported them in the election campaigns, circulated party literature, and, in general, promoted the Republican interest in their respective counties.[64]

Federalists reported in 1803 that Democratic associations had been formed in the counties of Hunterdon, Burlington, Gloucester, Salem, Cumberland, and possibly in Monmouth; and there was also a Democratic association in Cape May County.[65] Explaining that "the settled Democratic plan" was to form "*Combinations* . . . assuming the name of *Democratic* Associations," a Federalist leaflet denounced them as "political machines" and protested:

61. *Proceedings of the Democratic Association of Gloucester County, New-Jersey: at Several Meetings held in the Month of March, 1801, to which is added the Constitution of the Society* [n.p., 1801], pamphlet, Lib. Cong.

62. James Sloan, *An Address, delivered at a Meeting of the Democratic Association of the County of Gloucester, held in the Court-house at Woodbury, on the thirty-first of August, 1801*, by James Sloan, president (Trenton, [1801]), pamphlet, Lib. Cong. See also James Sloan, *An Oration, delivered at a Meeting of the Democratic Association of the County of Gloucester, held in the Court-house at Woodbury, on the fourth day of March, 1802* (Trenton, 1802), pamphlet, Hist. Soc. of Pa.

63. The Hunterdon articles of association are printed in George D. Luetscher, *Early Political Machinery in the United States* (Phila., 1903), 89-91.

64. Trenton *True American*, Sept. 20, Dec. 20, 1802.

65. Fee, *Transition from Aristocracy to Democracy in New Jersey*, 133.

They are Permanent bodies—self elected—extending over Counties and Townships. They have Presidents, Secretaries, and Committees—subscribe articles—and bind themselves to pursue the objects of the association, which are *political*. They annually elect Delegates—and have stated meetings, exercising jurisdiction and influence over greater or smaller districts. Tho' not elected by the people at large, and not composing a tenth part of the citizens, they assume power even greater than that of the Legislature.

Looking into the public prints, they are weekly seen filled with the Proceedings and Acts of these Associations. It would seem as if an entire *new* Government was organized.

These meetings pass general Votes of Censure against Officers, chosen by the people in Joint-Meeting—on courts of Justice—on Grand Juries—on particular Classes and Professions in society—affect to be the guardians of the elective privilege—to superintend, with their joint numbers and influence, the proceedings of our *Constituted Authorities*. . . . Above all they meet and *absolutely determine* who shall be elected into the public departments! And this in secret—without the participation of other citizens, or giving an opportunity for defence or exculpation.[66]

Despite the spread of the association plan, Republican party machinery in New Jersey remained a mixed system. Some counties retained their earlier committee organizations. Newspapers reported Republican tickets which were nominated by "the Republican Committees from the several townships" of Salem, by the "Republican Committee, from all the Townships of Morris," by the "Republican Electors of the county of Essex," and by other Republican meetings, as well as by Democratic associations.[67] As time passed, the Democratic associations appear to have been abandoned in favor of a return to committee systems. At least, the Gloucester Democratic association, which had been one of the earliest and most vigorous associations, was no longer active in 1807, though the same party leadership in the county continued. James Sloan, who had been president of the Gloucester association, was president of "a meeting of the Democratic Republicans of the county of Gloucester" convened to make nominations in August 1807.[68] The absence of newspaper reports

66. *Serious Considerations addressed to the Electors of New-Jersey concerning the Choice of Members of the Legislature for the Ensuing Year* [n.p., 1803], pamphlet, Lib. Cong.

67. Trenton *True American*, Sept. 20, 1802, Sept. 5, 26, 1803; Newark *Centinel of Freedom*, Oct. 4, 1803; Morristown *Genius of Liberty*, June 1, 1804.

68. *At a Meeting of the Democratic Republicans of the County of Gloucester, convened by Advertisement . . . 31st day of August, 1807* [n.p., 1807], pamphlet, Lib. Cong.

regarding the activities of the associations suggests their decline elsewhere in the state by 1808.

Party organization on the state level rested on the mixed system of county committees and associations. Republican party nominations for members of Congress, elected on a general ticket, and for presidential electors, also popularly elected on a general ticket in 1804 and 1808, were agreed upon at state party conventions. Since the delegates to these conventions were chosen in accordance with various county procedures, a certain amount of irregularity thus prevailed in the state party machinery, but the convention system appears to have operated without serious difficulty. In November 1803, "agreeably to public notice previously given, the Delegates from the several counties" of the state, with the exception of the county of Cape May, convened at Trenton; and, according to their report, "after a candid interchange of sentiment among the Delegates," a slate of Republican candidates for Congress was nominated. In recommending the ticket, the delegates urged that *"union* and *exertion"* prevail in its support.[69]

In 1804, a "State Convention," attended by "Delegates from the several Counties," was held at Trenton to nominate candidates for presidential electors and for Congress. In recommending the ticket agreed upon, the delegates emphasized that in the selection of candidates they had tried to accommodate the different parts of the state.[70] In 1806, delegates chosen by Republican county meetings met again in convention at Trenton and nominated the Republican ticket for Congress; the same delegates were also summoned by the president of that convention to convene, in February 1808, to nominate a congressional candidate for a special election to fill a vacancy caused by the death of one of New Jersey's representatives. This Republican convention passed resolutions calling for "Republican Delegates in the different counties to meet in convention" at Trenton in September 1808 to nominate candidates for the Eleventh Congress and for presidential electors.[71]

County delegates to this convention generally were appointed at the same time that county tickets were formed. The method of selection, as well as the number of delegates appointed, varied, though each county had

---

69. Newark *Centinel of Freedom*, Nov. 29, 1803.

70. Morristown *Genius of Liberty*, Sept. 13, Nov. 1, 1804; Newark *Centinel of Freedom*, Sept. 18, Nov. 6, 1804; Joseph Bloomfield to Jonathan Dayton, Nov. 12, 1804, Jonathan Dayton Papers, Rutgers Univ.

71. Newark *Centinel of Freedom*, Feb. 16, Mar. 1, Aug. 2, 1808.

two votes at the convention. A "Sussex Democratic Meeting" appointed two delegates; a "meeting of the Republican Committees of the different Townships of the county of Essex" chose five delegates; Morris County sent four delegates.[72] The Republican delegates from the various counties accordingly met in convention at Trenton on September 21, 1808, and nominated the Republican ticket for electors and representatives to Congress. An address in support of the ticket was also adopted and ordered to be published. The ticket was balanced to contain persons from different parts of the state in order to preserve "union and harmony in the Republican interest."[73] In Newark, a Republican meeting two weeks later passed resolutions agreeing to support the nominations made by the convention.[74]

New Jersey Republican party machinery was thus a complete system extending from township committees, through county committees, to a state convention. It was a decentralized organization, permitting variations of party procedures on the local and county level; and Republicans took pride in contrasting the public character of their party meetings and proceedings with the secret arrangements of the Federalists.[75]

Republican party machinery in Delaware rested on the party organization of the state's three counties, New Castle, Kent, and Sussex, in which similar systems operated. In 1800, at a county party meeting, the Republicans of New Castle County, where the party was strongest in the state, appointed a committee of two for each hundred in the county. In the following year a similar county meeting, in addition to appointing committees in the several hundreds, also appointed a four-member committee of correspondence and chose three delegates to meet those of other counties to nominate a Republican candidate for governor. Although there is no record of the assembling of this convention, county meetings in each of the three counties nominated David Hall for governor in September 1801, suggesting that correspondence among them was effectively organized.[76]

As party organization developed, the party machinery in each county

72. *Ibid.*, Aug. 30, Sept. 6, 13, 1808.
73. *Ibid.*, Sept. 27, Oct. 25, 1808; Elizabeth-Town *New-Jersey Journal*, Sept. 27, 1808.
74. Newark *Centinel of Freedom*, Oct. 11, 1808.
75. *Ibid.*, Nov. 6, 1804. On Federalist proceedings in New Jersey see Philadelphia *Aurora*, Nov. 5, 1804; Pole, "Jeffersonian Democracy and the Federalist Dilemma in New Jersey, 1798-1812," N. J. Hist. Soc., *Proceedings*, 74 (1956), 260-92.
76. Luetscher, *Early Political Machinery*, 147-48; Munroe, *Federalist Delaware*, 228-29.

came to consist of a county committee composed of members from each hundred, a county corresponding committee, and local committees in each hundred. Most of the county organization was initiated by the county party meeting, which appointed the county committee, the county corresponding committee, and at times the hundred committees.[77] In 1802, the Republicans of New Castle County resolved "that committees be chosen by the Republicans in each hundred . . . to consist of not less than twelve citizens whose duty it shall be to communicate and cooperate with the Committee of Correspondence and Arrangement."[78] A notice in the Wilmington *Mirror of the Times,* in July 1804, called a general meeting of the Republican citizens of New Castle to meet at the Red Lion Inn "in order to agree on the time, and number to be chosen as a Committee for each hundred in the county by the citizens of the several hundreds; also what number shall be chosen for the County Committee in the several hundreds."[79] Thus the hundred committees, in New Castle County at least, came to be chosen by each hundred rather than by the county meeting.

In the framing of Republican county tickets, there were some differences in nomination procedure among the county organizations. Some nominations were made at county meetings; others were made by county nominating committees.[80] Self-nomination of candidates was disapproved. The method of nomination which came to be adopted in New Castle County was exhibited at a meeting of "Democratic Republican Citizens," in September 1808, when it was recommended that on the day of hundred elections each hundred choose its delegates to nominate the county ticket for the legislature.[81]

On the state level, Republican organization was displayed in 1802, when a "Democratic Republican Meeting" composed of "delegates chosen at a meeting of the people of the several counties" was held at Dover and Caesar A. Rodney was nominated as the Republican candidate for

---

77. Washington *National Intelligencer,* Sept. 17, 1802; Wilmington *Mirror of the Times,* May 26, June 2, 23, 27, July 25, Sept. 15, 26, 1804; *The Address of the Democratic Republican Corresponding Committee of New-Castle County* [Wilmington 1804], signed by George Read and seven others, pamphlet, Lib. Cong.; Luetscher, *Early Political Machinery,* 96-97.

78. *Delaware Gazette,* July 17, 1802, quoted in Luetscher, *Early Political Machinery,* 96.

79. *Mirror of the Times,* July 25, 1804.

80. *Ibid.,* May 26, June 2, 23, Sept. 15, 1804; Luetscher, *Early Political Machinery,* 97.

81. *At a Very Numerous . . . Meeting of the Democratic Republican Citizens of New-Castle County,* Sept. 3, 1808, broadside, Lib. Cong.

Delaware's one seat in the United States House of Representatives.[82] In 1804, a similar convention, attended by "gentlemen selected as Conferees by the people from the several counties," nominated the Republican candidates for governor and for Congress. The names of the conferees were published in the newspapers, showing ten delegates from New Castle, seven from Kent, and nine from Sussex.[83]

This method of making state-wide nominations became the accepted Republican procedure.[84] When a similar convention at Dover in 1805 nominated a Republican candidate to run in a special election for Congress, a circular from the "President of the Democratic Republican corresponding committee for Newcastle County" to the hundred committees of the county urged activity in support of this nomination, explaining:

In appealing, on the approaching General Election, to the undiminished zeal and unwearied perserverance of the Democratic Republican Citizens of Newcastle County, through their regular organs, the Hundred Committees, the Corresponding Committee for the County, feel all the confidence inspired by a thorough knowledge of their firmness and devotion to the general interest. . . . A Representative to Congress for this state is to be chosen . . . and David Hall is the Candidate selected for the office by the Democratic Republican Conferees on the occasion of their late meeting at the town of Dover. The Conferees from Newcastle County were chosen by the people themselves, and made the selection, we firmly believe, with a disinterested view to the general good. In deliberately weighing the act, we are decidedly of opinion, that it is the duty as well as policy of every Democratic Citizen to afford it his utmost support. That each individual should be gratified with the selection for office of the man he most approves, is not to be expected; as much, if not more difference of opinion, existing among men with respect to fitness for office than almost on any other subject;—hence the necessity of adopting a method by which unanimity may be produced. The mode resorted to on this occasion (choosing Representatives to express the will of the people) conforms to the soundest principle of Democracy.[85]

82. Caesar A. Rodney to Jefferson, June 19, 1802; [Dover Address], Daniel Blaney, chairman, to Jefferson, June 5, 1802, Jefferson Papers, Lib. Cong.

83. Wilmington *Mirror of the Times,* June 30, 1804.

84. *At a Very Numerous . . . Meeting of the Democratic Republican Citizens of New-Castle County,* Sept. 3, 1808, broadside, Lib. Cong., reports the appointment of delegates to meet at Dover with delegates of other counties to nominate a Republican candidate for Congress.

85. *CIRCULAR, To the Democratic Republican Hundred Committees, of the Respective Hundreds of Newcastle County,* Sept. 14, 1805, broadside, Lib. Cong.

As this circular suggests, the county corresponding committees were the unifying forces which maintained contact among the Republican committees in the three counties and which encouraged and aided the hundred committees in their respective counties. They also sent general instructions such as the above circular's further recommendation to the hundred committees "to meet together on the 25th of this month in your respective Hundreds, and concert and determine on the general plan of operation, and the best means of bringing the people forward to the Election."[86] The corresponding committees also published addresses to the voters, discussing the issues in the election and recommending Republican candidates.[87] The hundred committees were largely election committees which superintended the party efforts in the campaign in each hundred.[88]

Judged in the light of later trends in the structure of parties in the United States, the middle states exhibited the most advanced party organization in the country at this time. In New Jersey and Delaware, state party conventions were being employed. In Pennsylvania, the delegate system prevailed in the operation of most party machinery below the state level, and on the state level the caucus was replaced in 1808 by a caucus-convention which employed the delegate principle. Only in New York did a state party caucus continue to supply the basic statewide party organization throughout the period, but in county and city organizations the system of delegates, generally referred to as committees, was widely used in making nominations and directing party affairs.

Thus, the Republican party machinery of the middle states, on the whole, displayed less centralization and more popular participation in party activities and decisions than that of the New England states. But the opportunity for the expression of the public will from the ground upward through the party structure did not, of course, eliminate the management of the party machinery by the same party leaders who had run the party when it was more informally organized. George Clinton

86. *Ibid.*
87. See "Address of the Committee of Correspondence of Kent County, to the Free Electors of said County," Sept. 4, 1802, in Washington *National Intelligencer*, Sept. 17, 1802; *Address of the Democratic Republican Corresponding Committee of New-Castle County* [1804], pamphlet, Lib. Cong.
88. Federalist party machinery in Delaware was very similar to that of the Republicans. See Wilmington *Monitor; or, Delaware Federalist*, Sept. 1, 1802; Wilmington *Federal Ark*, May 30, 1804; Munroe, *Federalist Delaware*, 235-37.

or DeWitt Clinton in New York, Michael Leib or William Duane in Pennsylvania, and James Sloan in New Jersey, still continued to play influential roles in party affairs, but the devices of party management made provision for an increasing public participation in the activities of the party.

Party machinery on the county and local levels in the middle states reflected varying degrees of local party vitality and organizational durability, but there was an extensive amount of formal party machinery throughout the states of the area. The disruptions of the regular party machinery by internal divisions, as in New York and Pennsylvania, also tended to multiply, at least temporarily, the machinery of parties. While the legitimacy of party organization in the New England states was still being questioned, party machinery in the middle states had come to be accepted as a normal part of the political system.

CHAPTER EIGHT

Party Machinery in the South and the West

The Republican party was strong in most areas of the South and the West, but formal party machinery was less fully developed there than in New England or in the middle states. The elaborate Republican machinery in Virginia stands out in contrast to the informal party organization that prevailed in most of the southern and western states.

In Maryland, where the governor was elected by the legislature and congressmen and presidential electors were chosen by districts, there were no state-wide elections. Under these conditions no formal state party machinery had been instituted. In cities, counties, and districts a variety of Republican party machinery was found in operation. This machinery reflected Maryland's border state location. While some candidates nominated themselves for office, as was common in the states south of Maryland, other candidates were chosen by conferees, conventions, or nominating committees, such as those found in Pennsylvania, Delaware, or New Jersey. The newspapers regularly published notices of candidates who were self-nominated or informally proposed by their friends, and some candidates announced their candidacies in handbills.[1] At the same time, in certain counties nominations were effectively controlled by organized party machinery.

Examples of formal party organization can be found in Prince George's and Anne Arundel counties. At a Republican meeting in Prince George's County in April 1804, it was agreed that "a general understanding of republicans, as far as practicable, would tend to ensure success at the ensuing elections of electors of president and vice-president, member of congress, and delegates to the general assembly." It was

---

1. Baltimore *American*, Sept. 4, 7, Oct. 5, 1804, Aug. 30, 31, 1808; Annapolis *Maryland Gazette*, July 21, Aug. 4, 1803, May 31, Aug. 23, 1804, Aug. 7, Sept. 18, 1806; David Kerr, *To the Voters of Talbot County*, Aug. 11, 1803, broadside, Maryland Historical Society.

therefore recommended that Republicans throughout the county meet at their respective places of election on the last Saturday of April and appoint seven delegates in each district. These delegates were to assemble and nominate the Republican candidates for the legislature. The same delegates were also to appoint committees to confer with similar committees in the congressional district and in the electoral district in order to choose the Republican nominees for Congress and for presidential elector. The Republican meeting which proposed this procedure pledged to support the candidates so nominated by "all fair and honourable means."[2] These nominating procedures were carried out in Prince George's County[3] and were imitated in neighboring Anne Arundel County, where soon after the Prince George's County Republicans had put their organization into operation a Republican meeting in Annapolis resolved to adopt the same procedures.[4]

The conferees from Prince George's and Anne Arundel counties who made the nomination of a congressional candidate defended this means of deciding the party's nomination in an address declaring:

Tis with concern and regret we hear a measure so necessary to the success of republicanism denounced as dangerous to liberty, and destroying the freedom of election, and this too by men who heretofore have been most forward in promoting committee meetings. It is true, that did there not exist among us two conflicting parties, divided in their views as to every leading measure of the general and state governments, there could be no necessity, previous to an election, to collect the sense of the people as to the candidate. . . . But while there does exist two such parties, we cannot but feel anxious to unite our friends. . . .

If it is necessary to collect the sense of republicans, in order to concentrate their efforts against their political opponents, who, on all occasions, act with unanimity, what better mode can be devised, than for the people to meet in the different election districts, and sending forward members to compose a general committee, to consult among themselves as to the characters, as candidates most likely to give satisfaction? This was done in most of the districts in both counties. If some of them were unrepresented, the fault was their own.[5]

These remarks indicate that such formalized party methods were not yet fully acceptable to all, but such organization in this instance did ef-

2. Annapolis *Maryland Gazette*, Apr. 19, 1804.
3. *Ibid.*, June 21, Aug. 30, Sept. 20, 1804.
4. *Ibid.*, May 3, 1804.
5. *Ibid.*, Sept. 20, 1804.

fectively decide the party nominee for Congress, and that nominee was elected.

Although there were no uniform procedures throughout the state, practices similar to those in Prince George's and Anne Arundel counties were found in other counties. "The conferees of Frederick, Washington and Allegany counties" nominated the candidate in 1804 to represent that district in Congress. In Charles County, a candidate for presidential elector was proposed at a general meeting of Republicans of the county, where a four-man committee was also appointed to solicit support for the nomination throughout the electoral district. In Frederick County, Republican committees in 1808 were chosen in each election district of the county to constitute a general committee which made nominations for the state assembly.[6]

Baltimore in 1804 presents a significant example of party organizational efforts in Maryland. In September, the editor of the Republican Baltimore *American* proposed a plan to promote Republican unity in the city. Suggesting meetings in the different wards for appointing conferees to agree on nominations, he explained:

> For instance, say that the democratic republicans of every ward shall meet *on the same evening in their own wards,* at which meeting nothing would seem necessary, but merely to appoint a chairman, and then proceed to nominate said two (or other number of) conferees. A general meeting of such conferees could afterwards take place, and a majority thereof determine on the candidates most proper to *recommend* to the republican voters. This plan holds forth nothing dictatorial, more than the offering of candidates, by individuals (as is common). On the score of propriety there is no difference, further than that a ticket formed by the immediate delegates of the citizens, would attach to itself more respect, and would to a certainty insure greater unanimity. If we adopt such measures we are secure, and the pretensions of candidates can be better investigated.[7]

These conferees were to make nominations for the state legislature, Congress, and presidential electors.

A few days later the *American* announced: "We are requested, by a number of democratic republicans, of different wards, to state that ward meetings will be held in the respective wards ... the 24th instant, for the

---

6. Baltimore *American*, Sept. 11, 1804, Aug. 11, 1808; see also Washington *National Intelligencer*, July 18, 1806, for report of nomination for Congress by Republican delegates of Frederick County.

7. Baltimore *American*, Sept. 13, 14, 1804.

purpose of appointing conferees to fix upon suitable characters to be supported at the ensuing election."[8] Thus the machinery was set into motion, but subsequent newspaper reports show that, although the ward meetings were held, they did not all follow in every detail the recommendations of the *American*. Some wards chose to meet on September 25, 26, or 27 rather than on the 24th; all but one of the eight wards recommended candidates for Congress and for the legislature; and, according to the newspaper accounts, three of the eight wards failed to appoint conferees. With one exception, the same candidates were proposed in all wards which made recommendations as to the nominees. On September 29, when the conferees appointed at the different ward meetings met, they recommended a ticket for Congress and the state assembly composed of the candidates previously proposed by most of the wards.[9] The conferees, however, did not make any recommendations in regard to presidential electors, and no subsequent nominations were made. As the presidential election approached, the *American* confessed: "We are sorry to find, that there is so little probability that any arrangement will be made, to insure union to the efforts of the friends of administration, at the approaching election." Two candidates had been proposed for the city, and "if both persist in a determination to stand as candidates, it may furnish the means of success to our political opponents."[10] But despite the pleas of the *American,* election day arrived with no arrangements having been made, and the Republican votes were divided. A Republican elector was nevertheless elected.[11]

In Baltimore in 1806, conferees chosen by wards again met to agree on Republican tickets for Congress and the assembly. From the newspaper reports, however, the system still did not seem to operate smoothly. Not all wards appear to have chosen conferees, nor was full support given to the nominations of the conferees.[12] If the absence of newspaper reports of ward meetings or the choosing of conferees can be accepted as evidence, the system of ward conferees introduced in 1804 appears to have been abandoned by 1808. There is no indication in the press as to how the Republican ticket in Baltimore was formed in 1808, and, in fact, there were two rival Republican slates for the assembly.[13] Formal party

8. *Ibid.,* Sept. 20, 1804.
9. *Ibid.,* Sept. 29, 1804.
10. *Ibid.,* Nov. 1, 1804.
11. *Ibid.,* Nov. 12, 13, Dec. 7, 1804.
12. *Ibid.,* Sept. 30, Oct. 2, 3, 4, 1806.
13. *Ibid.,* Aug. 17, 31, Sept. 12, 15, 23, Oct. 3, Nov. 14, 1808.

organization in Baltimore, as in other parts of the state, had not assumed a regular system of operation.

The irregularity of local party machinery and the absence of any state-wide party organization in Maryland left much of the party's success to informal party leadership and to the campaign efforts of individual Republican candidates.

Virginia Republicans in 1800 created state-wide party machinery consisting of a general standing committee in Richmond and a network of county committees. Both the general committee and the county committees were appointed by a Republican caucus composed of members of the state legislature and "other respectable persons." An active organization, the committee system directed the campaign to elect Jeffersonian presidential electors, chosen popularly on a general ticket in 1800.[14]

The system established in 1800 was renewed in 1804 and in 1808, as presidential electors continued to be elected on a general ticket. A "meeting of one hundred and thirty members of the Legislature, and a number of other respectable citizens," at the Capitol in Richmond, January 23, 1804, framed the Republican ticket of electors and re-established the committee organization.[15] A circular dispatched by the general committee to chairmen of the county committees, February 1, 1804, announced the appointment or re-appointment of members of the county committees and instructed:

We request that you will call a meeting of your committee immediately, and should any member refuse to serve, the remaining members can supply the vacancy, of which they will notify the General Committee. The Republican Meeting had the utmost reliance on the firmness and patriotism of the members of your committee, and we trust they will exert themselves with activity and zeal in their county, to give success to the Republican Ticket. Your committee will correspond with the General Committee, and will communicate from time to time anything which may occur in your county of importance and connected with the success of the Republican Ticket. This will enable the committee here to afford you any assistance in their power, in cases which require their co-operation. As soon as this committee shall receive answers from the persons fixed on as Electors, they will communicate to the county committees correct lists of the persons who will compose the Republican

14. For further details on the Virginia Republican machinery in 1800, see Cunningham, *Jeffersonian Republicans, 1789-1801*, 151-54.
15. Richmond *Virginia Argus*, Feb. 1, 1804; Fredericksburg *Virginia Herald*, Feb. 7, 1804.

RICHMOND, February 1st, 1804.

SIR

WE beg leave to inform you that the Republican Meeting in the city of Richmond, which was held for the purpose of fixing on proper persons to act as Electors of President and Vice President of the United States, and on the best means to promote the election of such persons, have appointed *John Ambler, Champion Travis, Wm. Lightfoot, William L. Allen & Wm. Walker* as a committee of correspondence in the county of *James City* of which committee you were made the chairman. We request that you will call a meeting of your committee immediately, and should any member refuse to serve, the remaining members can supply the vacancy, of which they will notify the General Committee. The Republican Meeting had the utmost reliance on the firmness and patriotism of the members of your committee, and we trust they will exert themselves with activity and zeal in their county, to give success to the Republican Ticket. Your committee will correspond with the General Committee, and will communicate from time to time any thing which may occur in your county of importance and connected with the success of the Republican Ticket. This will enable the committee here to afford you any assistance in their power, in cases which require their co-operation. As soon as this committee shall receive answers from the persons fixed on as Electors, they will communicate to the county committees correct lists of the persons who will compose the Republican Ticket. All communications to the General Committee, must be directed to their Chairman, in Richmond. You will be pleased as soon as you have a meeting of your committee, to acknowledge the receipt of this letter.

We are, respectfully, your fellow citizens,

PHILIP NORBORNE NICHOLAS, Chairman.
GEORGE HAY,
MERIWETHER JONES,
JOSEPH SELDEN,   Committee.
GERVAS STORRS,
SAMUEL PLEASANTS, Jr.

ATTEST,
JOHN H. FOUSHEE, Secretary.

To *John Ambler* Esq.
Chairman of the corresponding committee for the county of *James City*

Circular by the Republican General Committee of Virginia, 1804
(Courtesy of the Virginia Historical Society)

Ticket. All communications to the General Committee, must be directed to their Chairman, in Richmond. You will be pleased as soon as you have a meeting of your committee, to acknowledge the receipt of this letter.[16]

The general committee not only assumed the responsibility for circulating the Republican ticket among the county committees but also published in

---

16. [Circular], Richmond, Feb. 1, 1804, signed by Philip Norborne Nicholas, chairman, George Hay, Meriwether Jones, Joseph Selden, Gervas Storrs, Samuel Pleasants, Jr., committee, addressed to John Ambler, chairman of James City County committee, John Ambler Papers, Va. Hist. Soc. Reproduced above.

RICHMOND, *June* 25*th*, 1804.

SIR,

As the time approaches at which the election of Electors will be held in the several Counties, it will become the indispensible and sacred duty of the Corresponding Committees to use every possible exertion to advance the Republican Ticket.....Written tickets containing the names of the Electors, should be dispersed over each County, and active and intelligent Citizens in every neighbourhood should be prevailed on to attend the election, and to bring as many of their fellow-citizens as possible to give their suffrages.....The most convenient Newspapers should be employed by each Committee, to extend the knowledge of the characters who compose our Ticket, and to recommend the principles which we advocate.

The numerous and irresistible arguments which naturally present themselves in favor of the present administration, should be urged upon the people, and they should be induced to feel and appreciate their present state of happiness and prosperity, by contrasting it with the calamities brought upon us by the misconduct of former rulers. Virginia stood foremost in the struggle for freedom and for the triumph of correct principles; and it would be disgraceful and perfidious should she discover less zeal and less ardour than her sister States, in defence of that happy order of things which she so eminently contributed to establish. It is unnecessary for us to use any arguments to you in favor of the cause we espouse; you are known to be the zealous advocates of republican principles, and you have signalized yourselves in the worst of times in their defence......All we have to urge is, that you will now unite with us in giving so strong and decisive an expression of the public sentiment of our republican administration, as will strengthen the well founded confidence of our friends, and prove to the world that the government of the United States is now conducted conformably with the wishes of the great body of the American people.

Your Fellow-Citizen,
PHILIP NORBORNE NICHOLAS,
Chairman of the General Committee.

Attest, JOHN H. FOUSHEE, *Secretary.*

To *John Ambler* Chairman of the Corresponding Committee for *James City* County.

REPUBLICAN TICKET.

Richard Evers Lee,	*of Norfolk Borough.*	William Ellzey,	*of Loudoun.*
John Goodrich,	*of Isle of Wight.*	William Dudley,	*of Warwick.*
Edward Pegram,	*of Dinwiddie.*	Mann Page,	*of Gloucester.*
Dr. Richard Field,	*of Brunswick.*	John Taliaferro, jr.	*of King George.*
Thomas Read,	*of Charlotte.*	Richard Brent,	*of Prince William.*
Creed Taylor,	*of Cumberland.*	Hugh Holmes,	*of Frederick.*
William H. Cabell,	*of Amherst.*	James Dailey,	*of Hampshire.*
George Penn,	*of Patrick.*	James Allen,	*of Shenandoah.*
George Wythe,	*of City of Richmond.*	Archibald Stuart,	*of Augusta.*
John Taylor,	*of Caroline.*	James M'Farlane,	*of Russell.*
Larkin Smith,	*of King & Queen.*	Gen. John Preston,	*of Montgomery.*
John Minor,	*of Spotsylvania.*	William M'Kinley,	*of Ohio.*

Circular by the Chairman of the Republican General Committee of Virginia, 1804

(Courtesy of the Virginia Historical Society)

the newspapers official notifications, signed by the chairman and the secretary to the committee, listing the Republican ticket. The Richmond *Enquirer* published the slate with the request that Republican printers throughout the state insert the ticket for one month.[17]

In June 1804, the general committee mailed another circular to the county chairmen, instructing the committees on the distribution of party tickets and newspapers and stressing the "indispensible and sacred duty of the Corresponding Committees to use every possible exertion to advance the Republican-Ticket. Written tickets containing the names of the Electors, should be dispersed over each County, and active and intelligent Citizens in every neighbourhood should be prevailed on to attend the election, and to bring as many of their fellow-citizens as possible to give their suffrages. The most convenient Newspapers should be employed by each Committee, to extend the knowledge of the characters who compose our Ticket, and to recommend the principles which we advocate." The General Committee also suggested as campaign strategy that "the numerous and irresistible arguments which naturally present themselves in favor of the present administration, should be urged upon the people, and they should be induced to feel and appreciate their present state of happiness and prosperity, by contrasting it with the calamities brought upon us by the misconduct of former rulers." Virginians should also be urged to live up to their past record in defense of freedom and "correct principles."[18]

When the Republican party in Virginia split in 1808 over the question of whether to support Madison or Monroe for the presidency, similar committee organizations supported each candidate. The Republican legislative caucus representing a majority of the members nominated a ticket of electors in favor of Madison, appointed a "permanent corresponding committee" in Richmond, and named three-member county committees throughout the state.[19] The minority caucus which nominated a slate of electors in support of Monroe also created a "standing corresponding committee" in Richmond and corresponding committees of five members for each county. The standing committee was authorized to fill any

---

17. Richmond *Enquirer,* May 30, June 6, 13, 16, 20, 23, 27, 1804; *Petersburg Republican,* July 3, 1804.

18. [Circular], Richmond, June 25, 1804, signed by Philip Norborne Nicholas, chairman of the general committee, John H. Foushee, secretary, addressed to John Ambler, chairman of James City County committee, Ambler Papers, Va. Hist. Soc. Reproduced on p. 182.

19. Richmond *Enquirer,* Jan. 23, 1808; Richmond *Virginia Argus,* Jan. 26, 1808.

vacancies on the county committees.[20] In both organizations the Richmond committees were instructed to verify that the electors nominated would vote for the candidate for whom they were pledged and to substitute, if necessary, other names on the electoral ticket. A subsequent meeting of the Madison caucus also empowered the Richmond committee to increase the membership of county committees from three to seven.[21] Both committee systems followed the practices of 1800 and 1804, though the Madison committees regarded their organization as the regular successor to the previous committees.[22]

An examination of the membership of the general committee and of the county committees from 1800 to 1809 reveals that the committee system supplied a relatively stable party organization. Many of the same men who were committee members in 1800 were still committee members in 1808 (of the Madison organization), and others undoubtedly would have been members had they not turned their support to Monroe. Unfortunately the names of the county committees in 1804 do not appear to have survived except in a few scattered instances, but lists of the Republican committees in 1800 and of the Republican committees in support of Madison in 1808 are available. A comparison of these lists shows that there are seventy-eight counties for which party committee members are known for both 1800 and 1808; in fifty-one counties one or more of the three members in 1808 had been on the 1800 committee. In nineteen of these counties two of the three members had served in the same capacity in 1800, and in two counties three members had been on the 1800 committee. In thirty-two counties the chairman had been on the committee in 1800.[23] These statistics indicate a continuity of membership on county committees which gave them a certain amount of permanency even though new committees were appointed every four years.

The permanent character of the general committee is even more striking. Members of this committee were:[24]

20. Richmond *Enquirer*, Jan. 23, 26, 1808.
21. *Ibid.*, Jan. 26, 30, 1808; see also *ibid.*, Aug. 9, 1808.
22. See circular, Richmond, July 4, 1808, from standing committee to county committees, in *ibid.*, Aug. 9, 1808.
23. The names of the committees for 1800 are in W. P. Palmer *et al.*, eds., *Calendar of Virginia State Papers and Other Manuscripts* . . . , 11 vols. (Richmond, 1875-93), IX, 77-87; lists for 1808 are in Richmond *Enquirer*, Jan. 23, 1808, and Richmond *Virginia Argus*, Jan. 26, 1808.
24. [Circular], Richmond, Aug. 9, 1800, signed by Philip N. Nicholas and others, broadside, Lib. Cong.; [Circular], Richmond, Feb. 1, 1804, signed by Philip N. Nicholas and others, Ambler Papers, Va. Hist. Soc.; Richmond *Enquirer*, Jan. 23, 30, Aug. 9, 1808.

1800	*1804*	*1808*
Philip Norborne Nicholas, chairman	Philip Norborne Nicholas, chairman	William Foushee, chairman
Meriwether Jones	Meriwether Jones	Thomas Ritchie
Gervas Storrs	Gervas Storrs	Gervas Storrs
Samuel Pleasants, Jr.	Samuel Pleasants, Jr.	Samuel Pleasants, Jr.
Joseph Selden	Joseph Selden	Peyton Randolph
	George Hay	Abraham Venable

As this list shows, all of the five 1800 members were on the central committee in 1804, and two of them were still on the committee in 1808; this continuity of membership was an important factor in giving to the Richmond committee a dominating influence in the party organization throughout the state.[25]

Since the governor was chosen by the legislature and the members of the legislature and of Congress were elected in counties or districts, the selection of presidential electors provided the only state-wide election in Virginia. In county and district elections there was little formal party machinery in operation. Most candidates were either self-nominated or informally proposed by their friends. One reference has been found which reveals that the members of the House of Delegates of one district made the nomination for the upper house of the next legislature by caucusing during the session.[26] Undoubtedly the meetings of the legislature, bringing together party leaders from different counties, provided other opportunities for reaching agreements on district nominations, but no systematized procedure has been detected.

A few candidates announced their candidacies in newspaper notices.[27] Others published addresses to the voters in handbills offering their services and soliciting support. "In compliance with the wishes of some of the inhabitants of the district," announced John Mercer in a handbill nearly

---

John H. Foushee served as secretary to the committee in 1800 and 1804. The committee listed for 1808 was appointed by the caucus which supported Madison's candidacy. Meriwether Jones died before 1808. George Hay, who served on the 1804 committee, was a member of the Monroe standing committee in 1808, of which the other members were John Clarke, Edward C. Stanard, William Robinson, and John Brockenbrough. Richmond *Enquirer*, Jan. 26, Mar. 22, Sept. 30, 1808.

25. This political power was to be felt for a number of years. See Harry Ammon, "The Richmond Junto, 1800-1824," *Virginia Magazine of History and Biography*, 61 (1953), 395-418; *Letters on the Richmond Party, by a Virginian* (Richmond, 1823), pamphlet, Va. Hist. Soc.

26. Andrew Russell to David Campbell, [Jan. 25, 1804], David Campbell Papers, Duke Univ.

27. *Norfolk and Portsmouth Herald*, Mar. 14, 1805.

a year before the next election, "I inform you of my intention to become a candidate for your suffrages at the election to be held in April next."[28] Thomas Mann Randolph, seeking election to Congress in 1803, explained in another handbill: "Colonel Cabell offers his services to you again. I, also, tender you mine. . . . It has been your long established practice to choose among those who voluntarily offer themselves to your choice. It is not probable you will change that practice now, tho' I hope you will at some future time, take it into your consideration. I therefore place myself in your view. . . . The impossibility of personal communication with all of you, in the short time between this and the election . . . compels me to state, here, my pretensions to your approbation and confidence."[29]

Congressmen seeking re-election in Virginia also frequently indicated their willingness to serve again by means of circular letters to their constituents. "To have your assurance of undiminished confidence at the ensuing election, will be the most grateful reward for my past labors," wrote Burwell Bassett;[30] and John Clopton, issuing a pre-election report, concluded: "As the period will soon arrive when representatives are to be chosen for the next Congress, the custom of our country will justify me in noticing it to you; and my feelings will justify me in declaring, that should I be favored with a re-election, the honor will be accepted with grateful acknowledgements—the trust will be discharged with fidelity, and undeviating adherence to the same political principles, by which I have been heretofore actuated."[31]

A few public meetings were held to nominate candidates, but the practice appears to have been infrequent. In Wheeling, in September 1808, a party meeting resolved to support John G. Jackson for Congress and appointed a standing committee of three members to promote his election.[32] John Randolph reported that at the Prince Edward County courthouse, on September 24, 1808, "there was an assembly of the people

28. John Mercer, *To the Freeholders of the Congressional District composed of the Counties of Spotsylvania, Orange, Louisa and Madison*, May 3, 1806, broadside, Lib. Cong.

29. Thomas Mann Randolph, *To the Freeholders of Albemarle, Amherst, and Fluvanna*, [March, 1803], broadside, Lib. Cong. See also John Clopton, *To the Citizens of Henrico, Hanover, New-Kent, Charles-City, and James-City*, Mar. 30, 1801, broadside, Va. State Lib.

30. B[urwell] Bassett, [circular to his constituents], Feb. 26, 1809, broadside, Lib. Cong.

31. John Clopton, [circular to his constituents], Washington, Feb. 24, 1803, broadside, Va. State Lib.; see also Clopton, [circular to his constituents], Washington, Feb. 19, 1805, broadside, Va. State Lib.

32. *Address to the Freeholders of Ohio County, Virginia*, Wheeling, Mar. 6, 1809, signed by Joseph Tomlinson, Thomas Evans, and William M'Kinley, broadside, Lib. Cong.

called by my opponents, for the purpose of appointing a Committee which, in conjunction with other Committees as might be appointed by other Counties of the district, should fix upon a candidate in opposition to the present representative. . . . Caucussing however is not yet the vogue in *Congressional* elections. Out of upwards of 300 persons only seventeen or eighteen could be found who did not set their faces against the whole proceeding."[33] As Randolph suggested, this type of nominating procedure had not been widely used in Virginia. In general, nominations remained in the hands of party leaders who made the decisions with little formal public participation.[34]

In North Carolina there were no state-wide elections; the governor was chosen by the legislature, and congressmen and presidential electors were elected by districts. Under these conditions no formal state-wide party machinery developed, and party organization on the district and county level was informal. Most nominations were made informally, or political aspirants nominated themselves. It was not uncommon for candidates to announce their decision to seek office in newspaper notices or advertisements. For example, Abraham Gillean's advertisement, "To the freeholders of the County of Rowan," stated:

Being solicited by many of my friends whose opinions I feel myself bound to respect, I take this method of acquainting you that I offer my services as a Candidate for the Senate, at the approaching election for members of the General Assembly.

If I should be so happy as to meet the approbation and have the support of a majority of my fellow citizens upon this occasion, I flatter myself that they are assured my best efforts will be exerted to promote their interest, and that of my country.[35]

Candidates for presidential electors also publicized their intentions in the press. "Having taken the liberty of nominating myself a Candidate as an *Elector* for your division," announced one candidate, "I take this opportunity of soliciting your suffrages, and if honored with a sufficient number of them to elect me, I shall vote for Thomas Jefferson, Esquire, as *President,* and my choice of Vice-President will be governed by future

---

33. John Randolph to James M. Garnett, Sept. 25, 1808, Papers of John Randolph of Roanoke, Garnett transcripts, Lib. Cong.
34. See Alexander McRae to John Clopton, May 9, 1806, Clopton Papers, Duke Univ.
35. *North Carolina Mercury, and Salisbury Advertiser,* July 23, Aug. 6, 1801.

information."[36] Another notice informed the voters: "The Republican friends and neighbors of Joseph John Alston, Esq. of Chatham, nominate him Elector for the district composed of the Counties of Orange, Chatham and Moore, who pledges himself, if elected, to vote for Thomas Jefferson as President, and the most worthy candidate as Vice-President."[37]

Other candidates published circulars or handbills nominating themselves and seeking support. "The object of this address," wrote Duncan Cameron, "is to inform you, fellow-citizens, that I have presumed to become a candidate to represent you in the next Congress of the United States.... In tendering to you my services, I have only claimed the exercise of a common right, and put it into your power to make a choice."[38] Seeking re-election to Congress, Richard Stanford circulated a printed letter to his constituents, declaring: "Permit me, in this way, to make known to you that I am a Candidate for the honour of representing you again in the succeeding Congress, and to express the hope of your farther patronage and support."[39]

In such ways most of the names of political aspirants came before North Carolina voters, and formal party machinery was rare. An important exception, however, is found in Wilmington in 1808, indicating that more definite party machinery was making its appearance in the state. A meeting of the Republicans of Wilmington and its vicinity, February 27, 1808, recommended to the Republicans of the several counties composing the electoral district that four delegates from each county be sent to attend a meeting to nominate a presidential elector for the district. Delegates were chosen to represent Wilmington, and a five-member committee of correspondence was also appointed.[40] This com-

---

36. "To the Freemen of the Counties of Montgomery, Anson, Richmond, Robeson and Cumberland," signed A. Gilchrist, Sept. 20, 1804, in *Raleigh Register*, Oct. 8, 1804.

37. *Raleigh Register*, Apr. 16, 1804. For other examples, see *ibid.*, Apr. 14, July 7, Aug. 18, Oct. 6, 1808, *Edenton Gazette*, Mar. 30, 1808.

38. Duncan Cameron, *To the Freemen of the District Composed of the Counties of Wake, Orange and Chatham*, June 1808, broadside, Univ. of N. C.

39. Richard Stanford, [circular to his constituents], Orange County, June 24, 1808, broadside, *ibid*. For other examples see William Lenoir, *To the Citizens of the Twelfth Election District in the State of North Carolina*, Fort Defiance, July 30, 1806; M[ontfort] Stokes, *To the Freemen of the Counties of Rowan, Randolph and Cabarrus*, Salisbury, Sept. 6, 1804, broadsides, *ibid.*; William R. Davie, [circular], Halifax, May 2, 1803, in Kemp P. Battle, ed., "Letters of William R. Davie," *James Sprunt Historical Monographs*, 7 (1907), 55; William R. Davie to John Steele, Aug. 20, 1803, Wagstaff, ed., *The Papers of John Steele*, I, 405.

40. *At a Meeting of the Republicans of Wilmington . . . 27th February 1808*, broadside, Jefferson Papers, Lib. Cong.

mittee sent letters to Republican leaders in the counties of the district reporting the Wilmington proceedings and stressing: "As it is a matter of the utmost importance at the present crisis the Republicans should act in concert, we request you would be pleased to use your influence and best exertions to procure the delegation from your county of four decided Republicans to meet at South Washington for the purpose and at the time proposed."[41] Thus, following the example of Republicans in a number of other states, some beginnings were being made by 1808 in introducing formal party machinery into North Carolina.

As in North Carolina, there was little formal party machinery in South Carolina. Party leaders informally supplied most of the organization. There were no state-wide elections in the state: the governor and presidential electors were chosen by the legislature; congressmen and state legislators were elected in counties or districts. Nominations, largely decided by party leaders, were informally presented to the voters under such recommendations as "the Ticket agreed upon, to be supported by the Republicans generally," or by newspaper notices such as one announcing: "O'Brien Smith, Esq. is proposed by his friends as the Republican candidate, to represent the United Districts of Richland, Orangeburg and Colleton, in the Congress of the United States."[42]

When some Republicans proposed electing congressional representatives on a general ticket, the method met with strong opposition, and a new districting of the state was substituted and enacted. Federalists accused Republicans of "an iniquitous arrangement of districts . . . to stifle the voice of federalism," in redistributing the state so as to give advantage to the Republican party, and the charge was not without foundation.[43] In fact, Republicans, who had firm control of the state legislature, had privately boasted that whatever method was adopted, whether a general ticket or districts, "Federalism will be taken care of."[44] The Republican majority in the legislature also gave Republicans control of the selection of presidential electors both in 1804 and in 1808.

41. Christopher Dudley, Jr., secretary to the corresponding committee, to Maj. Gen. Benjamin Smith (of Brunswick County, N. C.), Mar. 1, 1808, in *ibid.*
42. Charleston *Carolina Gazette*, Aug. 31, 1804; Columbia *South-Carolina State Gazette*, Aug. 25, 1804; Charleston *Times*, Aug. 29, Sept. 9, Oct. 8, 1808.
43. Charles Cotesworth Pinckney to John Rutledge, Jan. 17, 1803, John Rutledge Papers, Duke Univ.; Henry W. DeSaussure to John Rutledge, Sept. [11?], 1801, Dec. 19, 1801, Rutledge Papers, Univ. of N. C.
44. Andrew Butler to Thomas Sumter, Dec. 9, 1802, Thomas Sumter Papers, Lib. Cong.

Although material relating to party operations in South Carolina is limited, a few hints have been uncovered to suggest something of these activities. A Federalist, for example, reported that in campaigning for the election of Joseph Alston to the legislature in 1801, Charleston Republicans "divided the Town into wards and went into them all to procure votes."[45] It may be assumed that similar measures were taken in other Charleston elections. A rare South Carolina broadside discloses that in the Pendleton District, August 18, 1804, "a meeting of Citizens from different quarters of this district, publicly assembled in the Courthouse . . . to consult, propose and agree on three proper persons to represent the said district in the state legislature." Two candidates were nominated and recommended to the voters.[46] Available evidence, however, does not indicate that South Carolina Republicans had taken many steps toward creating formal party machinery in the state.

Georgia politics displayed little party machinery as late as 1808. Nominations were made informally, with candidates offering themselves, being recommended by their friends, or being selected by party leaders. Announcements proposing individual candidates appeared irregularly in the newspapers, and Republican tickets published in the press rarely explained how they originated.[47]

In Savannah, however, Republicans appear to have given more attention to party organization than was common elsewhere in the state. A meeting of Savannah Republicans in September 1807 nominated candidates to represent Chatham County in both houses of the state legislature, agreeing that "every citizen present pledges himself to support the candidates nominated and chosen by a majority of this meeting," and recommending that the Republicans of the county be solicited to support the ticket. It was also decided to publish the proceedings of the meeting in the Republican newspapers of the city.[48] Similar organization was displayed in Savannah the following year, although the procedures were changed. In 1808 the "Democratic Republicans of Chatham county,"

45. Henry W. DeSaussure to John Rutledge, Charleston, Sept. [11?], 1801, Rutledge Papers, Univ. of N. C.
46. [Circular], Pendleton District, Aug. 16, 1804, broadside, Robert Anderson Papers, University of South Carolina.
47. Savannah *Georgia Republican*, Sept. 28, 1804, Sept. 26, 1807. For examples of individual candidacies being announced in newspapers, see Savannah *Republican*, Feb. 13, Aug. 11, 1808, *Augusta Chronicle*, Aug. 13, 1808.
48. Savannah *Republican*, Sept. 22, 1807.

called together by newspaper notices, appointed a committee of ten to nominate candidates for the legislature. This committee, composed of six members from Savannah and four from the county, was also instructed "to draft an address to the republican citizens of this county, stating reasons why such candidates should be supported at the ensuing general election." As directed, the committee met, made the nominations, and published an address in support of the candidates selected.[49] Although the party organization in Savannah clearly demonstrated that some party machinery existed in Georgia, it was not representative of the state as a whole.

Since the governor and the presidential electors were chosen by the Georgia legislature, the only state-wide election involved the choice of the state's four representatives to Congress, who were elected on a general ticket. Unlike most of the other states which held state-wide elections, Georgia did not evolve any party machinery to meet the demands of a state campaign. The private correspondence of party leaders in the state suggests that some party leaders felt that many of the voters did not consider the congressional elections important; in the absence of much public concern, therefore, they could be controlled by proper management. Obadiah Jones, an active Republican working for the election of Joseph Bryan in 1802, explained that "distant things, you know, make but slight impressions, not one in ten of our backwoods people knows (unless told) that Men to Congress are to be chosen, where they are to go, or what for." To promote Bryan's election he advised "proper address on the day of Election," elaborating:

> My plan is this, the people think so much of electing men for their own assembly that they think or care very little about Congress men, and a few Men of influence that will manage matters artfully may get a large number of Votes. In this County I think we shall do well in that particular. In Oglethorpe friend Crawford will do his endeavour for you, but the Members from that County are extremely severe against you. The rest of the Counties I have not been in since I knew you were a Candidate, but I shall be in some before the Election, and use my feeble exertions with the men whom I may meet that I think of influence in others ... all these things you know depend more upon the *art* of a few than the *general will*—And the door of address, I think, was hardly ever wider open than it is at present, for the small strip of land we have gotten of the Indians has set the Common people so *agog* that they do not care

49. *Ibid.*, Sept. 13, 17, 24, 1808. The ticket nominated by the committee was successful in the election. *Ibid.*, Oct. 4, 1808.

much if the Devil had the Congress, so the land is disposed of to please them.[50]

The role which influential men in various counties played in congressional elections is echoed in other private letters. "While at Screven Mr. Jones and myself were active in promoting your interest at the election . . . ," wrote Nicholas Ware to Thomas Carr, a candidate for Congress in 1806. "We have arranged this business with almost all the influential men in the County."[51] James Jackson credited John Milledge's election to Congress in 1801 to the endeavors of influential supporters who worked hard to promote his success. "Thank God for nothing," wrote Jackson as he named the men who had carried the election and emphasized that Milledge owed his victory to these men rather than to divine providence.[52]

These comments and those in other contemporary correspondence suggest that congressional elections in Georgia in this period were contests dominated by influential men in various counties.[53] Different combinations of candidates were supported in different counties, and there was no uniform Republican ticket throughout the state.[54] The absence of a strong Federalist threat permitted this attention to local interests and allowed personal partialities. Under these conditions, state-wide party machinery did not develop.

Republicans in Kentucky and Tennessee did not find it necessary to establish regular party machinery. Under no strong pressure from Federalist opposition, which had never been powerful in either state, party leaders found informal co-operation sufficient organization to keep political control in Republican hands. To guarantee Republican supremacy in Kentucky, the Republican-controlled state legislature in 1803 reduced the presidential electoral districts from six to two, with four electors to be popularly chosen in each district. Sponsored by the young

50. Jones to Bryan, Elberton, Ga., Sept. 1, 1802, Arnold-Screven Papers, Univ. of N. C.
51. Ware to Carr, Sept. 28, 1806, Thomas Carr Papers, Univ. of Ga.
52. Jackson to Milledge, Apr. 2, 1801, Harriet M. Salley, ed., *Correspondence of John Milledge, Governor of Georgia, 1802-1806* (Columbia, S. C., 1949), 70-71.
53. See James Jackson to Joseph Bryan, June 25, 1803, Obadiah Jones to Joseph Bryan, June 25, Sept. 24, 1803, July 18, 1804, Arnold-Screven Papers, Univ. of N. C.; James Jackson to Brig. Gen. Mitchell, Sept. 5, 1805, James Jackson Papers, Univ. of Ga.
54. Nicholas Ware to Thomas Carr, Sept. 28, 1806, Carr Papers, Univ. of Ga.; Savannah *Republican*, Sept. 28, 1804.

Henry Clay, the measure eliminated the possibility of a single Federalist electoral vote.[55]

Occasional local organization appeared, such as a corresponding society organized in Russellville, Kentucky, by supporters of Matthew Lyon. A hostile press protested in 1806 that "there are now in circulation a great number of hand-bills purporting to be the proceedings of a general meeting of a society denominated the corresponding society at Russelville ... for the avowed object of promoting Col. Lyon's election to Congress." Such newspaper criticism directed at "the extraordinary performance of this society" suggests that such organizations were uncommon in Kentucky.[56]

In both Kentucky and Tennessee, self-nomination for political office was an accepted practice. In Tennessee, some candidates circulated printed notices announcing their candidacy. John Rhea issued the following announcement dated October 16, 1801, printed on a slip of paper not much larger than a postal card:

CITIZENS *of the* STATE *of* TENNESSEE.

ON the last Thursday of this month, and the day following, an election is to be held in the several counties in this state, to elect a Representative to the Congress of the United States. I offer myself a candidate for the honor of the suffrages of my fellow citizens: Should I be elected, every exertion in my power shall be used to promote the interest and happiness of my fellow citizens of Tennessee and the honor and dignity of the United States.

I hope you will not deem it necessary for me to say any thing about my political opinions; those that I now hold, and for many years past have uniformly held, are well known, and to yourselves, on this subject, I do not refer.[57]

Other candidates issued campaign statements through the newspapers or were recommended by political friends. Newspapers often simply reported that they were "authorized to say" that certain persons were candidates.[58] A typical notice issued by a candidate announced:

55. Bernard Mayo, *Henry Clay: Spokesman of the New West* (Boston, 1937), 152-54; James F. Hopkins, ed., *The Papers of Henry Clay* (Lexington, Ky., 1959——), I, 123-24.
56. Frankfort *Palladium*, June 19, 1806.
57. Broadside, Amer. Antiq. Soc.; another similar notice, signed by John Cocke, Oct. 2, 1801, is also in the Broadside Collection, Amer. Antiq. Soc.; see also William Dickson, [circular to his constituents], Washington, Mar. 3, 1803, broadside, *ibid.*
58. Lexington *Kentucky Gazette*, Mar. 13, Apr. 3, 24, May 1, 8, June 12, 26, July 3, 31, 1804; Nashville *Tennessee Gazette*, May 23, Aug. 8, 1804; Frankfort *Western World*, Feb. 18, Apr. 21, Aug. 25, 1808; Frankfort *Palladium*, June 19, 1806.

To the Citizens of Kentucky.

I offer myself as a Candidate for the office of Lieutenant Governor at the ensuing Election. Should your suffrages be conferred on me, they will meet the grateful estimation of your

Fayette, 11th June 1804.
Fellow citizen,
Edm. Bullock[59]

At times candidates expanded their declarations of candidacy to include brief campaign appeals. A candidate for presidential elector in 1804 pointed out that he "always deprecated the unwarranted assumption and the tyrannical administration under Mr. Adams" and that he was "always a true friend to the mild, peaceful and economical conduct of the present administration."[60]

Some Kentucky candidates issued lengthy published addresses explaining their political views. A four-page circular by congressional candidate Robert H. Grayson began:

The time approaches when you will be called upon to choose a Representative to Congress. Having declared myself a candidate for your suffrages at the ensuing election, and having but a limitted personal acquaintance in many parts of the district, it may be necessary for your satisfaction, to disclose to you my political principles, and at the same time to notice the objections urged against me, by those in opposition to my election. I have preferred a written communication of my principles, as being a mode the least liable to perversion or misconstruction. Before I enter into a detail of them it may not be improper to make some preliminary remarks. When I came forward I was not insensible of the disadvantages which a candidate unknown to many of you, would have to encounter, nor was I unconscious of the importance and responsibility of the post for which I offer, and can with truth declare, in reply to those who charge me with being too aspiring, that it was not without the solicitations of several citizens of the district, aided by an inclination to serve my country, that I was induced to become a candidate. It was not with a view to oppose the election of any particular citizen; for it will be remembered, that at the time I declared myself a candidate, no other person had offered himself in that capacity.[61]

To counteract rumors concerning his candidacy, one aspirant in 1808 published the following announcement:

---

59. Lexington *Kentucky Gazette*, June 12, 1804.
60. *Ibid.;* see also *ibid.,* July 31, 1804.
61. Robert Harrison Grayson, *To the Voters of the Sixth Congressional District* . . . , April 14, 1804, broadside, Filson Club.

To the Sheriffs of the several counties of Kentucky.

Having been informed a report prevails that I have declined my pretensions as a candidate for the office of Lieutenant Governor, I take this method to contradict it, to request each of you to have a poll taken for me, and to assure my fellow-citizens that if favored with their suffrages, I will exert every power I possess in discharging the duties assigned to the office solicited.

Henderson, July 5, 1808   Saml. Hopkins

The Editors of news-papers in Kentucky, are requested to give this an insertion.[62]

Personalities played an important part in these states where party contests were not common, and the candidates seeking favor were frequently numerous. The *Kentucky Gazette* in 1804 listed sixteen announced candidates for presidential electors in the southern district and thirteen candidates in the northern district. Four electors were to be chosen in each district. Furthermore, the poll for the northern district showed that all thirteen candidates received votes, and most candidates registered more than a negligible number of supporters.[63] Similarly the Frankfort *Western World* published a "complete list of candidates" for presidential electors in 1808, naming fourteen candidates for the four electors elected in Kentucky's northern district, though listing only six candidates for the four electors chosen in the southern district. Another list in the *Argus of Western America,* naming candidates for the northern district, noted that with one exception it was presumed all would vote for Madison.[64] Once again there was a great scattering of votes.[65]

Such circumstances display not only the absence of party machinery, but also the absence of a party contest. The real decision concerning Kentucky's electoral votes, in fact, had been made at a Republican caucus of members of the legislature in February 1808, when, under the leadership of Henry Clay, Madison was recommended as Jefferson's successor to the presidency. "We are aware, fellow-citizens, that in the choice of his successor it is and ought to be your right to think and decide for yourselves," explained an address prepared by Clay and approved for

62. Frankfort *Western World,* July 1808 (date torn).
63. Lexington *Kentucky Gazette,* Sept. 25, Oct. 16, Nov. 27, 1804. All electors voted for Jefferson for president and George Clinton for vice-president.
64. *Western World,* Oct. 6, 1808; Frankfort *Argus of Western America,* Oct. 12, 1808.
65. Frankfort *Western World,* Nov. 17, 1808. Seven Kentucky electors voted for Madison for president and George Clinton for vice-president; one did not vote.

publication by the caucus. "We presume not to dictate to you, and we hope that we shall escape the imputation of arrogance, when we merely venture to recommend to your consideration, a suitable character in our judgements." Stressing Madison's qualifications for office, the address was signed by Governor Christopher Greenup as chairman of the meeting, by the speakers of both houses of the legislature, and by seventy-eight members of the legislature.[66] The decision of this caucus exerted a powerful influence in determining Kentucky's vote in the election of 1808.[67] No ticket, however, was presented by the caucus.

The content of various newspaper announcements, the self-nomination and informal designation of candidates, the large number of active candidates, the scattering of votes at elections, and the informal role of party leaders indicate the essential absence of formal party machinery in Kentucky and Tennessee.

Ohio entered the Union in 1803 with Republicans and Federalists active in competing for political dominance, but the superior strength of the Republicans had been clearly demonstrated in the election of the constitutional convention to organize the state government. Rejoicing that the Republican ticket had succeeded beyond his most sanguine expectations, Ohio Republican leader Thomas Worthington described the membership of the convention as composed of twenty-six "decided Republicans," seven Federalists, and two doubtful. Republican numerical superiority in the state continued throughout Jefferson's administration.[68]

In some parts of Ohio, Republicans had organized "Republican societies" previous to the admission to statehood. Some of the members of the state constitutional convention were nominated by delegates from these societies meeting in county conventions. In Hamilton County, for example, a ticket for the convention was nominated by "delegates from seventeen different Republican Societies throughout the county."[69] One active party worker reported that fifteen large societies had been established by August 1802.[70] With statehood accomplished, these so-

66. *Ibid.*, Feb. 25, 1808.
67. See John Monroe to James Monroe, June 18, 1808, Monroe Papers, Lib. Cong.
68. Worthington to Jefferson, Nov. 8, 1802, Jefferson Papers, Lib. Cong. See also John Smith to Jefferson, Dec. 27, 1802, *ibid.*
69. Cincinnati *Western Spy*, July 31, 1801, May 1, Aug. 28, 1802; John D. Barnhart, *Valley of Democracy; The Frontier versus the Plantation in the Ohio Valley, 1775-1818* (Bloomington, Indiana, 1953), 150.
70. Daniel Symmes to John C. Symmes, Aug. 5, 1802, Gallatin Papers, N.-Y. Hist. Soc.

cieties continued to supply the principal organization of formal party machinery; but they were far from universal throughout the state, and their influence varied in different parts of Ohio. In some areas the societies made the party nominations and were strong enough to elect the ticket. In other places accepted practices included nominations by informal means, by various party gatherings, and by self-nomination through newspaper announcements.[71]

Ohio Republicans were best organized in Hamilton County, in the Cincinnati area, where a system of Republican societies functioned much like the committee system in eastern states. Republican societies (also referred to as Republican corresponding societies) were organized on the township level, and each township society sent delegates to a county convention where the party nominations were made. Considerable regularity appears to have characterized the Hamilton County organization; notices of meetings were announced in the press, and delegates were required to present credentials from their township society at the county meetings.[72]

The 1805 election may be used to illustrate the operation of the Hamilton County Republican machinery. The Cincinnati *Western Spy* reported, September 11, 1805:

> At a meeting of Delegates from various Townships, at the house of Mr. Pittman on the 2d inst. 14 *delegates present*; they elected as chairman, the eldest present, viz. Jacob Skillman, and also selected as secretary, Othniel Looker.
> The delegates then produced their powers from the Republican Societies, to which they belong; after which the following citizens were duly nominated as candidates, to be supported by the Republicans, at the ensuing election.

After agreeing on the party slate, it was resolved that the ticket be published in the two Cincinnati newspapers until the time of the election.[73] Previous notices in the press show that the meeting of the Cincinnati Republican society had been called by an announcement in the newspaper and that, at the meeting of that society, the Cincinnati

---

71. Chillicothe *Scioto Gazette*, Aug. 27, Sept. 24, Oct. 1, 29, 1804, Apr. 24, May 1, 15, Aug. 28, 1806, Oct. 9, 1807; Cincinnati *Western Spy*, May 11, 18, 25, 1803.
72. Cincinnati *Western Spy*, Jan. 5, Sept. 7, 1803; Aug. 29, Sept. 10, 12, 1804; July 22, Aug. 7, 21, Sept. 11, 1805; Mar. 18, Apr. 17, July 22, 1806; Aug. 31, 1807; May 14, Aug. 13, 1808.
73. *Ibid.*, Sept. 11, 1805.

members instructed their delegates as to the candidates to be supported at the general county meeting.[74]

A critic of the Republican organization in Hamilton County protested in a newspaper attack that the county meeting was not representative of Republicans in the county. "I have it from the best authority, that not more than from four to six met in any one township to appoint their delegates to the aforesaid meeting," wrote "An Old American Farmer," "and they were principally persons materially interested, or that expected appointments at the next election."[75] But one of the delegates promptly called this charge "an *absolute falsehood*" and labeled it a Federalist maneuver to divide the Republicans. "Some of the certificates produced at the meeting of your delegates specified the majority by which some of them were elected," the delegate explained, "and that number was large and respectable, upwards of 40 or 50, to the best of my recollection, being given as the majority of votes from *one* township." Even if only four or six had attended, he pointed out, the meeting had been called by public advertisement two weeks in advance and all Republicans were welcome to attend.[76]

Although the Hamilton County Republican machinery generally appears to have functioned smoothly during the Jeffersonian era, it did not always operate without internal discord. In September 1808, "delegates from the different Republican Corresponding Societies of the county of Hamilton" met and agreed on nominations for presidential electors, for members of Congress and the state legislature, and for local officials.[77] Notices calling the "convention" had specified that it was "expected that the Delegates coming to represent the several societies in the County, will bring certificates of their appointment." Although this suggested efforts to safeguard against irregularities in the party procedures and to avoid internal party conflicts, the meeting produced a division. A number of the delegates walked out because they thought "the principles upon which the majority of the delegates acted, were not purely republican"; they then nominated a separate ticket.[78]

Problems of party unity were even greater on the state level. In state-wide elections, the co-operation of the various corresponding socie-

74. *Ibid.*, Aug. 7, 21, 1805.
75. *Ibid.*, Sept. 11, 1805.
76. *Ibid.*, Sept. 18, 1805.
77. Cincinnati *Liberty Hall*, Aug. 20, Sept. 3, 10, 24, supplement, 1808.
78. *Ibid.*, Sept. 3, 24, supplement, 1808.

ties appears to have been informal and lacking in central direction. Thomas Worthington, observing the Republican differences in regard to presidential electors in 1808, regretted that the nomination of Republican electors had not been made by a legislative caucus since it was "all important that the republicans should act in harmony."[79] Though a general agreement on Republican electors appears to have been informally arranged, there was still a considerable scattering of votes in the choice of electors in 1808.[80]

In the nomination of a Republican candidate for Ohio's one representative to Congress, no formal state-wide machinery was developed at this time, and Republicans in different parts of the state were not always united behind a candidate. In some areas, as in Hamilton County, the county convention of delegates from township Republican societies nominated a candidate for Congress; in other places, congressional nominations were informally presented or proposed at a general party meeting.[81] The Hamilton County organization attempted to exert a certain amount of state-wide leadership by having the reports of its meetings and recommendations published in newspapers in other parts of the state and through correspondence with Republicans in other counties. After proposing a candidate for Congress in 1806, the Cincinnati Republican society, for example, appointed a committee of correspondence to communicate the nomination to "republicans throughout the state, requesting their concurrence therein." On another occasion, to support their choice for Congress, "An Address from the Republican Corresponding Society of Cincinnati to the citizens of the state of Ohio" was published.[82]

The Hamilton County Republican machinery was at times admired by less well-organized Republicans in other counties. "A Republican," writing in the Chillicothe *Scioto Gazette* in November 1804, presented an outline "taken from the plan of organization adopted by your fellow citizens in Hamilton county" urging Republicans of Ross and Franklin counties to institute similar plans for "connecting your energies by a systimatical organization." He explained:

79. Worthington to Samuel Huntington, July 29, 1808, "Letters from Huntington Correspondence," Western Reserve Hist. Soc., *Tracts*, 95 (1915), 121-22; see also Huntington to Elijah Wadsworth, Aug. 25, 1808, *ibid.*, 123-24.
80. Cincinnati *Liberty Hall*, Nov. 25, 1808.
81. Cincinnati *Western Spy*, July 22, 1806, Aug. 13, 1808; Cincinnati *Liberty Hall*, Sept. 24, 1808, supplement; Chillicothe *Scioto Gazette*, Oct. 4, 1804, Apr. 24, May 1, July 10, Sept. 4, 1806.
82. Chillicothe *Scioto Gazette*, Apr. 17, 1806; Cincinnati *Western Spy*, Aug. 17, 1807.

This plan is simple. Let a Republican Society be constituted in each township, and one in the capital; previous to each election, or to any important constitutional measure, canvass the merits of your candidates, and the propriety of any measures you wish carried. In order to collect the sentiments of the whole in one focus, send one delegate from each township to meet two delegates from the society in Chillicothe, who shall have the power to express the general will. From the patriotism of the republicans in the capital, there is no doubt but they will take the lead, and correspond with other societies on every occasion interesting to the public welfare. By this organization, the whole republican strength will be directed to a single point. There will be an *union* and not a *division* of the same interest. . . .

Your fellow citizens in Hamilton county . . . will always be extremely pleased to find that you are disposed to promote similar measures; and their central committee will correspond with your committee, as soon as your committee thinks proper to open the correspondence.[83]

There is no indication in the newspapers that this plan was implemented immediately in Ross and Franklin counties,[84] but some progress was apparently made in that direction. Newspapers in 1807 report several township meetings where committees were chosen to meet with those of other townships in Ross County to agree upon party nominees.[85]

Republican party machinery was thus uneven on the county and local levels in Ohio, and on the state level it depended largely on informal arrangement by party leaders. That there was more formal Republican party organization in Ohio than in the other western states of Kentucky and Tennessee is reasonably explained by more active Federalist opposition there than in the states to the south.

Although the limitations of source material leave the political picture incomplete in several states, the available evidence summarized in the preceding survey of state party machinery supplies sufficient details to reconstruct an outline of the basic framework of Republican state party machinery. In every state north of Maryland, there was in operation by 1808 some system of state party machinery, although it varied from only a caucus organization in Vermont to the extensive manager-committee system of Connecticut. In all but two of these nine states—New Jersey and Delaware—a state legislative or semi-legislative caucus played a

---

83. Chillicothe *Scioto Gazette,* Nov. 19, 1804.
84. *Ibid.,* Apr. 24, May 1, 15, Aug. 28, 1806.
85. *Ibid.,* Aug. 21, Sept. 3, 1807.

prominent part in Republican machinery. In both New Jersey and Delaware, state party conventions were found instead of caucuses, and the caucus was also being replaced by a convention or a caucus-convention in Rhode Island and in Pennsylvania by 1808.

In general, the party machinery of the middle states was less centralized and permitted more popular participation in party affairs than the Republican systems in the New England states. In Pennsylvania, Delaware, New Jersey, and New York, local party committees chosen on the local level emerged in varying degrees to play an increasingly important role in state party affairs, while in most of New England local committees were appointed by the state party caucus or central party organization. The three largest New England states, Massachusetts, Connecticut, and New Hampshire, all had elaborate committee systems; although committees appointed by local initiative operated from time to time in Massachusetts, centralization of party machinery prevailed, and in most instances committee systems were appointed from the top downward. Vermont and Rhode Island had no state committee systems, but a state caucus directed Republican operations in both states throughout most of the period. The innovation of the convention in Rhode Island in 1808 was an important exception.

In Maryland and in the states to the south and in the West, formal party machinery which could compare in extent or maturity to that in the middle and eastern states was found only in Virginia. Republicans in Virginia operated a well-organized and highly centralized party machine directed by a semi-legislative caucus and a caucus-appointed central committee. But neither a state caucus nor a state committee system was found in any other southern state. Although a variety of local party machinery existed in Maryland, there was no formal state organization and no state party caucus. In Ohio, Republican societies acted in the capacity of committee systems, but state-wide organization was not systematized. In the Carolinas and in Georgia formal party organization did not exist on the state level, and local machinery was sparse. Similar conditions existed in the western states of Kentucky and Tennessee; although a caucus met in Kentucky in 1808 to recommend Madison for the presidency, it did not nominate a ticket for presidential electors.

Thus in ten states, of a Union of seventeen, Republican party machinery operated on a state-wide basis either through a caucus, a convention, a committee system, or a combination of these processes. These states included the largest and most influential states in the Union—Virginia, Pennsylvania, Massachusetts, and New York—together with Connecticut, New Hampshire, Vermont, Rhode Island, New Jersey, and Delaware. If the party organizations on a local level in Maryland and Ohio are added, in only five states—North Carolina, South Carolina, Georgia, Kentucky, and Tennessee—was formal party organization so occasional and scattered as to leave the direction of the party largely to informal influence and association.

Thus, though the process was not yet complete, by 1808 the control of the party within the various states and the direction of state party activities and campaigns was, taking the country as a whole, predominantly in the hands of formally organized party machinery. The structure of party machinery, varying as it did from state to state, determined that the participation of the voter in the affairs and the decisions of the party would differ widely throughout the country, but, in more and more places, party mechanisms were becoming a familiar part of American politics.

CHAPTER NINE

Problems of Party Unity

Party unity was one of the most difficult problems which faced the Republican party in the period from 1801 to 1809. The defeat of the Federalist party in 1800 removed from the Republicans the pressure of Federalist power which had cemented them together as an opposition party. As the party in power, the Republicans, enjoying a strong majority in Congress and in the country as a whole, found party discipline and unity difficult to maintain.

Signs of disunity appeared soon after the cheers of the Republican victory celebrations faded away. Differences over patronage policies were the first signals of disharmony. As early as August 1801, Governor Thomas McKean of Pennsylvania, where Republicans had been in power in the state government since 1799, was writing to Jefferson about Republican conflicts over offices. "When ever any party are notoriously predominant they will split," he concluded philosophically; "this is in nature; it has been the case time immemorial, and will be so until mankind become wiser and better. The Outs envy the Inns. The struggle in such a situation is only for the loaves and fishes."[1]

The first major problem of party unity centered around the Vice-President and his role in the Republican party nationally and in the state of New York. Because of Aaron Burr's position, Republican divisions in New York were intricately involved in national politics. The suspicions of many Republicans that Burr had intrigued to deprive Jefferson of the presidency in the election of 1800 had cast a heavy shadow over Burr's rising fortunes in the Republican party. The bright political prospects which had been produced by Burr's leading role in carrying New York for the Republican party in 1800 had been clouded by Burr's failure to announce that he would not accept the presidency even if the House decided the tie electoral vote in his favor.

As early as September 1801, Gallatin had expounded privately to

[1] McKean to Jefferson, Aug. 10, 1801, Jefferson Papers, Lib. Cong.

Jefferson the difficulties relating to Burr and the future course of the Republican party. There were two points, he said, "on which I wish the Republicans throughout the Union would make up their mind. Do they eventually mean not to support Burr as your successor when you shall think fit to retire? Do they mean not to support him at next election for Vice-President?" Gallatin confessed that "had I felt the same diffidence, I mean the total want of confidence, which during the course of last winter I discovered in a large majority of the Republicans towards Burr, I would have been wise enough never to give my consent in favor of his being supported last election as Vice-President. In this our party, those at least who never could be reconciled to having him hereafter as President, have made a capital fault, for which there was no necessity at the time, and which has produced and will produce us much embarrassment." Gallatin saw no easy solution to the dilemma. He disliked the idea of supporting a section of New York Republicans against Burr, because Burr was still considered the leader of the majority of Republicans in that state; and he felt that Republican factions in New York would bargain with Burr in order to control the state government by giving him support for his ambitions outside the state.[2] Jefferson, nevertheless, did not hesitate to repudiate the Vice-President by ceasing to follow Burr's patronage recommendations in regard to New York. Jefferson's refusal in 1801 to give office to Matthew L. Davis, one of Burr's chief lieutenants, when it was clear to Jefferson and to Republican politicians in New York that this refusal would be construed as a declaration of war on Burr, showed that Jefferson was unwilling to tie the future of the Republican party to Burr.[3]

In January 1802, as president of the Senate, Burr seemed to confirm his alienation from the administration by casting his tie-breaking vote to recommit to committee an administration-sponsored measure to repeal the Judiciary Act of 1801. On February 22, he appeared at a Federalist dinner in the capital to celebrate Washington's birthday and proposed a toast: "The union of all honest men!"[4] To many, no more proof was needed of Burr's apostasy. But Congressman John P. Van Ness of New York, a Burr adherent, explained privately that Burr had declined

2. Gallatin to Jefferson, Sept. 14, 1801, Adams, ed., *Gallatin Writings*, I, 51-53.
3. In regard to Burr and the patronage and Davis's application for office see pp. 38-44 above.
4. Burr to Joseph Alston, Feb. 2, 1802, Davis, *Memoirs of Burr*, I, 171; Burr to Charles Biddle, Feb. 2, 1802, Charles Biddle Papers, Hist. Soc. of Pa.; Adams, *History*, I, 280-83.

an invitation to dine with the Federalists. "After dinner, however, he went into their room, and to his astonishment found the whole corps there celebrating Washington's birthday; he immediately discovered the object and the business, not knowing it before, and after having sat for a moment or two retired. In the meantime, however, they called on him for a toast—and he gave the one you mention." Van Ness also pointed out that Burr attended the Republican celebration on March 4, and after he withdrew was toasted with three cheers—the same number accorded the President.[5] But whatever the circumstances of Burr's actions and the outward appearances of his relations with the two parties, Burr himself was feeling an isolation from the administration. "I dine with the President about once a fortnight, and now and then meet the ministers in the street," he wrote privately to his son-in-law. "They are all very busy: quite men of business. The Senate and the vice-president are content with each other, and move on with courtesy."[6] Federalists expectantly noted Burr's position. "I have the best evidence that Burr is completely an insulated man at Washington—wholly without personal influence," wrote Theodore Sedgwick.[7] Soon another was asking: "Is he to be used by the Federalists, or is he a two edged sword, that must not be drawn? I have sometimes inclined strongly to the opinion," said Harrison G. Otis, "that you ought to make use of him . . . that you cannot so conveniently carry hostility into your enemy's camp under any other general."[8]

In the summer of 1802, James Cheetham, editor of the New York *American Citizen,* openly attacked Burr, specifically charging him with improper activities designed to win the presidency for himself in the election of 1800.[9] In December 1801, Cheetham, in a lengthy letter to Jefferson, had explained his relations with Burr and his changing attitude toward him. Cheetham reported that Burr had tried to get him to establish a paper under his patronage, and, though he had not done so, he had remained on intimate terms with Burr for some months after entering into

5. John P. Van Ness to William P. Van Ness, Apr. 2, 1802, Van Ness Papers, N. Y. Pub. Lib.
6. Burr to Joseph Alston, Mar. 8, 1802, Davis, *Memoirs of Burr,* II, 185.
7. Sedgwick to Rufus King, Feb. 20, 1802, Theodore Sedgwick Papers, Mass. Hist. Soc.
8. Otis to John Rutledge, Jan. 29, [1803], Rutledge Papers, Univ. of N. C.
9. [James Cheetham], *A Narrative of the Suppression by Col. Burr, of the History of the Administration of John Adams* (N. Y., 1802), pamphlet, Lib. Cong.; [James Cheetham], *A View of the Political Conduct of Aaron Burr, Esq. Vice-President of the United States* (N. Y., 1802), pamphlet, Va. State Lib.

a partnership with David Denniston of the *American Citizen* in May 1801. From his contacts with Burr, Cheetham could affirm that since May 1801 Burr had frequently expressed his dissatisfaction with the administration and repeatedly criticized the President's appointments. "The end is obvious," Cheetham concluded. "It is to bring the present administration into disrepute, and thereby to place Mr. Burr in the Presidential Chair."[10]

Although Cheetham emphasized these considerations in explaining his turning against Burr, the public break in 1802 cannot be disassociated from the internal politics of New York State. A confidential letter from United States Senator John Armstrong to DeWitt Clinton, in June 1802, suggests that the New York Clintonians had decided that the time was right to destroy Burr. Armstrong was confident that Burr's New York strength was confined to the city and that there was little prospect of his gaining ground in the country or among the Federalists. "Can we look for any circumstances more auspicious to ourselves than the present?" he asked. "I think not. The cards are with us, and we should go the vote. An unbroken vote from this State does not merely disappoint Mr. B.—it prostrates him and his ambition forever, and will besides be a useful admonition to future schismatics. It is therefore well worth all the exertion, that may be necessary to effect it."[11]

As for Burr, he had no doubt that the responsibility for the Republican attacks upon him rested squarely with DeWitt Clinton, the governor's nephew and Cheetham's "colleague and instigator." "The charges which are of any moment will be shown to be mere fabrications," wrote Burr. "But there seems at present to be no medium of communication. The printers, called republican in this city (Denniston and Cheetham), are devoted to the Clintons, one of them (Denniston) being nephew to the governor, and, of course, cousin to DeWitt."[12] Burr's close friend John P. Van Ness explained that efforts were being made to refute the attacks on Burr, "but you must not be surprised at not seeing those publications in a Republican Paper, as there is only one of that description in this place and the Editor of it has very basely become one of the Banditti in this busi-

10. Cheetham to Jefferson, Dec. 10, 1801, Jefferson Papers, Lib. Cong. See also Cheetham to Jefferson, Dec. 29, 1801, Jan. 30, 1802, *ibid.*
11. Armstrong to DeWitt Clinton, June 26, 1802, DeWitt Clinton Papers, Columbia Univ.
12. Burr to Joseph Alston, July 3, 19, Aug. 2, 1802, Davis, *Memoirs of Burr*, II, 205, 208-9.

ness."[13] Before the summer of 1802 passed, the conflict between the Clintonians and the Burrites erupted beyond the warfare of the printed page, and a duel was fought between DeWitt Clinton and John Swartwout, a leading Burr supporter and a Jefferson-appointed United States marshal.[14]

The attacks made upon Burr in New York caused considerable concern among Republicans outside the state. "Appearances are stormy at New York; the schism disgusts many Republicans, [it] is fomented by the Federalists," observed Gallatin;[15] and Wilson Cary Nicholas wrote a lengthy letter to DeWitt Clinton expressing his fears that the attack "may produce a schism among the republicans, and that it may tend to lessen the confidence of the people in our leaders." Nicholas explained that "when we recommended Col. Burr for his present office he was very little known to a great proportion of the American people, he was taken up, upon our recommendation and responsibility; I fear his fall will attach some disgrace to those who induced the people to vote for him." Yet Nicholas concluded that the distrust of Burr was such that Republicans could never support him for the presidency and it was preferable to break with Burr now than on the eve of the next election. "Our situation was like that of a man who submits to the loss of a limb to save his life," he suggested, though hastening to add that he did not consider Burr so vital to the Republican party as a limb to a man. Thinking of the general interest of the party, Nicholas cautioned: "There are the most urgent reasons why every thing should be avoided that will induce a belief that personal regard to Mr. Jefferson has in any manner excited this attempt to unveil this modern Machiavel."[16]

In August, Jefferson expressed his concern to Gideon Granger, who had close ties with New York Republicans. "I see with sincere grief that the schism at New York is setting good republicans by the ears, and is attacking characters which nobody doubts," Jefferson lamented. "It is not for me to meddle in this matter; but there can be no harm in wishing for forbearance."[17] Before he could have received Jefferson's letter, Granger, passing through New York on his way to Connecticut, had breakfasted with Burr. But "not a word passed respecting what had

13. Van Ness to Samuel Smith, Aug. 2, 1802, Samuel Smith Papers, Lib. Cong.
14. Neither antagonist was seriously wounded. The duel was a subject of considerable controversy. *Ibid.*; Justin Foote to Ebenezer Foote, Aug. 2, 1802, Foote Papers, Lib. Cong.
15. Gallatin to Jefferson, Aug. 9, 1802, Adams, ed., *Gallatin Writings*, I, 83.
16. Nicholas to Clinton, Aug. 13, 1802, DeWitt Clinton Papers, Columbia Univ.
17. Jefferson to Granger, Aug. 29, 1802, Ford, ed., *Jefferson Writings*, VIII. 170-71.

happened in New York," he wrote to Jefferson. "I was prepared to converse, but not to open the conversation on that subject. Luckily I met with DeWitt Clinton and had a lengthy conversation—he avers the substantial facts charged in the Pamphlet can be proved." Granger also cautioned: "You will soon be visited by some principal people from New York and pardon me, Sir, for the liberty I take in recommending caution and circumspection while in their company. The visit to me appears inexplicable. I am not alone in this opinion."[18]

Meanwhile, Gallatin, visiting in New York, observed that Cheetham's attack on Burr had "deeply injured the Republican cause in this State," but his report to the President differed from that of Granger. He too had seen Burr, who had shown him a letter he had written to Governor Joseph Bloomfield of New Jersey containing "an explicit denial of the charges and assertions of his having either intrigued with the Federal party or in any other way attempted during the late election or balloting to counteract your election."[19] When he reached Connecticut, Granger spent a day with state Republican leaders Pierpont Edwards and Abraham Bishop. "They do not appear to believe the charges against Col. Burr," he reported, "but say that being once proved he will be abandoned by all."[20] It was evident that the attack on Burr affected the unity of the Republican party throughout the country, and, when even two members of the President's Cabinet on the scene tended to view the problem in a different light, Jefferson's position was not enviable.

It seems unnecessary in this study to examine the mass of charges and countercharges concerning Burr's conduct in the election of 1800, but it is important to notice that the charges of intriguing against Jefferson carried widespread conviction. In Virginia, "the dissatisfaction that existed as to Col. Burr's conduct made the people sufficiently ready to receive impressions to his disadvantage," observed Wilson Cary Nicholas.[21] From Pennsylvania, William Duane reported: "In this state all confidence in Mr. B[urr] is gone."[22] Tennessee Congressman William

18. Granger to Jefferson, Sept. 5, 1802, Jefferson Papers, Lib. Cong.
19. Gallatin to Jefferson, Sept. 21, 1802, Adams, ed., *Gallatin Writings*, I, 101.
20. Granger to Jefferson, Sept. 5, 1802, Jefferson Papers, Lib. Cong.
21. Nicholas to DeWitt Clinton, Aug. 13, 1802, DeWitt Clinton Papers, Columbia Univ. For an examination of the charges against Burr see Brant, *Madison, 1800-1809*, 23-24; Borden, "The Election of 1800: Charge and Countercharge," *Delaware History*, 5 (1952), 42-62.
22. Duane to Abraham Bishop, Aug. 28, 1802, William Duane Personal Papers Miscellaneous, Lib. Cong. See also Dallas to Gallatin, June 27, 1802, Gallatin Papers, N.-Y. Hist. Soc.

Dickson assured Andrew Jackson that "the Vice President has lost irretrivably the confidence of the American people";[23] and a Federalist colleague from North Carolina agreed: "He is given up by his party. They sincerely abhor him."[24] That these were not irresponsible or unrepresentative statements was soon to be proven by events.

Although outwardly displaying neutrality in the New York dispute, the President revealed his distrust of Burr and his sympathy with the Clintonians in his private correspondence and in the informal diary notes he made for himself. When a pamphlet published in reply to Cheetham charged George Clinton with improper conduct in regard to Jefferson's election in 1800, Clinton hastened to inform Jefferson that the charge was "abuse and dishonorable misrepresentation." But Jefferson assured Clinton that his explanations were unnecessary, that he had read enough of the pamphlet to know it was filled with falsehoods.[25] As the New York gubernatorial election of 1804 approached and Burr's ambitions for the governorship became clear, Jefferson, though refusing to give any direct support, assured DeWitt Clinton of his sympathy. "I should think it indeed a serious misfortune should a change in the administration of your government be hazarded before its present principles be well established through all its parts," he wrote. "Yet, on reflection, you will be sensible that the delicacy of my situation, considering who may be competitors, forbids my intermeddling. . . . I can therefore only brood in silence over my secret wishes."[26]

When Burr called on Jefferson in January 1804 to present his case to the President, he received a cool reception. Burr suggested that to prevent a Republican schism, he would be willing to retire from politics if some mark of favor were bestowed upon him to show that he retired with Jefferson's confidence. But Jefferson gave him no encouragement, and when Jefferson recorded the interview in his notes, he added he had

23. Dickson to Jackson, Dec. 10, 1802, John Spencer Bassett, ed., *Correspondence of Andrew Jackson*, 7 vols. (Wash., 1926-33), I, 64.

24. Archibald Henderson to John Steele, Jan. 16, 1803, Wagstaff, ed., *Papers of John Steele*, I, 357. See also Robert Johnson to Madison, Dec. 5, 1802, Madison Papers, Lib. Cong.

25. Clinton to Jefferson, Dec. 23, 1803, Jefferson to Clinton, Dec. 31, 1803, Jefferson Papers, Lib. Cong. The writing referred to was Aristides [pseud.], *An Examination of the Various Charges exhibited against Aaron Burr, Esq., Vice President of the United States* . . . (Phila., 1803), pamphlet, N.-Y. Hist. Soc. [written by Burr's close friend, William P. Van Ness]. This pamphlet was answered by James Cheetham in *A Reply to Aristides* (N. Y., 1804), pamphlet, Lib. Cong.

26. Jefferson to DeWitt Clinton, Dec. 2, 1803, Ford, ed., *Jefferson Writings*, VIII, 282.

long distrusted Burr and "habitually cautioned Mr. Madison against trusting him too much." "There never had been an intimacy between us," he said, "and but little association."[27]

After the names of Morgan Lewis and Aaron Burr had been placed in nomination for governor by the rival factions of the New York Republican party,[28] a number of prominent New York leaders called on the President to sound out his position in regard to the contest. Oliver Phelps, who had been nominated for lieutenant governor on the ticket with Burr, assured Jefferson that "the friends of Mr. Burr had been much misrepresented" and that many who would support him were "among the warmest friends to the administration of the general government." He wished to know in what light he would be considered by the administration if he supported Burr's election. "I understood you in reply," Phelps wrote in recalling the interview, "as taking the high and honorable ground of being superior to an interference in party dissensions."[29] Jefferson's answer appears to have been the same to all similar inquiries: he would not interfere in the New York election.[30]

But different interviewers attached different interpretations to Jefferson's statements, and when they repeated the President's remarks in their own words they sometimes unknowingly or purposely altered his meaning. The friends of Burr chose to interpret Jefferson's declaration of neutrality as meaning that Jefferson approved equally of Burr and of Lewis. A handbill, issued by the "Republican Albany Committee" in support of Burr, was headed in large type: "Jefferson & Burr, against the Clinton & Livingston Combination." It explained:

Our president THOMAS JEFFERSON, UNEQUIVOCALLY DECLARES THAT COL. BURR AND HIS FRIENDS ARE CONSIDERED, BY THE ADMINISTRATION OF THE GENERAL GOVERNMENT, AS EQUAL IN REPUBLICANISM AND INTEGRITY TO MORGAN LEWIS. This fellow citizens, is important information—it proves to every unbiassed mind that the contest is between Aaron Burr and his infuriated persecutors, and that Republicans may exercise their opinions with perfect security to the General Government, as they have the APPROBATION of Mr. JEFFERSON IF THEY SUPPORT Mr. BURR and Mr. PHELPS.[31]

27. Jefferson, "Anas," Jan. 26, 1804, *ibid.*, I, 301-4.
28. See pp. 149-52 above.
29. Phelps to Jefferson, Apr. 10, 1804, Jefferson Papers, Lib. Cong.
30. See Gideon Granger to DeWitt Clinton, Mar. 27, 1804, DeWitt Clinton Papers, Columbia Univ.
31. Broadside, [1804], signed Thomas Mather, chairman, N. Y. Pub. Lib.

Burr opponents charged misrepresentation and falsehood. Jefferson had said he would take no part in division among real Republicans, they argued, but he did not consider "the *little band*" as forming any part of the republican interest. Those who have confidence in the administration, said Lewis's supporters, "will oppose the elevation of a man to the governmental chair of this state, whose known principles are hostile to the general government."[32]

Gideon Granger, who had taken a position similar to that of the President in regard to the New York election, also found that the "most unwarrantable and unjust use is made of my name and pretended declarations relative to the pending elections."[33] It was clear that leaders on both sides placed great value on endorsement by the President or by members of his administration and would if necessary twist their words to give that impression. Burr adherents, visibly concerned about their political future, were anxious not to be read out of the national party for supporting Burr for governor. "I take this opportunity of again assuring you," wrote Oliver Phelps to Jefferson, "that a great number of influential and active republicans, warm and decided friends to the administration support Col. Burr—among them are the most uniform and zealous of those who formed the republican party previous to our success over the federalists. . . . That Col. Burr will be elected, I think most probable and am confident that his republican friends will furnish a steady and honorable support to the administration."[34] By the unauthorized use of his name the President was dragged through the New York campaign; yet in the middle of the contest Granger could still write: "In the midst of all these conflicts the President preserves the confidence of everyone."[35]

Although Burr leaders might attempt to confuse the voters as to Jefferson's sympathies in the election, there was clear evidence that Burr had been repudiated by the Republican party nationally. Reports that the Vice-President was "given up by his party" had come out of Washington for some time.[36] There was no question of this when the congressional caucus which met in February 1804 to nominate the Re-

32. *ELECTORS,* New York, Apr. 10, 1804, broadside, N. Y. Pub. Lib. See also *Albany Register,* Apr. 12, 1804, extra, broadside, N. Y. Pub. Lib.
33. Granger to Jefferson, Apr. 26, 1804, Jefferson Papers, Lib. Cong.
34. Phelps to Jefferson, Apr. 10, 1804, *ibid.*
35. Granger to DeWitt Clinton, Mar. 27, 1804, DeWitt Clinton Papers, Columbia Univ.
36. Archibald Henderson to John Steele, Jan. 16, 1803, Wagstaff, ed., *Papers of John Steele,* I, 357.

publican candidates for president and vice-president made its decision. The caucus was unanimous in its determination not to renominate Burr for vice-president. Burr did not receive a single vote. As the principal national organization of the Republican party, the congressional caucus's voice in regard to Burr's political future in the party nationally was decisive.[37] "It is worthy of particular notice that the name of Mr. Burr, was not introduced either in the meeting, or in a single vote," the *Aurora* pointed out in a piece that was quickly reprinted in Cheetham's *American Citizen.* "The fact that, among from one hundred to one hundred and twenty republican members of both Houses of Congress, there was not *one* individual who either nominated or voted for Mr. Burr, . . . is highly important. . . . We cannot but congratulate on this renunciation of Mr. Burr; we had rather his misconduct had not been such as to merit this great national chastisement, but having been detected and exposed . . . it became the representatives of the nation to strike his name off the list of citizens worthy the support of a free and *honest* people."[38]

The New York contest for governor in 1804 was of added concern to the Republican party nationally because of the support which the Federalist party gave to Burr. Federalists had long realized that their best hope of returning to power was to divide the Republican party, and they had carefully nourished Republican discords. Some Federalist leaders saw in Burr a chance to destroy the national dominance of the Jeffersonians. Some even thought in terms of a secession of New England and saw Burr as the only hope of including New York in the northern confederation.[39] Oliver Wolcott in a confidential letter written in New York, March 3, 1804, to Connecticut Congressman Roger Griswold, on the question of the Federalists supporting Burr, advised:

> Many who consider it no object, to decide between these Parties, with reference merely to the *internal concerns of this State,* will be governed by the opinion they form, of the probable effect of supporting Burr on the Interests of the Northern States collectively considered. They believe a crisis is impending which no skill or prudence can avert, and they are determined at all hazards, to free this part of the Country at least, from the abhorred domination of the perfidious Virginians. It is of the utmost consequence therefore, to ascertain whether the Northern Democrats in

---

37. See pp. 103-4 above, for details relating to the congressional nominating caucus.
38. Philadelphia *Aurora,* Mar. 1, 1804, New York *American Citizen,* Mar. 3, 1804.
39. Adams, *History,* II, 160-85.

Congress have begun to open their eyes, on the degraded condition of the Northern States and whether a *"Union of Parties"* is practicable with the view of opposing Virginia influence.[40]

Griswold replied that: "Many of the democratic members of Congress, from the Northern States have become sensible of the overbearing influence of Virginia. A few of them, appear disposed to attempt some union, which shall create a Northern interest and array it in opposition to Virginia—but this disposition is by no means universal. . . . Some attempts have been made to unite the Northern Representatives, but it has not succeeded. . . . The impossibility however of forming a Northern interest in Congress by the union of parties, ought not discourage exertions at home." Griswold, though expressing grave doubts as to what Burr's future policies might be, concluded that the only hope of the Federalists was to support Burr.[41] Although Hamilton used his influence against any Federalist support of Burr, he was not able to prevent the majority of New York Federalists from voting for Burr.[42]

Federalist support, however, was insufficient to elect Burr. Lewis's victory was decisive and was accompanied by the overwhelming defeat of Burrites for the New York legislature.[43] Burr's loss of the New York election ended not only his own political future but also the designs of those Federalists who cherished hopes of detaching northern Republicans from the national Jeffersonian party. It was also cause for Republican relief throughout the country. "This event I conceive must have a happy effect upon the republican cause generally throughout the Union," wrote former Senator Theodorus Bailey from New York. "Our republican fellow citizens cannot therefore restrain their joyful exultations on this auspicious occasion."[44]

In Philadelphia, at a Fourth of July celebration in 1804, a toast was drunk: "The advocates of Burrism and third party principles—May they be speedily shipped on board a British prison ship, and exported to the

40. Wolcott to Griswold, Mar. 3, 1804, William Griswold Lane Collection, Yale Univ.
41. Griswold to Wolcott, Mar. 11, 1804, *ibid.*
42. Adams, *History*, II, 183-86.
43. Theodorus Bailey reported to Jefferson that only 2 Burrites and 14 Federalists were returned to the Assembly consisting of 100 members. Bailey to Jefferson, June 9, 1804, Jefferson Papers, Lib. Cong.
44. *Ibid.* See also Samuel L. Mitchill to Madison, May 3, 1804, Madison Papers, Lib. Cong.

congenial regions of Nova-Scotia."⁴⁵ But, although Burr had been defeated in New York and the regular party organization had triumphed over a third-party challenge, the threat of Republican divisions and third-party movements was far from subsiding. Nowhere were local Republican divisions so critical as in Pennsylvania. Jefferson, at first, had tended to view the Republican discords there without alarm. In August 1802, he assured an anxious Governor McKean: "Despairing of success by their own strength, the only hope of the federalists is in dividing their opponents. This was to be expected, and we must count on it's not being always unsuccessful. So eager are men to carry their points that we shall often see minorities of republicans giving law to majorities by accepting the aid of the little band of federalists. The evil will however be less as it will take place, not between questions of republicanism or federalism, but only of more or less republicanism."⁴⁶

Republicans on the scene, however, were not so philosophical as the President. "The plan with the opposition is to divide and I am afraid they have in some measure effected their purpose," wrote Thomas Leiper, "but how can it be otherwise when our principle men are at daggers drawn."⁴⁷ William Duane agreed that "the jealousy among the principal republicans here requires a most vigilant attention," and presented Jefferson with "an outline of our leading men's dispositions towards each other":

1. Mr. [Alexander J.] Dallas—Offended with 2, unreservedly opposed to 4, cold to 3 and 5.
2. Dr. [George] Logan—Violently hostile to 1; unreservedly opposed to 3 and 5; good understanding with 4.
3. Dr. [Michael] Leib—Hostile to 2; familiar with 1 and 4; common cause with 5.
4. Mr. [Tench] Coxe—Estranged but willing to be friends with 1; friends with 2; familiar and friendly with 3 and 5.
5. Mr. [Peter] Muhlenberg—Friendly with all—but displeased with 2; and rather distant than familiar with 4.⁴⁸

Duane's summary strikingly illustrates the disunity among Pennsylvania Republican leaders and suggests how greatly these personal differences contributed to the party divisions in the state. Duane, who as

---
45. Wilmington *Mirror of the Times,* July 25, 1804.
46. Jefferson to Thomas McKean, Aug. 19, 1802, McKean Papers, Hist. Soc. of Pa.
47. Leiper to Jefferson, Sept. 19, 1802, Jefferson Papers, Lib. Cong.
48. Duane to Jefferson, Oct. 18, 1802, *ibid.*

editor of the *Aurora* and as an active participant in party affairs was in a position to know whereof he spoke, felt that "these five may be said to hold the principal weight" in the state. "I am sorry to say that no actual cause of *jealousy* exists with foundation between them, but what is *wholly political*," he concluded. "Each of them in one way or another considers his neighbor a rival! And the loss of any one of them would be to us a very serious evil. . . . The next two years will require all our strength of talents and activity—and Mr. Burr I make no doubt is laboring to assail every man's passions who he may conceive of weight, or likely to go into the erection of a third party."[49] Before long, others would be complaining to Jefferson that Duane was promoting Republican disunion by "denunciations of some of our best, and most influential friends."[50] Thomas Leiper, an active Philadelphia Republican leader, believed that patronage was a major factor in Pennsylvania divisions and recommended removals "to make room for some men whom I am afraid their habits of Republicanism will not be sturdy without an office. This I look upon as one of our greatest misfortunes," he confessed, "and the evil cannot be corrected but by a change in office notwithstanding anything Madison or Gallatin may say to the contrary."[51]

Although Pennsylvania Republicans managed to get along well enough in 1802 to re-elect Thomas McKean as governor and to choose a unanimous delegation of eighteen Republicans to Congress,[52] internal party squabbles soon became serious. Disagreement over Jefferson's patronage policy in Pennsylvania reached new heights early in 1803.[53] "I foresee a schism in Pennsylvania," Gallatin alerted the President in discussing appointments.[54] But once again, Jefferson replied calmly: "I have for some time been satisfied a schism was taking place in Pennsylvania between the moderates and high-flyers. The same will take place in Congress whenever a proper head for the latter shall start up, and we must expect division of the same kind in other States as soon as the Republicans shall be so strong as to fear no other enemy."[55]

John Beckley, the politically active clerk of the House of Representatives, wrote from Philadelphia in May 1803 that he was "laboring to

49. *Ibid.*
50. Andrew Ellicott to Jefferson, Dec. 1, 1803, *ibid.*
51. Leiper to Jefferson, Sept. 19, 1802, *ibid.*
52. McKean to Jefferson, Feb. 7, 1803, McKean Papers, Hist. Soc. of Pa.
53. See pp. 53-56 above; Higginbotham, *Keystone in the Domocratic Arch*, 58-59.
54. Gallatin to Jefferson, Mar. 21, 1803, Adams, *Gallatin Writings*, I, 118.
55. Jefferson to Gallatin, Mar. 28, 1803, Ford, ed., *Jefferson Writings*, VIII, 222-23.

effect an association and union of the principal characters now at variance," but his report to Madison was not promising. "There are great jealousies and divisions here among the democrats on the question of removals from office, although a decided majority are in the affirmative on that question," he wrote, "and great feeling is expected thereon pointed at Mr. Dallas here, and Mr. Gallatin at Washington, the alledged supporters of the system of moderation, as it respects Pennsylvania. It is difficult to restrain the turbulent spirits within any bounds of decency, and, as connected with other intrigues of some designing men, but little suspected, I know not where it will end."[56]

By 1804, the Republican party in Pennsylvania was hopelessly split: divided by personal rivalries, discord over federal patronage, disputes over judicial reform in the state, and increasing differences over the policies of Governor McKean.[57] Jefferson confessed that "our friends in Philadelphia seem to have got into such a jumble of subdivision that not knowing how they stand individually," he didn't know to whom he could write.[58] But he was reluctant to admit the existence of a third party. "That the rudiments of such a 3d party were formed in Pennsylvania and New York has been said in the newspapers, but not proved," he wrote. "Although I shall learn it with concern whenever it does happen, and think it possibly may happen that we shall divide among ourselves whenever federalism is compleatly eradicated, yet I think it the duty of every republican to make great sacrifices of opinion to put off the evil day."[59]

In August 1804, in a lengthy and detailed letter to Jefferson, Thomas Leiper blamed Tench Coxe, Jefferson-appointed purveyor of public supplies, for the division in Pennsylvania; and William Duane also singled out Coxe for attack as the leader of a third party.[60] Meanwhile, Alexander James Dallas, Jefferson-appointed federal district attorney, canceled his subscription to the *Aurora* and blamed its editor for the party discord. "The violence of Duane has produced a fatal division," he wrote to Gallatin. "He seems determined to destroy the republican

56. Beckley to Madison, May 5, 1803, Madison Papers, N. Y. Pub. Lib. See also Gideon Granger to Jefferson, May 6, 1803, Jefferson Papers, Lib. Cong.
57. For a detailed treatment of Pennsylvania politics in 1804 see Higginbotham, *Keystone in the Democratic Arch*, 65 ff.
58. Jefferson to Thomas Leiper, June 11, 1804, Ford, ed., *Jefferson Writings*, VIII, 305.
59. Jefferson to Joseph Scott, Mar. 9, 1804, *ibid.*, 305n.
60. Leiper to Jefferson, Aug. 16, 1804, Jefferson Papers, Lib. Cong.; Philadelphia *Aurora*, Aug. 23, 24, 1804.

standing and usefulness of every man, who does not bend to his will."[61] Finding a sympathetic ear in Gallatin, Dallas unburdened himself. He was convinced that the administration must "take decisive measures to discountenance the factious spirit." He believed that "unless some principle of political cohesion can be introduced into our public Councils, as well as at our elections," and men of character and talent brought into government, "the empire of Republicanism will moulder into anarchy." The time had come "to rally the genuine Republicans," he said. "At present we are the slaves of men, whose passions are the origin, and whose interests are the object, of all their actions: I mean, your Duanes, Cheethams, Leibs, etc., etc."[62]

Governor McKean was equally severe on Duane, writing to Jefferson that Duane "affects to consider his importance as an Editor of a Newspaper, to be superior to the Governor of a State, or even of the President of the United States."[63] Gallatin, who had felt the lash of Duane's pen, especially for his presumed influence over Jefferson in the administration's removal policies, thought Duane was "intoxicated by the persuasion that he alone had overthrown federalism" and resentful that he was "neither sufficiently rewarded nor respected." But Gallatin would not place all of the blame on Duane. Governor McKean by his removal policies, he thought, had encouraged a thirst for offices, and by his nepotism and indiscretion he had afforded an opportunity for divisions. Congressman Michael Leib, moved by ambition and envy, had fanned the flame. "Want of mutual forbearance amongst the best intentioned and most respectable republicans has completed the schism," Gallatin concluded.[64]

In the Pennsylvania gubernatorial election of 1805, two well-organized parties, both led by men who had once been co-workers in the Republican party, sought the Republican vote.[65] On one side were the Republicans who refused to support Governor McKean for re-election, nominated Simon Snyder, and advocated a constitutional convention to amend the state constitution. Prominent leaders of this group were William Duane, Michael Leib, Thomas Leiper, Matthew Lawler, and Joseph Clay. This

61. Dallas to Gallatin, Oct. 16, 1804, Gallatin Papers, N.-Y. Hist. Soc.; Dallas to William Duane, Aug. 20, 1804, Dallas Papers, Hist. Soc. of Pa.
62. Dallas to Gallatin, Jan. 26, 1805, Gallatin Papers, N.-Y. Hist. Soc. See also Dallas to Gallatin, Apr. 4, 1805, *ibid*.
63. McKean to Jefferson, Feb. 18, 1805, McKean Papers, Hist. Soc. of Pa. See also McKean to George Logan, Feb. 15, 1805, Logan Papers, Hist. Soc. of Pa.
64. Gallatin to Jean Badollet, Oct. 25, 1805, Gallatin Papers, N.-Y. Hist. Soc.
65. See pp. 162-63 above.

party, as the election proved, represented the majority of the Republicans in the state. The minority Republican faction following the leadership of Alexander James Dallas, Tench Coxe, William Jones, and George Logan supported the re-election of Governor McKean and opposed changing the state's constitution. Although this party assumed the name of Constitutional Republican, the term *Quid* was more familiarly used.

It was in Pennsylvania that the name *Quid*, which soon found usage in other states and in national politics, appears to have been first prominently employed in a political sense. Editor William Duane began consistently using *Quid* or *Tertium Quid* (meaning a third something of ambiguous status) in 1804 to refer to the rival faction within the Republican party.[66] Duane accused the Quids of being a third party akin to that of Burr in New York and pointed to Tench Coxe as "the principal contributor for the columns of a paper established by a *third party*. . . . Indeed *Mr. Coxe* may be emphatically called the *head* of the third party in this state," Duane proclaimed, "as *Mr. Burr* is that of the third party in the state of New York."[67] The Pennsylvania Quids and the New York Burrites were both third parties which commanded only a minority support within the Republican party. Both accepted the support of the Federalists. In New York in 1804, that support was not sufficient to elect Burr. In Pennsylvania in 1805, the combined strength of the Quids, or Constitutional Republicans, and the Federalists was strong enough to re-elect McKean. Gallatin estimated that the Quids commanded about one-fourth, or at most one-third, of the Republican vote in the state.[68]

Although Jefferson did not publicly take sides in the Republican divisions, his name was not kept out of Pennsylvania politics, just as it had not been kept out of New York politics. Opponents of Duane repeatedly protested that the editor of the *Aurora* endeavored to leave the impression that he was in the confidence of the President.[69] On the other hand, Duane's political ally Congressman Michael Leib complained to Jefferson during the 1805 election that Dr. George Logan was claiming that he had received a letter from the President exhorting him to use all his influence to re-elect Governor McKean on the grounds that to displace

66. Higginbotham, *Keystone in the Democratic Arch*, 69. The term was used as early as 1803 in the *Aurora*. *Ibid.*, 63.
67. Philadelphia *Aurora*, Aug. 24, 1804.
68. Gallatin to Jean Badollet, Oct. 25, 1805, Gallatin Papers, N.-Y. Hist. Soc.
69. Andrew Ellicott to Jefferson, Dec. 1, 1803, Jefferson Papers, Lib. Cong.; Alexander J. Dallas to Gallatin, Apr. 4, 1805, Gallatin Papers, N.-Y. Hist. Soc.; Andrew Ellicott to Madison, Oct. 2, 1805, Madison Papers, Lib. Cong.

him would be injurious to the Republican cause. Leib explained that he felt it his duty to apprise the President of "the use which is made of your name in the local affairs of Pennsylvania. You must be persuaded that great sensibility would be excited in this State, could it be believed that the President of the United States would interfere in our elections; and without any other authority than my confidence in you, I have flatly denied any such interference."[70] In assuring Leib that he had written no such letter to Logan, Jefferson made his usual explanation of neutrality:

I see with extreme concern the acrimonious dissensions into which our friends in Pennsylvania have fallen, but have long since made up my mind on the propriety of the general government's taking no side in state quarrels. And with respect to myself particularly, after eight and thirty years of uniform action in harmony with those now constituting the republican party, without one single instant of alienation from them, it cannot be but my most earnest desire to carry into retirement with me their undivided approbation and esteem. I retain therefore a cordial friendship for both the sections now so unhappily dividing your state.[71]

Before long Jefferson received an anonymous letter from Philadelphia:

Doctor Michael Leib is going from Beer House to Beer House in the City of Philadelphia and Northern Liberties showing a letter on the subject of our approaching election which he says he received from you. He enjoins secrecy on those to whom he shews it but cares not how many see the letter; perhaps near a thousand persons of the lowest class of society have already seen it. Those who are your *real* friends here cannot but regret that you should correspond in any shape whatever with so noted a liar and abandoned villain. His only aim is evidently to raise his own consequence by showing that he possesses so much of your confidence as to receive a letter from you.[72]

Though Jefferson's position was thus made difficult, he did not throw the weight of the presidency into the state party divisions, except to urge mutual concessions on both sides. Tench Coxe and Alexander J. Dallas, both federal officeholders and active Pennsylvania Quids, for example, kept their posts. Both Republican factions in Pennsylvania felt Jefferson should support them as the real Republicans. Alexander J. Dallas urged that the administration "take decisive measures to discountenance the factious spirit" of Duane and Leib, unaware that earlier Joseph Clay and

70. Leib to Jefferson, July 22, 1805, Jefferson Papers, Lib. Cong.
71. Jefferson to Leib, Aug. 12, 1805, Ford, ed., *Jefferson Writings*, VIII, 353-54n.
72. Unsigned letter to Jefferson, Philadelphia, Aug. 24, 1805, Jefferson Papers, Lib. Cong.

two other Pennsylvania congressmen had asked the President to appoint Leib to a federal office in Pennsylvania, thus demonstrating "some decisive countenance . . . to those who have heretofore braved the tempest" and effecting a "salutary influence" against the evil of a third party.[73] Meanwhile a supporter of McKean wrote: "Make some allowances for Mr. Jefferson—'it is heaven that has made us and not we ourselves,' and he perhaps observes a proper delicacy in not interfering in State politicks." But he concluded: "I own I should feel it a duty to express my sentiments against Jacobinism and Despotism at all times."[74]

The severity of Republican discord revealed in the Pennsylvania election of 1805 and the role played by the Federalists in bringing victory to the Pennsylvania Quids aroused an alarm in Jefferson not previously displayed in regard to party divisions. To Caesar A. Rodney, he wrote:

> How deeply to be regretted, my dear Sir, is the bitter schism which has lately split the friends of republicanism into two adverse sections in Pennsylvania! It holds up a melancholy prospect to the friends of liberty when they see two descriptions of sincere votaries to republican government let their passions get so far the mastery of their reason and patriotism, as that the one should drive, and the other hand into power the monarchical enemies of both, rather than use a little indulgence towards the opinions of each other. Is all reconciliation impossible? Have personal hatreds obtained such dominion over the breasts of both as to render every other sacrifice preferable? Every patriot on both sides who feels this should retire and suffer their more temperate brethern to come foward and endeavor a reconciliation. . . . He who would do to his country the most good he can, must go quietly with the prejudices of the majority till he can lead them into reason. . . . I cannot put pen to paper to a member of either party without scolding.[75]

Gallatin, noting that McKean owed his victory to the Federalists, confessed: "What will be the consequence I cannot even conjecture: my ardent wishes are for mutual forgiveness and a re-union of the republican interest; but I hardly think it probable."[76] In fact, it took nearly three more years for Republican unity to be restored in Pennsylvania.

Although on the state level Republican divisions were more critical in New York and Pennsylvania than elsewhere, party unity was disrupted

---

73. Dallas to Gallatin, Jan. 26, 1805, Gallatin Papers, N.-Y. Hist. Soc.; Joseph Clay, Jacob Richards, and Frederick Conrad to Jefferson, Jan. 23, 1804, *ibid*.
74. Thomas Law to George Logan, Aug. 29, [1805], Logan Papers, Hist. Soc. of Pa.
75. Jefferson to Rodney, Oct. 23, 1805, Jefferson Papers, Lib. Cong.
76. Gallatin to Jean Badollet, Oct. 25, 1805, Gallatin Papers, N.-Y. Hist. Soc.

in several other states. Republican discord flared in Delaware over the patronage early in Jefferson's administration.[77] Wilson Cary Nicholas reported party divisions in Virginia as early as 1804, particularly in the Norfolk area,[78] but serious state-wide division was not revealed until the election of 1808. In Rhode Island, a Republican split appeared in 1804, largely over the question of continued support or opposition to Governor Arthur Fenner.[79] Christopher Ellery, prominently involved in the party discords, provided Gallatin with a brief summary, written in 1807:

A schism has existed in the republican party, in this State, since the Fall of 1804. Parties have been three, nearly equal in numbers: The federalists, the friends of the late Governor Fenner, and the real republicans. The federalists have uniformly been in opposition to the General Government; the second named class have, at least, heretofore, worn the garb of republicanism; and the last, if I am not deceived, and I am proud of being one of the number, have been the sincere friends of the Union and its present Administration, at the same time that they have been determined opponents of factious and unprincipled men of whatever name, and have claimed, as they have deserved, the character of genuine republicans. In order to keep out of power the federalists, the real republicans have been forced to make great sacrifices, particularly in supporting for office persons unworthy of their support, both to fill the State departments and to fill seats in Congress.[80]

Rhode Island Republicans who carried their party troubles to the President met with Jefferson's sympathy but no help. "It is not for me to unravel the passions or the schisms which are so unhappily prevailing in your state. Still less am I disposed to take any side in this family quarrel," Jefferson wrote to one Rhode Island Republican. ". . . I hope there is sincere patriotism enough in all the parties to heal this schism, at least in all cases where the public interest is in question. Certainly I shall never know any difference between them."[81] To Virginia's Wilson Cary Nicholas, Jefferson confessed: "I did believe my station in March 1801 as painful as could be undertaken, having to meet in front all the

77. Thomas McKean to Jefferson, Aug. 10, 1801, Jefferson Papers, Lib. Cong.
78. Nicholas to Jefferson, Nov. 23, 1804, Mar. 10, 1805, *ibid.;* Jefferson to Nicholas, Dec. 6, 1804, Mar. 26, 1805, Ford, ed., *Jefferson Writings,* VIII, 338, 348-49.
79. David L. Barnes to Jefferson, Nov. 27, 1804, Jefferson Papers, Lib. Cong. See also Gideon Granger to Jefferson, Sept. 25, 1804, *ibid.*
80. Ellery to Gallatin, Apr. 27, 1807, Gallatin Papers, N.-Y. Hist. Soc.
81. Jefferson to David L. Barnes, Dec. 15, 1804, Jefferson Papers, Lib. Cong. See also Barnes to Jefferson, Nov. 27, 1804, Christopher Ellery to Jefferson, Nov. 19, 1804, Jefferson to Ellery, Nov. 22, 1804, *ibid.*

terrible passions of federalism. . . . But I consider that as less painful than to be placed between conflicting friends."[82]

The serious Republican divisions in the large and influential states of New York and Pennsylvania and party discord elsewhere created alarm of a national third-party movement. The worst fears appeared to have been realized when, early in 1806, John Randolph broke with the administration, announcing on the floor of the House of Representatives that "relative to what is generally called *quiddism*," he was "willing to meet gentlemen on that ground. If we belong to the third party, be it so."[83] Although Randolph thus associated himself with "quiddism," it is improper to use the name *Quid* as a synonym for *Randolphite*. *Quid* was a common term used to refer to third-party men and had no exclusive application to Randolph's followers. As has already been noted, *Quid* was being used prominently in a political sense in Pennsylvania in 1804. The Pennsylvania Quids, or Constitutional Republicans, constituted a third party which with the support of the Federalists was able to win the gubernatorial election of 1805. The term *Quid* also soon came into prominent usage in New York to refer to the Republican supporters of Governor Morgan Lewis after he was repudiated by the Clintonians. It is also important to note that when Randolph spoke of *the* third party, he was not being accurate, for there was no third party; instead there were several. More significant is the evidence that these third parties— these Quids in different states—did not support Randolph.

The important fact is that Randolph's schism did not lead to a third party of national proportions. The common description of "Randolph and the Quids" as the first third party in American history[84] is without foundation. There is no evidence to show that Randolph ever had a wide popular following, not even in Virginia. His schism, instead of cementing together a third party, left only a small group of dissatisfied "Old Republicans" in Congress. That Randolph did not lead a national party of Quids is clearly demonstrated by his relations with the party divisions in Pennsylvania and New York, the two states where third parties were strongest.

82. Jefferson to Nicholas, Mar. 26, 1805, Ford, ed., *Jefferson Writings*, VIII, 349.
83. *Annals of Congress*, 9 Cong., 1 Sess. (Mar. 13, 1806), 775. On *Quids* see Noble E. Cunningham, Jr., "Who Were the Quids?" *Mississippi Valley Historical Review*, 50 (1963).
84. See John D. Hicks, "The Third Party Tradition in American Politics," *Miss. Valley Hist. Rev.*, 20 (1933), 4-5.

In Pennsylvania, William Duane, who was a leading opponent of the Quids in that state, had at first appeared ready to support Randolph. In December 1805, Duane had expressed his concern over what he regarded in Washington as "a general disposition to favor the *spirit of the Quids*."[85] When reports circulated of Republican divisions and opposition to Randolph's leadership in the House, Duane began denouncing the opponents of Randolph as enemies of the administration,[86] much to the alarm of his close political associate Michael Leib, who as a member of Congress was in a better position to know what was happening than Duane. In February 1806, Leib wrote an urgent letter to Caesar A. Rodney asking him to caution Duane to be more guarded in his criticisms:

Some publications which have lately appeared in the Aurora have produced considerable sensation among the best friends of our cause and of Duane. Should these things be persisted in we shall be ruined at this place, and the interest taken in Pennsylvania affairs will be transferred to the quid faction. Unacquainted with the real state of things here, and how men are classed on the secret subjects which have been acted upon, Duane is laying about him, and is dealing his blows to those who have never been questioned as to their principles, or as to their interest in the honor of the present executive, and the success of the democratic cause. Before he condemns he ought to know what he is condemning; before he denounces he ought to know upon what ground the denunciation rests, and who are its objects. Our lips are sealed and he knows it, we cannot, therefore, apprise him of his errors; but surely he ought to have some certain data to proceed upon, before he utters reproach. I have no hesitation in saying, that the measures agreed upon will meet the approbation of the nation, and certain I am, that they are in accordance with our own principles, and will receive the sanction of the democratic party. How ill timed, how unfortunate, how ruinous then must be those articles of reprobation which have appeared in the Aurora! This paper is considered as the mirror of the sentiments of our party, every thing, therefore, which is reflected from it, the party is held responsible for. You will perceive what the operation of his late strictures must be, when compared with those on our own State politics. Men will be led to infer, that we must be as wrong in respect to Pennsylvania affairs, as we are in respect to those of the union, and an alienation of their friendly feelings towards us, must infallibly take place, should such conduct be persisted in.[87]

85. Duane to Joseph Clay, Dec. 12, 1805, Joseph Clay Papers, N. Y. Pub. Lib.
86. Higginbotham, *Keystone in the Democratic Arch*, 111-12.
87. Leib to Rodney, Feb. 8, 1806, Gratz Collection, Hist. Soc. of Pa.

It is clear that Leib was greatly alarmed that Duane might lead the Pennsylvania Republicans into following Randolph, leaving the Pennsylvania Quids in the more favorable position of being supporters of the administration.

On March 12, 1806, Duane reported to Jefferson various rumors that were circulating in Pennsylvania in regard to the administration. Although he professed his own disbelief and related his efforts to counteract them, he suggested that steps should be taken to dissipate doubts. "It is said here," wrote Duane, "that you have thrown yourself into the arms of a New England party, and given them your exclusive confidence; that the sturdy and independent republicans of the South are treated by you with coldness, and reserve. It is said in corroboration—that Mr. J. Randolph has openly attacked your administration, and censured the measures proposed by the administration to Congress." It was also alleged, Duane wrote, that Madison was the only member of the Cabinet not opposed to the President and that the President had announced that only moderate men of both parties would be appointed to office, "that in a word you had avowed an unqualified preference and predilection of those who are called Third party men or Quids."[88] It would appear that Duane still had doubts as to whether or not the President favored Quids, as Governor McKean in Pennsylvania had come to; certainly Duane did not think of Randolph as a Quid.

Jefferson, convinced of "an enemy somewhere endeavoring to sow discord among us," replied at length to Duane, explaining that because of accidental circumstances he had actually had less contact with eastern Republicans during the session than usual and that if there were any coolness between southern Republicans and himself it had not come from him. That Randolph "has openly attacked the administration is sufficiently known," he said, but the vote against him of eighty-seven to eleven Republicans demonstrates "which side retains its orthodoxy." Jefferson encouraged Duane to come to Washington "where alone the true state of things can be known, and where you will see republicanism as solidly embodied on all essential points, as you ever saw it on any occasion." As to Quiddism, Jefferson wrote: "That I have denounced republicans by the epithet of Jacobins, and declared I would appoint none but those called moderates of both parties, and that I have avowed

88. Duane to Jefferson, Mar. 12, 1806, Jefferson Papers, Lib. Cong.

or entertain any predilection for those called the third party, or Quids, is in every tittle of it false."⁸⁹

Before Jefferson's letter reached Duane, the warnings of his friends must have had some effect. The *Aurora* ceased to attack those who opposed Randolph, and Thomas Leiper reported to Jefferson that the *Aurora* had answered Randolph entirely to his satisfaction. Nevertheless, Duane did not join in direct attacks on Randolph, and Congressman Joseph Clay, one of Duane's close political associates, remained one of Randolph's strongest supporters.⁹⁰ As Randolph's criticisms of the administration continued, Congressman Michael Leib also appeared sympathetic to the dissidents, or at least "bewildered in the maze of the moment." The President's "course and his conduct have a suspicious aspect," he thought, but many were driven from acting with Randolph because of his violence. Leib advised Pennsylvania Republicans to adopt a neutral course in regard to the party split in Congress. "I wish our friends in Pennsylvania not to become partizans in the controversy," he wrote. "We have work enough on our hands, a neutral course, therefore, is indicated both by policy and interest. The quids [in Pennsylvania] are falling with us, and we shall only fan the dying embers and, perhaps, kindle a new flame, if we take a side."⁹¹

Contemporary evidence reveals more sympathy and support for Randolph among the Pennsylvania Republicans, led by Duane, Leib, and Clay, than among the Pennsylvania Quids. Alexander J. Dallas, a Quid leader, kept out of the dispute, explaining: "The opposition and speeches of Mr. Randolph are reprobated in some places, and applauded in others.... For my own part, I work as much, and think as little, as I can. But, I confess, I wish that I could see more confidence, co-operation, and system, among our political friends."⁹² In October 1806 the Philadelphia Quids, noticing attacks which had been made on the administration, sent an address to Jefferson, assuring the President of their confidence in him and in his Cabinet.⁹³ Of the six congressmen from Pennsylvania elected on the Quid ticket in 1806, one was a Federalist and the other five were regular Republicans in national politics. Although two of them

89. Jefferson to Duane, Mar. 22, 1806, Ford, ed., *Jefferson Writings*, VIII, 431-33.
90. Leiper to Jefferson, Mar. 23, 1806, Jefferson Papers, Lib. Cong.; Higginbotham, *Keystone in the Democratic Arch*, 112-13.
91. Leib to Caesar A. Rodney, Apr. 1, 1806, Gratz Collection, Hist. Soc. of Pa.
92. Dallas to Gallatin, Mar. 11, 1806, Gallatin Papers, N.-Y. Hist. Soc.
93. An address from the Constitutional Republicans of Philadelphia, signed by Samuel Wetherill, chairman, to Jefferson, Oct. 29, 1806, Jefferson Papers, Lib. Cong.

frequently voted with Randolph, none was his devoted follower in Congress.[94] None of them was to sign the 1808 protest of Randolph against the caucus nomination of Madison, a protest which was to be signed by Joseph Clay and four other Pennsylvania members, none of whom was a Quid.[95] While Randolph supported Monroe for president in 1808, the Pennsylvania Quids supported Madison. In short, the Pennsylvania Quids did not support Randolph, and his strongest support in Pennsylvania came from Republicans who were not Quids, notably Joseph Clay. Instead of either Republican faction in Pennsylvania lining up with Randolph, both continued to insist that they supported the President, though criticism of the President's Cabinet did continue in the *Aurora*. So strongly was Postmaster Gideon Granger attacked by Duane in regard to the Yazoo controversy that he offered to resign if it would "retard the storm which is now gathering round the administration," but the President was unwilling to sacrifice Granger.[96]

Jefferson still continued to "pray for a coalition between the two republican sections of Pennsylvania. They differ in no republican principle," he wrote, "while both differ from the federalists in points which are fundamental. I fondly hope that the good and disinterested of both sections will yield to the duty of suppressing all personal considerations and passions."[97] The President persisted in reaffirming his own neutrality in Pennsylvania politics: "With respect to the schism among the republicans in your state," he wrote to Thomas Cooper, "I have ever declared to both parties that I consider the general government as bound to take no part in it, and I have carefully kept both my judgment, my affections, and my conduct, clear of all bias to either."[98] It is apparent that neither Jefferson nor the Republican factions of Pennsylvania wished to get involved in each other's party discords. So far as Pennsylvania was con-

94. Republicans elected on Quid ticket in 1806 were Robert Jenkins, William Milnor, William Findley, Matthias Richards, John Hiester. Higginbotham, *Keystone in the Democratic Arch*, 119. William Findley reported: "Though Milnor and Jenkins were not Randolphites, yet on most leading questions they voted the same way." Findley to Joseph Hiester, Apr. 9, 1808, Papers of Joseph Hiester, Gregg Collection, Lib. Cong.

95. Pennsylvania signers of Randolph's protest were Joseph Clay, Samuel Smith, Daniel Montgomery, William Hoge, and Samuel Maclay. On the protest see p. 116 above.

96. Granger to Jefferson, Oct. 9, 1806, Jefferson Papers, Lib. Cong.; Samuel L. Mitchill to John Smith, Sept. 3, 1806, Papers of John Smith of Mastic, Long Island, Misc. Coll., N.-Y. Hist. Soc.

97. Jefferson to Timothy Matlack, Mar. 12, 1807, Jefferson Papers, Lib. Cong.

98. Jefferson to Cooper, Sept. 1, 1807, Ford, ed., *Jefferson Writings*, IX, 103n; see also Jefferson to Cooper, July 9, 1807, *ibid.*, 102; Cooper to Jefferson, June 23, 1807, Jefferson Papers, Lib. Cong.

cerned Randolph's schism was kept separate from the party divisions within the state, and, in 1808, reunion among Pennsylvania Republicans began to take place at the time when Randolph was refusing to support the party's presidential nominee.

New York also displays an absence of any alignment between the Quids of that state and Randolph. By the time of Randolph's insurgency in 1806, the New York Republicans who had elected Morgan Lewis governor in 1804 had divided again. The Clintonian faction led by DeWitt Clinton repudiated Governor Lewis for alleged sympathy to Federalists and labeled the supporters of Lewis as Quids. "There is now more real bitterness between the Clintonians and Lewisites," noted one observer, "than there ever has been between the democrats and federalists."[99] There is no evidence that the Lewisites, or New York Quids, supported Randolph any more than did the Pennsylvania Quids. In fact, it appeared for a time as if the Clintonians were going to join the Randolph revolt. John Nicholas, a Republican supporter of Lewis and thus in New York politics a Quid, noticed in February 1806 that DeWitt Clinton's standing toast was to "my countryman John Randolph,"[100] and Governor Lewis observed in March that Clinton had expressed approval of Randolph's opposition to the appropriation of two million dollars for the purchase of Florida.[101] In April, John Nicholas explained in regard to the Clintonians: "J[ohn] R[andolph]'s defection was eagerly caught at and he was puffed with the utmost assiduity until his speech appeared. That was so intemperate and especially so anti-commercial that they were obliged to draw back—not so far however but that they will join if he can rally any considerable opposition."[102] In July, Connecticut Republican Pierpont Edwards concluded:

> The Clintonians and Lewisites are friendly to the President and to his administration; but both these parties have their attention so entirely engrossed by local considerations, that neither of them trouble themselves much with respect to the President, or his administration. There is however this difference between the Clintonians and the Lewisites; the leaders of the former are very friendly to John Randolph and his party, the latter are hostile to him. The leaders of the Clintonian party are supposed to

99. Abraham Van Vechten to Ebenezer Foote, Apr. 7, 1806, Federalist Letters, Univ. of Va.
100. Nicholas to Gallatin, Feb. 26, 1806, Gallatin Papers, N.-Y. Hist. Soc.
101. Morgan Lewis to John Smith, Mar. 23, 1806, Papers of John Smith of Mastic, Long Island, Misc. Coll., N.-Y. Hist. Soc.
102. John Nicholas to Wilson C. Nicholas, Apr. 2, 1806, Nicholas Papers, Univ. of Va.

have strong motives for their predilection for Randolph, for it is considered here, as a firm point, that this influence, which is to exert itself to bring Mr. Monroe into the presidential chair, is also to exert itself to agrandize DeWitt Clinton.[103]

The Clintonians, nevertheless, soon abandoned their sympathies for Randolph. John Nicholas confirmed in January 1807: "In the beginning of last winter there was a settled purpose with the Clintonians to court him, but his principles were so anti-commercial that they feared it might injure their credit here."[104] More significant than the fact that the Clintonians did not line up with Randolph was the evidence that the Lewisites, or New York Quids, did not support Randolph either. Historical evidence thus demonstrates the impossibility of connecting Randolph with factions which in state politics were called Quids.

The presidential election of 1808 displayed Republican divisions but no clear-cut split nationally. Randolph's efforts to propel Monroe into the leadership of a third-party movement against the administration by supporting him as Jefferson's successor were unsuccessful.[105] Monroe had given no encouragement to Randolph's entreaties that he return from his ministerial assignment in England to take the field as a challenger to Madison's ambitions for the presidential nomination in 1808.[106] Jefferson himself had warned Monroe at the time of Randolph's assault on the administration in March 1806 to "be cautious what and to whom you write, that you may not be allied to operations of which you are uninformed."[107] Repeating the warning a few weeks later, he had explained: "The great body of your friends are among the firmest adherents to the administration; and in their support of you, will suffer Mr. R[andolph] to have no communications with them. . . . it is unfortunate for you to be embarrassed with such a *soi-disant* friend. You must not commit yourself to him."[108] Although Monroe returned home in December 1807 on the eve of the election and emerged as a presidential aspirant, he never committed himself to Randolph.

103. Edwards to Madison, July 31, 1806, Madison Papers, Lib. Cong.
104. John Nicholas to Wilson C. Nicholas, Jan. 28, 1807, Nicholas Papers, Univ. of Va.
105. Randolph to Monroe, Mar. 20, 1806, Monroe Papers, Lib. Cong., quoted p. 85 above.
106. Monroe to Randolph, June 16, 1806, Randolph to Monroe, Sept. 16, 1806, Monroe to Randolph, Nov. 12, 1806, Stanislaus M. Hamilton, ed., *The Writings of James Monroe* . . . , 7 vols. (N. Y., 1898-1903), IV, 466-68, 486-91.
107. Jefferson to Monroe, Mar. 16, 1806, Monroe Papers, Lib. Cong.
108. Jefferson to Monroe, May 4, 1806, Ford, ed., *Jefferson Writings*, VIII, 448.

The common assertion that "Randolph and the Quids" supported Monroe for president in 1808 is correct only so far as Randolph is concerned. To say that the Quids supported Monroe is both meaningless and inaccurate. The Pennsylvania Quids supported Madison, as did the New York Quids, although a confused South Carolina writer, who signed himself "A Clintonian," urged South Carolina voters to form a Quid party on the grounds that the Quids were the supporters of Clinton.[109] The New Yorkers who signed Randolph's protest against the caucus nomination of Madison did so because they favored not Monroe but George Clinton; and Clinton himself was convinced that the Quids were supporting Madison. Clinton denounced the caucus which selected Madison as "this pernicious Measure—this offspring of Quiddism." He referred to Washington as "this sink of Quiddism and corruption"[110] and accused Jefferson of favoring the Quids. "I did believe that after our late Election [in New York]," he wrote, "Quiddism had become unfashionable and would be discountenanced at Head Quarters but I am convinced I was mistaken. They are the marked confidants of the Executive in both Houses."[111] It was obvious that Clinton was referring to the New York Quids and not to Randolph's supporters. When in 1808 former Governor Morgan Lewis, defeated in 1807, was visiting Washington, Clinton repeatedly complained of the attention which he received. "He has experienced as much attention at the Palace as ever I did," he wrote, "and is caressed by the Quids and particular favorites of the Administration."[112] Clinton was very bitter in denouncing Quids because they were his political opponents in New York: "That Quiddism in our state is to be countenanced and supported by our beloved [President] cannot be doubted. It is the only chance his favourite has of acquiring the suffrages of New York."[113]

James Cheetham declared in the pro-Clinton New York *American Citizen* in May 1808: "Is it not an alarming fact that the *Quids* in this city and state, in the state of Pennsylvania, and indeed all over the union, are the most noisy, active, and distinguished supporters of the

109. *Charleston Courier*, Sept. 15, 1808.
110. Clinton to Pierre Van Cortlandt, Jr., Feb. 20, 1808, Van Cortlandt Papers, N. Y. Pub. Lib.
111. Clinton to Pierre Van Cortlandt, Jr., Feb. 5, 1808, *ibid*.
112. George Clinton to DeWitt Clinton, Feb. 13, 1808, DeWitt Clinton Papers, Columbia Univ.
113. George Clinton to DeWitt Clinton, Feb. 26, 1808, *ibid*.

election of Mr. Madison?"[114] But the editor of the New York *Public Advertiser* recognized the contradictions in using the term Quid when he replied: "The Quids, says Cheetham, are all for Madison—What say you, Jack Randolph?"[115]

Virginia was the only state in which strong support for Monroe was organized, but it is inaccurate to speak of this as Quid support. There was no Quid party in Virginia, and Monroe's strength in Virginia in 1808 was due not to Randolph's support but to Monroe's own popularity in his native state.[116]

Additional evidence of the failure of Randolph's schism to produce a third party is suggested by the unwillingness of some of his closest political friends to join any party movement. Nathaniel Macon would admit to no more than that he was a Republican of the "old school" whose principles were no longer in style. In 1808 he found his sentiments more in union with those of the President than two years before, and he refused to join in any partisan efforts to elect Monroe to the Presidency. "Perhaps no one knows less about the plans of all parties for the next election than myself," wrote Macon, "yet I am content with ignorance, as no one of the candidates would be my choice."[117] Another close political friend of Randolph, John Taylor of Caroline, also showed an unwillingness to support a Randolph-inspired third party. In August 1807, Taylor wrote to Wilson Cary Nicholas: "I begin to see strange sights in the atmosphere of the imagination. Lately a suspicion has crossed my brain, that the minority as they were called, have a party enmity to the president, instead of having only honorably differed from him in opinion as I supposed. It will give me great pain should it be verified."[118] Nicholas replied: "The 'suspicion that has lately crossed your brain as to what is called the minority' did long since take strong hold of mine, and to tell you the truth, my distress at what was passing was very much increased at hearing you gave your full support to that party. Although I never did give credit to this report, yet it gave me great uneasiness both on your own account

---

114. *American Citizen*, May 31, 1808. On another occasion Cheetham declared he was opposed to Madison "because in politics he is more of a *quid* than anything else." *Ibid.*, June 20, 1808.

115. *Public Advertiser*, May 31, 1808.

116. On support for Monroe in Virginia in 1808 see pp. 232-34 below.

117. Macon to Joseph H. Nicholson, Dec. 26, 1806, Nicholson Papers, Lib. Cong.; Macon to ———, Mar. 26, 1808, Nathaniel Macon Papers, N. C. Dept. of Archives and History; Macon to Joseph H. Nicholson, Apr. 6, Dec. 4, 1808, Dodd, ed., "Macon Papers," *Branch Historical Papers*, 3 (1909), 54, 56.

118. Taylor to Nicholas, Aug. 22, 1807, Edgehill-Randolph Papers, Univ. of Va.

and for the public interest." Nicholas then added what must have been the sentiments of many other Virginians: "I feel the utmost regret at the schism, both from personal and public considerations. No man could admire and respect J[ohn] R[andolph] more than I did; but I cannot go the length of abandoning all my old attachments, I cannot withdraw the confidence that I think so justly do to others, who are my personal and political friends, because he is out of humour with them."[119] Taylor was unwilling to become "a party man against the administration," and he was soon convinced that "poor Randolph is lost, and his party has vanished."[120] Although Taylor supported Monroe in the election of 1808, it was not because of partisanship for Randolph but because of his long-standing misgivings as to Madison's political principles.[121]

In the party divisions among Republicans within the states, it was common for all sides to claim to be genuine Republicans and to pledge their allegiance to Jefferson; few Republicans were willing to go so far as Randolph and break with the President. The danger of being read out of the party for following Randolph was demonstrated by the case of Congressman Thomas Sandford of Kentucky, who was defeated for re-election, according to two witnesses, because of his support for Randolph in 1806.[122] Even in Randolph's home district, there were strong, though unsuccessful, efforts to prevent Randolph's re-election, both in 1806 and 1808.[123] Randolph's close friend Joseph Bryan of Georgia, who advised him to present to the public the reasons for his opposition to the administration, explained: "The people want your motives. They are at a loss to conceive how you could oppose Madison and in some measure the president without swerving from your former (as they are pleased to style them) opinions."[124] Although Randolph wrote a series of papers for the press in defense of his position, his actions conveyed, as John Taylor reluctantly admitted, "party enmity" to the President. That Randolph could expect to attract a popular following among Republicans on the basis of opposition to Jefferson was an impossible presumption.

119. Nicholas to Taylor, Oct. 7, 1807, *ibid.*
120. Taylor to Nicholas, Oct. 26, Nov. 30, 1807, *ibid.*
121. Taylor to Nicholas, Apr. 13, 1805, May 14, June 10, 1806, *ibid.*
122. John Brown to Jefferson, July 25, 1806, John Smith to Jefferson, Aug. 10, 1806, Jefferson Papers, Lib. Cong.
123. Randolph to Joseph H. Nicholson, June 3, 1806, Nicholson Papers, Lib. Cong.; Randolph to James M. Garnett, May 27, Sept. 25, 1808, Garnett to Randolph, Aug. 12, 1808, Randolph Papers, Garnett transcripts, Lib. Cong.
124. Bryan to Randolph, June 3, 1806, Bryan Family Papers, Va. State Lib.

Monroe's candidacy in 1808 presented a peculiar problem of party unity, aside from its relationship to Randolph; for, although he never committed himself to Randolph, Monroe allowed his name to be kept in contention against Madison for the presidency. As described in an earlier chapter, Monroe's supporters in the Virginia Assembly had attempted to win control of the state Republican caucus, which pledged support to Madison, but, failing in that, they persisted in placing Monroe's name in nomination by a minority caucus.[125] Monroe's candidacy appealed to a small group of dissident Republicans who sided with Randolph, to some Federalists, and to a sizable number of Republicans who thought of Monroe as a stronger personality than Madison. John Beckley, who had no sympathy for Randolph, confidentially reported to Monroe in the summer of 1806: "Madison, is deemed by many, too timid and indecisive as a statesman, and too liable to a conduct of forbearance to the federal party, which may endanger our harmony and political safety. It is believed that in you, with equal knowledge of and talents to direct our foreign relations, the known energy and decision of your character would effectually put down all federal views of disuniting us, and ruling themselves."[126] A great deal of Monroe's Virginia support appears to have rested on similar convictions that Monroe would make a more effective president. Some reflective individuals were also uneasy about Madison's political principles. John Taylor of Caroline had doubts about Madison which, he said, "arise chiefly from an opinion, still continuing, that the book called the federalist, is full of federalism, if I understand what federalism is." Taylor found views in *The Federalist* "nearly resembling the obnoxious doctrines in John Adams's book"; thus he confessed: "My inclination towards Col. Monroe's election, turned upon the supposition, that his principles differed from those in the Federalist, which I thought wrong."[127]

Unlike Randolph's backing, much of Monroe's other support, though anti-Madison, was not anti-Jefferson nor anti-Republican. Indeed, Monroe had been repeatedly cautioned by many of his Virginia friends that he would have no chance if he appeared to be an anti-administration candidate. During the maneuvering in the Virginia Assembly to put through Monroe's nomination, one of the Monroe strategists wrote frankly to

125. See pp. 109-12 above. For a detailed examination of Monroe's candidacy see Harry Ammon, "James Monroe and the Election of 1808 in Virginia," *William and Mary Quarterly*, 3d Ser., 20 (1963), 33-56.
126. Beckley to Monroe, July 13, 1806, Monroe Papers, N. Y. Pub. Lib.
127. Taylor to Wilson C. Nicholas, Feb. 5, 1808, Edgehill-Randolph Papers, Univ. of Va.

him: "You are in my opinion still gaining ground here; but a number of those who express themselves to be most warmly attached to you, declare, that they would in a moment, abandon you, 'if they could suppose you capable of countenancing the opposition made to the administration.' I have thought it necessary, without delay, to give you this information."[128]

A similar view was indicated by another Richmond observer who explained: "The democratic party in our Legislature have divided between Madison and Monroe for President. . . . As far as opinions are expressed by them at all, a preference appears for Monroe, on a calculation, drawn from *unexplained* occurrences, that he is less bigotted to the errors which have enthralled us in our present difficulties. The election however has not been placed by his friends on any ground of opposition to the present course of administration."[129] John Taylor also emphasized the impossibility of Monroe's winning support in Virginia on an anti-administration platform, writing to him: "The opinion of all your friends whom I have seen is, that a difference with Mr. Jefferson will destroy your popularity. Many have never even conceived its possibility. And a multitude would desert you, if it was avowed that you would change, and Mr. Madison adhere to, the system of his administration."[130]

Because of the apparent hopelessness of challenging Jefferson's administration, some of Monroe's friends, who had backed him before the official nomination of a Republican candidate for president, urged him to withdraw after Madison had received the nomination of the Republican congressional caucus and the support of the Virginia Republican caucus. Virginia Congressman Matthew Clay wrote to Monroe at the end of February 1808:

Nothing but the importance of the subject, and a sincere regard for public good, and your wellfare could justify the liberty, I am now about to take. The ensuing Presidential Election has caused much party spirit, and has assumed a shape to be viewed with extreme regret. You had sincere and firm friends in Congress but finding they could not run you to advantage, deemed it best for the present, not to hazard the possibility of dividing the republican party—and believing an attempt with little probability of success, would rather prove unfavourable, than honorable:

128. Alexander McRae to Monroe, Richmond, Dec. 31, 1807, Monroe Papers, N. Y. Pub. Lib.
129. Edward Carrington to Timothy Pickering, Jan. 30, 1808, Pickering Papers, Mass. Hist. Soc.
130. Taylor to Monroe, Mar. 20, 1808, William E. Dodd, ed., "Letters of John Taylor, of Caroline County, Virginia," *Branch Historical Papers*, 2 (1908), 294-95.

have therefore thought best for the present to withhold from placing you among the Candidates. This we do from a firm conviction it is the best policy for the public good, and your future prospects. If then a friend may be permitted to advise, put a stop to the contest."[131]

Jefferson himself had already written to Monroe that he saw "with infinite grief a contest arising between yourself and another, who have been very dear to each other, and equally so to me." The President pledged his own neutrality in the contest, but he expressed his deep concern about the consequences of a political controversy between the friends whom he had always viewed as the "two principal pillars" of his happiness.[132]

Monroe could not have been unaware of the potential damage to the party that his continued candidacy might produce, but he did not withdraw. He took the stand that "in regard to the approaching election I have been and shall continue to be an inactive Spectator of the movement. Should the nation be disposed to call any citizen to that station it would be his duty to accept it. On that ground I rest. I have done nothing to draw the attention of any one to me in reference to it, nor shall I in future. No one better knows than I do the merit of Mr. Madison, and I can declare that should he be elected he will have my best wishes for the success of his administration."[133]

Monroe maintained this position until the fall of 1808, when in the closing weeks of the election contest he unexpectedly moved into the active campaign by publishing, with the President's permission, the correspondence which had passed between them in regard to the election and Monroe's recent diplomatic service.[134] In this exchange of letters, Jefferson had expressed his admiration for Monroe, his continued confidence in him, and his neutrality in the contest with Madison.[135] Coming as it did late in the campaign, the publication was apparently of little consequence and seems to have been more of an effort at personal vindication on Monroe's part than a serious bid for the presidency. The main subject of the correspondence was, in fact, not Monroe's candidacy

131. Clay to Monroe, Feb. 29, 1808, Monroe Papers, Lib. Cong.
132. Jefferson to Monroe, Feb. 18, 1808, Ford, ed., *Jefferson Writings*, IX, 177-78.
133. Monroe to Jefferson, Feb. 27, 1808, Hamilton, ed., *Monroe Writings*, V, 26.
134. See Monroe to Littleton W. Tazewell, Sept. 25, 1808, Tazewell to Monroe, Oct. 8, 1808, Monroe Papers, Lib. Cong.
135. *The following interesting correspondence between the President of the United States and Mr. Monroe, is published by consent of the president, at the request of Mr. Monroe,* Office of the Spirit of "Seventy-Six," Richmond, Oct. 27, 1808, circular in Rives Collection, Madison Papers, Lib. Cong.

but his diplomatic mission to Great Britain. Monroe had returned to the United States in December 1807 after having negotiated in association with William Pinkney the treaty of 1806 with Great Britain. As minister to Britain, Monroe had resented the appointment of Pinkney to assist him in the negotiation; and, when the President judged the treaty to be so unsatisfactory that he did not submit it to the Senate, Monroe felt his reputation was severely damaged.[136] "In rejecting the treaty it [the administration] had by implication censured me," he wrote.[137] Although Jefferson found the treaty highly objectionable, particularly because it contained no provision regarding impressment, he assured Monroe that he was confident that the best possible terms had been secured under the circumstances.[138] It was this presidential approval of his conduct that Monroe wanted to get before the public. Indeed, Monroe's attitude toward his candidacy was inseparable from his differences with the administration on foreign policy centering around the rejection of the treaty. He believed that withdrawal from the contest would suggest an unwillingness to stand on the record of his public achievement, thus implying an admission of failure on the British mission. "In regard to the election," he wrote later, "it is known, that I allowed the nomination to be made and persevered in, as a trial of my character, and in support of my independence, of the administration, and of all others, and not in the expectation, or desire of being elected."[139] Regardless of Monroe's reasons for remaining in the contest, his conduct posed a threat to party unity and became an embarrassment to the administration. Jefferson, however, patiently tolerated Monroe's actions and was rewarded when Madison, who was unquestionably the President's choice as his successor, decisively carried Virginia.

Party unity was a constant problem throughout Jefferson's administration, but Republican loyalty to Jefferson was not seriously endangered. The party never was so united while in power as it had been in opposition, but aided by the massive popular support which the President commanded and his policy of forbearance toward intra-party disputes, factionalism was kept in check so long as Jefferson remained in office.

136. See Monroe to Jefferson, Feb. 27, Mar. 22, 1808, Hamilton, ed., *Monroe Writings,* V, 24-26, 27-35.
137. Monroe to Littleton W. Tazewell, Oct. 30, 1808, *ibid.,* 71.
138. Jefferson to Monroe, Mar. 10, 1808, Ford, ed., *Jefferson Writings,* IX, 178n-81n. An examination of the Monroe-Pinkney treaty of 1806 critical of the administration is in Bradford Perkins, *Prologue to War: England and the United States, 1805-1812* (Berkeley, 1961), 114-39.
139. Undated memorandum by Monroe, Monroe Papers, Miscellany, Lib. Cong.

CHAPTER TEN

The Party and the Press

Fully conscious of the power of public opinion and the influence of the press in molding popular sentiment, Republican party strategists were constantly alert to the problems and the uses of the press. The party had utilized the instrument in winning political power and could be expected to look to the party press to support and advance the Republican administration.

There were some 234 newspapers, mostly weeklies, published in the United States in 1800.[1] By 1808 the total had reached about 329. Many of the papers published in 1800 were no longer being printed in 1808, and numerous papers had come and gone in the few years between. A contemporary observed in 1803: "The increase of Gazettes is excessive. I have several times attempted to count the whole number, but they appear and disappear and change places so often that the exact number I cannot ascertain."[2] The historian, faced with the same problem in trying to determine the number of papers and aware also that many files have not survived, cannot obtain completely accurate statistics. As far as can be discovered, there were published, at some time during the year 1808, 260 weeklies, 31 semi-weeklies, 14 tri-weeklies, and 24 dailies, though all of these did not survive the year.[3] Nearly half of all the newspapers published in 1808 were printed in Pennsylvania, New York, and Massachusetts; but every state could claim at least six papers, except Delaware with only one weekly. The twenty-four dailies were published in five cities—Philadelphia, New York, Baltimore, Alexandria, and Charles-

---

1. As tabulated by Donald H. Stewart, *Jeffersonian Journalism: Newspaper Propaganda and the Development of the Democratic-Republican Party, 1789-1801* (unpubl. Ph.D. diss., Columbia Univ., 1950), 24-27, there were 178 weeklies, 29 semi-weeklies, 3 tri-weeklies, and 24 dailies.

2. William Bentley, *The Diary of William Bentley* . . . , 4 vols. (Salem, Mass., 1911), III, 54-55.

3. These totals are compiled from Clarence S. Brigham, *History and Bibliography of American Newspapers, 1690-1820*, 2 vols. (Worcester, Mass., 1947); Clarence S. Brigham, *Additions and Corrections to History and Bibliography of American Newspapers, 1690-1820* (Worcester, Mass., 1961).

ton—but there were important non-daily papers in most of the principal cities. Jefferson believed in 1804 that Federalists controlled three-fourths of the nation's papers,[4] and it is certain that their control of the press was proportionately greater than their party strength. However, by 1808 the Republicans appeared to have a slight lead in the total number of papers, although this total did not necessarily indicate influence; and, while the Republicans had the support of more weekly papers, the Federalists could claim more dailies. As far as party affiliations can be discovered, Republicans in 1808 had the support of 114 weeklies, 11 semi-weeklies, 9 tri-weeklies, and 8 dailies, while Federalists controlled 97 weeklies, 15 semi-weeklies, 5 tri-weeklies, and 14 dailies. Neutral papers and those whose politics are unknown numbered 49 weeklies, 5 semi-weeklies, and 2 dailies.[5]

Although some newspapers tried to maintain a position of political neutrality, the great majority of papers displayed a clear party attachment. In most instances this political alignment was openly and readily acknowledged. David Denniston and James Cheetham, in announcing their partnership to publish the New York *American Citizen,* declared: "The American Citizen . . . shall be DECIDEDLY republican—a defender of liberty—an advocate of the constitution—and a sedulous and zealous detector of those sentiments which tend to sap its foundation and overturn the comely structure."[6] In a similar vein, the editors of the Trenton *True American* pledged that it was firmly attached to the Republican party, "which it will support as far as its influence extends. It lays no claim to the character of impartiality. It will be exclusively Republican."[7] Whether a statement of political affiliation was issued or not, most papers made it known where they stood in regard to parties by the candidates whom they supported and by the positions which they took on issues that were before the public. There could be no doubt of where the Richmond *Examiner* stood when, in reporting the results of a congressional election,

4. Jefferson to William Short, Jan. 23, 1804, *Amer. Hist. Rev.,* 33 (1928), 834.
5. Party affiliation, where files have not been examined, is based on Isaiah Thomas, *The History of Printing in America, with a biography of Printers, and an account of Newspapers,* 2d ed., 2 vols. (Amer. Antiq. Soc., *Transactions and Collections,* 5 and 6 [1874]), II, 296-305. Thomas, who published the first edition of his work in 1810, carefully compiled a list of all newspapers published in the United States between January and June 1810, indicating the party affiliation of most of them. Supplemental information on New England newspapers has been obtained from a manuscript list, "Presses in New England," [1808], in Harrison Gray Otis Papers, Mass. Hist. Soc.
6. *American Citizen,* May 1, 1801.
7. *True American,* Dec. 20, 1802.

the two contestants were referred to as "the enlightened republican candidate" and "the ignorant tory candidate."[8] Enclosing the first number of the *Georgia Republican,* publisher James Lyon assured the President: "The political object of this paper, is to inculcate the principles of Representative democracy, and to defend the present administration against its natural enemies, error and falsehood."[9]

Newspaper editors were frequently prominently involved in state and local politics. William Duane, editor of the influential Philadelphia *Aurora,* was deeply involved in Pennsylvania politics. Meriwether Jones, editor of the Richmond *Examiner,* was appointed to the state Republican committee in 1800, reappointed in 1804, and after his death succeeded on the committee in 1808 by Thomas Ritchie, editor of the Richmond *Enquirer.* Samuel Pleasants, Jr., editor of the Richmond *Virginia Argus,* was named to the same committee in 1800, and renamed in both 1804 and 1808. Elisha Babcock, editor of the Hartford *American Mercury,* worked closely with Connecticut Republican leaders. Peter Freneau, editor of the Charleston *Carolina Gazette,* and James Cheetham, of the New York *American Citizen,* were actively engaged in the politics of their respective states. These examples from a list which could be greatly expanded are representative of the active involvement of editors in party politics.

When Republicans came to power in 1801, party leaders appeared to regard the need for more Republican presses as one of the greatest demands of the party. Although Elbridge Gerry assured the President soon after the inauguration that "republican presses ... are continually multiplying,"[10] Jefferson received frequent reports on the necessity for more papers. From Massachusetts, Levi Lincoln explained: "The Palladium printed at Boston is undoubtedly supplied to the ministers very generally and very extensively without any expense to them, except that of the trouble of spreading them among their parishioners and procuring subscriptions for their more extensive circulation. The Port Folio, printed at Philadelphia, is, I believe, sent to some gentlemen free of expense for similar purposes. The effects of these measures must be counteracted by establishing some more republican presses in the eastern states."[11] Postmaster General Gideon Granger likewise expressed his concern over the lack of Republican papers. "In my tour from Washington to Philadelphia

---

8. *Examiner,* Apr. 13, 1803; see also *ibid.,* Apr. 27, 1803.
9. Lyon to Jefferson, Oct. 5, 1802, Jefferson Papers, Lib. Cong.
10. Gerry to Jefferson, Apr. 29, 1801, *ibid.*
11. Lincoln to Jefferson, July 5, 1801, *ibid.*

I took the back road, through Montgomery, Frederick, York, Lancaster, etc.," he wrote in 1802. "I found on the road a very general circulation of federal papers. They were to be seen at most of the Public houses while on the whole route—say 190 miles, through the best farming Country, I saw but one republican Paper. This was not altogether pleasing to one who believes that public opinion will in a great measure be governed by that Vehicle of Intelligence."[12] Writing to Connecticut Republican leader Ephraim Kirby, Granger stressed that "the Federalists have associated in an organized body to destroy the reputation of the present administration by every species of Slander and Calumny which they have ingenuity to invent.... We therefore ardently solicit our friends and all friends of the Republican Principles to be instant in season and out of season in repelling their attack by counter Publications in the Republican News Papers from time to time as they appear."[13] Similar views were expressed by Secretary of War Henry Dearborn when he wrote to a New England friend in 1802: "The leading characters among the federalists appear to have abandoned every idea of any thing like a compromise . . . they appear to rely principally on writing down (as they term it) the present administration through the channell of their newspapers. The industrious and unremitting application of the tallants they possess, may, in a country like this, where newspapers are so generally circulated, produce very important effects, unless eaqual industry is used on the opposite side."[14]

Republican leaders, recognizing the influence of the press and the Federalist use of that instrument, made continual efforts throughout Jefferson's administration to establish more Republican newspapers.[15] Massachusetts Republican Barnabas Bidwell reported in the summer of 1801: "In the District of Worcester . . . from all appearances, I conclude nothing is wanted in that County, to insure success to Republican-

12. Granger to Jefferson, Sept. 5, 1802, *ibid*.
13. Granger to Ephraim Kirby, Mar. 8, 1802, Kirby Papers, Duke Univ.
14. Dearborn to James Bowdoin, Apr. 10, 1802, "Bowdoin and Temple Papers, Part II," Mass. Hist. Soc., *Collections*, 7th Ser., 6 (1907), 226.
15. Although Republicans concentrated their efforts upon the establishment of Republican papers rather than upon the suppression of the Federalist press, there are several examples of Republican efforts in certain states to counteract the Federalist press by court actions for seditious libel. Three cases have so far come to light: against Harry Croswell, editor of the Hudson, New York, *Wasp*; against Joseph Dennie, editor of the Philadelphia *Port Folio*; and against six defendants in Connecticut, among them Brazillai Hudson and George Goodwin, editors of the Hartford *Connecticut Courant*. These cases and their implications are discussed in Leonard W. Levy, *Legacy of Suppression: Freedom of Speech and Press in Early American History* (Cambridge, Mass., 1960), 297-307.

ism, but a good Paper. I had much conversation with Dr. [William] Eustis and others, respecting the means of introducing and establishing Republican Papers in Worcester and Hampshire and the Province of Maine. The first and last may be easily done, if attempted with prudence and spirit."[16] About the same time, Levi Lincoln wrote from Worcester: "If Massachusetts gets right, all will be right. The other eastern states will be with her. A few more republican newspapers, and the thing is accomplished. Exertions are making to obtain them. Editors alone are wanting, sufficient encouragement would be given them. I mean soon to spend some time in Boston, shall improve the opportunity to political purposes."[17]

Throughout the country, Republican leaders were involved in the establishment and maintenance of party presses. Only six weeks after the death of editor John E. Smith of the *Augusta Chronicle*, Georgia Senator James Jackson had engaged the services of Dennis Driscol, of the Baltimore *American Patriot*, to edit the paper. Introducing him to Republican Governor John Milledge, he explained:

His character, is that of a Man of Learning, integrity, and sound principle precisely such an one, as we needed at Augusta; and I hope he will be properly supported. I have taken the liberty to promise him yours—as well as as much of the publick work, as is consistent with your duty. I shall procure him all the subscribers, I can. . . . I have also assured him, that if necessary he shall be assisted in the purchase of the Smith establishment, at the expiration of the year agreeably to Mr. Smiths desire.[18]

From Wilmington, Delaware, former Congressman Caesar A. Rodney reported in 1805: "We are about to give new life to our torpid Republican paper by obtaining a new editor, who though he cannot be of sounder principles than the present, will have more time to attend to it. A firm, prudent and spirited paper would produce a wonderful change in this State."[19]

In Philadelphia, book publisher Mathew Carey, active in Republican politics, sought to give increased vigor to one of the party's most successful and influential papers, the *Aurora*. Writing to the President in 1802, he explained: "For a considerable time past, it has been strongly

16. Bidwell to Aaron Burr, July 6, 1801, Gratz Collection, Hist. Soc. of Pa.
17. Lincoln to Jefferson, July 28, 1801, Jefferson Papers, Lib. Cong.
18. Jackson to Milledge, Baltimore, Mar. 16, 1803, Salley, ed., *Correspondence of John Milledge*, 100.
19. Rodney to Jefferson, June 3, 1805, Jefferson Papers, Lib. Cong.

impressed on my mind, that notwithstanding the goodness of our cause, we have suffered, and are suffering very severely, by the industry, the talents, the zeal, and the abominable, though plausible, misrepresentations, of the federal Editors, throughout the union, but particularly in this city. There are four daily and two weekly papers printed here, which are hostile to the cause of republicanism. We have only one paper in our defence. That the war is waged on very unequal terms, no man in his senses can dispute or deny." Although Carey praised William Duane's *Aurora* for its great services to the Republican cause, he felt that Duane needed help. He thus proposed to raise by subscription $520 yearly to pay a suitable writer $10 per week "for writing paragraphs and essays, to refute the groundless charges brought against the republicans, and to occasionally carry the war into the enemy's quarters." The chief part of his production would be furnished to the *Aurora,* but occasionally pieces would be sent to Boston, New York, and Baltimore. Carey proposed that Jefferson suggest the plan to some members of Congress to raise the subscription.[20] Jefferson expressed approval of Carey's proposals but replied that in his position he could not take a prominent part in anything of that kind and could not therefore initiate the plan as Carey had suggested. Since editor Duane was not pleased by Carey's dissatisfaction, Carey's efforts, without the President's assistance, apparently collapsed.[21]

In 1801, James Lyon, whom Jefferson described as "a young man of bold republicanism in the worst of times . . . son of the persecuted Matthew Lyon,"[22] attempted to implement a plan to establish a network of Republican presses. Lyon proposed to establish a weekly newspaper in Washington to be printed in pamphlet form, containing "general information upon politicks, the economic arts, and miscellaneous Literature, together with a weekly abstract of intelligence." This would be sent to local printers who would add a cover sheet containing local news and advertisements. Lyon estimated that one hundred subscribers in a district would support a local printer and suggested that under such an arrangement local Republican printing offices could be established with almost as much facility as post offices. "I hope I have convinced you of the practicability of this plan," he wrote in presenting his scheme to the President; "and if so there is no need of a comment to show the immense

20. Carey to Jefferson, Apr. 24, 1802, *ibid.*
21. Jefferson to Carey, May 4, 1802, *ibid.;* Duane to Gallatin, Mar. 15, 1802, Gallatin Papers, N.-Y. Hist. Soc.
22. Jefferson to Gideon Granger, Dec. 5, 1801, Jefferson Papers, Lib. Cong.

advantage of it, as it relates either to the diffusion of knowledge, uniformity of public sentiment or strengthening of the republican cause."[23] Jefferson apparently encouraged Lyon in the project for Lyon thankfully acknowledged "the assistance which Mr. Jefferson has rendered to the Washington Printing and Bookselling Company," and he promised that every effort would be made to establish a branch office in Lynchburg, Virginia, in response to Jefferson's suggestion of the need for a press there.[24] Lyon issued a prospectus, offered five thousand shares of stock in his company at five dollars per share, printed the first number of *Franklin; Or a Political, Agricultural and Mechanical Gazette*, and even prepared circulars to be supplied to local printers by which they could advertise the establishment of their local papers.[25] But Lyon, who had failed in several earlier publishing efforts, was apparently ahead of his times in this well-conceived but ambitious plan, and the venture collapsed. Jefferson believed that "though of real genius, he has not succeeded in his newspapers, owing to his making them vehicles of other kinds of information, rather than of news, which is not within the general object in taking newspapers." Nevertheless, Jefferson continued to encourage Lyon's subsequent publishing efforts.[26]

In the fall of 1808 a group of Newport, Rhode Island, Republicans organized the Newport Republican Association for the purpose of establishing a Republican newspaper. "How can a virtuous government endure, unless its virtues are protected from the blighting influence of calumny, perversion and falsehood," declared the preamble to the articles of association; "and how can those virtues be thus protected, otherwise than by the means of diffusing truth? It becomes indispensable, therefore, to establish a REPUBLICAN NEWSPAPER in this part of the State." For this purpose a fund was raised by issuing shares at five dollars, "each subscriber assuming one or more shares at his option—the money to be paid on or before the *thirty-first day of December*, 1808." The fund was to be administered by a board of nine directors who would procure a "printing-press, types and apparatus, sufficient for the establishment of a printing office, to be the immediate property of the said

23. Lyon to Jefferson, July 23, 1801, *ibid.;* Lyon to Madison, July 2, 1801, Madison Papers, Lib. Cong.
24. Lyon to Jefferson, Oct. 22, 1801, Jefferson Papers, Lib. Cong.
25. [Circular], Washington, Oct. 17, 1801, by James Lyon, "principal agent of the Washington Printing and Bookselling Company," Lyon to Jefferson, Oct. 22, 1801, *ibid.*
26. Jefferson to Gideon Granger, Dec. 5, 1801, Lyon to Jefferson, Oct. 5, 1802, *ibid.*

Association." The newspaper published was to be called the *Rhode-Island Republican* and was to be under the control of the directors who would see that "nothing unbecoming, illiberal or improper, is communicated through its medium; the primary object of which being to discuss political subjects with dignity and fairness; to vindicate the Constitution, and constitutional laws; and to defend the principles of the American Revolution."[27] The plan was evidently successful, for in March 1809 the *Rhode-Island Republican* began publication in Newport.[28]

The Trenton *True American* in November 1808 also published a "Plan for the establishment and support of a firm decided Republican paper in the city of New Brunswick." This proposal recommended that Republicans in each township of the various counties in the vicinity of New Brunswick form a committee of ten to raise the capital to start the paper, to procure subscriptions and advertisements, and to aid in distributing and circulating the paper. A fund of fifteen hundred dollars was to be raised by advances of $1.50 or more to be repaid in the fourth year of publication. When the capital fund was raised and five hundred subscribers were obtained, the paper was to be issued as the *New Jersey Intelligencer and Republican Advertiser*.[29] This plan apparently collapsed since there is no evidence that the paper was ever published.[30] It illustrates, nevertheless, the methods which were attempted in establishing Republican presses.

Party leaders contributed money out of their own pockets to found and maintain Republican papers. In reference to the Worcester *National Aegis,* established in December 1801, Levi Lincoln wrote to the President, after a mixup over printing of the laws: "I need say nothing of the necessity or utility of supporting a republican paper, in this place, nor of its character, after mentioning that Gov. Sullivan, Messrs. Gerry, Bowdoin, S. Brown, the two Messrs. Austins, Doct. Eustis, etc. etc. were among the individuals who subscribed from $50 to 100 dollars each, at first, to establish, and that most of them, with others about fifteen months since . . . contributed then further sums for purchasing new [type] and continuing the establishment."[31] The proprietors of the Republican *Political*

27. *Republican Association,* [1808], pamphlet, Newport Historical Society.
28. Brigham, *History and Bibliography of American Newspapers,* II, 1004.
29. Trenton *True American,* Nov. 21, 1808.
30. No record of it is found in Brigham, *History and Bibliography of American Newspapers* or in Brigham, *Additions and Corrections to History and Bibliography of American Newspapers.*
31. Lincoln to Jefferson, Apr. 1, 1808, Jefferson Papers, Lib. Cong.

Observatory, established in Walpole, New Hampshire, in 1803, solicited support even from distant party leaders. A printed circular, addressed to Kentucky Senator John Breckinridge, explained:

A small number of persons have united, and at a great expense, procured a new press and types, and hired, upon a liberal salary, an Editor and a Printer, and are now enabled to present to the public the first-fruits of their labor. But, to proceed further in the business and carry into complete effect the object of their undertaking, the aid of their political friends is *absolutely* necessary. And it is believed, that the subscribers will find themselves amply compensated for their generous advances, by the satisfaction they will receive from the weekly contents of the Observatory.[32]

Many congressmen contributed to the party press through the letters which they sent to editors and friends back home. Writing to the editor of the *Raleigh Register*, North Carolina Representative James Holland concluded a summary of the proceedings of Congress by stating: "I have no objections to your giving these communications a place in your register."[33] His letter was accordingly published. John Clopton of Virginia suggested that certain paragraphs of a letter to a Richmond friend be published in the *Virginia Argus* under the heading "extract from a member of Congress to his friend in Richmond."[34] The editor of the *Augusta Chronicle* explained in 1808: "The readers of the Chronicle are, from the commencement of the present Session of Congress, indebted to our worthy representative, Doctor [Dennis] Smelt, for the early intelligence they have received from time to time, through the medium of this paper."[35]

In addition to informal party support through the efforts and contributions of party leaders, Republican presses in some areas could count on organized official party support. A convention of Republican delegates from the congressional district embracing Salem, Massachusetts, resolved in 1802: "That it be most seriously recommended to all Republicans to exert themselves to obtain subscriptions for THE SALEM REGISTER,

---

32. [Circular], Walpole, Nov. 19, 1803, signed "The Proprietors," Papers of Breckinridge Family, Lib. Cong. The *Political Observatory* survived until 1809. Brigham, *History and Bibliography of American Newspapers*, I, 490.

33. *Raleigh Register*, Apr. 20, 1802.

34. Clopton to Alexander McRae, Dec. 25, 1807, Monroe Papers, Lib. Cong.

35. *Augusta Chronicle*, Mar. 19, 1808. Federalist Senator William Plumer supplied weekly reports for publication in the *Portsmouth Oracle*, published under the heading "Extracts of letters from Washington." Plumer to Daniel Treadwell, Nov. 6, 1804, Plumer Papers, Lib. Cong.

as a free and well conducted paper, devoted to the republican cause—and particularly that the committees interest themselves in this behalf."[36] Elsewhere Republicans were urged to support the Republican paper in their locality. A party circular in western New York in 1808 declared:

> We invite your attention to another subject—*the support of the Press*. . . . By the invaluable art of printing, the PRESS has become the vehicle of knowledge—and knowledge the sheet anchor of FREEDOM. Republicans must support their *Presses*, or their Presses cannot support *Republicanism*. If public patronage fail them, designing and wealthy men will buy them up to mislead and pervert public opinion. . . . The federalists and British partizans have years since correctly appreciated the influence of the Press on public opinion, and have better patronized it. Their printers acknowledge they are better paid by their party than the Republican printers are—and we have other evidence—that with the large majority of Republicans in this country, yet there are two Federal papers to one Republican in it. This is a severe reflection on the Republicans for their remissness; and we hope it will invite them to extend their patronage by liberal subscriptions and payments for papers. Let every Republican make it a matter of principle and honor to pay his printer when due, and it would greatly aid him in his resources.[37]

In some areas, especially in New England, party newspapers were extensively and gratuitously circulated by party workers during election campaigns. Instructions to Republican committees in Connecticut in 1801 advised that "each town committee be directed to make every exertion to procure a general circulation of republican newspapers." Another Connecticut Republican circular in 1803 urged "that Babcock's *Mercury* be most extensively circulated without delay. The town of New-Haven has lately added 93 to their weekly stock of these papers. They are the only republican papers in the State, which can gain a general circulation. They are cheap and easily obtained."[38] Other towns also secured the *Mercury* in quantity. Ephraim Kirby, chairman of the Litchfield Republican committee, ordered fifty copies to be continued for seventeen weeks during the period of the 1803 elections; and editor Elisha Babcock of the *Mercury* reported in March 1803 that he was printing nearly four

---

36. [Circular], Salem, Sept. 24, 1802, signed John Hathorne, chairman, broadside, Amer. Antiq. Soc.

37. (*Circular*), Canandaigua, Mar. 23, 1808, broadside, N.-Y. Hist. Soc. The number of Federalist papers was exaggerated; see p. 237 above.

38. Republican circular, Oct. 1801, printed in Boston *New-England Palladium*, May 10, 1803; [Circular], New Haven, Feb. 1, 1803, printed in New Haven *Connecticut Journal*, Feb. 24, 1803.

thousand papers weekly.[39] Federalist protests against "an almost gratuitous and universal distribution of the concentrated wisdom of their party, as it beams in the *Mercury*,"[40] suggest that Connecticut Republicans carried out their plans for wide circulation of party papers. By 1805, the party distribution of Republican papers in Connecticut had been well organized. Republican State Manager Alexander Wolcott, in his instructions to county Republican managers, advised: "You will be supplied with newspapers for every town, which the town managers will distribute to the district managers, and these will circulate them among the republicans and federalists in their districts. A correct knowledge of our cause will go a great way towards removing the prejudices, which the devices of our enemies have produced."[41]

In Massachusetts, a district party convention, in 1802, "resolved, That the Printer of the SALEM REGISTER be requested to print an extra number of papers from this time to the time of election, to be distributed GRATIS among the people by committees of the various towns, and that these committees be EARNESTLY REQUESTED to send by all opportunities to Salem for the same, in as great a number as they can use advantageously, and that the same be delivered to said committee FREE OF EXPENCE."[42] The Republican *Independent Chronicle* of Boston proposed in 1808: "To disseminate useful information, and genuine American feelings among the people, *free of expence*, let the republicans unite in forming A PATRIOTIC FUND, to defray the charges of printing and distributing *gratis*, handbills, pamphlets and other papers, containing just views of the causes of our present embarrassments, and such occasional information as may be deemed necessary to enlighten the people on their best and dearest interests. A dollar a man from every one who could afford it, would be amply sufficient."[43] Enthusiastically supporting the proposal, the Boston *Democrat* soon reported that one former Federalist, recently converted to Republicanism, had offered the Patriotic Fund the annual interest on eight hundred and fifty dollars.[44]

39. Elisha Babcock to Ephraim Kirby, Feb. 3, Mar. 29, 1803, Kirby Papers, Duke University. See also Babcock to Kirby, Sept. 17, 1801, acknowledging an earlier order for 50 copies of the *Mercury, ibid.*
40. Boston *New-England Palladium*, Oct. 11, 1803.
41. [Circular], Nov. 1, 1805, printed in Hartford *Connecticut Courant*, Nov. 27, 1805.
42. [Circular], Salem, Sept. 24, 1802, signed John Hathorne, chairman, broadside, Amer. Antiq. Soc.
43. *Independent Chronicle*, Sept. 15, 1808. See also Boston *Columbian Centinel*, Nov. 12, 1808.
44. *Democrat*, Sept. 24, 1808; see also Boston *New-England Palladium*, Sept. 23, 1808.

Printers who supported the party cause expected to receive help from the party. Newspaper publishing was far from lucrative. Printers frequently had great difficulty in collecting subscriptions, and income from advertisements was small. "Subsisting by a country news-paper, is generally little better than *starving*," declared the Trenton *True American* in 1802.[45] City presses had difficulties also and frequently supplemented their income by other types of printing. Under the Federalist administration's sedition law a number of Republican printers had suffered great personal and financial distress. When Republicans took control of the national administration, Republican printers naturally looked to the federal government for patronage, especially in the printing of the laws. Even before Jefferson was elected by the House, the editors of the Boston *Independent Chronicle,* one of whom had spent thirty days in jail under the sedition act, were writing Massachusetts Republican Congressman Joseph B. Varnum in regard to publishing the laws of the United States: "It is generally believed here . . . that those powerful engines of State, which have been laboring so long, and with so much success to sap the foundation of our happy Constitution . . . that those presses or their Editors, cannot, in the nature of things, receive the countenance and support of that Government, which is so obnoxious to them and their party." Congressman Varnum passed the letter on to Jefferson and the printing of the laws was transferred from the Federalist Boston *Columbian Centinel* to the *Independent Chronicle*.[46]

Since the publication of the laws seemed to imply the confidence of the federal government, Republicans were anxious that the federal printing be transferred immediately to Republican printers. Less than three weeks after Jefferson was inaugurated, Maryland's Representative Samuel Smith was pointing out that the laws were still being printed "*By authority*" in a Federalist Baltimore paper; he expressed the hope that the Baltimore *American* "which we have established at great Expense will have the Public Business given it."[47] When federal officers in state posts continued to give their printing business to Federalist presses, there were strong Republican protests. In reply to Anthony Haswell, a Vermont Republican printer who complained of such practices in his state, Jefferson explained the administration's position: "I am sorry to

---

45. *True American,* July 26, 1802.
46. Abijah Adams and Ebenezer Rhoades to Joseph B. Varnum, Jan. 20, 1801, endorsed by Jefferson, Appointment Papers, Nat. Archives.
47. Smith to Levi Lincoln, Mar. 22, 1801, *ibid.*

learn ... that the officers in the public employment still use the influence and the business of their offices to encourage presses which disseminate principles contrary to those on which our constitution is built," he wrote. "This evil will be remedied. We proceed with circumspection to avoid doing any wrong. Your press having been in the habit of inculcating the genuine principles of our constitution, and your sufferings for those principles, entitle you to any favors in your line which the public servants can give you; and those who do not give them, act against their duty. Should you continue in the business you will have the publication of the laws in your state, and probably whatever else of business any of the offices within your state can give."[48]

The policy of rewarding Republican printers with federal patronage suggested by Jefferson in his letter to Haswell was followed by the administration. However, it took longer to make changes than some printers and local Republicans thought necessary, and not a few of them expressed their concern to some member of the administration. A Pittsburgh Republican wrote to Gallatin in August 1801 that "the Anglo printer here although he continues to throw as much odium on the President as he can, and misses no opportunity of Scandalizing him and Republicanism, yet he is employed to do all the printing for the United States in this place. You know sir there is a Republican Press here and I presume the President nor you will approve of Mr. Sculls having the public Printing to do in preference to the Republican Press here, which you know has been a support to the Republican Interest and the Presidents Character and Election."[49] Charles Holt, editor of the New London, Connecticut, *Bee* and a sufferer under the sedition act, pleaded for public printing in November 1801, explaining:

In consequence of my attachment to the principles of the present administration, and my exertions, as a printer, to establish them, I have suffered such a deprivation of business in the line of my profession as to be unable any longer to execute it in this place without further aid and encouragement. Not only have every man in office or under authority under the State government withheld all the printing under their controul from me, but the federal Custom House, Post office, (deputy) supervisor's, Navy and Army business in my calling, has with the most scrupulous care been kept from me,—(and been given to one who makes

48. Jefferson to Haswell, Sept. 11, 1801, Haswell to Jefferson, July 20, 1801, Jefferson Papers, Lib. Cong.
49. Nathaniel Irish to Gallatin, Aug. 14, 1801, Gallatin Papers, N.-Y. Hist. Soc. John Scull edited the Federalist *Pittsburgh Gazette*.

it his weekly task to traduce the character of the President and his friends). From these causes, which have operated against me with increased vigour since Mr. Jefferson's inauguration, I have sunk, within twelve months past, a sum equal to the whole value of my property, and continued in my present situation upon the sole hope that the happy events which have lately taken place in the United State would restore me to the common privileges and employments of Printers, and enable me to gain an honest livelihood by my profession.[50]

Although there were some instances of public printing being given by mistake to Federalist printers,[51] only occasional letters of complaint after 1801 regarding the public printing are found in the papers of Jefferson, Gallatin, and Madison—the latter officer handling the publication of the laws. On the other hand, there are numerous letters from Republican printers to Madison acknowledging their appointments to publish the laws of the United States.[52] Once inaugurated, the policy of supporting Republican presses with printing patronage appears to have been consistently applied throughout the Jeffersonian administration.

In 1804, James Cheetham, editor of the New York *American Citizen*, protested to the President that David Gelston, Jefferson-appointed collector of the port of New York, refused to give him any of his printing business, estimated at seven hundred dollars per year. Cheetham explained that Gelston, a Burrite, divided his patronage between a Federalist and a Burrite and gave him none because the *American Citizen* had abandoned Burr. A committee of Republicans had met with Gelston, and he had promised to give all of his printing to Cheetham; but, wrote Cheetham: "Mr. Gelston *has not* fulfilled the promise which he solemnly made to the Committee, and it has therefore become a Question . . . whether my press is to be destroyed by his continuance in, or preserved by his removal from, office, and the appointment in his place of a Citizen more *friendly* to the *Republican party?*"[53] Jefferson was much disturbed by Cheetham's complaint and instructed Gallatin, spending his summer vacation in New York, to put pressure on Gelston to give his printing to Cheetham. He wrote:

50. Holt to Gallatin, Nov. 29, 1801, Gallatin Papers, N.-Y. Hist. Soc.
51. See Woodbury Langdon to Madison, Feb. 6, 1802, Madison Papers, Lib. Cong.; Levi Lincoln to Jefferson, Apr. 1, 1808, Jefferson Papers, Lib. Cong.
52. See Jesse R. Lucke, ed., "Letters from John Quincy Adams and Others Dealing with the Printing of the Federal Laws in Virginia, 1802-1821," *Va. Mag. of Hist. and Biog.*, 59 (1951), 34-50.
53. Cheetham to Jefferson, July 25, 1804, Jefferson Papers, Lib. Cong.

The inclosed letter to me from Cheetham is very embarrassing. Were competition for the public printing to lie between a Burrite and Clintonian, certainly a decision on our part might be declined. But between a Clintonian and a federalist there cannot be a moment's hesitation; and Mr. Gelston ought certainly to have no hesitation. Yet I ought not to write either to him or to Cheetham on the subject. As you are on the spot, and in communication with Mr. Gelston cannot you find means of setting him to rights in this matter, and that he should use no further delay? I have no objection to his understanding that I consider Cheetham as the most unquestionably republican printer in New-York and therefore having better title than any other.[54]

As this letter demonstrates, Jefferson was determined that Republican printers should be supported by the patronage of the printing business of the federal government and of federal officials.

The greatest embarrassment to the Republican party in relation to the press was provided by James Thomson Callender, who, as one of the most scurrilous writers to support the party, had been convicted under the sedition law and was lodged in the Richmond jail at the time of Jefferson's election. On several occasions Jefferson, while Vice-President, had answered Callender's appeals for support by sending him money—fifty dollars at two different times—and he had given encouragement to his writings by reading some of Callender's proof sheets and confiding to him that "such papers cannot fail to produce the best effect. They inform the thinking part of the nation; and these again, supported by the taxgatherers as their vouchers, set the people to rights."[55] Jefferson had also helped to arrange assistance for Callender at his sedition trial.

Upon becoming President, Jefferson adopted a policy of granting pardons to those convicted under the sedition law and halting prosecution in pending cases. Under this policy, the President granted a pardon to Callender on March 16, 1801, and directed the remission of his fine of two hundred dollars. However, David M. Randolph, United States marshal of Virginia and a Federalist, refused to refund the fine, creating a situation which became increasingly intolerable to Callender and embarrassing to the administration. Randolph was removed from office on

---

54. Jefferson to Gallatin, Aug. 3, 1804, Gallatin Papers, N.-Y. Hist. Soc.
55. Jefferson to Callender, Oct. 6, 1799, Ford, ed., *Jefferson Writings*, VII, 395. For additional details see Cunningham, *Jeffersonian Republicans, 1789-1801*, 169-72; Malone, *Jefferson and the Ordeal of Liberty*, 331-33, 468-71.

March 24, but the issue of refunding Callender's fine remained unsettled.[56] On April 12, Callender protested to the President about the delay in receiving the two hundred dollars. He complained of the "unexampled treatment which I have received from the party" and lamented that he had not profited from the victory of Republicanism.[57] Two weeks later he was extremely critical of Jefferson for not getting his fine remitted when he wrote to Madison seeking appointment as postmaster at Richmond. "And surely, Sir," he added, "many syllogisms cannot be necessary to convince Mr. Jefferson that, putting feelings and principles out of the question, it is not proper for him to create a quarrel with me."[58] About the same time, he complained to Attorney General Lincoln that he had "never had any communication from Mr. Jefferson, which I could regard as amounting to *a serious mark of attention*."[59] Twice he appeared to protest to Governor Monroe in Richmond. He condemned the President for not giving a positive order for refunding his fine. When Monroe tried to explain the legal technicalities involved in the question of the authority of the marshal to return the money, Callender only shook his head and talked of his services to the party and "the ingratitude of the republicans who after getting into power had left him in the ditch." Monroe at first thought of trying to raise money by subscription to pay Callender, but discarded the idea after Callender's second visit. He feared that Callender might use "these circumstances or advances, to the discredit of the government and its friends." Since Callender talked of going to Washington, Monroe warned Madison: "Be assured that the President and yourself cannot be too circumspect in case he comes to Georgetown in your conversations with him; for I think nothing more doubtful than his future political course. If from charitable motives either of you advance him money, it merits your consideration whether he ought to know from whom it came."[60]

Meanwhile, Jefferson decided that Callender should be pacified by refunding his fine by private contributions, and he sent Monroe fifty dollars as his donation.[61] But before this project matured, Callender

56. Albert Gallatin to [Samuel H. Smith], Aug. 20, 1802, copy of pardon and order remitting fine, Mar. 16, 1801, Gallatin Papers, N.-Y. Hist. Soc.
57. Callender to Jefferson, Apr. 12, 1801, Jefferson Papers, Lib. Cong.
58. Callender to Madison, Apr. 27, 1801, Madison Papers, Lib. Cong.
59. Callender to Levi Lincoln, Apr. 29, 1801, Gallatin Papers, N.-Y. Hist. Soc.
60. Monroe to Madison, May 23, 1801, Monroe Papers, N. Y. Pub. Lib.
61. Jefferson to Monroe, May 26, 1801, Worthington C. Ford, ed., *Thomas Jefferson and James Thomson Callender, 1798-1802* (Brooklyn, N. Y., 1897), 38.

appeared in Washington. The President sent his private secretary, Meriwether Lewis, to Callender with fifty dollars and assurances that efforts were being made to return his fine. As Jefferson recounted it to Monroe: "His language to Capt. Lewis was very high toned. He intimated that he was in possession of things which he could and would make use of in a certain case: that he received the 50. D. not as a charity but a due, in fact as hush money; that I knew what he expected, viz. a certain office, and more to this effect. Such a misconstruction of my charities puts an end to them forever." Instructing Monroe not to use the fifty dollars he had forwarded to him, Jefferson concluded: "He knows nothing of me which I am not willing to declare to the world myself. . . . I gave to him from time to time such aid as I could afford, merely as a man of genius suffering under persecution, and not as a writer in our politics. It is long since I wished he would cease writing on them, as doing more harm than good."[62] The cautious Monroe was much alarmed that Lewis had paid the money after what Callender had said and warned Jefferson: "It will be well to get all letters however unimportant from him."[63]

Although Callender's fine was officially returned to him on June 20,[64] he did not receive the postmastership at Richmond, and in the summer of 1802 Monroe's worst fears were realized when Callender turned against the administration. In the midst of his scurrilities against the President, he disclosed the letters and money which he had earlier received from Jefferson.[65] Republicans tried to counteract the embarrassment which the President suffered from having given assistance to so notorious a writer, displaying Callender's attack on the President as the result of the administration's virtuous refusal to accede to Callender's demand for an office.[66] Jefferson privately explained that his gifts to Callender were "mere charities, yielded under a strong conviction that he was injuring us by his writings,"[67] but the fact remained that he had earlier commended Callender for writings designed "to produce the best

62. Jefferson to Monroe, May 29, 1801, *ibid.*, 38-39.
63. Monroe to Jefferson, June 1, 1801, *ibid.*, 39.
64. Copy of receipt signed by Callender, June 20, 1801, in Gallatin Papers, N.-Y. Hist. Soc.
65. Monroe to Jefferson, July 7, 26, 1802, Hamilton, ed., *Monroe Writings*, III, 355-56.
66. Trenton *True American*, Aug. 23, 1802.
67. Jefferson to Monroe, July 15, 1802, Ford, ed., *Jefferson Writings*, VIII, 165-66; see also Jefferson to Mrs. John Adams, July 22, 1804, *ibid.*, 309*n*.

effect." The president's afterthoughts did little to relieve the uncomfortable position in which his prior support of Callender had placed the administration.

When Federalist Congressman John Rutledge, of South Carolina, suggested that Callender be employed by the *Washington Federalist,* one of the proprietors replied:

> It is conceived, that however the spirit of the paper might be increased by such an arrangement, its reputation would certainly be lost. It would be found very difficult to support, much more to associate with a man whose character has been so completely damned to infamy. His present situation is the only one, in which he can be of use; he now stands upon his own grounds with full liberty to shoot his arrows at pleasure. Those against the federalists have been long since exhausted, he can now wound those, by whom he has heretofore been upheld; and he has proven himself to be a much more dangerous friend than enemy.[68]

Callender remained an embarrassing Republican liability until July 1803, when, while drunk, he drowned in the James River.[69]

During his presidency, Jefferson subscribed extensively to newspapers throughout the country. He received the leading Republican papers from various sections, a few Federalist papers, and some miscellaneous Republican sheets to which he subscribed in order to encourage Republican editors. While in office Jefferson apparently never failed to subscribe to any Republican newspaper whose editor was bold enough to solicit the President's patronage. A newspaper account sheet, dated March 31, 1804, in Jefferson's papers shows that he paid out at that time $70.50 for fourteen different papers. In February 1809, he paid $28.50 for previous subscriptions to Georgia newspapers alone.[70] In 1807 Jefferson reported in his possession in Washington fifty-one volumes of newspapers representing more than twenty-three different papers for the years 1797-1807.[71] Other files were at Monticello. Receipts and correspondence in Jefferson's papers and the files of newspapers which he assembled for his library indicate that between 1801 and 1809 President

---

68. Elias B. Caldwell to Rutledge, Aug. 17, 1802, Rutledge Papers, Univ. of N. C.
69. Charles A. Jellison, "That Scoundrel Callender," *Va. Mag. of Hist. and Biog.,* 67 (1959), 295-306.
70. Jefferson, "Newspapers to be paid for," Mar. 31, 1804, Jefferson to John Milledge, Feb. 6, 1809, Jefferson Papers, Lib. Cong.
71. Jefferson to Joel Barlow, Dec. 19, 1807, *ibid.*

Jefferson subscribed for varying periods to at least thirty-three different newspapers.[72]

Although Jefferson subscribed to leading Republican and Federalist papers to keep informed of what was being published on both sides, it is clear that the large number of newspapers which he received, and for which he paid from his personal funds, was prompted by the desire to aid Republican printers. It was with considerable relief that he closed out most of his subscriptions when he retired from office. "These little newspaper accounts scattered all over the union have been extremely troublesome to me," he confessed, "and it is a great consolation to me that I am closing them for ever, and approaching the term when I shall cease to read newspapers."[73] He had no desire to aid Federalist editors even by his own subscription. In 1802 he explained to Republican editor James Cheetham, of the New York *American Citizen*:

It is proper I should know what our opponents say and do; yet really make a matter of conscience of not contributing to the support of their papers. I presume Coleman sends you his paper, as I understand the printers generally do to one another. I shall be very glad to pay you for it, and thus make my contribution go to the support of yours instead of his press. If therefore, after using it for your own purposes you will put it under cover with your American citizen to me, it shall be paid for always with yours. I shall not frank this to avoid post office curiosity, but pray you to add the postage to your bill.[74]

Cheetham accordingly forwarded to the President the *New-York Evening Post*, edited by William Coleman, and received payment for it from

---

72. Boston: *Independent Chronicle, Democrat,* and *Constitutional Telegraphe;* Salem *Register;* Worcester *National Aegis;* Hartford *American Mercury;* New York: *American Citizen, New-York Evening Post, Morning Chronicle,* and *Republican Watch-Tower;* Hudson *Bee;* Poughkeepsie *Political Barometer; Albany Register;* Philadelphia: *Aurora, Aurora, for the Country, Poulson's American Daily Advertiser, Freeman's Journal, Spirit of the Press, Philadelphia Repository,* and *Hope's Philadelphia Price-Current;* Baltimore *American;* Fredericktown *Republican Advocate;* Washington: *National Intelligencer,* and *Universal Gazette;* Georgetown *Cabinet; Alexandria Expositor;* Richmond: *Virginia Argus, Enquirer, Examiner,* and *Virginia Gazette, and General Advertiser;* Staunton *Political Mirror;* Savannah: *Georgia Republican,* and *Public Intelligencer.* This list has been compiled from the following sources: John S. Lillie to Jefferson, Oct. 12, 1803, and receipt, Oct. 12, 1803, Jefferson, "Newspapers to be paid for," Mar. 31, 1804, Jefferson to John Vaughan, Jan. 14, 1806, June 22, 1808, Jefferson to Joel Barlow, Dec. 19, 1807, Jefferson to John Milledge, Feb. 6, 1809, Jefferson Papers, Lib. Cong.; Jefferson to Levi Lincoln, June 22, 1808, Levi Lincoln Papers, Mass. Hist. Soc.; E. Millicent Sowerby, comp., *Catalogue of the Library of Thomas Jefferson,* 5 vols. (Wash., 1952-59), I, 267-85.

73. Jefferson to John Vaughan, July 10, 1808, Jefferson Papers, Lib. Cong.; see also Jefferson to Vaughan, June 22, 1808, *ibid.*

74. Jefferson to Cheetham, Apr. 23, 1802, *ibid.*

Jefferson.[75] Jefferson also aided Republican printers by purchasing numerous pamphlets. His bill from James Cheetham for the period April 1802 to June 1803 totaled $53.93 for pamphlets and newspapers; from August 1803 to April 1805, it amounted to $44.80 1/2.[76]

In 1798, Jefferson had written: "At a very early period of my life I determined never to put a sentence into any newspaper. I have religiously adhered to the resolution through my life, and have reason to be contented with it."[77] Previously, Jefferson had made similar declarations in reference to Philip Freneau's *National Gazette,* and during the election of 1800 he rigidly refrained from participating in the newspaper controversy of the campaign.[78] These earlier declarations have been cited by some writers to suggest that Jefferson while President adhered to the policy of not writing anything for the press. Frank L. Mott in his monograph on *Jefferson and the Press* indicated that Jefferson did not depart from his rule against contributions to newspapers until 1817, long after his retirement.[79] The evidence, however, is conclusive that Jefferson did on several occasions while President write pieces which were anonymously published in several different newspapers.

In June 1803, Jefferson wrote to Attorney General Levi Lincoln:

On reading a paragraph in the N. Y. Evening post, I took up my pen to write a squib on it; but the subject run away with me till I found I had written a treatise. It is one on which I have a great desire to reconcile the parties among republicans.... The interest I take in the question made me willing to hazard a few lines for the press, although I have through life scrupulously refrained from it; inasmuch that this is but the second instance of my being willing to depart from my rule. I have written it under the character of a Massachusetts citizen, with a view of it's appearing in a paper there; the Chronicle I suppose is most read. But how to get it there divested of the evidence of my handwriting? Think of this if you please; correct the paper also to make it what it should be, and we will talk of it the first time we meet. Friendly salutations, and religious silence about it.[80]

75. Cheetham to Jefferson, Apr. 24, 1805, July 1, 1807, *ibid.*
76. Cheetham to Jefferson, [June 22, 1803], Apr. 24, 1805, *ibid.*
77. Jefferson to Samuel Smith, Aug. 22, 1798, Andrew A. Lipscomb, ed., *The Writings of Thomas Jefferson* ..., 20 vols. (Wash., 1903), X, 58.
78. Jefferson to Washington, Sept. 2, 1792, Ford, ed., *Jefferson Writings*, VI, 106-7; on election of 1800 see Cunningham, *Jeffersonian Republicans, 1789-1801*, 139, 199.
79. Frank L. Mott, *Jefferson and the Press* (Baton Rouge, 1943), 25-26. Worthington C. Ford, "Jefferson and the Newspaper," Columbia Historical Society, *Records*, 8 (1905), 108, concluded that Jefferson "had never written for the newspapers."
80. Jefferson to Lincoln, June 1, 1803, Jefferson Papers, Lib. Cong.

In the issue of June 27, 1803, the Boston *Independent Chronicle* published the article which Jefferson had written. Signed "FAIR PLAY," the piece differed only in minor alterations from the original draft made by Jefferson, and it was published, as Jefferson had designed, as having been written by a resident of Massachusetts. A contemporary reader of the *Independent Chronicle* would have had no suspicion that the lengthy discussion of appointments and removals and the strong defense of the administration's patronage policy had been written by the President himself.[81]

What Jefferson considered his first departure from his rule against writing for the press, to which he referred in his letter to Lincoln, is not clear. On May 23, 1803, the *National Intelligencer* published a piece which was essentially written by Jefferson. On May 21, the President had supplied editor Samuel H. Smith with a brief analysis of a recent Connecticut election. He cited election returns and showed that, although the Republicans had elected fewer members to the state legislature in 1803 than in the previous year, the Republican percentage of the vote had risen from 29 to 35 per cent. "Would it not be worth presenting to the public in this concise view?" he asked. Editor Smith responded by publishing Jefferson's summary as a leading piece headed "Plain view of the Politics of Connecticut."[82] Since this was only a brief notice, not a prepared article, it is questionable that this was the earlier writing that Jefferson had in mind when writing to Lincoln. In any case these were not the only times that Jefferson, while President, wrote pieces for newspapers.

On June 18, 1803, Jefferson wrote to Meriwether Jones, editor of the Richmond *Examiner,* that a published statement made by Gabriel Jones concerning certain financial transactions with the President some twenty years before was incorrect. He explained:

> Although I have made it a point to disregard the various calumnies by which the federalists have endeavored to wound republicanism through me, yet when a respectable man, as Gabriel Jones, comes forward. . . . I have thought it would not be remiss that a just statement should be made, in order to satisfy candid minds. I have therefore made the inclosed, thinking I could not do better than commit it to your friendship

---

81. The article from Jefferson's draft is printed in Ford, ed., *Jefferson Writings*, VIII, 234-39n.

82. Jefferson to Smith, May 21, 1803, Henley-Smith Papers, Lib. Cong.; Washington *National Intelligencer*, May 23, 1803.

to publish it in such form, with such alterations or abridgements as you think proper, whether too as an anonymous communication, or with a feigned name, or as the editor's own observations is left to yourself, as you are sufficiently apprised of the utter impropriety of it's being in any form which should engage me in that field, or if you think it better to repress it, I leave it to your judgment. There is no fact in it but what is stated by Mr. Jones, and the historical references are known to everyone. . . .

P. S. I will thank you to destroy the original and this letter.[83]

Jefferson's statement, signed "Timoleon," was published in the *Examiner*, June 25, 1803.

Among the most important material which Jefferson prepared for the press was that published as an answer to a series of publications by Decius, written by John Randolph. The articles of Decius—which apparently left no one in doubt that they came from Randolph's pen—treated the question of the administration's foreign policy, especially in relation to the appropriation to purchase Florida, and the issues upon which Randolph justified his break with the administration.

Editor Thomas Ritchie, who originally published Randolph's series in his Richmond *Enquirer,* wrote shortly after their publication to William A. Burwell, Jefferson's former private secretary, requesting that Burwell prepare an answer to Decius.[84] Burwell in turn wrote to Jefferson, who opened his letter in the company of Madison and Dearborn. "I therefore, with them, took up Decius and read him deliberately," he explained to Burwell; "and our memories aided one another in correcting his bold and unauthorized assertions. I shall note the most material of these in order of the paper." In the detailed explanation which followed, Decius was strongly rebuked in such language as to leave no doubt that it was directed at Randolph. "He speaks of secret communications between the executive and members, of backstairs' influence, etc.," wrote Jefferson. "But he never spoke of this while he and Mr. Nicholson enjoyed it almost solely. But when he differed from the executive in a leading measure, and the executive, not submitting to him, expressed it's sentiments to others, the very sentiments (to wit, the purchase of Florida) which he acknowledges they expressed to him, then he roars out upon backstairs' influence." Jefferson concluded: "It remains now to consider

---

83. Jefferson to Jones, June 18, 1803, and enclosed 3-page statement of transaction [letter press copies], Jefferson Papers, Lib. Cong.
84. William A. Burwell, Memoir [1804-1808], Burwell Papers, Lib. Cong.

on what authority these corrections of fact can be advanced without compromitting the Executive. It would seem to be best that the writer should assume the mask of a member of the Legislature. . . . These, my dear Sir, are the principal facts worth correction. Make any use of them you think best, without letting your source of information be known."[85] Jefferson's facts became the substance of remarks which Burwell sent to Ritchie and which filled two columns in the Richmond *Enquirer* of October 24, 1806. Published as "Important Facts," they appeared to be the editor's own reply to Decius. It is doubtful that any reader outside the confidence of the President suspected that these facts came from Jefferson.

The above examples are ample proof to explode the myth of Jefferson's disassociation from the press and to show that as President he wrote, on more than one occasion, important pieces for newspaper publication. He also made unsolicited suggestions to newspaper editors, such as when he explained his removal policies to Peter Freneau, of the Charleston *Carolina Gazette,* adding: "I explain them to no one more willingly than yourself because I am sure you will use them with prudence and sincerity for the information and satisfaction of others when occasions may lead you to an expression of sentiment."[86] Appealing to Attorney General Lincoln to answer a newspaper attack on the administration, he suggested that "each must do his part. You are directly attacked by name in this paper, that the defense seems yours of right."[87] And about the same time the President wrote to Gallatin: "I must have a conference with you on the subject of defending ourselves regularly in the newspapers."[88] Additional evidence of Jefferson's connection with the party press can be found in his relationship to the *National Intelligencer,* which was established in Washington by Samuel Harrison Smith in October 1800 and after Jefferson's inauguration became the most important administration organ in the country.

Party leaders recognized the need for an authoritative national party newspaper which could be relied upon to present the administration's position and to mark out the official party line. In July 1801, Massa-

85. Jefferson to Burwell, Sept. 17, 1806, Ford, ed., *Jefferson Writings,* VIII, 468-72.
86. Jefferson to Freneau, May 20, 1803, Jefferson Papers, Lib. Cong. See also Freneau to Jefferson, June 17, 1803, *ibid.*
87. Jefferson to Levi Lincoln, Mar. 4, 1802, Lincoln Papers, Mass. Hist. Soc.
88. Jefferson to Gallatin, May 1, 1802, Gallatin Papers, N.-Y. Hist. Soc.

chusetts Republican Barnabas Bidwell wrote to Vice-President Burr in regard to such an official party newspaper:

An opposition, not yet very much systematized, is intended against the present administration. Every popular prejudice will be seized and wielded with as much effect as possible. I trust the measures of administration will bear a strict examination; but people at large have not the means of examining. They must judge from impressions, communicated thro News-papers principally. The true explanations of controverted measures should be communicated and circulate. They should be uniform in all parts of the United States. I mean essentially so. For this purpose there ought to be one authentic paper, from which the Republican editors can take their Texts, on which they and their correspondents may comment, with all their variety of amplifications. It is not to be expected that they will otherwise act in any good degree of concert, in explaining, defending and enforcing, to the people, the views and measures of government, so as to counteract false impressions on the public mind. . . .

Upon the subject of my preceding observations respecting an authentic newspaper, I have wished to know, on my own account, and for the benefit of our Republican Editor in this County, whether the National Intelligencer is to be relied on. If so, as some gentlemen at Boston suppose, it may be an useful guide to our country Papers.[89]

To Bidwell's inquiry regarding the *National Intelligencer,* Burr replied firmly: "The Washington paper edited by Smith has the countenance and support of administration. His explanations of the Measures of Government and of the Motives which produce them are, I believe, the result of information and advice from high Authority."[90]

Federalists also recognized the *National Intelligencer* as "the official paper of the Administration" and as "a paper which is unquestionably under the direction of Mr. Jefferson and his party."[91] But Jefferson, who was irritated by being held responsible for all that was published in the *National Intelligencer,* protested: "That Tory printers should think it advantageous to identify me with that paper, the Aurora, etc., in order to obtain ground for abusing me, is perhaps fair warfare. But that any one who knows me personally should listen one moment to such an insinuation is what I did not expect. I neither have, nor ever had, any more connection with those papers than our antipodes have; nor know what is to be in them until I see it in them, except proclamations and

89. Bidwell to Burr, July 6, 1801, Gratz Collection, Hist. Soc. of Pa.
90. Burr to Bidwell, Oct. 15, 1801, Henry W. Taft Collection, Mass. Hist. Soc.
91. James A. Bayard to Richard Bassett, Jan. 31, 1806, Donnan, ed., *Bayard Papers,* 165; Hartford *Connecticut Courant,* July 6, 1808.

other documents sent for publication."[92] Although it was indeed true that Jefferson exercised no control over the *National Intelligencer,* and editor Smith was completely his own agent in determining the policies and publications of his paper, Jefferson's suggestion that he had no more connection with it than his opponents is misleading. There was indeed no formal connection, but informally Smith was very close to the President, and there is ample proof that the administration on a number of occasions employed the *National Intelligencer* as its spokesman. That the role of Smith's paper was more accurately described by Burr in the remarks quoted above than by Jefferson can be seen by examining the party role of this paper and its relationship to the administration.

Smith and Jefferson had become acquainted in Philadelphia as members of the American Philosophical Society while Vice-President Jefferson served as president of the society and Smith, then editor of the weekly *Universal Gazette,* was the secretary. According to Mrs. Smith, Jefferson had been a major influence in her husband's decision to move his paper to the new capital where he began publication on October 31, 1800, of the tri-weekly *National Intelligencer.*[93] Smith's move to Washington having taken place before the election of 1800 was decided (and thus at a risk since there was no assurance that the Republican party would be victorious) placed him in an advantageous position to receive government favors when the Republicans came to power on March 4, 1801.

Early on the morning of his inauguration, Jefferson sent to editor Smith an advance copy of his inaugural address, enabling Smith to have copies of it ready for distribution as the crowd left the Capitol following the inauguration. Since Jefferson had delivered his speech in a voice so low that few heard it, the printed copies were in much demand.[94] This small mark of attention was followed by numerous more important favors. Smith was given the printing of the laws and the printing of every department. Secretary of the Treasury Gallatin recalled that Smith "was promised by myself and others every reasonable encouragement."[95] When the Republican-controlled Seventh Congress in December 1801 restored the ardent Republican John Beckley to the clerkship of the House, Beckley gave Smith the entire printing of the

92. Jefferson to Thomas Paine, June 5, 1805, Ford, ed., *Jefferson Writings,* VIII, 361.
93. Reminiscences of Mrs. Samuel Harrison Smith, in Hunt, ed., *First Forty Years of Washington Society,* 9.
94. Mrs. Samuel H. Smith to Susan B. Smith, Mar. 4, 1801, *ibid.,* 26.
95. Gallatin to Jefferson, [received Dec. 15, 1801], Jefferson Papers, Lib. Cong.

House. In view of the other printing which Smith had been given, many Republicans, including Gallatin, felt that Beckley should have divided the House printing between Smith and William Duane, who had also established a printing shop in Washington and had been promised government patronage.[96]

At the outset of his administration, Jefferson endorsed the *National Intelligencer* as a source of correct information relating to the proceedings of the administration. "I recommend to you to pay not the least credit to pretended appointments in any paper, till you see it in Smith's," the President wrote in denouncing false rumors published in other papers. "He is at hand to enquire at the offices, and is careful not to publish them on any other authority."[97] As his term progressed, Jefferson on many occasions relied on the *National Intelligencer* to present the administration's position. From time to time, the President supplied Smith with material for publication. Forwarding to the editor an anonymous piece which he had received, Jefferson explained: "The inclosed paper seems intended for the legislative as well as Executive eye; but certainly not to be laid before the former in a regular way. The only irregular one would be in the newspapers. . . . Do with it as you may think of it worth or want of it."[98] Jefferson also wrote several pieces for publication in the *National Intelligencer*. In May 1803, he furnished Smith with a short notice regarding Connecticut politics which was promptly printed.[99] When editor William Coleman of the Federalist *New-York Evening Post* during the election of 1804 attacked the President's Revolutionary record, Jefferson appealed to Smith. "Is it worth while to contradict the barefaced falsehoods of Coleman in the 2d. page 5th. column of the inclosed paper," he asked, in supplying Smith with specific refutations of the charges. Smith accordingly published Jefferson's statements "on the authority of a friend of Mr. Jefferson, who has long enjoyed his confidence, and acted with him in many of the important scenes of the revolution."[100]

96. *Ibid.*
97. Jefferson to John W. Eppes, Mar. 27, 1801, Jefferson Papers, Univ. of Va.
98. Jefferson to Smith, Oct. 23, 1802, Henley-Smith Papers, Lib. Cong. For another example see Jefferson to Smith, Oct. 8, 1803, *ibid.*
99. Jefferson to Smith, May 23, 1803, *ibid.; National Intelligencer*, May 23, 1803, see p. 256 above.
100. Jefferson to Smith, July 19, 1804, Henley-Smith Papers, Lib. Cong.; *National Intelligencer*, July 23, 1804. When, after investigation, Jefferson wished to correct his statements published by Smith, this was done in a subsequent article. Jefferson to Smith, July 31, 1804, Henley-Smith Papers, Lib. Cong.; *National Intelligencer*, Aug. 10, 1804. The charges related to Jefferson's having signed a laudatory address to the King of Great

Jefferson also used the *National Intelligencer* to promote policies which he favored. He strongly advocated a policy of classifying the militia, in order to have available for duty, if needed, a selected corps for a year's national service. When he discovered a discussion of the subject in a pamphlet, he suggested to Madison, "Could S. H. Smith put better matter into his paper than the 12 pages above mentioned, and will you suggest it to him? No effort should be spared to bring the public mind to this great point."[101] On another occasion he wrote an article defending the naval policy of employing gunboats; this piece appeared with only minor changes in the *National Intelligencer*.[102] Reading an article on the gunboat policy adopted by Denmark, he sent it to Smith with a covering note explaining:

Th: J. present his compliments to Mr. Smith and considering it as rendering an essential service to the nation to fix them in the *defensive* system of gunboats, and draw them off from the *offensive* one of a navy, submits to him the propriety of publishing the Copenhagen article of the within paper, inclosed in crotchets.[103]

Two days later the piece was published in the *National Intelligencer*.[104] During the period when the administration was experiencing difficulties in enforcing the Embargo, the President sent the following note to Smith:

Th: Jefferson salutes Mr. S. H. Smith with esteem, and thinks that some such paragraph as the following published in his paper would do good.
      Removal by the President.
  ——— Pope, Collector and Inspector of the port of New Bedford in Massachusetts for not using due diligence in the execution of the embargo laws. Isaiah Weston is appointed in his place.
I do no recollect Pope's Christian name. It can be known at the office of state.[105]

Editor Smith added the first name of Edward Pope but otherwise published the notice as Jefferson had written it.[106]

Britain ten months before writing the Declaration of Independence. Jefferson at first flatly denied it, thinking the reference was to a Virginia address, but finding it referred to a document sent by Congress, he agreed that he had signed it as it was the custom of members to sign all papers that passed the Congress.

101. Jefferson to Madison, May 5, 1807, Jefferson Papers, Lib. Cong.
102. *National Intelligencer*, Jan. 11, 1808; Jefferson's draft of the article is printed in Ford, ed., *Jefferson Writings*, IX, 24-25n.
103. Jefferson to Smith, Mar. 2, 1808, Henley-Smith Papers, Lib. Cong.
104. *National Intelligencer*, Mar. 4, 1808.
105. Jefferson to Smith, Aug. 1808, Henley-Smith Papers, Lib. Cong.
106. *National Intelligencer*, Aug. 8, 1808.

The administration also on occasion used the *National Intelligencer* to make public information which the government was not prepared to announce officially. Following the *Chesapeake* incident, Madison wrote to the President in September 1807: "Would it not be proper to let Smith publish in the words of Canning, without quoting them, the disavowal of the pretension to search ships of war, and promising satisfaction for the attack on the Chesapeake. This will enable the public to appreciate the chance of peace, and put all on an equal footing." Jefferson agreed: "I think it would be well for Smith to be furnished with the declaration of Mr. Canning only taking care that it should not appear to have been furnished by us." A week later the *National Intelligencer* announced in large type that the British government had, "it appears," disavowed the right to search ships of war and had indicated that reparations for the *Chesapeake* attack would be made.[107]

Secretary of the Treasury Gallatin in at least one instance wrote an important piece for anonymous publication in the *National Intelligencer*. "On reading the enclosed piece in Poulson's paper, I was induced to answer it," he explained to the President, "as a similar misrepresentation has already appeared in the Boston Centinel. . . . My idea was that Smith should obey the request of 'a plain citizen,' by reprinting his piece, and should add as his own remarks the substance of what I have written dressed in his own way and corrected as he may think fit. Will you be good enough to look at it and to see whether it wants any additions, corrections or curtailing? I mean as to facts and arguments, not as to style—this Smith must modify."[108] The President "entirely approved" Gallatin's article, which related primarily to the remission of the fine of James Thomson Callender, and it was published in the *National Intelligencer* as Gallatin had suggested. Revisions incorporated by the editor included material which Gallatin had explained in private letters to editor Smith.[109]

The evidence, therefore, is sufficient to establish the fact that the association of the administration with the *National Intelligencer* was not merely a Federalist invention. It may also be assumed that the President's in-

---

107. Madison to Jefferson, Sept. 21, 1807, Jefferson to Madison, Sept. 22, 1807, Jefferson Papers, Lib. Cong.; *National Intelligencer*, Sept. 28, 1807.

108. Gallatin to Jefferson, [received Oct. 6, 1802], Jefferson Papers, Lib. Cong. The draft of Gallatin's article is in the Gallatin Papers, N.-Y. Hist. Soc.

109. Jefferson to Gallatin, Oct. 6, 1802, Gallatin Papers, N.-Y. Hist. Soc.; *National Intelligencer*, Oct. 20, 1802; Gallatin to [Samuel H. Smith], Aug. 20, 1802, Gallatin to Smith, [1802], Gallatin Papers, N.-Y. Hist. Soc.

fluence on Smith extended well beyond the specific examples cited above, for the editor was included among those invited to dine at the executive mansion and apparently had easy access to the President.[110]

In view of the extensive use made of the press by Jefferson and by the Republican party to advance the policies and interests of the party and to maintain popular support, a letter which Jefferson wrote to John Norvell in June 1807 appears highly inconsistent. The President wrote:

> To your request of my opinion of the manner in which a newspaper should be conducted, so as to be most useful, I should answer, "by restraining it to true facts and sound principles only." Yet I fear such a paper would find few subscribers. It is a melancholy truth, that a suppression of the press could not more compleatly deprive the nation of it's benefits, than is done by it's abandoned prostitution to falsehood. Nothing can now be believed which is seen in a newspaper. Truth itself becomes suspicious by being put into that polluted vehicle. The real extent of this state of misinformation is known only to those who are in situations to confront facts within their knoledge with the lies of the day. I really look with commiseration over the great body of my fellow citizens, who, reading newspapers, live and die in the belief that they have known something of what has been passing in the world in their time: whereas the accounts they have read in the newspapers are just as true a history of any other period of the world as the present, except that the real names of the day are affixed to their fables. General facts may indeed be collected from them, such as that Europe is now at war, that Bonaparte has been a successful warrior, that he has subjected a great portion of Europe to his will, etc., etc., but no details can be relied on. I will add, that the man who never looks into a newspaper is better informed than he who reads them, inasmuch as he who knows nothing is nearer to truth than he whose mind is filled with falsehoods and errors.[111]

This was indeed a sobering indictment from an ardent champion of the freedom of the press and a practical politician who had given much attention to the political uses of the press. The letter was apparently written at a moment when Jefferson had reached the limit of his endurance of newspaper attacks on him. Smarting under some particularly painful attack, as one writer has suggested, "he wrote not as a philosopher but as a shamefully persecuted man."[112] Jefferson's actions,

---

110. Jefferson to Samuel H. Smith, Apr. 23, 1803, Henley-Smith Papers, Lib. Cong.; Mrs. Samuel H. Smith to Maria Bayard, May 28, 1801, Hunt, ed., *First Forty Years of Washington Society*, 29.

111. Jefferson to Norvell, June 11, 1807, Jefferson Papers, Lib. Cong.; printed, under date June 14, 1807, in Ford, ed., *Jefferson Writings*, IX, 71-75.

112. Mott, *Jefferson and the Press*, 57.

rather than this highly quotable denunciation of newspapers, must stand as the better evidence of his attitude toward the press.

Samuel Harrison Smith made it plain in the *National Intelligencer* that he supported the administration and the Republican party. In an address to the subscribers on the second anniversary of the establishment of the paper, he emphasized that "the editor does not claim an exemption from decided political convictions." Reviewing his policies, he wrote:

Believing the freedom of speech and of the press to be one of the great bulwarks of our liberties, it has been and shall be vigorously sustained. That freedom consists in the temperate discussion of all principles and measures on which the general happiness depends. While, on the one hand, it holds no principle too sacred for examination, it forbids all personal slander and vulgar language. The National Intelligencer, therefore, has not, and will not enter into personal warfare with any wretch who by his crimes has abandoned himself to infamy, nor will it, elated with editorial consequence, make the nation the theatre of the petty feuds of hostile prints. . . .

Believing that our happiness essentially depends upon a republican government, and that such government is alike susceptible of abuse and improvement, whatever increases a love and respect for it, whatever tends to destroy its abuses or promises its amelioration shall be admitted.

Believing that the measures of the late administration tended to draw into disrepute the republican system by incorporating numerous and dangerous abuses, which were calculated with great rapidity to hurry us into the common vortex of ruined nations, those measures have been held up to public opinion as unworthy of imitation; while the measures of an administration, zealously attached to the republican system, and resolutely bent on keeping this country apart from foreign connection, have been enforced as the offspring of a wise and honest policy.[113]

Restating his editorial policies again in 1807, Smith explained: "The same principles, which have hitherto guided the discharge of his Editorial duties, remain unshaken. . . . He conscientiously believes the existing administration have uprightly and wisely discharged their duties. He is, therefore, the friend of that administration, and whatever new dangers may environ them, from the injustice of foreign powers, or from internal machinations, he shall view in the light of new motives to exertion."[114]

Although Smith was thus a thoroughgoing party editor and an unwavering supporter of the administration, the *National Intelligencer*

---

113. *National Intelligencer*, Oct. 6, 8, 11, 13, 15, 18, 1802.
114. *Ibid.*, Sept. 7, 1807.

was not a violent party sheet. Smith lived up to his promises not to engage in petty feuds with hostile editors, and he did not resort to personal abuse and irresponsible attacks. William Duane, the more passionate editor of the *Aurora*, once referred to Smith's "*silky milky way*,"[115] and Smith himself appealed to other Republican editors to be more moderate.[116] He supported the administration with a rational rather than a partisan tone. Burr, however, thought that "he sometimes shows too much eagerness and solicitude to defend and explain every thing, even things which require neither defense nor explanation; and in this way he invites animadversion which would not otherwise be meditated."[117]

The *National Intelligencer* published the fullest reports of the debates in Congress of any paper in the country, and Smith prided himself in "rigid impartiality" in their publication.[118] Federalists, however, accused him of omitting Federalist speeches and of softening language. George Hoadley, the Washington correspondent of the Federalist *United States Gazette*, declared that "Smith, who reports more fully than any one else, does not publish more than one third, and at most, one half of what is spoken. He also omits or softens many expressions which bear hard on the ruling powers."[119] Federalist Congressman Killian K. Van Rensselaer also accused Smith of omitting "every good speech delivered by our federal speakers, with the exception of a few unimportant remarks."[120] Yet it is doubtful that Smith was responsible for all the modifications which appeared in the printed version of debates and speeches. The task of recording the debates was a tremendous chore, since Congress provided for no verbatim record of its deliberations and its journals provided only a mere outline of proceedings. Smith thus employed his own stenographer and depended on members to furnish him reports. One method used by Smith was indicated by Senator John Quincy Adams, who recorded in his diary in 1803: "The editor of the National Intelligencer, S. H. Smith, came to me and desired me to give

115. New York *American Citizen*, Jan. 11, 1804, reprinted from the *Aurora*.
116. *National Intelligencer*, Nov. 16, 1801.
117. Burr to Barnabas Bidwell, Oct. 15, 1801, Henry W. Taft Collection, Mass. Hist. Soc.
118. *National Intelligencer*, Oct. 6, 1802.
119. Hoadley to Jeremiah Evarts, Feb. 5, 1807, photostat, Va. Hist. Soc.
120. Van Rensselaer to ————, Jan. 29, 1802, Killian K. Van Rensselaer Papers, Misc. Coll., N.-Y. Hist. Soc. Senator William Plumer remarked in regard to the publication of Randolph's anti-administration speech against the Gregg resolution: "Samuel H. Smith is to be the printer, and I fear its strong language will be too much softened." Plumer to William Plumer, Jr., Mar. 11, 1806, Plumer Papers, Lib. Cong.

him the substance of what I said on the debate yesterday, for publication, as other gentlemen on both sides of the question had promised him they would. I agreed to furnish him with it."[121] Working in such fashion it was unlikely that the printed version of debates would correspond exactly to the recollection of everyone who had heard the spoken word.

The *National Intelligencer* as a party organ of nationwide influence gave the Republican party an important advantage over the Federalists, who, though supported by a powerful press, did not have a paper of such national stature and influence. Federalist leaders recognized this disadvantage and attempted to remedy it. Fisher Ames urged that the Boston *New-England Palladium* be supported as the national party organ of the Federalists, but this ambition was never realized.[122] Other efforts were directed toward making the *Washington Federalist* the Federalist counterpart of the *National Intelligencer*. In 1808, a committee organized to support the paper and extend its operation and influence sent circulars to Federalist leaders throughout the union requesting aid and support of the paper. "The local position of the *Washington Federalist* will give it obvious advantages as a steady Centinel on the measures of the present Administration," the circular emphasized, and promised that if properly supported a stenographer would be hired to report the debates of Congress and furnish proof sheets to Federalist editors throughout the nation.[123] The *Washington Federalist*, however, ceased publication in 1809.[124]

At no time during Jefferson's administration did the Federalists have a national party paper which could seriously rival the *National Intelligencer*. Republicans, moreover, had the support of another paper of national influence, the Philadelphia *Aurora*, edited by William Duane. Neither the *National Intelligencer* nor the *Aurora* would yield first place to the other. When an announcement calling for a national festival to celebrate the acquisition of Louisiana carried a notice that the date would

121. Adams, ed., *Diary of John Quincy Adams*, entry of Nov. 4, 1803, I, 271.
122. Ames to John Rutledge, July 30, 1801, Rutledge Papers, Univ. of N. C.; Ames to Jeremiah Smith, Dec. 14, 1802, Ames to Christopher Gore, Feb. 24, 1803, Seth Ames, ed., *Works of Fisher Ames, with a Selection from his Speeches and Correspondence*, 2 vols. (Boston, 1854), I, 314-15, 318-19.
123. Printed circular, signed by Archibald Lee and Robert Beverly, Sept. 15, 1808, to John Rutledge, Rutledge Papers, Univ. of N. C.; another copy also signed by Lee and Beverly, dated Sept. 16, 1808, and addressed to Dwight Foster, is in the Broadside Collection, Amer. Antiq. Soc.
124. Brigham, *History and Bibliography of American Newspapers*, I, 95-96.

be announced in the *Aurora,* "as the most complete channel of republican communication in the United States," Smith protested that "the National Intelligencer does not yield in the extent of circulation or in the mass of republican information to any print on the continent." To this Duane responded by calling attention to the fact that the *National Intelligencer* was not in existence during the dark days from 1797 to 1800.[125]

The *Aurora's* past support of the Republican party and its active influence throughout the country in promoting the party triumph in the election of 1800 gave Duane strong claims for favor when the Republican administration came to power. Accordingly Duane opened a stationery, bookselling, and printing shop in Washington with the view of supplementing his income from the *Aurora* by supplying stationery to the government offices, selling books to the Library of Congress, and securing congressional printing work. He solicited the President and department heads for support of his establishment, and Jefferson wrote in response: "As to your proposition on the subject of stationery I believe you may be assured of the favor of every department here. . . . My custom is inconsiderable and will only shew my desire to be useful to you."[126] By September 1801, Duane was writing of his "having now the contract for serving the public offices of Government with stationery, and the Congress," and was seeking to establish an arrangement with a bookseller in London.[127]

In his expectations of securing congressional printing, Duane met with disappointment, however, when House Clerk John Beckley awarded all House printing to Samuel Harrison Smith. Duane wrote dejectedly to Gallatin:

> I came here under an expectation of obtaining the Printing of the Journals but other arrangements have disappointed that hope, which was founded principally on an intimation given me last winter by Mr. Macon, that if I bought a press, I should have the printing of the House. There were other grounds upon which it was not unreasonable in me to expect the preference in this branch of business. . . . Before the removal of the Government to this place, I had issued proposals for a newspaper to be

---

125. New York *American Citizen,* Jan. 3, 11, 1804.

126. Duane to Jefferson, May 10, June 10, 1801, Duane to Madison, May 10, 1801, Worthington C. Ford, ed., "The Letters of William Duane," Mass. Hist. Soc., *Proceedings,* 2d Ser., 20 (1906), 263-64; Jefferson to Duane, May 23, 1801, Ford, ed., *Jefferson Writings,* VIII, 54.

127. Duane to Joseph Nancrede, Sept. 30, 1801, William Duane Personal Papers Misc., Lib. Cong.

published and meant to establish myself here. Upon that occasion it was intimated to me that if I would relinquish that object, and sustain the Aurora at Philadelphia, that some means would be found to recompense me. I immediately relinquished the project of a paper here, although I had a very handsome list of Subscribers, and I may fairly presume might have stood here against any competitor whatever.

... The public, of all parties looked as certain to my obtainment of the printing for Congress, and I have been questioned by many influential members of Congress how it came to pass that I did not. In Philadelphia it was particularly expected, not from any declaration of mine, but from the simple act of removal and the ample printing establishment and book bindery provided by me.[128]

Duane stressed the debts that he had incurred in establishing his business in Washington and suggested that the public offices purchase a half year's supply of stationery in order to enable him to put his affairs in order and maintain his family. Duane's remonstrance met the sympathy of Gallatin, who declared in forwarding the letter to the President:

Why Mr. Beckley did not divide the printing between Mr. Duane and Mr. Smith I do not know; but I am sure that most of our friends are so chagrined at it, that they speak of altering the rules of the house, so as to have the printer appointed by the House and not by the clerk. Mr. Smith came here before the fate of the election was ascertained and at a risk. He was promised by myself and others every reasonable encouragement. But this cannot be construed into an exclusive monopoly. He has already the printing of the laws and of every department; and the Congress business might have been divided.

I wish however that Mr. D[uane]'s application for purchase of his stationary might be communicated to the several heads of Department; and, if you think it proper, the letter being transmitted by you may be better attended to. We may in the Treasury purchase a part but cannot until Congress shall have made an appropriation; our's being exhausted.[129]

Duane had already been given a contract to deliver 400,000 sheets of paper to the Treasury Department by November 15, 1801, but had not completed the order. By February 1802 he was still 172,500 sheets short, according to the department's books, and Gallatin informed the President that the Treasury had a surplus of paper and would not extend the contract with Duane after the 400,000 sheets were delivered.[130] In

---

128. Duane to Gallatin, Dec. 13, 1801, Gallatin Papers, N.-Y. Hist. Soc.
129. Gallatin to Jefferson, [received Dec. 15, 1801], Jefferson Papers, Lib. Cong.
130. William Miller to Gallatin, Treasury Department, Feb. 8, 1802, Gallatin to Jefferson, Feb. 9, 1802, *ibid.*

August 1802, Duane complained to Gallatin that he had received reports that the Secretary of the Treasury had purchased a considerable quantity of stationery from someone else, and questioned Gallatin's friendship. "With regard to my two branches of business in Washington," he wrote, "if the heads of Departments mean not to patronize me, it will be an act of common justice to apprize me of it. I will neither complain nor reproach them. But I will silently withdraw my two establishments from Washington."[131]

Duane was awarded a part of the congressional printing, but he still remained dissatisfied with his share of the printing patronage. In October 1803, seeking the printing of the Senate journals, he sent printed circulars to members of the Senate soliciting their support for his application. "Three years since, upon the invitation and persuasion of distinguished republicans," he explained, "I established here a printing office adequate to the execution of any quantity or any kind of printing, and have executed a part of the work for Congess, to general satisfaction. Circumstances did not admit of the fulfilment of the purposes of my friends, with regard to the printing for the Senate, and the Journals have been hitherto printed by a person of adverse politics with whom however, I did not think it delicate to be a competitor before this period."[132] Duane's appeal was successful. Two Federalist Senators, William Plumer and John Quincy Adams, reported that Samuel A. Otis, a Federalist holdover who had been clerk of the Senate since 1789, was given to understand that, if he wished to retain his post, the Senate printing should be given to Duane.[133] This was accordingly done, and Otis kept his office. It is perhaps not without significance that Otis took the trouble in November 1804 to notify the President that three hundred copies of the President's message to Congress had been secured from Duane for the use of the Senate.[134]

Jefferson personally patronized Duane as he did other Republican printers. His account with Duane for books, stationery, printing, and writing supplies for one year, October 1803 to November 1804, amounted

131. Duane to Gallatin, Aug. 12, 1802, Gallatin Papers, N.-Y. Hist. Soc.
132. [Circular], Washington, Oct. 14, 1803, signed William Duane, addressed to John Breckinridge, Papers of Breckinridge Family, Lib. Cong.
133. Brown, ed., *Plumer's Memorandum*, entry of Oct. 27, 1803, 28-29; Adams, ed., *Diary of John Quincy Adams*, entry of Oct. 21, 1803, I, 264.
134. Otis to Jefferson, Nov. 9, 1804, Jefferson Papers, Lib. Cong.

to $121.49 1/2. This was in addition to the President's subscriptions to both the daily *Aurora* and the tri-weekly *Aurora, for the Country*.[135]

The relations between the administration and the *Aurora* were never so intimate as with the *National Intelligencer*. The *Aurora* was a far more violent paper, and Duane, passionate and intolerant in temperament, was deeply involved in the turbulent politics of Pennsylvania. Yet, although the administration was at times roughly handled by the *Aurora* and Duane developed a bitter antipathy toward Secretary of the Treasury Gallatin, Jefferson remained tolerant of Duane's behavior and never questioned the basic Republicanism of the *Aurora*. "Duane is honest, and well intentioned, but over zealous," he wrote in 1803. "These qualities harmonise with him a great portion of the republican body. He deserves therefore all the just and favorable attentions which can properly be shewn him."[136] Yet at the same time he explained: "I think Duane's zeal merits tenderness and satisfaction, while his precipitancy makes him improper to be considered as speaking the sense of the government."[137] Later during Duane's involvement in the Republican schism in Pennsylvania Jefferson excused an attack made by the *Aurora* on an administration appointment by explaining: "Though Duane is friendly, he could not lose the opportunity of smiting a Quid as he calls them."[138]

Although the *Aurora* was not employed as an administration spokesman as was the *National Intelligencer,* Duane on occasion received confidential information from the administration. When, in 1803, he sought documents concerning England's reaction to the Louisiana Purchase, both Jefferson and Madison felt that no official communication should be given him but agreed that his request should receive attention. Madison politely explained that "it is not thought proper that the document itself should be given out for the press. But there is no objection to its being affirmed, without allusion to the particular authority for the fact, that the British Government instead of obstructing in any way the cession of Louisiana to the United States, has evinced the most perfect satisfaction

---

135. Duane to Jefferson, Nov. 27, 1804, account for Oct. 18, 1803-Nov. 27, 1804, Jefferson Papers, Lib. Cong. Receipts show that Jefferson paid Duane $52.00 for newspapers, May 1, 1802-May 1, 1806, and $26.26 for supplies, June 6, 1805-Feb. 15, 1806. Duane to Jefferson, Mar. 8, 1806, *ibid*.
136. Jefferson to Madison, Aug. 29, 1803, Madison Papers, Lib. Cong.
137. Jefferson to Madison, Aug. 16, 1803, *ibid*.
138. Jefferson to Henry Dearborn, Aug. 22, 1805, Jefferson Papers, Lib. Cong.

at the event."[139] On another matter, the President wrote confidentially to Duane in 1807: "I have often wished for an occasion of saying a word to you on the subject of the Emperor of Russia, of whose character and value to us, I suspect you are not apprized correctly." He then went on to explain that Alexander I had taken a peculiar affection and attachment to the United States and that both countries had the same interests in regard to neutral rights. At any peace conference the United States would be assured of a friend in the Emperor. "I have gone into this subject," Jefferson concluded, "because I am confident that Russia (while her present monarch lives) is the most cordially friendly to us of any power on earth, will go furthest to serve us, and is most worthy of conciliation. And although the source of this information must be a matter of confidence with you, yet it is desirable that the sentiments should become those of the nation."[140]

Although Jefferson privately confided that Duane should not be considered as speaking the sense of the government, it was widely believed that the *Aurora* had the support and confidence of the administration, a factor which strengthened Duane's position in the factional struggle among Pennsylvania Republicans. Andrew Ellicott, of Pennsylvania, deplored "an opinion generally prevailing in this state, and probably in some others, that, that paper is the organ of the will, and wishes, of the administration of the general government."[141] Alexander James Dallas, politically aligned against Duane in Pennsylvania politics, protested against "Duane's assertions, that he possesses the confidence, and acts at the instance, of the President."[142] Another anti-Duane Republican, lamenting that there was "no paper having an extent of circulation or a standing with the community capable of rebutting his pernicious doctrines," feared "the extensive circulation of the Aurora, and the implicit confidence put in it may do infinite mischief."[143]

Outside of Pennsylvania most Republicans appear to have regarded the *Aurora* as useful to the Republican party. Jacob Crowninshield, Representative from Massachusetts, extolled: "In the Aurora I see the

139. Duane to Madison, Aug. 3, 1803, Madison to Duane, Aug. 20, 1803, Madison Papers, Lib. Cong.; Madison to Jefferson, Aug. 13, 1803, Jefferson Papers, Lib. Cong.
140. Jefferson to Duane, July 20, 1807, Ford, ed., *Jefferson Writings*, IX, 120-21.
141. Ellicott to Jefferson, Dec. 1, 1803, Jefferson Papers, Lib. Cong. See also Ellicott to Madison, Oct. 2, 1805, Madison Papers, Lib. Cong.
142. Dallas to Gallatin, Apr. 4, 1804, Gallatin Papers, N.-Y. Hist. Soc.
143. John Kean to Alexander J. Dallas, Mar. 20, 1805, Dallas Papers, Hist. Soc. of Pa.

hand of a master. Its columns often delight me and although I am not bound to approve of every thing in the republican papers I am free to acknowledge Mr. Duane has done more in favour of the republican cause than any other editor in the U. S. His paper stands high in my estimation. It is sometimes too severe however, but I believe we may always trust to the purity of the intention."[144] After being attacked by the *Aurora,* Senator Wilson Cary Nicholas of Virginia avowed that he had not the least confidence in the *Aurora;* but John Taylor declared in reply: "As to Duane, I need no caution against his authority; and yet I can appreciate his utility. To lop off his press, and supply the dismemberment by a federal press, would be like lopping off republican minorities as they appear, and supplying the dismemberments with sections cut off from federalism. A strong arm may wither, but who voluntarily parts with it in its full vigour, and in the midst of combat."[145] Thomas Truxton, a supporter of Madison for President in 1808, thought that no efforts should be spared to secure the influence of Duane. "Duane's press," he wrote, "with all its indecency, is worth for our purposes all others. The circulation of his paper is so universal throughout the United States—and in every hovel of Pennsylvania it is to be found and read."[146]

Duane was not always a consistent champion of the administration; at one time or another, he attacked directly or indirectly most of the President's Cabinet. Gallatin was the main object of attack, but Gideon Granger was so strongly attacked on one occasion that he offered to resign to save the administration embarrassment.[147] Duane almost followed in support of John Randolph when the latter broke with the administration, until warned of the folly of his course by close political allies.[148] At periods during Jefferson's two terms, the *Aurora* was so involved in the state politics of Pennsylvania that its national influence was lessened. Yet it was a powerful paper in a key state, and it retained its national audience. It was of great national importance when the *Aurora* in

144. Crowninshield to Caesar A. Rodney, Aug. 5, 1805, Ferdinand J. Dreer Collection, Hist. Soc. of Pa.
145. Nicholas to John Taylor, Oct. 7, 1807, Taylor to Nicholas, Oct. 26, 1807, Edgehill-Randolph Papers, Univ. of Va.
146. Truxton to Thomas Tingey, Mar. 17, 1808, Truxton to Madison, Mar. 17, 1808, Madison Papers, Lib. Cong.
147. Granger to Jefferson, Oct. 9, 1806, Jefferson Papers, Lib. Cong. Samuel L. Mitchill to John Smith, Sept. 3, 1806, Papers of John Smith of Mastic, Long Island, Misc. Coll., N.-Y. Hist. Soc.
148. See pp. 223-25 above.

1808 endorsed Madison for the presidency.[149] Despite the irritations which Duane had caused members of the administration, the President continued to regard him as worthy of support—a fact confirmed when Jefferson commissioned Duane a lieutenant colonel in July 1808. That this feeling was shared by other Republicans was seen when his commission was confirmed by the Senate by a vote of 21 to 10. "I owe you the expression at least of my thanks for your goodness on this occasion, and for the general benignity with which I have always been honored and favored by you," Duane wrote the President; "it is to me a very great solace, that exposed as I have been and daily am to the persecutions of the most malignant of men, I yet hold a place in your esteem and regard."[150]

The practical relationships between the party and the press form an essential part of the total picture of the operation of the Jeffersonian party. Jefferson was not so disassociated from the press as has frequently been asserted; the *National Intelligencer* was, as most contemporaries believed, an administration organ even if not controlled by the President, and it gave the Republican party the important advantage of having a national party newspaper. The President's contacts with other editors and newspapers were frequent. He encouraged the efforts of Republican editors, personally contributed on occasion to the party press, and directed the patronage of the federal government to Republican printers. From the President on down to the local party leaders, the party press was supported, often established and maintained, by the party faithful. In return the party press supported the party cause with enthusiasm and frequently with excessive partisanship.

149. Duane, who had previously displayed antipathy toward Madison and favored the nomination of George Clinton for the presidency, had earlier taken a somewhat equivocal position, but finally in May 1808 came out strongly for Madison. See Higginbotham, *Keystone in the Democratic Arch*, 156-59.
150. Duane to Jefferson, Feb. 4, 1809, Ford, ed., "Duane Letters," Mass. Hist. Soc., *Proceedings*, 2d Ser., 20 (1906), 317.

CHAPTER ELEVEN

The Party and the Voter

The machinery and organization of the Jeffersonian party and the methods and practices of its leaders reflected, in the final analysis, the power of the American voter. The devices of party, geared to the functioning of democratic government, reaffirmed the voter's ultimate authority. By the nature of the American political system, the party's record and program were always presented to the electorate in the form of political candidates aspiring to office. Just as party machinery varied from state to state, so the methods and campaign practices of candidates seeking political preferment were adapted to the customs and practices of local political life. Persons from one section of the country were frequently surprised by the campaign and election practices of other regions. Observing a day of electioneering in South Carolina, Edward Hooker, a Connecticut-born Yale graduate, found himself "an astonished spectator of a scene, the resemblance of which I had never before witnessed." On the other hand, Henry W. DeSaussure, a South Carolinian attending an election in Hartford, Connecticut, observed that "it was a singular spectacle, unlike all other elections I ever saw."[1] The South Carolina scene which astonished Hooker, as it would have equally amazed many other New Englanders, was direct solicitation of votes by political candidates. It was Saturday afternoon in Pickensville, in western South Carolina, in September 1806, and the fall campaign was in full swing. Let Hooker describe the day:

Several hundreds of people came together: the houses and streets were thronged. The three candidates for Congress, Alston, Hunter and Earle were present electioneering with all their might—distributing whiskey, giving dinners, talking, and haranguing, their friends at the same time making similar exertions for them. Besides these, there was a number of Candidates for the Assembly. It was a singular scene of noise, blab and

1. J. Franklin Jameson, ed., "Diary of Edward Hooker, 1805-1808," entry of Sept. 27, 1806, American Historical Association, *Annual Report, 1896*, (Wash., 1897), I, 900; DeSaussure to John Rutledge, Sept. 21, 1802, Rutledge Papers, Univ. of N. C.

confusion. . . . Handbills containing accusations of federalism against one, of abuse of public trust against another—of fraudulent speculation against a third—and numerous reports of a slanderous and scurrilous nature were freely circulated. Much drinking, swearing, cursing and threatening—but I saw no fighting. The minds of uninformed people were much agitated—and many well-meaning people were made to believe that the national welfare was at stake and would be determined by the issue of this back-woods election."[2]

Hooker, who had attended church services in the region on the previous Sunday, had also witnessed an electioneering scene outside the church door: "The candidates had stationed themselves conveniently, and were now very busy in saluting every man in the crowd, taking care to call by name as many as possible, and putting themselves on the terms of old acquaintance. Col. Alston was perfect master of the art, and played his game with so much adroitness as almost to persuade one that nobody could have a more cordial attachment to him, or feel a greater interest in his welfare."[3] At another time, Hooker expressed surprise that "a person told me he had seen letters from a person to several voters, announcing himself a candidate, and soliciting their patronage and influence. To such a height does the fondness for office and power rise."[4] Although a New Englander might be shocked at such electioneering practices in South Carolina, open campaigning by candidates in their own behalf was common in most of the region from Delaware and Maryland southward.

In Maryland, the stump-speaking political canvass was the accepted practice. Candidates for office toured the state or district, speaking at public meetings, militia reviews, barbecues, or wherever a crowd could be assembled. Opposing candidates frequently spoke or debated from the same platform. A contemporary report of one of these campaign gatherings near Baltimore in 1808 described a Saturday militia review followed by electioneering speeches. "A considerable number of citizens had collected both from the city and county," it was reported. "Between 3 and 4 o'clock, a circle was formed around a stump, on which Mr. Pollock mounted, and addressed the auditory in his usual vein of humor and pertinacity declaring himself a candidate for a seat in Congress." Pollock

2. Jameson, ed., "Diary of Edward Hooker," entry of Sept. 27, 1806, Amer. Hist. Assn., *Annual Report, 1896*, I, 900.
3. *Ibid.*, entry of Sept. 21, 1806, 897.
4. *Ibid.*, entry of Sept. 6, 1806, 892.

was followed by a Mr. Winder who also offered himself as a candidate for Congress and "commenced a philippic on the great *stalking horse* of federalism, the Embargo." Several other candidates also spoke soliciting suffrages.[5] So accepted had such campaign practices become in Maryland that one candidate felt called upon to explain: "My present engagements, and the necessary attention to my private affairs, will not allow me to appear at every public meeting which is held for the purpose of *Electioneering*." It was therefore his hope that "as Free and Independent Men, you are not to be *cajoled* by the show of great *personal respect,* nor caught with the miserable bait of *entertainment*."[6] This candidate was not elected, however, and most men who sought public favor in Maryland found it necessary to engage in a canvass.

Campaign practices in Delaware followed those in Maryland, as Caesar A. Rodney explained in writing to Madison in October 1801. "I returned late last evening from a political tour of about two weeks in the lower counties of this State," he reported. "I travelled with the acts of Congress, the annual reports of the Secretary of the Treasury and other documents in my hands to meet the Federalists on their strongest grounds. We have followed the example of the worthy Duvall and the other Republicans of Maryland in addressing the people on the state of affairs at the various public assemblies and I trust with the same good effect."[7] Self-nomination which was acceptable in Maryland, however, was considered improper in Delaware.

Political candidates in Virginia campaigned openly, making speeches, attending county court days, and soliciting the suffrages of the voters on the day of the election.[8] A successful candidate for the state legislature in 1801 explained:

Two months before the Election were almost exclusively appropriated to electioneering. I traversed every part of the County, and became acquainted with almost the whole of the people, with whom before that Time I was wholly unacquainted. I had a good opportunity of observing the state of their Manners, and Sentiments. Many of them I found to be

5. Baltimore *American*, Sept. 26, 1808; for details of similar electioneering practices in Maryland in 1800, see Cunningham, *Jeffersonian Republicans, 1789-1801*, 190-94.
6. David Kerr, *To the Voters of Talbot County*, Aug. 11, 1803, broadside, Md. Hist. Soc.
7. Rodney to Madison, Oct. 5, 1801, Madison Papers, Lib. Cong. See also Rodney to Jefferson, Aug. 11, 1801, John Vaughan to Jefferson, Oct. 10, 1801, Rodney to Jefferson, May 16, June 19, 1802, Jefferson Papers, Lib. Cong.
8. Richmond *Enquirer*, Apr. 26, 1805; John W. Eppes to Jefferson, Feb. 10, 1803, Edgehill-Randolph Papers, Univ. of Va.; John G. Jackson to Madison, Apr. 29, 1803, Madison Papers, Lib. Cong.

ignorant, brutified and totally indifferent to the Exercise of their most important Rights. The only stimulus with them to that Exercise was through the medium of their palates. Grog, strong Grog was to them of much more Consequence than the giving their Votes for this or that man. These persons I generally neglected, having determined not to gain my Election by such means, and I succeeded, for I believe I did not spend two Dollars during the two Months, in which I canvassed. Some I found to be extremely independent, and intelligent, and it was by the Votes of these men, and the neighborhood Influence which they possessed, that I was elected. Others again, not so bad as the first, although they put on the appearance of Independence, yet possessing it not in Reality, required a great Deal of courting.[9]

This candidate found a two-month canvass more successful than treating the voters with grog; but it was clear that he found campaigning necessary for election.

John Randolph in 1805 boasted: "I have been to none of the election or public meetings since my return, but the *good people* have again deputed me to serve them."[10] However, in 1808 when a strong opposition was made to his re-election, Randolph was compelled to campaign. His opponent, as a friend warned Randolph, adopted the practice of "following you about in your District, replying at one Court-House to speeches which you had made at another."[11] Randolph disclosed more about the campaigning in this election when he reported in regard to his opponent that "an electioneering barbacue was given to him (or rather against me) where at he was present and declared off. I was not there."[12]

Something of the conduct of a Virginia candidate can be concluded from a contemporary comment on current political practices in the state published in the Richmond *Examiner* in 1803, in which the writer declared that "in choosing a representative, we look for qualities, often adverse to, and at best, accidentally associated with political merit. Has a candidate an easy exterior, condescending manners, and is he equally polite to all? Does he recollect your names, the names of your wives and children, and greet you with the meretricious smile of continued

---

9. William Brockenbrough to Joseph C. Cabell, June 18, 1801, Cabell Papers, Univ. of Va. Harry Ammon quotes this letter in The Republican Party in Virginia, 1789 to 1824 (unpubl. Ph.D. diss., Univ. of Va., 1948), 33-34.

10. Randolph to Joseph H. Nicholson, Apr. 18, 1805, Nicholson Papers, Lib. Cong.

11. Randolph to James M. Garnett, May 27, 1808, Garnett to Randolph, Aug. 12, 1808, Randolph Papers, Garnett transcripts, Lib. Cong.

12. Randolph to Garnett, July 24, 1808, *ibid*.

placidity and universal good humour? He is too often the man of your choice."[13]

In Kentucky, "flattery" and "barbecues" were listed by a contemporary observer as high among the "electioneering arts" in that state,[14] and one Kentucky politician recalled in regard to Matthew Lyon's success in winning elections to four terms in Congress: "He was a man of Herculean frame and constitution—could drink Grog all the day long without getting drunk; tell pretty good rough anecdotes and take him altogether was a good 'Electioneerer.' "[15] Robert H. Grayson, an unsuccessful candidate for Congress, condemned "the practice of treating and feasting for votes, a practice which I think every independent voter will condemn, and which however it may be smoothed over is the worst kind of corruption in elections." Grayson's remarks on election practices in Kentucky afford a rare contemporary commentary:

It is a misfortune, sir, for this country, that electioneering (as it is called) has been so compleatly reduced to a science, as with us. Candidates are in the habit of making appeals to the passions and prejudices, not the reason of the voter. Duplicity, flattery and the most shameful political and religious hypocricy are frequently resorted to. To prevent a *fair expression* of the public voice, they frequently act over the whole comedy of tricks and maneuvres, and he who plays his part the best is praised for his *address*. Cameleon like, you see them changing colors, and in order to please, they are saints and sinners by turns, as occasion may require. Treating some of the voters, in open violation of the laws of our country, is practised under pretence of *sociability*. The whole dictionary of insipid jokes is consulted and these jokes dealt out with great profusion upon all occasions and in all companies', as if men were to be sent to Congress, or to the assembly, to act the part of Buffoons or jesters. Intemperance, it seems, is not always an improper qualification for a candidate. A pack of cards, a keg of whisky, and a game cock, have on some occasions (it is said) been a good electioneering apparatus, for a man, who if elected, was to assist in making laws for a nation. But this is not all, the candidate according to the present mode of electioneering, if he wishes to succeed, must, for at least a year before the election, totally neglect his private affairs, however inconvenient it may be to him, and instead of having that necessary time for preparing himself, to discharge properly the trust reposed in him by the people, if elected, he has perpetually to take the rounds, through the district with the velocity of a race rider. If he does not do this, there are not wanting men to accuse him of

13. *Examiner*, Mar. 23, 1803.
14. James Brown to Wilson C. Nicholas, Aug. 23, 1803, Nicholas Papers, Univ. of Va.
15. "Memoirs of Micah Taul," Kentucky State Hist. Soc., *Register*, 27 (1929), 364-65.

neglect and pride. These measures to obtain an election cannot long be countenanced. They are pursued in no other state in the Union. The people will open their eyes, and ask why men adopt these extraordinary means to obtain success if they had nothing in view but the good of their country?[16]

In Tennessee, as in Kentucky, campaigning for office was openly conducted, and the outcome of elections depended heavily on the exertions of a candidate, his friends, and party supporters in directly soliciting votes. Considerable last-minute canvassing appears to have taken place at the polls, and these activities were not always above suspicion. "To vote by ballot is subject to corruption much more than viva voce suffrages," wrote one Tennessee observer who witnessed the canvassing on election day at Rutledge and "understood the carryings on at most other Court-Houses in this District was much the same." He concluded: "An active impudent Man with some address and could write with facility and always have pen, ink, and paper at hand, was worth more than fifty common Voters to his party."[17]

In North Carolina, electioneering speeches were made "at the Courthouse door," candidates "spoke on the fence" in support of their elections, and active solicitation of votes on election day at times became clamorous.[18] Nathaniel Macon, a popular and often re-elected congressman from North Carolina, could write: "I have never solicited any man to vote for me or hinted to him that I wished him to do so, nor did I ever solicit any person to make interest, for me to be elected to any place."[19] But though Macon adhered to such a mode of political conduct, most candidates in North Carolina by 1800 did not appear to have regarded open electioneering activities as improper.

In Georgia, political candidates and their friends also campaigned

16. Robert H. Grayson, [Circular], Mason County, June 5, 1806, broadside, Filson Club. The Kentucky Constitution of 1799 contained a prohibition against treating which apparently was frequently circumvented. This was indicated in the following resolution passed by the Kentucky House of Representatives in 1809: "*Resolved,* That the provision in the constitution, against a treating by candidates for the House of Representatives, as much forbids an union and agreement amongst all the candidates of a county, to treat, and divide the expence equally between themselves, with a view of affecting the election, as it does a treating by an individual candidate." Hopkins, ed., *Papers of Henry Clay,* I, 429-30.
17. Arthur Campbell to David Campbell, Aug. 22, 1803, Campbell Papers, Duke Univ.
18. William Lenoir, Memorandum Book from Mar. 1, 1802, to Mar. 15, 1804, in Fletcher Green, ed., "Electioneering 1802 Style," *North Carolina Historical Review,* 20 (1943), 243-44.
19. Macon, brief autobiographical sketch, Macon Papers, Duke Univ.

openly. John Milledge was supported in his race for Congress in 1801 by friends who "rode day and night" and "worked like a Horse," as one of them said, to promote his election.[20] Joseph Bryan, running for Congress in 1803, was advised by a close political friend to make a campaign tour. "I think you would do well to spend a few weeks in the *upcountry* the latter part of this summer," wrote Obadiah Jones, "in which case, I give it as my opinion your Election would be pretty certain." And Jones himself proposed to visit the "upcountry" before the election: "I wish much to get up, before the great day of the feast . . . for I conclude I should do your Election no injury."[21] Bryan evidently made an electioneering tour, and so did his opponent, for Jones reported after Bryan's victory that Bryan's opponent "had gone over the same ground after you electioneering, and had made use of means that I think very unjustifiable, I mean that of lying (at least telling untruths) and publishing some specious pieces in the papers."[22] During another election it was a matter of political concern that "Mr. Spalding has been a Considerable time in the up Country; he is a man of talents and information, of smooth and insinuating manners and address."[23] Electioneering in Georgia also took place at county seats when courts were in session, at militia musters, and at the polls on election day.[24]

Electioneering by the candidates themselves was more open and direct in the South than in the middle states or in New England. In these regions, self-nomination—widely accepted in the South—was regarded as improper. A meeting of Republicans in Woodbury, Pennsylvania, in 1804, resolved: "That this meeting highly disapprove of the practice, so inimical to republican principles of individuals announcing themselves in the public prints as candidates for office in the gift of the people, and pledge themselves to oppose, by all proper means in their power, the election of any person persisting in such indelicate practice."[25] But although the candidate himself maintained a more reserved position in these states, the voters were no less exempt from some form of electioneer-

20. James Jackson to Milledge, Apr. 2, 1801, Salley, ed., *Correspondence of John Milledge*, 70-71.
21. Jones to Bryan, June 25, Sept. 24, 1803, Arnold-Screven Papers, Univ. of N. C.
22. Jones to Bryan, Jan. 20, 1804, *ibid*.
23. Jones to Bryan, July 18, 1804, *ibid*.
24. Nicholas Ware to Thomas Carr, Sept. 28, 1806, Carr Papers, Univ. of Ga.; Obadiah Jones to Joseph Bryan, Jan. 20, 1804, Sept. 1, 1802, Arnold-Screven Papers, Univ. of N. C.
25. Wilmington *Mirror of the Times*, Sept. 15, 1804.

ing than the electorate in the southern states. The growth of political parties had brought electioneering to all parts of the union. A New England writer protested early in 1801: "Elections to office, in New England, have been always, till very lately, *free* beyond any example that can be found elsewhere. . . . It was not prudent for any man to express a wish for promotion. . . . Unhappily, however, our democrats have already had some influence in changing this truly republican state of things among us. The detestable practice of electioneering is, by their means, indirectly gaining ground, in these states."[26]

The development of party machinery in the New England states brought well-organized electioneering campaigns to that region. Although stump speaking does not appear to have yet become acceptable, the solicitation of suffrages by a candidate's friends and by party committees, employing personal contacts, party handbills, and the press, was extensive. Dr. Nathaniel Ames in his diary, March 20, 1808, noted: "Electioneering opened. Pamphlets flying like wild geese in a storm."[27] Massachusetts elections were becoming particularly tumultuous. Thomas Dwight confessed in 1802: "If my conscience would allow me to be the occasion of losing one vote in the federal cause I would not go into Boston to attend the Election—it is always a noisy business of parade. To have seen this scene acted over once is enough—enough—to see it done over and over year after year is painful or at the least irksome to me."[28] Another explained: "So loud and so indecently rude, is the noise made by the distributers of ballots for the different candidates, and such the illiberal reflections and uncandid remarks upon their respective characters, as cannot but excite painful sensations in every delicate mind."[29] Although Federalists claimed to disdain electioneering, both parties were actively engaged. James Sullivan, Republican candidate for governor in 1806, protested: "The arts, frauds, bribes and calumnies used by the federalists this year were never equalled but in one instance. Bribery is boasted of without a blush, and the most attrocious slanders smoothed over with an apology that they were only for an electioneering purpose."[30]

26. Hartford *Connecticut Courant*, Feb. 2, 1801.
27. Warren, *Jacobin and Junto*, 243.
28. Dwight to John Williams, May 21, 1802, Dwight Papers, Mass. Hist. Soc.
29. Boston *New-England Palladium*, Feb. 10, 1801.
30. Sullivan to Jefferson, Apr. 21, 1806, Jefferson Papers, Lib. Cong. See also Barnabas Bidwell to Jefferson, June 21, 1806, *ibid*.

Election campaigns in New York and Pennsylvania were consistently among the most vigorously contested races in the country. The divisions between Federalists and Republicans had early turned these states into party battlefields. Party machinery was extensive, newspapers were numerous and politically active, and public participation in party affairs was unusually extensive. There are far more extant political handbills from New York elections than from any other state, attesting to the extensive use of that method of campaigning in New York. Handbills were also widely circulated in Pennsylvania. Campaigns in which there were party splits with Republicans fighting Republicans were among the most bitter of the period, and nowhere were Republicans more plagued by divisions than in New York and Pennsylvania. Perhaps the most abusive campaign waged during the period was the gubernatorial election of 1804 in New York when Burr and his followers challenged the regular Republican organization.[31]

In New Jersey, elections were accompanied by considerable campaigning by party committees, and, as a result of last-minute electioneering and the availability of grog on election days, there was frequent tumult at the polls.[32] One New Jersey observer declared in 1804:

Look at an election scene and the steps preparatory to it. Behold characters torn into tatters and scattered to the winds. Committees of lies to tell the truth to the people.... What changing of votes and tricks and impositions upon electors? ... What bribery, perjury, and corruption? Lo! a voter, brimful of freedom and grog, marching up to the election box, guarded by two or more staunch patriots, lest the honest soul should mistake, lose his way or be surprised by the other party and lost.[33]

Although party machinery varied and election procedures and campaign practices differed, there were certain common patterns of political behavior that can be ascribed to party workers in all parts of the country. The immediate aim of every party worker was, of course, to win the election at hand and in so doing to contribute to the over-all success of the party in securing or maintaining control of the state and national administrations. To accomplish this purpose the party machinery described in earlier chapters was put into operation. Whatever its con-

31. See collections of broadsides for 1804 at N. Y. Pub. Lib. and N.-Y. Hist. Soc.; see also Dixon Ryan Fox, *The Decline of Aristocracy in the Politics of New York* (N.Y., 1919), 63-67.
32. McCormick, *History of Voting in New Jersey*, 114.
33. New Brunswick *Guardian*, Sept. 27, 1804, quoted in *ibid.*, 115.

struction, Republican party machinery aimed at common objectives through similar means: nominating or approving of party candidates, publicizing the party program and defending the party record, familiarizing the electorate with the party's candidates and appealing to the interests and the sentiments of the voters to support them, arousing public interest especially in getting out to vote, and maintaining party unity.

Appeals to voters to exercise their suffrage were frequent in Republican party literature. An editorial in the Newark *Centinel of Freedom,* on the eve of the election in November 1804, urged:

> Let it be remembered that one hour, or a day spent in making the choice of proper persons to represent us in our national councils, and electing persons for to chuse the President and Vice-President of the U. States, is of more importance to a farmer than the same time spent following his plow, or a mechanic at his anvil, or the merchant behind the counter. If our information is true, our opponents are organizing in secret, with a view of making a bold push, at a late hour, in hopes of finding the republicans off guard. Fellow freemen of the state of New Jersey, we again intreat you to come out; do not sleep, do not slumber on the days of election. However secure we may feel ourselves; let it be remembered that we have enemies.[34]

In Connecticut, where Federalists were firmly in control of the state government, a circular issued by the Republican party state manager in 1805 declared: "Those, who talk against federalism through the year, and yet neglect to attend proxies, do worse than nothing. Those, who profess to be republicans, and yet vote for federalists on any occasion, do us irreparable mischief. Federalism cannot be talked down or flattered down; IT MUST BE VOTED DOWN."[35] Republicans were regularly urged by party spokesmen to vote the party ticket. "It is our duty, *one and all,* to be *vigilant and united* in support of the [Republican] ticket," Republicans were told;[36] and one of the most frequently repeated party slogans was "United we stand, divided we fall."[37]

That Republican leaders sought to encourage a feeling of popular participation in the affairs of the party and to keep alive popular en-

---

34. *Centinel of Freedom,* Nov. 6, 1804.
35. [Circular], Nov. 1, 1805, printed in Hartford *Connecticut Courant,* Nov. 27, 1805. For other examples, see Elizabeth-Town *New-Jersey Journal,* Sept. 27, 1808; Newark *Centinel of Freedom,* Nov. 1, 1808.
36. Baltimore *American,* Aug. 31, 1808.
37. Boston *Independent Chronicle,* Feb. 23, Mar. 29, 1804, Mar. 24, 1808; *United We Stand—Divided We Fall,* Boston, Feb. 20, 1807, broadside, Hist. Soc. of Pa.

thusiasm for the party was well demonstrated by the frequency of party celebrations held throughout the country. Many of the Republican celebrations which accompanied the inauguration of Jefferson on March 4, 1801, were well-planned, elaborate demonstrations which featured parades, dinners, orations, balls, and other festivities.[38] These celebrations were repeated in many places in March of each year throughout Jefferson's administration.[39] "The 4th of March forms an epoch in the political history of the United States, which ought always to awaken the purest sensations of the American Patriot," declared a Richmond Republican meeting in announcing "the celebration of that day, which restored to us the genuine principles of '76, and removed the alarms which had clouded the fairest prospects of American Liberty and Independence."[40] Reporting the Republican celebration in New Haven in March 1803, Abraham Bishop enthusiastically pointed out that "the procession extended in close columns through two sides of the public square and consisted of 1108 men. The whole company far exceeded that on commencements and Elections."[41] The Boston *Independent Chronicle* on Monday, March 5, 1804, announced: "This Day, the anniversary of the renovation of *Republicanism* in the United States, in the inauguration of the patriot, the sage, the inflexible Republican, will be celebrated in the most splendid manner."

In addition to the March 4th celebrations, there were also the July 4th festivities which came to be separately observed by the two parties in many places.[42] A July 4th celebration planned and controlled by Republicans meant, as explained by Levi Lincoln, "a republican orator, republican prayers, republican music, republican toasts, and republican songs."[43] Special celebrations were also held, the most elaborate and extensive being the celebration of the acquisition of Louisiana. From Washington,

38. Richmond *Examiner*, Feb. 6, 27, Mar. 13, 1801; Richmond *Virginia Argus*, Mar. 13, Apr. 14, 1801; *Alexandria Advertiser*, Mar. 5, 16, 1801; *Raleigh Register*, Apr. 14, 1801. See pp. 5-6 above.
39. See Richmond *Examiner*, Mar. 2, 30, 1803, Richmond *Virginia Argus*, Feb. 22, Mar. 7, 1804; Hartford *American Mercury*, Mar. 7, 1805; Washington *National Intelligencer*, Feb. 9, 1803; New Haven *Connecticut Journal*, Feb. 24, 1803; Portland *Eastern Argus*, Mar. 9, 1804. See also pp. 127-28 above.
40. *Petersburg Intelligencer*, Feb. 17, 1804.
41. Bishop to ———, Mar. 23, 1803, Misc. Coll., N.-Y. Hist. Soc.
42. *Raleigh Register*, July 20, 1802; Boston *Independent Chronicle*, July 7, 1808; Boston *Columbian Centinel*, July 6, 1808; [Circular], Worcester, June 20, 1808, signed by Edward Bangs and others, broadside, Amer. Antiq. Soc.; Nathaniel Cogswell to Jefferson, July 11, 1808, Jefferson Papers, Lib. Cong.
43. Lincoln to Madison, July 5, 1801, Madison Papers, Lib. Cong.

Federalist Congressman Manasseh Cutler reported in January 1804: "There is a *Jubilee* proclaimed here by the Democrats. . . . There is to be such a feast, it is said, as was never known in America, on account of taking possession of *Louisiana*. There is to be diners—suppers—balls—assemblies, dances, and I know not what. . . . The *Jubilee* is to begin here—but they expect it will run—like *wildfire*, to every dark and benighted corner of America."[44] And spread it did. Republican newspapers called for a national festival, and Republicans in many parts of the country organized celebrations. So tremendous was the Philadelphia celebration that it must have dominated the life of the city for days, even weeks, before the May 12 festival.[45]

Federalists replied to the Republican celebrations by observing Washington's birthday, just before the March 4th festivals, and in other ways calling attention to the first President. The Worcester *Massachusetts Spy,* obviously trying to counteract recent Republican demonstrations, devoted most of the issue of March 7, 1804, to publishing Washington's Farewell Address.

Although every election had its own peculiar set of circumstances and many voters were influenced in their suffrages by considerations often of a local or personal nature, there were certain appeals voiced sufficiently frequently and universally by Republican candidates and party spokesmen that they may be correctly referred to as party appeals. These Republican appeals reveal the issues or lack of issues which were presented to the voters, as well as the methods by which party workers sought to advance the Republican cause.

First of all, the Republicans who had successfully turned out John Adams in 1800 campaigned against Adams as long as they could keep alive the memories of the unpopular measures of his administration. A circular in support of Republican candidates for the legislature of Maryland in September 1802 declared:

> Sir, you cannot have forgotten the unjust and oppressive measures of the late administration.

---

44. Cutler to Francis Low, Jan. 21, 1804, "Cutler Letters," Essex Institute, *Hist. Collections,* 39 (1903), 325; see also Simeon Baldwin to Mrs. Baldwin, Jan. 22, 1804, Baldwin Family Papers, Yale Univ.

45. Philadelphia *Aurora,* Mar. 29, Apr. 6, 20, 26, May 10, 14, 1804; Richmond *Virginia Argus,* Feb. 25, 1804; New York *American Citizen,* Jan. 11, Feb. 3, 1804; Lexington *Kentucky Gazette,* May 15, 1804; Bishop, *Oration in Honor of the Election of President Jefferson, and the National Festival,* in Hartford on the 11th of May, 1804, pamphlet, Lib. Cong.

WHO imposed, unnecessarily, upon the people a debt of upwards of ten millions?—The Federalists.
WHO laid and continued the tax on your stills?—The Federalists.
WHO taxed your dwelling houses?—The Federalists.
WHO taxed your lands?—The Federalists.
WHO imposed on you a Stamp-Act, and created an *host of officers* to collect the excise duties?—The Federalists.
WHO imposed on you an alien law, a Sedition Act, and a new and unnecessary Judiciary law. . . ?—The Federalists.
WHO raised a useless standing army?—The Federalists. . . .
The *principal* actors in the Federal measures approve of the former, and are dissatisfied with the present administration. . . .
The question before you is, do you wish those measures of extravagant Taxation pursued by the Federalists re-established?[46]

Republican delegates from the various counties of New Jersey in recommending the Republican ticket for Congress in 1803 explained: "It is not necessary . . . to recall to the recollection of their fellow-citizens, the extravagant, oppressive, and unconstitutional measures of the late administration; or to direct their attention to the economical, pacific, and equitable conduct of the present. Every friend to a republican government, in form and substance, must wish to avert a recurrence of the scenes that marked Mr. Adams's administration, and to perpetuate the system practised by the administration of Mr. Jefferson."[47] The Democratic Republican Corresponding Committee of New-Castle County, Delaware, in 1804, announced that "the Committee would be willing to rest the fate of the approaching general election in the State of Delaware on the comparative review . . . of the measures and policy of the *former* and *present* administrations, believing that the public suffrages will give a decided preference to the friends of the *latter* who are candidates for office—and this on the score of economy alone, if there were no other

---

46. *Circular*, Frederick-Town, Sept. 23, 1802, broadside, Lib. Cong. For other examples of campaigning against the Adams administration see *To the Electors of the Middle District*, Poughkeepsie, Apr. 3, 1801, *To the Electors of the Southern District of the State of New-York*, By order of the General Committee in New York, N. Y., Apr. 7, 1801, broadsides, Lib. Cong.; *Authentic Information relative to the Conduct of the Present and Last Administrations of the United States* (Wilmington, Del., 1802), pamphlet, Lib. Cong.; Washington *National Intelligencer*, Sept. 17, 1802; Chillicothe *Scioto Gazette*, Oct. 29, 1804; Thomas Sumter, [circular to his constituents], Washington, May 1, 1802, Sumter Papers, Lib. Cong.; Richard Stanford, [circular to his constituents], Washington, Feb. 26, 1803, broadside, Lib. Cong.

47. Newark *Centinel of Freedom*, Nov. 29, 1803.

reasons."[48] The Democratic Republicans of Gloucester County, New Jersey, in 1807, authorized the printing and distribution of five hundred copies of an address, "containing a brief narrative of the most oppressive laws passed during the federal administration, their extravagant expenditure of the public money, prosecutions, fines and imprisonments, to prevent freedom of speech, or an investigation of their conduct; contrasted with the conduct of the present administration."[49]

In the election of 1808, when the Federalists, hoping to take advantage of the unpopularity of the Embargo, made their strongest efforts thus far to regain popular support, the issues of the Adams administration were revived with increased vigor. A Republican reply to William Gaston, who was running as a Federalist elector in support of Charles Cotesworth Pinckney in North Carolina, concluded:

General Pinckney, as to political principles, is just such a man, Fellow-Citizens, as you dismissed from office eight years ago, on account of those principles. If you elect Mr. Gaston, he will endeavor to give you a Federal President. If this should take place, it is reasonable to conclude, that under similar circumstances, he would act as the former President did. Therefore ... you must expect—"Alien and Sedition Laws—Direct, —Stamp,—Still and other Internal TAXES."[50]

A notice printed in Republican newspapers called attention to the difference between the Adams and Jefferson administrations in the following comparison:

LOOK ON

THIS PICTURE	AND ON THIS.
During *four* years of Adams' administration the National Debt was *augmented* eleven millions of dollars; a host of judges appointed to receive large salaries and carry the sedition law, etc., into execution, and so intimidate a free people; four hundred tax-gatherers	During Jefferson's republican administration, the *whole system* of internal taxes has been abolished; the superfluous and useless judges dismissed; and even the duties on imports in some cases diminished. No tax is paid to the general government;—yet near 30 *millions* of

48. *The Address of the Democratic Republican Corresponding Committee of New-Castle County*, pamphlet, Lib. Cong.

49. *At a Meeting of the Democratic Republicans of the County of Gloucester ... 31st day of August, 1807*, pamphlet, Lib. Cong.

50. *Remarks, on Mr. Gaston's Address to the Freemen of Wayne, Green, Lenoir, Jones, Craven and Carteret* (Newbern, N. C., 1808), pamphlet, Lib. Cong., replying to William Gaston, *To the Freemen of the Counties of Wayne, Green, Lenoir, Jones, Craven and Carteret* (Newbern, N.C., 1808), pamphlet, Univ. of N. C.

were employed to collect the internal direct taxes on lands, houses, stills, carriages, sugar, and domestic distilled spirits. Navies were built, armies were raised; and loans were obtained at the enormous interest of eight per cent.—to maintain the system of direful waste and extravagance.

the public debt has been redeemed; and Louisiana purchased for *fifteen* millions of dollars—though it is worth sixty millions of dollars, renders us secure on the S. W. border of the Union, and produces cotton and sugar in great abundance. And of the 15 millions, three went to compensate our own merchants for spoliations.[51]

The preceding illustrations not only indicate how Republicans throughout the country campaigned against the previous administration, but they also show how Republicans in both national and state elections stood on the record of the administration. Printed circular letters sent by Republican congressmen to their constituents also were filled with glowing praise of the accomplishments of the administration which they supported and which they pledged themselves to continue to support if re-elected.[52]

As the presidential election of 1804 approached, party spokesmen and the party press called attention to the accomplishments of Jefferson's first years in office. The following summary published in the Republican press included the major points which Republicans emphasized when appealing for the support of the electorate. The record of the administration, Republicans claimed, showed:

It has taken off the whole internal taxes, among which were the duties on stills, on stampt paper, etc. and the people now pay no tax, only to support their state Governments.

It has dispensed with several thousand unnecessary officers, who were before fattening upon the labor of the people.

It has reduced the land forces employed on our frontiers, and as much of the navy as could safely be dispensed with.

It has lessened the expences in every department of Government, by employing no unnecessary agents, and allowing no improper expenditures.

It has reduced, several millions of dollars, the National Debt, which had increased under Mr. Adams; and has made provision by law for its entire discharge in about fifteen years.

51. Charleston *Carolina Gazette,* Oct. 14, 1808, reprinted from Baltimore *Whig.*
52. Thomas Sumter, [circulars to his constituents], Washington, May 1, 1802, Mar. 4, 1803, Sumter Papers, Lib. Cong.; John Clopton, [circulars to his constituents], Washington, Feb. 24, 1803, Feb. 19, 1805, broadsides, Va. State Lib.; Richard Stanford, [circular to his constituents], Washington, Feb. 26, 1803, broadside, Lib. Cong.; John Claiborne, [circular to his constituents], Washington, Apr. 18, 1806, broadside, Duke Univ.

It has preserved peace, even when its opposers declared for instant war; and has effected by negociation in a few months what it would have taken years of hostilities to acquire; and have purchased for fifteen millions of dollars, a territory which is worth ten times the sum, and which would have cost an hundred millions of dollars, and thousands of lives, if it had been taken by force, as its opposers proposed and insisted.[53]

The conscious Republican emphasis on the Jeffersonian retrenchment policies was succinctly confessed by James Cheetham, editor of the New York *American Citizen,* when he remarked: "The reduction of our taxes and the diminution of the public debt, are arguments which the worst reasoner in the union can justly appreciate."[54]

Seeking election as a Jeffersonian elector in the presidential contest of 1804, Montfort Stokes appealed to North Carolina voters to "take a retrospective view of the successful operations of our Government for the last four years," affirming:

We enjoy peace and respect abroad, happiness and tranquility at home. With many burdens lightened, and no new impositions laid we have yet been enabled ... to diminish the public debt.... Without the aid of a standing army or a burthensome naval force, our commerce is less embarrassed by the depredations of foreign powers, and our frontiers less disturbed by our Indian neighbours, than at any period since we became an Independent nation.... We have no alien or sedition law.... By the repeal of the excise laws and other internal taxes, we have got rid of a host of revenue officers, who were fattening on the spoils of the industrious.

Much praise was also lavished on the Louisiana purchase. These were but "a few of the many blessings we have experienced by the wise policy of Mr. Jefferson."[55]

Republicans campaigned on the administration record not only in presidential elections but also in state contests. Robert H. Grayson, a Kentucky candidate for Congress in 1804, announced in an electioneering circular reviewing the accomplishments of Jefferson's administration:

I am a friend to those political measures recommended and pursued by the enlightened statesman who now fills the presidential chair; a statesman who has given us the best theory, and is now exhibiting the

---

53. Windsor *Spooner's Vermont Journal,* Oct. 25, 1803, reprinted from *Alexandria Expositor.*
54. Cheetham to Jefferson, May 30, 1803, Jefferson Papers, Lib. Cong.
55. Stokes, *To the Freemen of the Counties of Rowan, Randolph, and Cabarrus, in the State of North Carolina,* Sept. 6, 1804, broadside, Univ. of N. C.

best practical exposition of the essential principles of our free government ever attempted. It would exceed the limits, and perhaps be travelling a little out of the usual course of an address, to pass in review the various benefits we have received from his administration. My solicitude, however, that they should be known to every American citizen, will, I hope, plead my apology for noticing some of the most important, and contrasting them with the evils we sustained from those unwise principles of policy pursued by the last administration.[56]

Caesar A. Rodney, seeking re-election to Congress in 1804, assured the President: "I stand upon the single and solid ground of being a supporter of you and your administration."[57] A Republican convention in New Jersey in 1808 nominated candidates for Congress who had "uniformly and steadily, supported the measures of the present administration of our General Government:—Measures, in our opinion, founded in wisdom and sound policy."[58]

Standing on the administration's record was a position easy to adopt during Jefferson's first term, when the President enjoyed an immense popularity climaxing in the enthusiastic reception given to the purchase of Louisiana; but it was a stand more difficult to take during his last years in office, when the administration was burdened with increasing problems in regard to foreign affairs. The President's handling of the crisis with England over neutral rights provided a major issue which the Federalist opposition could effectively exploit, and it also became an issue among Republicans. The Embargo Act of December 1807, the capstone of the administration's attempt to bring England to terms through economic coercion, was a measure which demanded much sacrifice while conferring only the negative benefit of avoiding something worse—war or the surrender of the American position in regard to neutral rights.

The Embargo was unquestionably the most prominent issue in the election of 1808; it pervaded not only the presidential contest but state elections as well. It was a principal issue in the gubernatorial elections in Massachusetts and in Pennsylvania, in both of which contests the Republicans defended the administration's foreign policy and the Em-

56. Robert Harrison Grayson, *To the Voters of the Sixth Congressional District* . . . , April 14, 1804, broadside, Filson Club.
57. Rodney to Jefferson, June 14, 1804, Jefferson Papers, Lib. Cong.
58. Elizabeth-Town *New Jersey Journal*, Sept. 27, 1808.

bargo.[59] There was probably no state election in 1808 in which the Embargo issue did not play a part. Federalists clearly hoped to profit from the distress created by the halting of trade, and Republican opponents of Secretary of State Madison likewise used the issue, especially in support of Clinton in New York. Despite some open Republican attacks and considerable equivocation on the Embargo policy, the majority of Republicans still campaigned on the Jeffersonian record, standing by the Embargo; and Madison emerged victorious in the election of 1808 as the candidate running squarely on the administration's record.

The prominence of the Embargo issue and the repeated attacks on the administration's foreign policy resulted in widespread Republican efforts to make it clear to the voters that the party supported the administration. Numerous party meetings throughout the country passed resolutions expressing confidence in the administration and support for the Embargo. In Essex County, Massachusetts, a Republican county convention "*Resolved,* That we fully approve of the present administration under the direction of THOMAS JEFFERSON, in whom we recognize the inflexible patriot, the great philosopher, and the friend of Man." It also "*Resolved,* That we consider the embargo, at the present crisis, as a measure best calculated to preserve our property from plunder, our Seamen from impressment, and our nation from the horrors of War."[60] In September 1808, "A General Meeting of the Republicans of the City of New York" passed the following resolutions "with but few dissenting voices":

Resolved, That this meeting continues to repose full confidence in the patriotism and wisdom of the PRESIDENT and of the *Republican majority* in both houses of the Congress of the United States.

Resolved, That in our opinion the EMBARGO is a prudent, just and politic measure, rendered necessary by the rapacity and depredations of the principal belligerent nations, and not originating from any events within the power of our government to have controuled—that a repeal of the same, under existing circumstances, would probably involve us in the calamities of WAR; and, that it is therefore the duty of every faithful citizen to afford the Administration his firm and decided support.[61]

---

59. Boston *Independent Chronicle,* Feb. 29, Mar. 28, 1808; Boston *Democrat,* Feb. 27, Mar. 26, 1808; Delegates of the Democratic Citizens of the Fourteen Wards of Philadelphia, *The New Crisis of American Independence* (Phila., 1808), pamphlet, Amer. Antiq. Soc.

60. Boston *Independent Chronicle,* Feb. 29, 1808, Boston *Democrat,* Feb. 27, 1808.

61. New York *Public Advertiser,* Sept. 16, 1808; *Address of the Republicans of the City and County of New-York, to their Republican Fellow-Citizens of the United States* (N. Y., 1808), pamphlet, N.-Y. Hist. Soc.

Similar resolutions were passed elsewhere.[62]

Although the Republican party was at times seriously disturbed by party disunity, Republican factions ordinarily claimed to be supporters of the national administration when the divisions were confined to state politics. John Randolph's schism and the Republican divisions in the election of 1808 conspicuously extended party divisions into national politics, and Republicans then took conflicting stands on the Jeffersonian record. However, John Randolph failed to attract any sizable Republican following in his anti-administration movement; and the anti-administration position adopted by the supporters of George Clinton in the election of 1808 won him but six presidential electoral votes.

Republicans who appealed to the voters on the basis of principles, politics, and interests also spoke to their passions and prejudices. In the election of 1808, the Federalists were denounced as attached to Great Britain, and frequent reminders of the Revolutionary War, designed to arouse anti-British sentiment, appeared in Republican party literature. A Republican handbill circulated in the Massachusetts gubernatorial election in 1808 made a passionate appeal:

> As in the days of HANCOCK and ADAMS, you have among you the emissaries of Britain. They are anxious to restore the DESCENDANTS of the OLD TORIES, and degrade the patriots of our Revolution. They are in favor of men who wish to hazard our Commerce to the depredation of the European powers—who are desirous to have our ships BURNED ON THE OCEAN—who wish to expose our SEAMEN to every outrage of impressment and murder, just to gratify their British masters. They seek to DIVIDE YOU FROM YOUR GOVERNMENT, so that British Aggressions may find less opposition. They even have the audacity to declare, in *recommendation* of their candidate, that he is opposed to our national government—at this time, too, when foreign encroachments make union so necessary. These men are devoted friends to the nation who set CHARLESTOWN in flames—who destroyed thousands of American prisoners on board the British GUARD Ships—who attempted to starve the people of Boston by a cruel PORT bill. They are familiarized to massacres and murder. They advocated the Boston Massacre.

---

62. For other examples of meetings at which resolutions were passed in support of the Embargo see: Philadelphia *Aurora*, June 22, Aug. 9, 1808; Newark *Centinel of Freedom*, Aug. 23, 1808; *At a Very Numerous . . . Meeting of the Democratic Citizens of New-Castle County*, Sept. 3, 1808, broadside, Lib. Cong.; [Circular], State of New-Hampshire, July 4, 1808, signed by Richard Evans, broadside, N.-Y. Hist. Soc.; Portsmouth *New-Hampshire Gazette*, Aug. 23, 1808; *Republican Convention*, Essex County, Massachusetts [1808], pamphlet, Amer. Antiq. Soc.

They approve the sanguinary action of KILLING AMERICAN SEA-MEN. They thirst for the Blood of Republicans.[63]

Although this was an exceptionally extreme appeal, similar efforts to associate the Federalists with British sympathizers and the Tories of the Revolution were common Republican tactics.[64]

Republicans also sought to direct sentiment in favor of national unity to party advantage by arguing that state governments should have the confidence of the national administration. A Republican appeal in support of Israel Smith for governor of Vermont in 1807—the year of the Burr trial and of the *Chesapeake* affair—explained:

> At this eventful period, when we are on the eve of a war with Great Britain, when rebellion stalks abroad in our land, union of sentiment, union of energies of the nation are peculiarly necessary. United, we have nothing to fear from any nation on earth—divided, we may become an easy prey to any invader.
>
> You cannot be insensible of the necessity at all times, but more especially in the time of war and rebellion, that a perfect confidence subsist between the general and the respective state governments. . . .
>
> . . . Let it be remembered that the question is not men but principles; that is, not whether Israel Smith or Isaac Tichenor shall be Governor; but whether Vermont will unite and cooperate with the government of the United States in the present moment, or whether in the hour of danger we will basely desert our country's rights, and by our vile example excite discord and division, and thereby encourage the machinations of foreign foes and domestic traitors.[65]

A circular, distributed by the Republican Central Committee of Massachusetts in 1806, opposing the re-election of Federalist Governor Caleb Strong similarly argued:

> It is a fact, which neither our present Chief Magistrate, or those who support him, will deny, that he never has, and we confidently believe, never will, harmonize with the present Administration of our National Government. And at a time when our foreign Relations with the Belligerent powers of Europe have become extremely critical . . . we hold it to be most essentially necessary, that every State Government in the

---

63. *National Honor and Permanent Peace, or a Glorious Struggle for Independence*, [Apr. 4, 1808], broadside, Amer. Antiq. Soc.

64. See Bennington *World*, Aug. 8, 1808; Philadelphia *Aurora*, Oct. 10, 1808; Boston *Independent Chronicle*, Nov. 7, 1808; *British Barbarity and Piracy!!*, Boston, Mar. 25, 1808, broadside, Lib. Cong.; *The Last Day*, Apr. 1807, broadside, N.-Y. Hist. Soc. Reproduced on p. 295.

65. *To the Freemen of Vermont*, [1807], broadside, N.-Y. Hist. Soc.

The Last Day.

Every shot's a vote, and every vote kills a **TORY !**

This is the last day of the election—Shall it close gloriously for Republicans, or in TORY triumph?
Every American will cling to his
COUNTRY ;
Every true whig will oppose with all his might
The Tories ;
Every man in whose veins there runs a drop of republican blood will
SUPPORT THE
Republican Ticket :
He who wishes not this State and the Union to be governed by
Britiſh Politics,
Will leave no honorable effort untried to defeat the
Britiſh Ticket,
at the head of which stands the name of
RUFUS KING,
The friend of Tory principles—the pander of the British government—the enemy of our republican institutions.
Bad Weather
Will be no excuse for the triumph of a
Bad Cause ;
Every man to his tent, O Israel!
An Old Soldier.

APRIL, 1807

Republican Campaign Handbill, New York, 1807
(Courtesy of the New-York Historical Society)

Union should be ready cordially to unite, in support of the measures, which may be adopted by the National Administration.

Knowing, as we do, that the Republican Candidates for the two first offices for the Executive department in this State have the disposition to unite their Energies with those of the General Government, and possess their Confidence, and that their Opponents have neither the one, nor possess the other; we consider this alone to be a sufficient reason for a Change at the present moment.[66]

Although Republicans were anxious to keep the name of John Adams associated with the Federalists, they were unwilling to allow the Federalists to claim President Washington. Federalists made repeated efforts to keep Washington's name before the public in connection with their party. They conspicuously celebrated Washington's birthday. Federalist party tickets were labeled the "Washington Ticket," the "Washington and Anti-Embargo Ticket," and "Washington and Adams Nominations."[67] Recommending the Washington ticket for Congress, New Hampshire Federalists claimed: "The political principles of these gentlemen are those which ever actuated our beloved and revered Washington, during his administration of the Federal Government. They are all Federalists—they are all Republicans: Not of the *French* school, but of that of WASHINGTON."[68] Republicans in Vermont reacted to Federalist use of Washington's name by designating their ticket the "Washington and Jefferson Ticket" and referring to the Federalist slate as the "Adams and Hamilton Ticket."[69] The Boston *Columbian Centinel,* however, replied:

The democrats still continue to *profane* the revered name of WASHINGTON, by opposing it to that of JOHN ADAMS, and uniting it with that of JEFFERSON. *Let it be remembered,* that in 1796, JOHN ADAMS was the Federal, and THOMAS JEFFERSON, the antifederal candidate for Presi-

66. [Circular], Boston, Feb. 20, 1806, signed Thompson J. Skinner and others, broadside, Amer. Antiq. Soc. For other examples, see: *United We Stand—Divided We Fall,* Boston, Feb. 20, 1807, signed "The Central Committee," broadside, Hist. Soc. of Pa.; *To the Electors of the Southern District of the State of New-York,* New York, Apr. 7, 1801, broadside, Lib. Cong.; *New-York Address: To the Republican Electors for Governor and Lieutenant Governor* . . . , [1804], broadside, N.-Y. Hist. Soc.; Hartford *American Mercury,* Mar. 21, 1805.

67. Concord *Courier of New Hampshire,* July 25, Aug. 1, Oct. 3, 1804; Boston *Columbian Centinel,* Mar. 3, 1804, Oct. 8, 1808; *Trenton Federalist,* Oct. 10, 1803; *Providence Gazette,* Oct. 29, 1808, *Newport Mercury,* Oct. 8, 1808.

68. Concord *Courier of New Hampshire,* July 25, 1804. For similar examples see Boston *Columbian Centinel,* Sept. 5, Nov. 3, 1804.

69. Bennington *Vermont Gazette,* Aug. 27, Sept. 3, 1804; Walpole (N. H.) *Political Observatory,* Aug. 25, 1804.

dent of the United States. In that year, all the electors of *Virginia, save only one*—voted for THOMAS JEFFERSON:—That one was Colonel POWELL, and he voted for JOHN ADAMS—*And be it also remembered,* that GEORGE WASHINGTON, then in the 66th year of his age, rode from *Mount Vernon,* to *Alexandria,* a distance of 8 miles to give his vote for Col. POWELL, *the Federal Candidate. Facts are knotty things!*⁷⁰

Federalists were still using this same appeal in 1808.⁷¹

Federalist claims of having received the blessing of the "immortal Washington" brought Republican reminders that Jefferson had been Washington's Secretary of State and that Madison had been active in support of the Constitution.⁷² Aroused by the use of Washington's name by South Carolina Federalists, the Charleston *Carolina Gazette* vigorously protested:

The Tories and Disorganizers who have constantly abused and vilified the government and its laws . . . now have the impudence to call themselves *Followers of Washington*—this fetch will not do, gentlemen Tories; disguise yourselves under what names you please, you are, in fact, nothing else than followers and faithful servants of George the third. You know not Washington but as a man whose life was spent in freeing his country from such evil doers as yourselves.⁷³

Republicans flatly refused to give up claims to Washington. Declared the Boston *Independent Chronicle*:

The most glorious things of which our country can boast, claim Washington, Jefferson, and Madison for their authors:
Washington fought and conquered for Liberty:
Jefferson composed the Declaration of Independence, and confirmed its principles by his administration—
Madison originated the present admirable constitution of the U. States, and has victoriously supported it against all its foes.⁷⁴

Party leaders and active party workers fully realized that the voter was influenced in sundry ways, and they hoped not to leave any means

70. *Columbian Centinel,* Oct. 3, 1804; see also *ibid.,* Nov. 3, 1804.
71. *Ibid.,* Apr. 2, 1808.
72. *Republican Address to the Electors of New-Hampshire, on the Choice of Electors of President and Vice-President* (Walpole, N. H., 1804), pamphlet, N.-Y. Hist. Soc. This pamphlet was written in reply to [William Plumer], *An Address to the Electors of New Hampshire* [n.p., 1804], pamphlet, N.-Y. Hist. Soc.
73. *Carolina Gazette,* Aug. 12, 1808; see also Charleston *Times,* Oct. 7, 1808; *Now or Never! Disciples, Pupils, Friends of Washington,* Charleston, Oct. 14, 1806, broadside, Lib. Cong.
74. *Independent Chronicle,* July 14, 1808.

of arousing his support neglected. Effective organization and aggressive campaigning through newspapers, party literature, and personal contacts were directly aimed at winning and maintaining the support of the voter, who made the ultimate decisions in the American political system. The meaningfulness of the alternatives from which the voter had to choose varied according to local contests; but, in the broad perspective, the Republican party offered to the voter a program of government action with which the voter could identify and of which a majority could, and did, approve.

CHAPTER TWELVE

A Broad View

On March 4, 1809, a Washington visitor—one of the fortunate among the ten thousand who sought entrance to the Capitol—recorded in her diary: "Mr. Madison this day took the inauguration oath and read a short speech to the most numerous assembly that I ever saw—Mr. Jefferson appeared one of the most happy among this concourse of people. The foreign Ministers were at the Capitol the gallery and every part of the house was crowded and the number of carriages was so great that it was difficult to get to the door—from there a great number went to Mr. Madison's and from there some few went to pay Mr. Jefferson a visit."[1] In the *National Intelligencer,* editor Samuel Harrison Smith noted that the day "was marked by the liveliest demonstrations of joy. It appeared as if the *people,* actuated by a general and spontaneous impulse, determined to manifest, in their strongest manner, the interest excited by this great event, and their conviction of the close connection between it and their happiness."[2]

As Madison thus moved to the center of the nation's attention and Jefferson prepared to slip quietly into retirement, the Republican party added a new triumph to its record. The party had achieved a successful party succession. If Jefferson's happiness on this occasion was noticeable, it must have been inspired primarily by the pleasing anticipation of returning to Monticello, but he could also have found satisfaction in the renewed confidence which the nation had expressed in the party with which he had for so long been so intimately connected. Now, after eight years of Republican rule, the party had survived the verdict of public approval and weathered the test of its own internal strength—which some informed party leaders feared might not withstand the strain once Jefferson withdrew from the party battle.

1. Noble E. Cunningham, Jr., ed., "The Diary of Frances Few, 1808-1809," *Journal of Southern History,* 29 (1963).
2. Washington *National Intelligencer,* Mar. 6, 1809.

The functioning of the party as a political mechanism during these years in office revealed a close attention to party organization and methods, a utilization of the power of the press and of the patronage, and a deference to the ultimate power of the voter. The Jeffersonians exhibited a thoroughly realistic organization aimed at maintaining the support of the electorate and perpetuating the political power of the party. The institutions, mechanisms, and methods directed to this end were remarkably successful, yet it remains clear that these would have been unavailing had not the party pursued the policies and produced the leaders that conformed to the temper of the nation. Conversely, the aspirations of the electorate might never have found effective implementation without the device of party.

The party which Jefferson turned over to Madison's guidance was, as it had been since its formation, a national party held together by the goal of controlling the national administration through which its programs and interests could be translated into action. The party members in Congress continued, as they had since the beginning, to form the basic national party organization, assisted under conditions of power by the party leaders in the executive branch. The nominating caucus, though still challenged as it had been since its first usage, established by repeated performance its control over the party's nominations for president and vice-president. As a national party, the Republican structure was, however, always dependent upon its component parts in the states, and its national strength and unity were severely strained by the local party schisms which had broken out once the party was firmly in power. State and local issues and little-known personalities always affected the sum total of the party's success.

While the national party machinery remained little altered during Jefferson's years in office, state party organizations, reflecting the varying conditions and issues of the federated union, exhibited a variety of growth and activity. Yet, although the party organization within the various states differed in many details, there are certain patterns of party development which stand out when the two decades before 1809 are viewed as a whole. The development of formal party machinery was plainly influenced by the extent of party conflict. Party organization developed most rapidly in those states which were most closely divided between Republicans and Federalists. Thus in the period before Jefferson's election, the closest contests between Republicans and Federalists had occurred in the middle states, especially New York and Pennsylvania, and including also New Jersey in 1800. Party organization in these states by 1800 was the most advanced and extensive in the nation. During the period of Jefferson's presidency, the most extensive party organizational efforts took place in the New England states, where Republicans were more vigorously challenged by the Federalists than anywhere in the country.

The development of party machinery was also directly influenced by state electoral procedures, particularly the presence or absence of state-wide elections. The demands of waging state-wide political campaigns produced state-wide organizations which otherwise would not have been deemed necessary. The states which exhibited the least amount of formal party machinery, principally the states south of Virginia and in the West, either displayed little party conflict or lacked state-wide elections. When there were neither state-wide elections nor substantial party opposition, party organization remained largely informal.

The first party organizations of the 1790's centered primarily in the hands of political leaders and influential local citizens; a state party caucus of members of the legislature and other party leaders commonly exercised the decisive voice in state nominations and the affairs of the party in the state. Early machinery generally was initiated by party leaders and tended to develop from the top down. This was largely true of party organization before 1800, and the same pattern continued after 1800 in most states where formal party machinery was then being initially introduced. In the years from 1801 to 1809, the New England states went through the initial stage of erecting party machinery on an extensive scale. Most of this organization came from the top down: it was commonly headed by a legislative caucus; the state committees tended to dominate the state organization and to pass instructions down to the county and local committees. In Connecticut the state party manager had unusually wide powers. What took place in the New England states in these years was basically what had taken place in states such as New York and Pennsylvania in the previous decade. There state party caucuses, state committees, and centralized control from influential party leaders had set the pattern for party organization and largely determined the operations of the party. Differences in details of party structure were many, but the general pattern was similar.

Once party machinery was established and regularized procedures adopted for making party nominations and conducting party campaigns, these procedures, by the nature of the political process, directly involved not only party leaders but also ordinary voters. As the voter became more active politically and more familiar with the operations of the party, his role became increasingly important in party procedures. Party leaders in the early stages of party development frequently organized public participation, much of which was so completely directed from the top down as to afford very superficial popular participation. However, this activity, though guided, controlled, and used to advance the decisions of the party leaders, accustomed the voters to taking part in party affairs. This participation and experience in party matters tended to produce within states in which party machinery was well developed a trend toward more democratic procedures within the party. Thus a pattern of increasing intra-party popular participation emerged.

In the period from 1801 to 1809, the greatest degree of popular involvement in party affairs took place in the middle states—most of all in Pennsylvania, and to a slightly lesser extent in New York and New Jersey—where the voters had had the most practical experience in party affairs. In these states the political leadership was now forced to operate within a more democratic framework. The trend toward more democratic party procedures was also beginning to emerge in New England in the county conventions of Massachusetts and in the state convention of Rhode Island in 1808. Throughout the country, popular participation was also stimulated by the regular practices of holding Republican celebrations.

But if a pattern of evolution from party machinery dominated by influential leaders to machinery reflecting more popular participation is discernible within certain states, such a transition had not as yet begun on the national scene during Jefferson's years in office. National party machinery continued to be controlled by the party leaders; the party role of the administration and of the members of Congress dominated the national party organization, formulated party policy, and determined the party's nominees for the nation's highest offices. Although state caucuses were in the process of being modified by such developments as the caucus-convention in Pennsylvania in 1808 or the Rhode Island convention of 1808, the national caucus remained unchanged. Its dominance was to survive until 1824, when it too was soon to follow the pattern of development marked out by state processes as the national convention emerged to replace the congressional caucus.

When Jefferson returned to Monticello in March 1809, he ended nearly two decades of active participation in national political life, broken only by three years of retirement, from 1794 to 1797. In these formative years of the American party system no man stood longer in the center of political activity than Jefferson. Although in the early development of the Republican party Madison more than Jefferson had been the party organizer, it was Jefferson who emerged as the chief party leader and the symbol of the aspirations of the Republican interest. It was Jefferson who inspired and led the mobilization of the Republican party which turned the Adams Federalists out of power in 1800, and it was Jefferson who guided the party under the initial critical test of holding the reins of power.

Jefferson in 1798 wrote that "in every free and deliberating society there must, from the nature of man, be opposite parties and violent dissensions and discords; and one of these, for the most part, must prevail over the other for a longer or shorter time. Perhaps this party division is necessary to induce each to watch and delate to the people the proceedings of the other."[3] Despite the advanced conception of parties that can be inferred from this statement, it is not at all clear that Jefferson thought in terms of a permanent party system such as developed in the United States. He never recognized the validity of the Federalist party either while Adams was in office or as an opposition party during his own administration. His initial efforts to consolidate the two parties, though soon abandoned, appear genuine. There is every reason to believe that Jefferson was sincere when he said: "We are all republicans—we are all federalists." But the party system had become more permanent by 1801 than Jefferson himself realized.

If Jefferson, like most of his contemporaries, may not have clearly foreseen the American party system as it was to develop, he was far from naïve about the realities of politics of his own day. He clearly recognized the usefulness of party devices to advance and implement the aims of the Republican interest which he conceived of as representing the aspirations of a majority of the American people—a verdict confirmed by the election of 1800 and reaffirmed in 1804 and 1808. Although Jefferson would have been among the first to admit the importance and usefulness of party machinery, he would never have suggested that party organization and

3. Jefferson to John Taylor, June 4, 1798, "The Jefferson Papers," Mass. Hist. Soc., *Collections*, 7th Ser., I (1900), 62-63.

campaign methods alone would determine the outcome of any political contest; rather, he would have stressed the party's ability to express and implement the aims and the interests of the majority.

As President, Jefferson clearly demonstrated the abilities of an effective politician. He well understood the nature of a national political party which reflected regional differences, diverse interests, and clashing personalities. His ability to hold the Republican party together nationally when it was rocked by state party divisions and to retain the attachment of virtually all sides involved in the internal divisions of state politics was an accomplishment that only a superb politician could achieve. His patient toleration of party schisms on the state level reflected a realistic comprehension of local politics. His success in preventing the Randolph schism from spreading into a crippling disruption of the party nationally likewise revealed his understanding of the importance of a strong national party organization in support of his administration. Jefferson's efforts to develop a workable relationship with a party floor leader in Congress spoke clearly of his practical political sense. His close relationship with the Republican party press revealed his appreciation of that instrument for party purposes; at the same time, it indicated his basic commitment to an informed public opinion as the strength of democratic government. That Jefferson fully realized the power of party patronage and did not hesitate to use it for party advantage was demonstrated, but that he also realized the responsibilities of using that power was evident. His patronage policy, which was neither moderate enough to suit some nor sweeping enough to please many, was to a large extent the result of his efforts to balance the conflicting pressures which he felt as the leader of a national party with the broad interests of the nation.

Although Jefferson recognized his position as the head of the Republican party, he never acted as if that place gave him the commanding voice in party affairs. His party leadership was always exercised through persuasion rather than by dictation. He was invariably accessible to party leaders throughout the nation, but he never attempted to dictate to them nor to plan and manage their local party machinery. Although his sympathies in regard to state Republican schisms were sometimes evident, or confidentially revealed, he never publicly threw the weight of his party leadership nor that of the presidential office into local party disputes.

Under Jefferson the Republican party proved the workability of the party system and demonstrated the procedures for changing national policy through the operation of parties. In presenting the voters with meaningful alternatives and in implementing the electorate's decision through governmental action, the party established its utility and validity.

When Jefferson turned over the presidential office to Madison on March 4, 1809, there was proof that the Republican party had survived the test of power. In so doing, the party had done much to engrain into American political life the party system, to make party government acceptable, to make party machinery a normal part of political activity, to make party and patronage inseparable, and to make the voter more conscious of political action and more active in party affairs. Jefferson retired to Monticello carrying with him the memories of the bitter rivalries with Hamilton, Adams, and other Federalist leaders, deeply scarred by the violent personal attacks made upon him by the Federalist opposition, and disappointed by his own failure to reconcile the Federalists to his administration. But more important than such outward manifestations of the party conflict through which Jefferson had moved for nearly two decades was the development of the party system which was to endure as a vital part of the American heritage.

Bibliographical Note

Manuscripts

The slow means of transportation and communication of the Jeffersonian era dictated that political leaders and party workers fashion many of their plans and conduct much of the party's business through correspondence. Thus the letters of active participants in the political scene afford a particularly rich source of early party history. While there are important published collections of the writings of most of the prominent political figures of the era, until current editorial projects—such as the Jefferson Papers and the Madison Papers—are completed, these sources must be supplemented by unpublished manuscripts. The older publications are incomplete and rarely include the incoming correspondence. Also unpublished are the manuscripts of many lesser men, frequently providing invaluable evidence concerning the operation of parties.

The two most important manuscript collections for the subject of this study are the Thomas Jefferson Papers in the Library of Congress and the Albert Gallatin Papers in the New-York Historical Society. Important additional collections of Jefferson manuscripts are at the University of Virginia and the Massachusetts Historical Society. The major collections of the papers of James Madison and of James Monroe are in the Library of Congress, and valuable supplements to both collections are in the New York Public Library. The Wilson Cary Nicholas Papers in the Library of Congress contain some particularly important material relating to the election of 1808, and other Wilson Cary Nicholas papers are at the University of Virginia. The Henley-Smith Papers in the Library of Congress are revealing on Jefferson's relationship with the press. The Joseph H. Nicholson Papers, Library of Congress, contain numerous correspondence with important Republican leaders. Among the most useful collections of Federalist correspondence are the William Plumer Papers, Library of Congress; the Baldwin

Family Papers, Yale University; and the John Rutledge Papers, University of North Carolina. An extremely valuable and little-used collection, the Appointment Papers, in the National Archives, throws important light on the patronage problems of Jefferson's administration. Among other major collections containing significant political material are the DeWitt Clinton Papers, Columbia University; the Creed Taylor Papers and the Edgehill-Randolph Papers, University of Virginia; and the Ephraim Kirby Papers, Duke University.

Manuscript material for the period is widely scattered. In addition to the collections mentioned above, the following collections, listed by depositories, were found to be the most useful: *Duke University:* David Campbell Papers, John Clopton Papers, Edwin Gray Papers, Joseph Jones Papers, Nathaniel Macon Papers, John Rutledge Papers; *Filson Club:* John Breckinridge Papers; *Georgia Department of Archives and History:* William Few Papers; *Historical Society of Pennsylvania:* Charles Biddle Papers, Alexander J. Dallas Papers, Ferdinand J. Dreer Collection, Simon Gratz Collection, William Jones Papers in Uselma Clarke Smith Collection, Lea and Febiger Collection, Logan Papers, Thomas McKean Papers, William Meredith Papers, George Read Papers, Jonathan Roberts Papers; *Library of Congress:* Papers of Breckinridge Family, William A. Burwell Papers, William C. Cabell Personal Papers Miscellaneous, George W. Campbell Papers, Henry Dearborn Papers, William Duane Personal Papers Miscellaneous, William Eustis Papers, Ebenezer Foote Papers, Papers of Gideon and Francis Granger, Papers of Joseph Hiester in Gregg Collection, Papers of John Randolph of Roanoke, Papers of Caesar A. Rodney, John Cotton Smith Papers, Papers of Samuel Smith, Thomas Sumter Papers; *Massachusetts Historical Society:* Autograph Collection, Thomas Dwight Papers, Harrison Gray Otis Papers, Levi Lincoln Papers, Timothy Pickering Papers, Winthrop Sargent Papers, Theodore Sedgwick Papers, Henry W. Taft Collection, Alexander C. Washburn Collection; *New-York Historical Society:* Abraham Bishop Papers in Miscellaneous Collection, Papers of John Smith of Mastic, Long Island, in Miscellaneous Collection, Killian K. Van Rensselaer Papers in Miscellaneous Collection; *New York Public Library:* Joseph Clay Papers, Emmett Collection, Papers of Pierre Van Cortlandt, Jr., William P. Van Ness Papers; *North Carolina Department of Archives and History:* Hayes Collection, Nathaniel Macon Papers; *Rutgers University:* Jonathan Dayton Papers, William Paterson Papers; *University of Georgia:* Abraham Baldwin Papers, Thomas Carr

Papers, James Jackson Papers; *University of North Carolina:* Arnold-Screven Papers, William Gaston Papers; *University of South Carolina:* Robert Anderson Papers; *University of Virginia:* Cabell Papers, Carter-Smith Family Papers, Federalist Letters, Madison-Todd Family Papers, John Randolph of Roanoke Papers; *Virginia Historical Society:* John Ambler Papers, Ellis Papers; *Virginia State Library:* Bryan Family Papers, Tazewell Family Papers; *Yale University:* Brown Papers, William Griswold Lane Collection, John Cotton Smith Papers.

Contemporary Pamphlets, Broadsides, and Newspapers

Printed communications of party proceedings, party literature publicizing campaign appeals and political issues, and newspaper reports of party activities provide important sources of party history, although such publications are never so revealing as private correspondence or personal memoranda. Most valuable of the contemporary printed material are campaign handbills, party circulars, and political pamphlets, especially those which were issued under official party auspices. Also notable are the printed circular letters which members of Congress sent to their constituents. Political broadsides are extensive for New York, available in moderate numbers for Pennsylvania, Massachusetts, and Virginia, and rare for all other states. Of the broadsides examined for this study, some two hundred were considered pertinent to the party history of the years 1801 to 1809; of these, approximately one half relate to New York politics. The best broadside collections for the period are in the Library of Congress, the New York Public Library, the New-York Historical Society, and the American Antiquarian Society. Although the majority of all political pamphlets were published in a few principal cities, these publications circulated throughout the country. The best collections of political pamphlets are in the Library of Congress, the Historical Society of Pennsylvania, and the New-York Historical Society. Depositories for all broadsides and pamphlets cited have been indicated in the footnotes.

For newspapers published in the major cities of the eastern seaboard, extant files are abundant and generally accessible in several major libraries. The newspaper press in remote and newly settled areas was often very limited, and surviving files for many such areas are poor and widely scattered. Forty-four cities and towns in seventeen states and the

District of Columbia are represented in the sixty-seven newspaper files cited in the footnotes. All issues may be conveniently located in Clarence S. Brigham, *History and Bibliography of American Newspapers, 1690-1820*, 2 vols. (Worcester, Mass., 1947).

Other Major Sources and Selected Secondary Writings

Published collections of the papers of Thomas Jefferson, James Madison, and Albert Gallatin afford the most pertinent printed correspondence, which can be supplemented by published papers of numerous other contemporaries. These publications can be conveniently located in Oscar Handlin *et al., Harvard Guide to American History* (Cambridge, Mass., 1955). Full citations of the publications used in the present study have been given in the footnotes. The most useful contemporary diaries are Everett S. Brown, ed., *William Plumer's Memorandum of Proceedings in the United States Senate, 1803-1807* (N. Y., 1923) and Charles Francis Adams, ed., *Memoirs of John Quincy Adams, comprising portions of his Diary from 1795 to 1848*, 12 vols. (Phila., 1874-77).

Henry Adams, *History of the United States of America during the Administrations of Thomas Jefferson and James Madison*, 9 vols. (N. Y., 1889-91), remains the most extensive treatment of the Jeffersonian era but deals only slightly with the practical operation of political parties. The best recent political summary of the period of Jefferson's administration is Irving Brant, *James Madison, Secretary of State, 1800-1809* (Indianapolis, 1953). Also important for general coverage of the period and the treatment of key personalities are Leonard D. White, *The Jeffersonians: A Study in Administrative History, 1801-1829* (N. Y., 1951); William Cabell Bruce, *John Randolph of Roanoke, 1773-1833*, 2 vols. (N. Y., 1922); and Raymond Walters, Jr., *Albert Gallatin: Jeffersonian Financier and Diplomat* (N. Y., 1957).

The most useful studies of parties on the state level are Sanford W. Higginbotham, *The Keystone in the Democratic Arch: Pennsylvania Politics, 1800-1816* (Harrisburg, Pa., 1952); John A. Munroe, *Federalist Delaware, 1775-1815* (New Brunswick, N. J., 1954); William A. Robinson, *Jeffersonian Democracy in New England* (New Haven, 1916); Harry Ammon, The Republican Party in Virginia, 1789 to 1824 (unpubl. Ph.D. diss., University of Virginia, 1948); Norman L. Stamps, Political Parties in Connecticut, 1789-1819 (unpubl. Ph.D. diss., Yale University, 1950). Old, but still useful for the middle states, is George D. Luetscher, *Early Political Machinery in the United States* (Phila., 1903). Additional writings relating to the period may be located in the *Harvard Guide to American History*.

Index

A

Adams, John, 8, 10, 67, 95, 232, 305; and election of 1796, 4-5; midnight appointments of, 14-15, 23, 62; Republican campaigning against, 194, 286-87, 288-89, 296
Adams, John Quincy, 72, 114, 140; appraisal of Republican strength, 7-8; and impeachment of Chase, 81; on Randolph, 84-85; on Giles, 93; on Jefferson's influence on Congress, 94; on caucuses, 99; attends caucus of 1808, 111, 112; on Samuel H. Smith, 266-67; on patronage, 270
Adams, Thomas Boylston, 16
Albany Register, 27, 254n
Alexander I of Russia, 272
Alexandria Expositor, 254n
Allen, James, 182
Allen, William L., 181
Alston, Joseph, 190
Alston, Joseph John, 188
Alston, Lemuel J., 275-76
Alston, Willis, 77
Ambler, John, 181, 182
American (Baltimore), 178, 254n
American Citizen (New York), 17-18, 212, 237, 238, 254n. *See also* Cheetham, James; Denniston, David
American Mercury (Hartford), 128, 245, 254n. *See also* Babcock, Elisha
American Patriot (Baltimore), 240
American Philosophical Society, 260
Ames, Fisher, 6, 267
Ames, Dr. Nathaniel, 133, 134, 135-36, 282
Anderson, Joseph, 114
Argus of Western America (Frankfort, Ky.), 195
Armstrong, John, 39, 206
Augusta Chronicle, 240, 244
Aurora (Philadelphia), 216; on Republican patronage policy, 17, 27; defends congressional caucus, 107-8; on Burr's repudiation, 212; and Mathew Carey, 240-41; Jefferson subscribes to, 254n, 271; as Republican paper, 267-68, 271; and Republican administration, 272-73. *See also* Duane, William
Aurora, for the Country (Philadelphia), 254n, 272. *See also* Duane, William
Austin, Benjamin, Jr., 243
Austin, David, 31-32
Austin, Jonathan L., 243

B

Babcock, Elisha, 128, 245; as Republican editor, 238. *See also* American Mercury (Hartford)
Bailey, Theodorus, 38, 39, 213
Baldwin, Abraham, 98, 105
Baldwin, Simeon, 53, 77, 102, 131
Baltimore, Md., Republican organization in, 178-80
Bank of the United States, 63-64
Barnet, Oliver, 33
Bayard, James A., 6, 48-49, 75, 93, 99-100; on Randolph, 73-74, 83
Beckley, John, 30, 86, 215-16, 232; and Republican patronage, 260-61, 268, 269
Bee (Hudson, N. Y.), 254n
Bee (New London, Conn.), 248-49
Bidwell, Barnabas, 239-40, 259; as party leader in Congress, 84, 88-89, 90-91, 92, 94
Bishop, Abraham, 6, 15-16, 23, 127, 285; on Conn. Federalists, 132; and Burr, 208
Bishop, Samuel, 15-16, 20, 22-23
Bloomfield, Joseph, 208
Bowdoin, James, 243
Bradley, Stephen R., 104, 112, 113-14, 115
Breckinridge, John, as Republican leader in Senate, 93, 101, 102-3, 105, 244; and Jefferson, 96-97; and Cabinet, 98; as vice-presidential candidate in 1804, 104, 108

Brent, Richard, 182
Brockenbrough, John, 185n
Brockenbrough, William, 277-78
Broome, John, 149, 150, 151, 153
Brown, Mr., of Mass., 243
Bryan, Joseph, 77, 87, 191, 231, 281
Bryan, Samuel, 32
Bullock, Edmund, 194
Burr, Aaron, 5, 106, 128, 294; electoral tie with Jefferson, 3-4; and patronage, 15, 18, 38-39, 40-41, 42-43; charges of intrigue against, 39; and Jefferson, 42-43, 205, 209-10; repudiated by Republicans in Congress, 103, 104, 211-12; and N. Y. election of 1804, 151-52, 210-11, 213, 283; position in Republican party, 203-13; Federalist support of, 212-13; William Duane on, 215, 218; on *National Intelligencer*, 259; on Samuel H. Smith, 266
Burwell, William A., 84, 257

C

Cabell, Samuel J., 186
Cabell, William H., 110, 182
Cabinet (Georgetown), 254n
Callender, James Thomson, 80, 250-53, 263
Cameron, Duncan, 188
Campaign practices. See Adams, John; Elections; Jefferson, Thomas; names of individual states
Campbell, Arthur, 33
Campbell, George W., 88, 99
Canning, George, 263
Carey, Mathew, 240-41
Carolina Gazette (Charleston), 238, 258, 297
Carr, Thomas, 192
Caucuses, status of congressional, 99-100, 123, 124, 302; and Republican nominations in 1804, 103-8, 109; and Republican nominations in 1808, 108-19, 120, 121, 122; in Va. in 1808, 111-12, 183-84; in Conn., 127; in Mass., 133, 137; in N. H., 142; in Vt., 145-46; in R. I., 146; in N. Y., 148; in Pa., 161, 164
Centinel of Freedom (Newark), 26-27, 284
Chase, Samuel, 79-81
Cheetham, James, 209; on congressional caucus of 1808, 119-20; Madison supporters attack, 120-21; opposes Burr, 205-6, 208; Alexander J. Dallas attacks, 217; on Quids and Madison, 229-30; as Republican editor, 237, 238; and public printing, 249-50; and Jefferson, 254, 255, 290. See also *American Citizen* (New York); Denniston, David
Chesapeake incident, 263, 294
Claiborne, William C. C., 16, 96
Clarke, John, 185n
Clay, Henry, 193, 195
Clay, Joseph, 162, 217, 219; supports Randolph, 88, 116n, 225, 226
Clay, Matthew, 233-34
Clinton, DeWitt, 40, 74, 97; and N. Y. patronage, 42-44; as Republican leader in N. Y., 122, 175; and N. Y. election of 1804, 149, 150-51, 209; and N. Y. election of 1807, 152, 154; and Burr, 206, 208; duel with John Swartwout, 207; opposes N. Y. Quids, 227; and Randolph, 228
Clinton, George, 59, 152, 174, 209; and Republican patronage, 18, 39-40; and election of 1804, 103-4, 105, 106, 108; and election of 1808, 109, 114-23 passim, 140, 147, 165-66, 229, 292-93
Clinton, George, Jr., 116n
Clopton, John, 101-2, 244
Cocke, William, 105
Coleman, William, 254, 261
Columbian Centinel (Boston), 26, 140, 141, 247, 296-97
Condit, John, 88, 105
Congress, Seventh Congress, 9, 10, 71, 72, 73-75; Eighth Congress, 71; early party leadership in, 73; role of committees in, 90-91; circular letters by members of, 101-2, 186, 289; role of members in party machinery, 101, 103, 105, 114, 300, 302; newspaper reports of debates in, 266. See also Caucuses
Connecticut, 106, 115; Federalists in, 7, 19, 21, 129, 131, 132; patronage policy in, 19-24; Republicanism in, 20-21; Republican party machinery in, 125-30, 200-202, 301; caucus in, 127; Republican newspaper circulation in, 245-46; campaign practices in, 275, 284; Republican celebrations in, 285
Constitutional Telegraphe (Boston), 254n
Coxe, Tench, 214, 216, 218, 219
Crowninshield, Jacob, 71-72, 104, 138, 272
Cutler, Manasseh, 79, 286

D

Dailey, James, 182
Dallas, Alexander J., and Republican party in Pa., 162, 214, 218, 219; opposes Wil-

liam Duane, 216-17, 272; and Randolph, 225
Davenport, John, 78
Davis, Matthew L., 38-43 *passim*, 204
Davis, Thomas T., 102
Dawson, John, 97
Dearborn, Henry, 4, 29, 68-69, 114, 239, 257
Delaware, 7, 9, 109, 115, 117; elections in, 9, 46, 47-48; and patronage, 16, 36-38, 44-49; Republican machinery in, 148, 171-74, 200, 202; Republican discord in, 221; newspapers in, 236, 240; campaign practices in, 277, 287
Democrat (Boston), 246, 254n
Democratic associations, in New Jersey, 166-70
Democratic Society of Friends of the People, in Pa., 162-63
Denniston, David, 206, 237. See also *American Citizen* (New York); Cheetham, James
DeSaussure, Henry W., 28, 275
Dickinson, John, 36, 37
Dickson, William, 102, 208-9
Driscol, Dennis, 240
Duane, William, 238; and patronage in Pa., 55, 59, 261, 268-70; and election of 1808, 118, 165; and intra-party strife in Pa., 162, 175, 214-15, 216-17, 218, 219; on Burr, 208; and Jefferson's administration, 218, 224, 226, 270-72, 273; and Randolph, 223, 224, 225; Mathew Carey supports, 241; on Samuel H. Smith, 266; praised by Jacob Crowninshield, 272-73. See also *Aurora* (Philadelphia); *Aurora, for the Country* (Philadelphia)
Dudley, William, 182
Duvall, Gabriel, 137, 277
Dwight, Thomas, 282

E

Earle, Elias, 275
Eastern Argus (Portland), 142
Edwards, Pierpont, 19, 22-23, 208, 227-28; and Conn. Republicans, 125-26, 127, 131
Eggleston, Joseph, 15
Eichelberger, Frederick, 160
Election of 1796, presidential, 4-5
Election of 1800, presidential, 3-4, 5, 6, 7, 109
Election of 1804, presidential, 9, 103-8, 109, 180-85, 284, 289-90
Election of 1808, presidential, 108-24, 140, 147, 166, 183-85, 195-96, 226-35, 273-74, 288; electoral vote in, 9, 123; campaign issues of, 291-93. See also names of individual states
Ellery, Christopher, 64-65, 221
Ellicott, Andrew, 272
Ellzey, William, 182
Embargo Act of 1807, 9, 98, 119; supported by Republicans in middle states, 121, 166; supported by Mass. Republicans, 135, 140; enforcement of, 262; Federalists oppose, 277; as campaign issue, 288, 291-92
Enquirer (Richmond), 111, 183, 238, 254, 257. See also Ritchie, Thomas
Eppes, John Wayles, 79, 95
Eustis, William, 140, 240, 243
Evans, Richard, 143
Examiner (Richmond), 237-38, 254n, 256-57, 278-79

F

Federalist, The, 232
Federalist party, 5; strategy after 1800 elections, 6-7; in election of 1804, 9; Jefferson's attitude toward, 10, 52-53, 303; in Conn., 19, 21, 129, 131; on Republican patronage policy, 53; in Congress, 93; in Mass., 141-42; in Vt., 145; attitude toward Burr, 212-13; and third parties, 218; and newspapers, 237, 239n, 267; and Washington, 286, 296-97; Republican charges against, 287; effect on Republican party organization, 300-301
Fenner, Arthur, 221
Fenner, James, 146
Ferguson, Hugh, 30
Few, Frances, 299
Field, Richard, 182
Foushee, John H., 181-83, 185n
Foushee, William, 185
Franklin, Jesse, 114
Franklin; Or a Political, Agricultural and Mechanical Gazette (Washington), 242. See also Lyon, James
Freeman's Journal (Philadelphia), 254n
Freneau, Peter, 238, 258. See also *Carolina Gazette* (Charleston)
Freneau, Philip, 255
Fries, John, 80

G

Gallatin, Albert, 4, 84, 102; and patronage, 25, 29, 38, 52, 55-70 *passim*, 215, 216; on appointment of Matthew L. Davis, 41-42; reports on federal revenue officers, 60; and Bank of the United States, 63-64;

and state banks, 64-65; on Yazoo commission, 78; relationship with Congress, 73, 98, 99; on Burr, 203-4, 208; on N. Y. politics, 207; and William Duane, 217, 269-70, 271, 273; on Pa. politics, 218, 220; and public printing, 249; and Samuel H. Smith, 260; writes for press, 258, 263
Garnett, James M., 88, 116n
Gaston, William, 288
Gelston, David, 15, 38, 39, 40, 249-50
Genesee Messenger (Canandaigua, N. Y.), 155
Georgia, 240, 253; and Yazoo land controversy, 78; Republican organization in, 190-92, 201, 202; campaign practices in, 281
Georgia Republican (Savannah), 238, 254n. See also Lyon, James
Gerry, Elbridge, 238, 243
Giles, William B., 13, 17, 81, 111, 114; as party leader in Congress, 73-75, 93, 98
Gillean, Abraham, 187
Goddard, John, 142
Goodrich, Elizur, 19-20, 23
Goodrich, John, 182
Granger, Gideon, 4, 65, 104, 131; and party patronage, 20, 21-22, 63; Randolph attacks, 79; on Burr, 207-8; and N. Y. election of 1804, 211; William Duane attacks, 226, 273; on newspapers, 238-39
Gray, Edwin, 113, 116n
Grayson, Robert H., 194, 279-80, 290-91
Great Britain, 235, 291, 293, 294
Greenup, Christopher, 196
Gregg, Andrew, 83, 105
Griswold, Roger, 10-11, 74, 212-13
Grove, William Barry, 75, 106

H

Habersham, Joseph, 61
Hall, David, 44, 46, 171, 173
Hall, John, 31
Hamilton, Alexander, 6, 213, 305
Hanna, John A., 13
Hargrove, Rev. John, 33
Harris, John, 116n
Haswell, Anthony, 247-48
Hay, George, 181, 185
Helms, William, 84, 85
Henderson, Archibald, 94
Hiester, Joseph, 30
Hillhouse, James, 94, 99
Hoadley, George, 266
Hoge, William, 116n, 226n

Holland, James, 244
Holmes, Hugh, 182
Holt, Charles, 248-49
Hooker, Edward, 275-76
Hope's Philadelphia Price-Current, 254n
Hopkins, Samuel, 195
Howland, Benjamin, 114
Hunter, John, 13

I

Independent Chronicle (Boston), 139, 246, 247, 285, 297; Jefferson subscribes to, 254n; publishes Jefferson article, 256

J

Jackson, Andrew, 209
Jackson, James, 192, 240
Jackson, John G., 186
Jefferson, Thomas, inauguration in 1801, 3, 5, 128, 285; and Burr, 3-4, 42-43, 204, 205-6, 209-10; and appointments, 4, 15-16, 30-31, 33, 35-36, 52-53, 60-63; and election of 1796, 4-5; and election of 1800, 4, 6; inaugural address (1801), 8, 9, 12-13, 260; attempts to reconcile parties, 8-9; and election of 1804, 9, 108, 187; message to Congress in 1801, 10; and development of Republican party after 1800 election, 11; patronage policy of, 12-14, 17-19, 29, 49-51, 304; reply to the New Haven remonstrance, 19-20, 23-29, 50; and Del. patronage, 36-38, 44-49; and N. Y. patronage, 38-44; patronage policy in Pa., 55-56; and the Bank of the United States, 63-64; removal policy, 69-70; on federal patronage to banks, 64; and army, 66-68; calculates party strength in Seventh Congress, 71; and Randolph, 75, 76, 83-84, 86-87, 90, 224, 304; and party leaders in Congress, 75-76, 89-90, 91-92, 93-97, 304; and impeachment of Justice Chase, 80, 81; and Barnabas Bidwell, 89-91; nomination in 1804, 104, 105, 106; urged to seek third term, 109; supported by Mass. Republicans, 140; and Republican schism in N. Y., 152, 207, 209-11; and Republican divisions in Pa., 166, 214, 215, 216, 218-19, 220, 226; on Republican divisions in R. I., 221; accused of favoring Quids, 224, 229; warns Monroe of Randolph, 228; and Monroe-Pinkney treaty of 1806, 235; and election of 1808, 234-35; and Republican divisions, 231, 235, 304; and Republican newspapers, 238-39, 241-42, 253-54; policy on print-

ing of laws, 247-48, 249-50; and James Thomson Callender, 250-52; relationship to *National Intelligencer,* 256, 258-63; publications of, in newspapers, 255-58; comments on newspapers, 264; and William Duane, 270-72, 274; on Alexander I of Russia, 272; Republican campaigning for, 287, 288-89, 297; Republican view of administration of, 288-91, 292; retirement of, 299, 305; attitude toward parties, 303-4; evaluation of, as party leader, 303-5
Jones, Gabriel, 256
Jones, Meriwether, 181, 185, 238, 256-57
Jones, Obadiah, 191-92, 281
Jones, William, 162, 218

K

Kentucky, 108; Republican organization in, 192-96, 201, 202; campaign practices in, 193-96, 279-80, 280n
Kentucky Gazette (Lexington), 195
King, Rufus, 31, 295
Kirby, Ephraim, 63, 125-26, 131, 245
Kirkpatrick, William, 114
Kitchell, Aaron, 114

L

Langdon, John, 104, 114, 123
Latimer, George, 48
Lawler, Matthew, 59, 162, 217
Lee, Richard Evers, 182
Leib, Michael, and Republican patronage in Pa., 31, 53-54, 59; and Republican divisions in Pa., 160, 162, 175, 214, 217, 219, 220; and 1808 election in Pa., 165; and Randolph schism, 223, 225
Leiper, Thomas, 58, 217, 225; and Republican divisions in Pa., 160, 162, 214, 216; and 1808 election in Pa., 165; and Republican patronage in Pa., 215
Lewis, Joel, 36, 37, 38
Lewis, Meriwether, 252
Lewis, Morgan, 149, 150, 151, 152-53, 222, 227; and New York election of 1804, 210-11, 213; George Clinton repudiates, 229
Lightfoot, William, 181
Lincoln, Levi, 4, 89, 125, 285; and Republican patronage in Conn., 21, 28; on Yazoo commission, 78; as vice-presidential candidate in 1804, 104; and Republican newspapers, 238, 240, 243, 258
Linn, James, 16
Livingston, Brockholst, 103, 149

Livingston, Edward, 15, 38, 39
Livingston, Robert R., 15
Logan, George, 162, 214, 218
Louisiana purchase, 52-53, 96, 267, 271-72, 285-86; as campaign issue, 289, 290, 291
Lyon, James, 238, 241-42. See also *Georgia Republican* (Savannah); *Franklin; Or a Political, Agricultural and Mechanical Gazette*
Lyon, Matthew, 193, 241, 279

M

McFarlane, James, 182
McKean, Thomas, 28, 54, 103; and party divisions in Pa., 161, 162, 163, 203, 215-18 *passim,* 224; Federalists support, 220
McKinley, William, 182
McLane, Allen, 44-49
Maclay, Samuel, 104, 116n, 226n
Macon, Nathaniel, 73, 105, 108, 280; and Randolph, 77, 86, 87-88, 230
McRae, Alexander, 110
Madison, James, 4, 9, 72, 78, 98, 297; and patronage, 25, 34, 36, 38, 42, 58-59, 215, 249; Randolph opposes, 83, 84, 109; and Republican divisions in election of 1808, 85-86, 108-12, 115-24, 140, 147, 165-66, 183-84, 195-96, 226-35 *passim,* 273-74; nominated for president, 114; James Cheetham attacks, 119; elected President, 123; and Burr, 210; and Jefferson, 224, 257; and John Taylor of Caroline, 231, 232; and Louisiana purchase, 271; and Embargo Act of 1807, 292; inauguration of, 299, 305; as party leader, 73, 303
Marshall, John, 3, 79
Maryland, 7, 9; Republican machinery in, 176-80, 201, 202; campaign practices in, 276-77, 286-87
Mason, Stevens Thomson, 8, 92
Massachusetts, 57, 68, 106, 285, 291; Republican machinery in, 133-40, 201, 202, 302; Federalist party in, 141-42; newspapers in, 236, 238, 239-40; campaign practices in, 282, 292, 293, 294, 296-97
Masters, Josiah, 112-13, 116n
Mercer, John, 185-86
Merchant, George, 150
Milledge, John, 114, 192, 240, 281
Minor, John, 182
Mirror of the Times (Wilmington, Del.), 172
Mitchill, Samuel L., 105
Monroe, James, and election of 1808, 85-86,

109-18 *passim*, 123, 183-84, 226-35 *passim;* and Monroe-Pinkney treaty of 1806, 235; and James T. Callender, 251
Montgomery, Daniel, 30, 116n, 226n
Montgomery, John, 114
Morning Chronicle (New York), 254n
Morris, Gouverneur, 44
Muhlenberg, Peter, 16, 31, 214
Mumford, Gurdon S., 116n

N

National Aegis (Worcester, Mass.), 243, 254n
National Gazette (Philadelphia), 255
National Intelligencer (Washington), 51, 108, 263; and Jefferson, 254n, 256, 258-63, 274; editorial policy of, 265-66; as official Republican paper, 267, 271. *See also* Smith, Samuel Harrison
Nelson, Roger, 79
New England, campaign practices in, 9, 22, 282; Republican machinery in, 147, 201, 301, 302. *See also* names of individual states
New-England Palladium (Boston), 267
New Hampshire, Republican machinery in, 106, 142-45, 201, 202
New Haven, Conn., remonstrance of merchants of, 19-20, 60; reply to remonstrance by merchants of, 23-24, 25-29, 50
New Jersey, 7, 17, 284; Republican machinery in, 148, 166-71, 174, 200, 202, 301, 302; campaign practices in, 283-84, 287, 288, 291
New Jersey Intelligencer and Republican Advertiser (New Brunswick), 243
Newspapers, statistics on, 236-37; party support of, 243-46; patronage to, 247-50. *See also* names of individual newspapers
New York, 6, 7; patronage problems in, 17-18, 38-44; opposition to Burr in, 103; and congressional caucus, 117-18; support for George Clinton in, 118, 119, 120; support for Madison in, 120-21; election of 1808 in, 121, 122; Republican machinery in, 148-56, 202, 301, 302; gubernatorial election of 1804, 148-52, 209-13; Republican divisions in, 151, 152-53, 203-13, 216, 218, 227-28; gubernatorial election of 1807, 152-54; newspapers in, 236; campaign practices in, 283, 295. *See also* Burr, Aaron; Clinton, George; Quids
New-York Evening Post, 254 and *n*, 261
Nicholas, John, 153-54, 227

Nicholas, Philip Norborne, 10, 121, 123; chairman of Republican state committee in Va., 181, 182, 183, 185
Nicholas, Wilson Cary, 56, 105, 111, 273; and Jefferson, 91-92, 96; and George Clinton, 121-23; on Burr, 207, 208; on Republican divisions in Va., 221; and Randolph schism, 230
Nicholson, Joseph H., 73, 96; party leadership in Congress, 74, 75, 257; and Randolph, 77, 79, 86
North Carolina, 9, 187-88, 201, 202, 280, 290
Norvell, John, 264

O

Ohio, 106; Republican machinery in, 196-200, 201, 202
Old Republicans, 85, 222
Olin, Gideon, 105
Osgood, Samuel, 39, 40, 44
Otis, Harrison G., 28, 205
Otis, Samuel A., 270

P

Page, Mann, 182
Parker, Nahum, 114
Pegram, Edward, 182
Penn, George, 182
Pennsylvania, Federalist strength in, 7; and Republican patronage, 17, 53-55, 58-59, 65-66; presidential election of 1808 in, 118, 119, 122; Republican machinery in, 148, 156-66, 174, 201, 202, 301, 302; Republican divisions in, 160-61, 162-64, 214-20; gubernatorial election of 1805 in, 162-63, 217-18; and Randolph schism, 223-27; newspapers in, 236; campaign practices in, 281, 283; gubernatorial election of 1808 in, 291; caucuses in, 302. *See also* Quids
Phelps, Oliver, 210, 211
Philadelphia, Republican machinery in, 156
Philadelphia Repository, 254n
Pickering, John, 80
Pickering, Timothy, 80-81, 94, 140
Pinckney, Charles, 15
Pinckney, Charles Cotesworth, 9, 123, 288
Pinkney, William, 235
Pitkin, Timothy, 83
Pleasants, Samuel, Jr., 181, 185, 238. *See also Virginia Argus* (Richmond)
Plumer, William, 56, 75, 96, 102; on Randolph, 77, 78, 82, 83-84; on Chase impeachment, 81; on William B. Giles, 93;

INDEX 317

on caucuses, 99; on printing patronage, 270
Political Barometer (Poughkeepsie, N. Y.), 254*n*
Political Mirror (Staunton, Va.), 254*n*
Political Observatory (Walpole, N. H.), 243-44
Pope, Edward, 262
Pope, John, 114
Port Folio (Philadelphia), 238
Post Office, patronage in, 63
Potter, Jared, 125-26
Poulson's American Daily Advertiser (Philadelphia), 254*n*
Powell, Leven, 297
Preston, John, 121-22, 182
Public Advertiser (New York), 19-20, 230
Public Intelligencer (Savannah), 254*n*

Q

Quids, in Pa., 58, 162, 218, 219, 220, 223, 224, 225-26; relationship of Randolph to, 222-31; in N. Y., 227, 228, 229; and election of 1808, 229, 230; and William Duane, 271

R

Raleigh Register, 244
Randolph, David M., 250
Randolph, John, of Roanoke, appointed chairman of Ways and Means Committee, 73-74; as party leader in Congress, 74-78, 92, 95, 304; opposes Yazoo compromise, 78-79; end of leadership in Congress, 79, 87-88; and Chase impeachment, 79, 80, 81; breaks with Jefferson, 82-83, 94, 222, 224, 231, 293; opposes Madison, 83, 84, 85-86; and Monroe, 85-86, 109, 228, 230, 232; attacks Bidwell, 89; defends caucuses, 99, 107; and caucus of 1804, 104, 116; and caucus of 1808, 115-16; on campaign practices, 186-87, 278; and Quids, 222-35; and William Duane, 224-25, 273; and election of 1808, 228-29; articles of Decius by, 257
Randolph, Peyton, 185
Randolph, Thomas Mann, 84, 91, 92, 95, 185
Read, Thomas, 182
Republican Advocate (Fredericktown, Md.), 254*n*
Republican societies, in Ohio, 196-98
Republican Watch Tower (New York), 121, 254*n*. See also Cheetham, James
Rhea, John, 193

Rhode Island, patronage in, 56; establishment of Republican bank in, 64-65; Republican machinery in, 146-47, 201, 202, 302; Republican divisions in, 221; establishment of Republican press in, 242-43
Rhode Island Republican (Newport), 243
Ritchie, Thomas, 112, 116-17, 185, 238, 257
Robinson, William, 185*n*
Rodney, Caesar A., 10, 28-29, 220, 223; as Republican leader in Del., 36, 37, 38, 45-46, 47; as party leader in Congress, 75, 76, 92, 94, 105; candidate for Congress, 172-73, 277, 291; on Del. newspapers, 240
Rogers, Richard, 41
Rogers, Thomas J., 157
Roger Williams Bank, Providence, R. I., 64-65
Russell, John, 116*n*
Russell, Jonathan, 16
Rutledge, John, 99, 253

S

Salem Register, 139, 244-45, 246, 254*n*
Sandford, Thomas, 231
Scioto Gazette (Chillicothe, Ohio), 199
Scull, John, 248
Sedgwick, Theodore, 205
Selden, Joseph, 181, 185
Shee, John, 58
Shipman, Elias, 20
Simkins, Eldred, 132
Sloan, James, 169, 175
Smelt, Dr. Dennis, 244
Smilie, John, 114
Smith, Israel, 294
Smith, John, of Pa., 30-31
Smith, John, of Va., 82
Smith, John E., 240
Smith, Larkin, 182
Smith, O'Brien, 189
Smith, Robert, 4, 97
Smith, Samuel, of Md., 15, 105, 247; and Allen McLane incident, 48-49; party leadership in Congress, 74, 75; on Randolph, 82, 83
Smith, Samuel, of Pa., 116*n*, 226*n*
Smith, Samuel Harrison, 51, 71, 266; and Jefferson, 256, 258-66; receives printing patronage, 260, 268, 269; on Madison's inauguration, 299. See also *National Intelligencer* (Washington)
Smith, Mrs. Samuel Harrison, 3, 260

Snyder, Simon, 162, 163, 164, 166, 217
Society of Constitutional Republicans, 162, 163, 165. *See also* Quids, in Pa.
South Carolina, 189-90, 201, 202, 275-76, 297
Spalding, Thomas, 281
Spayd, John, 165
Spirit of the Press (Philadelphia), 254n
Stanard, Edward C., 185n
Stanford, Richard, 188
Stanton, Joseph, Jr., 56-57, 105
Steele, John, 58, 60
Stokes, Montfort, 290
Storm, Thomas, 153
Storrs, Gervas, 181, 185
Strong, Caleb, 135, 294
Stuart, Archibald, 182
Sullivan, James, 91, 243, 282
Sumter, Thomas, 31, 71, 105
Swart, Peter, 116n
Swartwout, John, 15, 38, 39, 40, 207

T

Taggart, Samuel, 79, 88-89
Taliaferro, John, Jr., 182
Taylor, Creed, 70, 110, 182
Taylor, John, of Caroline, 33, 100, 182, 230-31, 273; and Monroe, 232, 233
Taylor, John, of S. C., 114
Taylor, Richard, 34
Tazewell, Littleton W., 106-7
Tennessee, 192-96, 201, 202, 280
Thompson, John, 116n
Tichenor, Isaac, 294
Tiffin, Edwin, 114
Tilton, James, 36-37
Tompkins, Daniel D., 153
Tracy, Uriah, 93
Travis, Champion, 181
Trigg, Abram, 116n
True American (Trenton), 237, 243, 247
Truxton, Thomas, 273

U

United States Army, 66-69
United States Gazette (Philadelphia), 266

Universal Gazette (Philadelphia), 260
Universal Gazette (Washington), 254n
Upham, Edward, 57

V

Van Ness, John P., 43, 49-50, 204-5, 206-7
Van Rensselaer, Killian K., 266
Varnum, Joseph B., 68, 88, 90, 101, 114, 247
Vaughan, Dr. John, 36, 37, 38
Venable, Abraham, 185
Vermont, 9, 22; Federalist party in, 145; Republican machinery in, 145, 200, 202; campaign practices in, 294, 296
Virginia, election of 1800 in, 5-6; election of 1808 in, 110-12, 118, 121-23, 183-85, 221, 230, 232-35; election of 1804 in, 180-83; Republican machinery in, 180-87, 201, 202; campaign practices in, 185-87, 277-78; opposition to national leadership of, 212-13; Republican divisions in, 221
Virginia Argus (Richmond), 238, 244, 254n. *See also* Pleasants, Samuel, Jr.
Virginia Gazette and General Advertiser (Richmond), 254n

W

Walker, William, 181
Ware, Nicholas, 192
Washington, George, 4, 10, 286, 296-97
Washington Federalist, 253, 267
Western Spy (Cincinnati), 197
Western World (Frankfort, Ky.), 195
Weston, Isaiah, 262
Willett, Marinus, 40
Williams, David R., 95-96, 116n
Williams, Col. Jonathan, 97
Wolcott, Alexander, 128-30, 246
Wolcott, Oliver, 53, 212-13
Worthington, Thomas, 196, 199
Wythe, George, 182

Y

Yazoo land controversy, 78

www.ingramcontent.com/pod-product-compliance
Lightning Source LLC
Chambersburg PA
CBHW021353290426
44108CB00010B/228